BLUE GUIDE

ISTANBUL

John Freely

Edited and revised by
Annabel Barber

Somerset Books • London

4

Sixth edition 2011

Published by Blue Guides Limited, a Somerset Books Company
Winchester House, Deane Gate Avenue, Taunton, Somerset TA1 2UH
www.blueguides.com
'Blue Guide' is a registered trademark.

© John Freely and Blue Guides 2011
The rights of John Freely and Annabel Barber to be identified as
author and editor of this work have been asserted by them in accordance with
the Copyright Designs and Patents Act, 1988.

ISBN 978–1–905131–40–2

A CIP catalogue record of this book is available from the British Library.

Distributed in the United States of America by
W.W. Norton & Company, Inc.
500 Fifth Avenue, New York, NY 10110.

The editor and publisher have made reasonable efforts to ensure the accuracy of all the
information in *Blue Guide Istanbul*; however, they can accept no responsibility for any loss,
injury or inconvenience sustained by any traveller as a result of information or advice
contained in the guide.

Statement of editorial independence: Blue Guides, their authors and editors, are prohibited
from accepting payment from any restaurant, hotel, gallery or other establishment for its
inclusion in this guide, or on www.blueguides.com, or for a more favourable mention than
would otherwise have been made.

All other acknowledgements, photo credits and copyright information
are given on pp. 6 and 336, which form part of this copyright page.

Your views on this book would be much appreciated. We welcome not only specific
comments, suggestions or corrections, but any more general views you may have: how this
book enhanced your visit, how it could have been more helpful. Blue Guides authors and
editorial and production team work hard to bring you what we hope are the best-researched
and best-presented cultural, historical and academic guide books in the English language.
Please write to us by email (editorial@blueguides.com), via the comments page on our website
(www.blueguides.com) or at the address given above. We will be happy to acknowledge
useful contributions in the next edition, and to offer a free copy of one of our titles.

CONTENTS

THE GUIDE

MAPS & PLANS

contd. from p. 4

Maps: Dimap Bt
Ground plans: Imre Bába
Line drawings: Annabel Barber (p. 34);
Gabriella Juhász and Michael Mansell RIBA (pp. 302–11)
Watercolours: Edit Nagy

Photo research, editing and pre-press: Hadley Kincade
(for individual image credits, see p. 336)

Acknowledgements
Special thanks are due to **Bill Greenwood**, formerly at *Cornucopia* magazine and now at the
Museum of Islamic Art in Qatar, for valuable suggestions and additions
to the text and for checking much of the information on the ground.

Thanks also to Faruk Boyacı and his staff, Juliet Daher Bory, Andrew Finkel,
Caroline Finkel, Michael Metcalfe, İlhan Olam, Bob Ousterhout, Peter Read, Emin Saatçi,
John Scott, Gencay Üçok, Jim Urquhart, Linda Vadász.

John Freely was born in Brooklyn, New York in 1926. He joined the US Navy at the age of 17 and was on active duty during the last two years of the Second World War, serving in the Pacific, India, Burma and China. After the war he resumed his education and received a PhD in Physics from New York University in 1960, later doing post-doctoral studies in the History of Science at Oxford. He first went to Istanbul in 1960 to teach physics at the old Robert College, now Boğazici University, to which he returned in 1993 after intervals of living and working in New York, Boston, London, Athens and Venice. His first book was *Strolling Through Istanbul*, co-authored by the late Hilary Sumner-Boyd, which was published in 1972. Since then he has written more than 40 books. *Istanbul, the Imperial City* (1996) is the only modern single-volume treatment of Roman, Byzantine and Ottoman Istanbul. *Inside the Seraglio, Private Lives of the Sultans in Istanbul*, an intimate family biography of the Ottoman sultans and their women and favourites, was published in 1999. His recent work has concentrated on the subject of Islamic contributions to science (*Aladdin's Lamp: How Greek Science Came to Europe Through the Islamic World* and *Light from the East*, a history of Islamic science). In preparing this edition of *Blue Guide Istanbul* he was assisted by his son, **Brendan Freely**, who is currently writing a book about Beyoğlu.

Annabel Barber is Editor-in-Chief of the Blue Guides.

Material prepared for press by Anikó Kuzmich
Printed in Hungary by Dürer Nyomda Kft., Gyula

ISBN 978–1–905131–40–2

HISTORY OF ISTANBUL

The founding of Byzantium

Although archaeological evidence of human settlement in Istanbul dates back to Neolithic times, the history of the city as we know it begins with the founding of the colony of Byzantium, by mainland Greeks from Megara, in the 7th century BC. According to tradition, the founder was Byzas, who established a city named after himself on the high ground above the confluence of the Bosphorus and the Golden Horn c. 660 BC. Before setting out, Byzas had consulted the Delphic oracle, who advised him to settle 'opposite the Land of the Blind'. This was taken to mean Chalcedon, a Greek colony established about 15 years before on the Asian side of the water. The implication is that the settlers must have been blind not to have spotted the greater advantages of the site on the European side. A city built there would be more defensible, since the steep hill was bounded by deep waters on two sides and its short landward exposure could be protected by walls. The city would then be in a position to control all shipping passing between the Aegean, the Propontis (Sea of Marmara) and the Pontus (Black Sea), while its situation on the principal crossing-point between southeast Europe and Asia Minor would put it astride the main land routes between the continents. Byzantium became a centre for trade and commerce, acquiring wealth from its fisheries and from the customs duties it charged on shipping through the Bosphorus.

The Classical period

In 512 BC the Persian king Darius crossed the Bosphorus on a bridge of boats, at the outset of his campaign against the Scythians. On his way he captured the city of Byzantium, which remained in Persian hands until 477 BC, when it was freed by an allied Greek force under the Spartan general Pausanias. Byzantium was alternately allied with Athens and Sparta during the Peloponnesian War, which was fought in the years 431–404 BC. The Athenians took Byzantium from the Spartans in 409 BC, at which time Athens founded Chrysopolis, the City of Gold, on the site of the modern Üsküdar. Byzantium retained its independence throughout the rest of the Classical period, withstanding a year-long siege by Philip II of Macedon (father of Alexander the Great) in 341–340 BC. Despite their spirited resistance to King Philip, the Byzantines avoided conflict with his son, who began his invasion of Asia with a victory over the Persians at the Battle of the Granicus in 334 BC.

The Hellenistic and Roman periods

After Alexander the Great's death in 323 BC, his vast empire was dismembered and divided among his successors, who found themselves pitted against the inexorable eastward expansion of Rome. Byzantium became part of the Roman province of Asia after its establishment in 129 BC, and for more than three centuries afterwards it enjoyed a respite from war, sheltered by the mantle of the *Pax Romana*.

In the closing years of the 2nd century AD Byzantium became embroiled in the civil war between the emperor Septimius Severus and his rival, Pescennius Niger. Byzantium supported the latter, and Septimius, after defeating and killing him in 194, returned to punish the Byzantines, putting their city under siege. After finally taking Byzantium in 196, the emperor tore down the city walls, massacred all those who had supported his rival, and burned the city to the ground. But Septimius realised the imprudence of leaving so strategic a site undefended, and rebuilt the city on an enlarged scale, enclosing it on its landward side with a new line of walls. The walls of Septimius Severus are thought to have begun at the Golden Horn a short distance downstream from the present Galata Bridge, and to have ended at the Marmara below the Hippodrome. The area thus enclosed was twice as great as in the original town of Byzantium, which had comprised little more than the acropolis itself.

At the beginning of the 4th century BC Byzantium played an extremely important role in the climactic events then taking place in the Roman Empire. After the retirement of Diocletian in 305, his successors in the Tetrarchy, the two co-emperors and their caesars, fought bitterly with one another for supreme control. This struggle was eventually won by Constantine, Emperor of the West, who in 324 defeated Licinius, Emperor of the East. The final battle took place in the hills above Chrysopolis (Üsküdar), where Licinius had his last base. On the following day Byzantium surrendered and opened its gates to Constantine, now sole ruler of the Roman Empire.

During the first two years after his victory, Constantine conceived and put into operation a scheme that was to influence the world for the next millennium: reorganising the Roman Empire and shifting its capital to Byzantium. Once the decision was taken, Constantine set out to rebuild and enlarge the old town to suit its imperial role. The project began on 4th November 326, when the emperor personally traced out the limits of his new city. The defence walls with which he enclosed his capital extended in a great arc from the Golden Horn to the Sea of Marmara, more than quadrupling the area of the city. The imperial building programme proceeded rapidly, and in less than four years the new capital was completed. On 11th May 330, in a ceremony in the Hippodrome, Constantine dedicated the city of New Rome and proclaimed that thenceforth it would be the capital of his empire. However, in popular speech the new capital soon came to be called Constantinople, capital of the Byzantine Empire.

Constantinople, the city of Constantine

The empire ruled by Constantine and his successors turned out to be quite different from the old Roman Empire. The new realm, which later historians called the Byzantine Empire, adopted Christianity as the state religion and Greek as the official language. The last emperor to rule over both the eastern and western halves of the Empire was Theodosius I (r. 379–95). After his death his son Arcadius succeeded as Emperor of the East and another son, Honorius, became Emperor of the West. Theodosius is recognised as a saint in the Orthodox world, for theologically he was a very great emperor. He convoked the Council of Constantinople in 381 to address the rift in the Church caused by debates over the nature of Christ, human or divine. At the council Theodosius enshrined the Nicene Creed in law, thereby officially declaring that God and Christ are 'one substance', that Christ is 'begotten not made', and that the Holy Ghost 'proceedeth from the Father'. As a result of the council Constantinople became the second city of Christendom after Rome, superseding older Christian cities such as Alexandria and Antioch. Theodosius had pulled off an adroit political coup.

By the time of Theodosius II (r. 408–450) the capital had grown considerably in population, expanding well beyond its Constantinian limits. Because of this, and also because of the threat of barbarian invasions, the emperor decided to build a new and stronger line of walls a mile farther out into Thrace. The first phase of these walls was completed in 413 and the final phase in 447, just in time to turn aside the advancing hordes of Attila. Theodosius II also built a splendid new cathedral dedicated to Haghia Sophia, the Divine Wisdom. Completed in 415, it replaced an earlier church of the same name which had been built by the emperor Constantius (r. 337–61) and burned down during a riot in 404.

The reign of Justinian the Great

A new epoch in the history of the city began in 527, with the reign of Justinian I. A few years before becoming emperor, Justinian fell in love with a reformed circus artiste named Theodora, and in 525 he married her. After his accession, Theodora became his empress and shared power with her husband.

Even before his accession, when he served as Caesar under his uncle Justin I, Justinian laid the foundation for the grand design that would be carried out during his reign, the reconquest of the lost dominions of Rome. He was fortunate to have in his service one of the greatest generals in Byzantine history, Belisarius, who in 526 began his illustrious career by leading Justin's army against the Persians. This campaign was prosecuted with even greater vigour the following year, when Justinian became emperor.

In 532 Justinian was very nearly overthrown in a revolt that broke out among the factions in the Hippodrome. This insurrection is known as the Nika Revolt, from the rallying-cry of 'Nika' (Victory), yelled by the mobs as they stormed the Great Palace. At the height of the insurrection, when the rebels were almost in control of the capital, Justinian was on the point of giving up his throne and fleeing for his life. But Theodora persuaded him that it would be nobler to stay and fight on, even if it meant their death. After five days of bloody fighting the revolt was put down by Belisarius, who trapped and slaughtered 50,000 of the rebels in the Hippodrome.

When the revolt ended most of the buildings on the old acropolis were in ruins, including the royal palace and the church of Haghia Sophia. Justinian immediately began a programme of reconstruction, and within five years he had rebuilt everything, erecting a new church of Haghia Sophia, which he dedicated on 26th December 537.

During the course of Justinian's long reign Belisarius and his other generals succeeded in regaining much of the former territory of the Roman Empire. By 565 the borders of the realm extended around the Mediterranean and included Palestine, Syria, Asia Minor, Greece, the Balkans, much of Italy, southern Spain, the North African littoral, Egypt and the Mediterranean islands, an area only slightly smaller than that of the Roman Empire

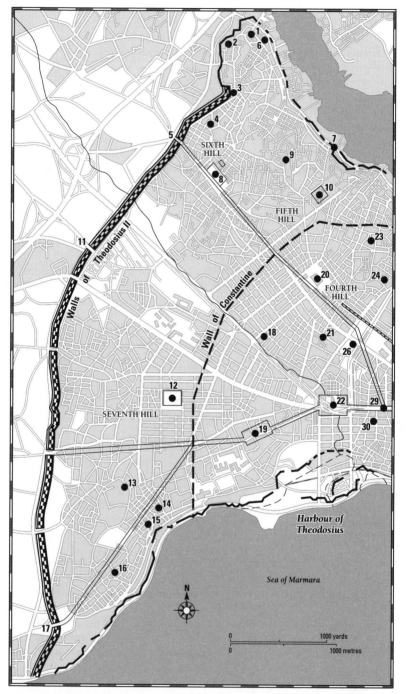

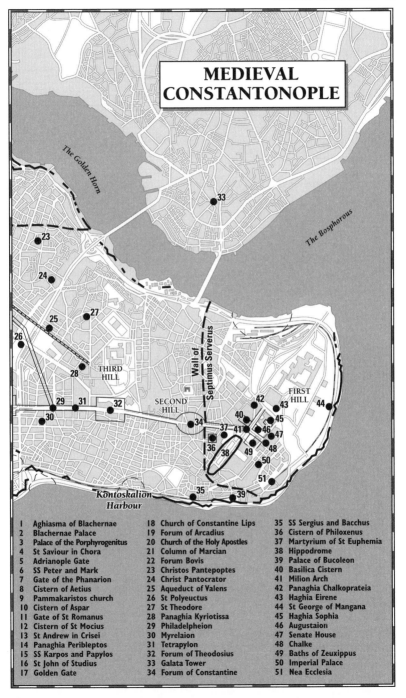

MEDIEVAL CONSTANTONOPLE

The Golden Horn

The Bosphorous

Wall of Septimus Serverus

THIRD HILL

SECOND HILL

FIRST HILL

Kontoskalion Harbour

1 Aghiasma of Blachernae	18 Church of Constantine Lips	35 SS Sergius and Bacchus
2 Blachernae Palace	19 Forum of Arcadius	36 Cistern of Philoxenus
3 Palace of the Porphyrogenitus	20 Church of the Holy Apostles	37 Martyrium of St Euphemia
4 St Saviour in Chora	21 Column of Marcian	38 Hippodrome
5 Adrianople Gate	22 Forum Bovis	39 Palace of Bucoleon
6 SS Peter and Mark	23 Christos Pantepoptes	40 Basilica Cistern
7 Gate of the Phanarion	24 Christ Pantocrator	41 Milion Arch
8 Cistern of Aetius	25 Aqueduct of Valens	42 Panaghia Chalkoprateia
9 Pammakaristos church	26 St Polyeuctus	43 Haghia Eirene
10 Cistern of Aspar	27 St Theodore	44 St George of Mangana
11 Gate of St Romanus	28 Panaghia Kyriotissa	45 Haghia Sophia
12 Cistern of St Mocius	29 Philadelpheion	46 Augustaion
13 St Andrew in Crisei	30 Myrelaion	47 Senate House
14 Panaghia Peribleptos	31 Tetrapylon	48 Chalke
15 SS Karpos and Papylos	32 Forum of Theodosius	49 Baths of Zeuxippus
16 St John of Studius	33 Galata Tower	50 Imperial Palace
17 Golden Gate	34 Forum of Constantine	51 Nea Ecclesia

at the time of Augustus. But the strength of the Empire had been sapped by the enormous expenditure of money and manpower in the campaign of reconquest. Taxation had been exorbitant and many lives had been lost in the endless wars of Justinian's reign.

The struggle for survival

During the half-century after Justinian's death the great empire that he created was almost destroyed, attacked by enemies on all sides and torn apart by internal strife. The low point came with the reign of Phocas (r. 602–10), perhaps the worst emperor ever to sit upon the Byzantine throne. Phocas was overthrown and succeeded by Heraclius, who defeated the Persians and the Avars when they were almost on the point of capturing Constantinople in 626. During the remaining years of the reign of Heraclius he won back from the Persians all of the territory they had conquered, and at the same time he drove the Avars out of the southern Balkans, so that the empire seemed secure at the time of his death in 641.

After the final defeat of the Persians the next enemies to appear were the Arabs, who first swept across Asia Minor in 674, led by Yazid, son of the Umayyad Caliph. They besieged Constantinople for four years. The Byzantines withstood this siege, driving off the Arab fleet with their flame-throwers spewing the terrible 'Greek Fire' (*see p. 205*). Among the besiegers was the aged Abu Ayyub, a companion of the Prophet, who died and was buried outside the Theodosian walls in what is now the great shrine that bears his name (in Turkish, Eyüp). The Arabs besieged the capital a second time in 717–18, during the reign of Leo III, but once again they were driven off with heavy losses.

When Leo III (r. 717–41) ordered the removal of the great icon of Christos Chalkites from above the Chalke Gate at the Great Palace of Byzantium, he marked the beginning of the most serious internal conflict in Byzantine history: the Iconoclastic Crisis, which was to last for more than a century. The iconoclasts were opposed to the presence of figurative representations of Christ or the saints and while the iconoclast emperors were in power, virtually all such icons were destroyed. At the same time many of the monasteries of the Empire were closed and their monks imprisoned and persecuted. The crisis came to an end in 845, when a council of the Greek Orthodox Church permanently restored icons to the churches of the Empire and reopened the monasteries.

The next threat came from the Bulgars, who rose to dominance in the Balkans early in the 9th century, besieging Constantinople unsuccessfully in 814, 913 and 924. The climax of this struggle came with the campaigns of Basil II, who ruled from 976 until 1025, the longest reign in the history of the Byzantine Empire. In 995–1001 Basil defeated the Arabs and drove them out of southern Asia Minor forever, and in 1014 he annihilated the Bulgar army, a feat for which he received the title of Bulgaroctonus, the 'Bulgar-Slayer'. When Basil died in 1025 he left behind him an empire that stretched from the Caucasus and Persia to the Adriatic and from the Holy Land to the Danube. This represented the zenith of Byzantine power in the late medieval period.

The dynasty of the Comneni

The death of Basil II marked a turning-point in the history of the Byzantine Empire.

His passing was followed by a half-century of steady decline, in which a series of weak and ineffective emperors proved unable to deal with the mounting internal troubles of the Empire, at a time when new and stronger enemies were appearing on all sides and threatening the very existence of Byzantium. The nadir came in 1071, when a Byzantine army led by the emperor Romanus IV Diogenes was annihilated by the Seljuk Turks at Manzikert in eastern Asia Minor. This opened up all of Asia Minor to the Seljuks, who overran it as far as the Sea of Marmara. With them came hordes of nomadic Turcoman tribesmen, who divided up the former Byzantine territory into a patchwork of Turkish *beyliks*, or principalities. In the same year, 1071, the Normans captured Bari, thus ending Byzantine rule in Italy.

Although the Empire had now lost its possessions in Italy forever, the Byzantines still maintained political and economic ties with certain Italian city-states, particularly Venice. During the reign of Basil II, Doge Pietro Orseolo obtained commercial concessions for Venice in Constantinople, a development that had important consequences. These concessions included reduced customs fees for Venetian traders, and also gave them a small strip of territory extending from the Golden Horn, where they could build docks for their ships, warehouses for their goods, and houses for their merchants. The Byzantines later gave similar concessions to Amalfi, Pisa and Genoa. Amalfi and Pisa acquired strips of territory on the Golden Horn beside those of the Venetians, while the Genoese were given Galata. The Byzantines derived some commercial and political advantage from these concessions at first, but later the Italians and other Latins in Constantinople became virtually independent of the Empire. This was particularly true in Galata, which became a semi-autonomous city-state governed by an official sent out annually from Genoa. With their stronger fleets, the Italians were able to flout the Empire's laws and restrictions with impunity. This led to friction between the Byzantines and the Latins, and was a contributory factor in the eventual downfall of Byzantium.

In 1081, a decade after the catastrophic defeat at Manzikert, Alexius I Comnenus succeeded to the throne of Byzantium. Throughout the next century he, and his son and grandson in turn, successfully defended the Empire against the incursion of the forces that were hemming it in on all sides, using diplomacy and an enlightened foreign policy to great advantage. When Alexius first came to the throne, the Seljuk Turks and their Turcoman vassals were in complete control of virtually all Asia Minor, with their capital at Nicaea (modern İznik). When the armies of the First Crusade reached Constantinople in 1096, on their way to the Holy Land, Alexius took the opportunity to use their help in regaining the territory that Byzantium had lost to the Turks. Their first success came in June 1097, when they captured Nicaea. The Crusader leaders returned the city to Alexius and marched on, while the emperor and his troops hastened to occupy all of the former Byzantine cities abandoned by the fleeing Turks.

Alexius I died in 1118 and was succeeded by his son John II, who has been acclaimed both by his contemporaries and by modern historians as the finest ruler in the illustrious dynasty of the Comneni. John continued his father's foreign policy, applying clever diplomacy and the judicious use of military force against his opponents. When he died in 1143, all of the territory bequeathed to him by his father was intact, and in addition he had regained southern Asia Minor, extending his borders as far as Syria. John was succeeded by his son, Manuel I, who in a reign of 37 years (1143–80) preserved the lands he had inherited and added to them Dalmatia, Croatia and Bosnia. When he died his borders stretched from Syria to Hungary and from central Asia Minor to the Adriatic, including Cyprus, Crete and the Aegean islands.

Manuel Comnenus was succeeded by his 12-year-old son, Alexius II. Since Alexius was too young to rule in his own right, his mother, Mary of Antioch, acted as regent. This led to a power vacuum that was filled by Andronicus Comnenus, younger brother of the late emperor Manuel, who was serving as governor of the Pontus. Andronicus rose up and took control of Constantinople, and in September 1183 he was crowned as co-emperor with Alexius, whom he murdered shortly afterwards. Two years later Andronicus himself was overthrown and murdered, an ignominious end to the once-illustrious dynasty of the Comneni.

The dynasty of the Angeli and the Fourth Crusade

Andronicus was succeeded by Isaac II Angelus, founder of the short-lived dynasty of the Angeli. Isaac was a totally incompetent ruler who gave free play to the corrupt and divisive elements that were threatening to destroy the Empire. In 1195 he was deposed by his elder brother, Alexius III, who imprisoned him along with his eldest son, Prince Alexius, and blinded him so that he would not be tempted to try to regain power. Then in 1202 Prince Alexius escaped and fled to the West, where he sought help in restoring his father and himself to the throne.

He went first to Pope Innocent II, who earlier that year had preached another Crusade, the Fourth, to free the Holy Land from the Muslims. When Pope Innocent proved unwilling to help him, Alexius went to the court of Philip of Swabia, his brother-in-law. Philip agreed to support him, and suggested that Alexius should present his case to the leaders of the Fourth Crusade; Enrico Dandolo, Doge of Venice, and Count Boniface of Montferrat. The Crusaders had assembled in Venice, from where the Doge's fleet would transport them to Egypt to begin their campaign. But the Crusaders proved unable to pay for their passage, and there was an impasse until Dandolo suggested that they might make good the deficiency by helping the Venetians recapture the Dalmatian seaport of Zara (the modern Zadar), a former possession of theirs that had gone over to the Hungarians. The Crusaders agreed, and in November 1202 began their 'sacred mission' with the capture and sack of the Christian city of Zara, an outrage for which they were all excommunicated by the pope. The Latins (as the Western Christian army is known) were wintering in Zara when a messenger arrived from the court of Philip of Swabia, carrying Alexius's appeal that the Crusaders restore his father and him to the throne of Byzantium. Alexius promised enormous sums of money to the Latins for their support, and Dandolo persuaded the Crusaders to agree.

The Latins set sail from Zara in the spring of 1203, arriving in the port of Constantinople on 24th June of that year. As soon as their fleet appeared, Alexius III fled with the imperial treasury and the crown jewels. The Crusaders captured Galata and encamped outside the land walls, while Dandolo and the other Latin leaders negotiated with the

Byzantines. Threatened by the vastly superior force of the Crusaders, the Byzantines agreed to restore Isaac II and to make his son co-emperor as Alexius IV. Immediately after his coronation, when it came to paying off the indemnity that he had promised the Crusaders, Alexius found that his treasury was empty. Under pressure from Dandolo, he attempted to raise the money by imposing confiscatory taxes on the Greek population of the capital. But this lost him what little public support he had, and in January 1204 he and his father were deposed and lost their lives in a popular revolt. They were replaced by Alexius V Ducas Mourtzouphlos ('the Beetle-Browed'), who repudiated the agreement that Alexius IV had made with the Crusaders. This gave the Latins an excuse to attack Constantinople, and on 13th April 1204 they breached the sea walls along the Golden Horn and took the city by storm. They proceeded to sack the capital, stripping it of its wealth, its art treasures and its sacred relics, sending their loot back to Western Europe and leaving the city a burned-out ruin. The Latins then began their occupation of Constantinople, a hiatus in the history of the Byzantine Empire.

The Latin occupation and the Empire of Nicaea

Soon after their capture of Constantinople, the Latins divided up the territory they had seized. The Venetians were awarded three-eighths of the capital and the church of Haghia Sophia, along with various ports and islands. Half of the conquered Byzantine territory outside the capital was given to various Crusader knights as fiefs, while the other half and the remaining five-eighths of Constantinople became the property of Count Baldwin of Flanders. On 16th May 1204 Baldwin was crowned in Haghia Sophia, by then a Roman Catholic cathedral, and took the title of Emperor of Rumania, as the Latins called their new empire. The territory of this empire originally consisted of Thrace and the northwest corner of Asia Minor, as well as a few Aegean islands. But in the subsequent half-century the Latin Empire steadily lost territory to its neighbouring states in Europe and Asia, so that by the middle of the 13th century it was so small and weak that it lay open to conquest by those around it.

When Constantinople fell to the Latins in 1204, fragments of the Byzantine Empire continued in existence in several parts of Greece and Asia Minor, ruled by various members of the former royal families of Byzantium. As the Latin Empire progressively weakened, these Byzantine principalities contended with one another for the great prize, the recapture of Constantinople and the restoration of the Empire. The most fortunately placed of these states was the Empire of Nicaea, which was founded in 1204 by Theodore I Lascaris, a son-in-law of Alexius III Angelus. Nicaea was only a short distance from Constantinople, and to the north its territory shared a common border with the Latin Empire. Under the able leadership of Theodore I (r. 1204–22) and his son-in-law and successor, John III Ducas Vatatzes (r. 1222–54), the Empire of Nicaea flourished and its boundaries expanded, so that by the middle of the 13th century it consisted of western Asia Minor from the Black Sea to the Aegean as well as most of the offshore islands. By that time the Latin Empire had shrunk to little more than Constantinople itself, with the European littoral of the Sea of Marmara, the Bosphorus and the Dardanelles.

When John III died in 1254 he was succeeded by his son, Theodore II (r. 1254–58). Theodore was an effective ruler and a highly cultured man, a student of the scholar Nicephorus Blemmydes. During his brief but brilliant reign Nicaea became a cultural centre of such importance that scholars of the time referred to it as a second Athens. The cultural revival that started there later gave rise to a renaissance of learning in Byzantium. But Theodore died of epilepsy at the age of 37. He was succeeded by his seven-year-old son, John IV, for whom a regent, George Mouzalon, had been appointed by Theodore on his death-bed.

But Mouzalon was extremely unpopular with the aristocracy, and nine days after his appointment he was murdered. The aristocracy appointed as regent the ablest and most distinguished man among them, Michael Palaeologus. Early in 1259 he was crowned co-emperor as Michael VIII, the young John IV by then being a virtual prisoner. Two years later, on 25th July 1261, Michael's commanding general captured Constantinople with a small force and with hardly any opposition, for the Latin Empire had been moribund and was now dead. On 15th August Michael VIII made his triumphal entry into Constantinople with his court and army, after which he rode at the head of a joyous procession to Haghia Sophia, where a service of thanksgiving was held. The legitimate emperor, the young John IV, took no part in the celebrations connected with this great event, for he remained a prisoner, and a few weeks later Michael had him blinded and sequestered in a monastery, where he spent the rest of his days in obscurity.

The Byzantine renaissance and the rise of the Osmanlı Turks

The cultural renaissance that had started in Nicaea continued in Constantinople during the reigns of Michael VIII and his successors, the Palaeologi, the last dynasty to rule Byzantium. This renaissance gave birth to scholars like the great Neoplatonist Gemistos Plethon, who were important influences on the Italian Renaissance; and it also produced masterpieces of art far surpassing anything created in the history of the Empire. But the Empire under Michael VIII was merely a fragment of what it had been in its prime, comprising only western Asia Minor, Thrace, Macedonia, parts of the Peloponnese, and a few of the Aegean islands.

At the beginning of the 14th century a new power arose in western Asia Minor, one which would eventually destroy the Byzantine Empire and all of the other surviving medieval states in western Asia and southeastern Europe. These were the Osmanlı Turks, better known to Westerners as the Ottomans. The Osmanlı were named after their first leader, Osman Gazi (*Gazi* is an honorific title meaning 'Warrior for the Faith'). Between 1288 and 1326 Osman Gazi headed a small tribe of nomadic Turks from central Asia who had been settled in western Asia Minor by the Seljuks in the first half of the 13th century. At that time the Osmanlı controlled a few square miles of farmland and pasturage as vassals of the Seljuks, and their little *beylik* shared a common border with the Empire of Nicaea, whose capital was only a day's ride from their territory.

The Osmanlı gained their independence when the power of the Seljuks was broken by the Mongols in the second half of the 13th century. Under Osman Gazi they began to expand their borders westward, and by the time he died in 1326 their forces were besieging the Byzantine city of Brusa (Bursa), a few miles from the Sea of Marmara. Shortly after Osman's death, Brusa was captured by his son and successor, Orhan Gazi, who established his capital there. Orhan Gazi is considered to be the first Ottoman Sultan, for during the 36 years of his reign the Osmanlı forces conquered most of western Asia Minor and penetrated Europe as far as Bulgaria.

The Byzantines could do little to stop this expansion; when the Turks began to move into Europe, the Empire was engaged in the most serious civil war in its history. In this struggle, which lasted from 1341 to 1347, the forces of the legitimate emperor, John V Palaeologus, were arrayed against those of the usurper, John Cantacuzenus, who actually brought the Turks over into Europe as his allies. John V eventually emerged victorious, but by that time the Turks had established a permanent foothold in Thrace and were beginning to move northward. In 1361, the year before Orhan Gazi died, his son Murat captured the Byzantine city of Adrianople on the border between Thrace and Bulgaria. Murat succeeded his father as sultan in 1362 and soon afterwards shifted his capital from Brusa to Adrianople (which in Turkish became Edirne), for the Thracian city now became the base for the annual campaigns in which the Ottoman armies penetrated ever deeper into southeastern Europe

The last Byzantine century

From the mid-14th century onwards the fortunes of the Byzantines declined with the rise of the Osmanlı, who extended their empire deep into the Balkans. Allied Christian armies fell to the 'red wind' of the Turkish scimitars at Kosovo polje (in modern Kosovo) in 1389 and Nicopolis (in modern Bulgaria) in 1396. Beyazıt I besieged Constantinople in 1394, building the fortress of Anadolu Hisarı on the Asian side of the Bosphorus at the narrowest point of the strait. The siege was lifted in 1402, when Beyazıt was defeated by Tamerlane at the Battle of Ankara and died in captivity. This gave Byzantium a reprieve as Beyazıt's sons fought a war of succession that lasted until 1413, when Mehmet I became sultan. The Ottomans resumed their expansion under his successor Murat II (r. 1421–51), who decisively defeated allied Christian armies at Varna in 1444 and at the second battle of Kosovo in 1448.

During the first half of the 15th century Byzantium made several futile attempts to obtain help from western Europe. The most notable of these efforts began in 1437, when John VIII Palaeologus travelled to the West to ask for assistance from Pope Eugenius IV and the princes of Western Europe. At the Council of Ferrara-Florence, which met from April 1438 until July 1439, Emperor John and his Patriarch, Joseph II, agreed to the pope's terms, promising to bring the Greek people and clergy with them into union with Rome. But the emperor gained nothing from this surrender, for not only did help for Byzantium never materialise in the West, but his own people and clergy completely repudiated the agreement.

John died childless and was succeeded by his younger brother Constantine XI. At the time of his accession Constantine was Despot of the Morea (the Peloponnese), the only remaining Byzantine possession outside the capital. He was crowned Emperor of

Byzantium in Mistra on 6th January 1449, after which he set out for Constantinople by sea, arriving there two months later. He took up the hopeless task that had occupied his late brother all through his long reign, attempting to gain help from the West to save Byzantium from the Turks who encircled it. He tried to persuade the people and clergy of the capital to agree to union with Rome, but the Greek hatred of the Latins was so great that this only turned the populace against him. As one of the highest court officials said, when asked to support the emperor's policy of union with Rome: 'I would rather see the Muslim turban in the midst of the city than the Latin mitre.'

The fall of Byzantium

Murat II died on 13th February 1451 and was succeeded by his son, Mehmet II, then only 19 years old. Immediately after his accession Mehmet began preparations for the long-awaited siege of Constantinople. After organising his government and his military forces, Mehmet set up his headquarters in Thrace, just a few miles from Constantinople. There, in the summer of 1452, he proceeded to build an enormous fortress called Rumeli Hisarı, just opposite Anadolu Hisarı. These two fortresses enabled him to control the Bosphorus and cut off Constantinople from the Black Sea, depriving the city of the shipments of corn that were its main food supply.

In March 1453 the Ottoman navy sailed through the Dardanelles and the Sea of Marmara and anchored within sight of Constantinople, which was now completely cut off from the outside world. During the first week of April, Mehmet massed his forces in Thrace and marched them into position before the Theodosian walls, beginning the siege of the city with a tremendous bombardment from his artillery park of giant cannon. The siege continued for seven weeks, with almost continual bombardment and with frequent attacks on the walls by the Turkish infantry. The Byzantines and their Genoese allies, outnumbered more than ten to one, defended the city valiantly, commanded by the emperor and his Genoese commander, Giustiniani. In the early weeks of the siege the Byzantines were able to keep the Turks out of the Golden Horn by stretching an enormous chain across its entrance (three sections of it survive, in the Maritime, Military and Archaeological museums), but one night the sultan had the ships of his fleet placed on rollers and pulled across the ridge above Galata, so that by morning they were all in the Golden Horn. This put the Byzantines at an even greater disadvantage, for they were now forced to take men from their already inadequate ranks on the Theodosian walls to defend the sea walls along the Golden Horn. But they fought on, though the walls were breached in many places, repelling attacks that often took the Janissaries, the elite corps of the Turkish army, into the inner line of defences.

The sultan decided to make a final all-out attack in the early hours of Tuesday, 29th May. The attack began with a heavy artillery barrage, followed by repeated attacks by waves of Turkish infantry who hurled themselves against the walls, but still the defenders managed somehow to repel them. The sultan then threw in his main reserve, the Janissaries, one contingent of which managed to scale the walls at their weakest point. During the fighting there, Giustiniani received a fatal wound and was carried away by his men. This proved to be the turning-point in the battle, for the defenders now became disheartened and were no longer able to hold back the Janissaries, who poured through a breach in the walls near the Adrianople Gate (Edirne Kapı; *see p. 200*). Constantine fought on with his men until he was killed beneath the walls of his fallen city.

Istanbul: capital of the Ottoman Empire

All resistance ceased within a few hours, and by noon the city was completely in Turkish hands. Then, in keeping with Muslim practice, the Sultan turned his soldiers loose to loot and pillage for three days. They stripped the city of all its wealth and took as slaves most of the young and able Greeks who had survived the siege. Early in the afternoon Sultan Mehmet rode triumphantly into the city, acclaimed by his soldiers as 'Fatih', or the Conqueror, the name by which he would thenceforth be known. He rode to Haghia Sophia, which was filled with terrified refugees who were being carried off into slavery by Turkish soldiers. Fatih had the building cleared and ordered that it be converted into a mosque at once. This was done, and on the following Friday the sultan attended the first Islamic service in Aya Sofya Camii, the Mosque of Haghia Sophia.

Soon after his capture of Constantinople, Fatih began to repair the damage it had sustained during the siege and in the decades of decay before the Conquest. A year or so later he transferred his government from Edirne to Constantinople, which thus became the capital of the Ottoman Empire. He constructed a palace on the Third Hill, in the quarter later known as Beyazıt. Some years later he built a second and more extensive palace, Topkapı Sarayı, on the acropolis above the confluence of the Bosphorus and the Golden Horn. By 1470 he had completed the great mosque complex that bears his name, Fatih Camii, the Mosque of the Conqueror. Many of Fatih's viziers followed his example, building mosques and pious foundations of their own, each of which soon became the centre of its neighbourhood, together developing into the new Ottoman city that the Turks came to call Istanbul. Fatih also repeopled the city, forcibly transplanting thousands of his subjects to the new capital. Thus the city took on the patchwork complexion—Turks, Greeks, Albanians, Armenians—for which it was famous for so long. During the last decade of the 15th century, large numbers of Sephardic Jewish refugees from Spain were welcomed to the empire by Beyazıt II (r. 1481–1512), Fatih's son and successor. By the end of the century Istanbul was a thriving and populous city, once again the capital of an empire.

The reign of Süleyman the Magnificent

Beyazıt II was succeeded by his son Selim I (r. 1512–20), who extended the bounds of the Ottoman Empire through the Middle East into Egypt with his capture of Cairo in 1517, after which he and his successors added the title of Caliph to that of Sultan.

Selim was succeeded by his eldest son, Süleyman, known in the East as 'the Lawgiver' and in the West as 'the Magnificent'. During Süleyman's long reign, 1520–66, the Ottoman Empire reached the peak of its fortunes and became the most powerful state in the world. Süleyman personally led his armies in a dozen victorious campaigns, failing only in his attempt in 1529 to take Vienna, which thereafter set the limit to Ottoman expansion into Europe. At the same time his fleet, commanded by pirate-admirals like Kılıç Ali Pasha (*see p. 232*) and Barbarossa (*see p. 250*), was conquering the Aegean islands and extending the borders of the empire along the coast of North Africa as far as Tunis and Algiers. Loot from these campaigns, and tribute and taxes from conquered territories, enormously enriched the Empire, and much of this wealth was used by Süleyman and his viziers to adorn Istanbul with palaces, mosques and pious foundations. The grandest of the structures built during this epoch is the Süleymaniye, the mosque complex completed for the sultan in 1557 by his Chief Architect, the great Sinan.

According to Islamic law, the sultan, like any other Muslim, is allowed four wives, though he may have as many slave concubines as he can maintain. The two women who headed a sultan's harem were his mother, the Valide Sultan, and his chief 'wife', the First Kadın. Early in his reign, Süleyman took as his First Kadın a woman whom he called Hürrem, 'the Cheerful One', better known in the West as Roxelana (*see p. 135*). She worked hard to secure the line to the throne for her son, Selim, who, like many a son of a brilliant father, failed to live up to expectations. He succeeded to the throne on Süleyman's death in 1566. Historians consider this to be a turning-point in the history of the Ottomans, for with Selim's reign the Empire began its long and steady decline.

THE OTTOMAN SUCCESSION

There was no hereditary aristocracy in Ottoman Istanbul. Positions of power were filled by ministers who were more often than not Christian Greeks and Armenians who had risen through the ranks and converted to Islam. And though the early sultans had entered into dynastic marriages with the daughters of neighbouring beys and khans, after the reign of Selim I they stopped doing this. The sultans did not marry; instead they could take their pick of a harem full of slave concubines. None of these women was originally a Muslim, for Islamic law does not permit the enslavement of the faithful, only of infidels. So the mothers of a whole succession of sultans were Greeks, Circassians, Armenians, Georgians, Jews, Serbians, even Frenchwomen. There was no law of primogeniture: when a sultan died he was succeeded by whichever of his sons got to Istanbul first and physically claimed the throne. Needless to say, this caused panic and feuds among the harem ladies. All the mothers of sons hoped to become Valide Sultan, their only chance of making something of their lives. For otherwise, on the accession of another man's son, they would be relegated to obscurity in the 'Palace of Tears', the Eski Saray at Beyazıt. Not only that, but in accordance with the fratricide law introduced by Fatih, a new sultan would order all his brothers to be strangled, and pregnant harem ladies (who might be bearing sons) were executed. The strangling sentence was commuted to house arrest in the reign of Ahmet I (*see p. 82*). Later still, in the reign of Süleyman II (acceded 1687), a law of seniority was introduced, whereby the succession first exhausted all the claimants of the older generation before embarking on the younger.

The reign of the women

During Selim II's reign, 1566–74, the sultan left all affairs of state to his Grand Vizier, Sokollu Mehmet Pasha, while he himself caroused with his women and his favourites in the Harem. Sokollu Mehmet was a Bosnian who had become Grand Vizier in the last year of Süleyman's reign. He was one of the most capable men who ever held that office, and it was because of his leadership that the empire still continued to expand under Selim, who was pleasure-loving, famously addicted to the bottle, and little interested in affairs of state. Nevertheless, during the course of his reign, the Ottomans conquered Cyprus and Georgia.

Selim's First Kadın was a Venetian, who went under the palace name of Nurbanu ('Lady of Light'). She used his drunkenness to take complete charge of the Harem, running its affairs and those of the palace to her own advantage. Historians refer to this as the beginning of the 'Reign of the Women', a period in which a series of strong and determined Harem ladies seized control from their weak and dissolute sultans. The two most powerful women in the Harem were invariably the Valide Sultan and the First Kadın, the mother of the reigning sultan and his principal 'wife', between whom there were often violent struggles for power.

When Selim died on 21st December 1574, after a drunken fall in the Harem bath, Nurbanu had all but one of his five sons strangled so that her own child, Murat III, would succeed him. Nurbanu corrupted her son by supplying him at a very early age with all of the beautiful women that she could buy in the Istanbul slave market, so that while he spent his time with them she would be free to run the palace. Sokollu Mehmet Pasha continued to serve as Grand Vizier during the early years of Murat's reign, but when he was assassinated in 1578 Nurbanu became the power behind the throne. She eventually lost power to her son's First Kadın, another Venetian girl, known as Safiye ('Untainted'), whose influence over Murat was so great that she persuaded him to adopt a more favourable policy toward her native city.

When Murat died, on 16th January 1595, Safiye had all but one of his 19 brothers strangled so that her son, Mehmet III, would become sultan. Safiye ruled the palace as Valide Sultan until 1602, when she herself was strangled by one of her rivals in the Harem. The mosque that she had begun, the Yeni Cami, was to remain unfinished for half a century. Mehmet III died the following year and was succeeded by his eldest son, Ahmet I, this time without bloodshed. Ahmet, who was only 13 years old at the time of his accession, soon fell under the influence of his First Kadın, a Greek girl named Kösem (see p. 107), who was herself only in her early teens when she first entered the Harem. Kösem ruled the Harem throughout her husband's reign, as well as through those of her first son Murat IV and her second son İbrahim (1640–48). She even managed to cling to power during the early years in the reign of her grandson, Mehmet IV (1648–87), but in 1651 she was strangled on the orders of Mehmet's mother, Turhan Hatice (who completed the Yeni Cami). Thus ended the Reign of the Women.

The decline of the Ottoman Empire

Another turning-point in Ottoman history came in 1683, when the Turks failed in their second attempt to take Vienna. The tide of Ottoman expansion had turned, and thereafter the Turks began to lose more battles than they won. By the end of the 17th century the fortunes of the Empire had declined to the point where its basic problems could no longer be ignored, even in the palace. The Empire gave up large parts of its territories in the Balkans and Carpathian Basin after losing wars with European powers. Within, the Empire was weakened by anarchy and rebellion, particularly among the subject Christians in the Balkans, who now began to nourish dreams of independence.

Disastrous wars and recalcitrant Janissaries (*see box*), coupled with repeated outbreaks of fire and plague, eventually led to a movement of reform in the Ottoman Empire, in the reign of Selim III (r. 1789–1807). Influenced by the advice of a trusted Armenian, who had been in Paris and was full of enthusiasm for the French Revolution, Selim attempted to restructure the Ottoman army along European lines. By this means he hoped to protect the Empire from further encroachments on the part of foreign powers and from anarchy and rebellion within its own borders. But Selim's efforts were resisted and eventually frustrated by the Janissaries, who felt that their privileged position was being threatened by the reforms. Selim was at heart a gentle man, a poet and a gifted musician. He was assassinated in Topkapı, and it was not for another two decades that the power of the Janissaries was finally crushed.

THE JANISSARY CORPS

The Janissaries, in Turkish *Yeni Çeri*, the 'new troops', were an infantry corps who formed the sultan's household platoon and bodyguard. Formed in the reign of Murat I, their ranks were fed by the *devşirme*, the conscripting of Christian youths from all over the Empire. These boys, if they served well, could look forward to satisfying careers and positions of influence and trust. As a result, they felt loyal to their sultan. But by the late 18th century the situation had changed. The Janissaries had almost become a guild, a closed order, with new recruits being furnished by the sons or relatives of existing members. They had a stranglehold on the government and the army, though their skill in arms was out of date. They were prone to mutiny: when roused to revolt, they traditionally upturned their rice cauldrons and banged them. The hollow sound of these improvised gongs became a sign for any sultan to tremble and then capitulate, if he didn't want to find himself overthrown in favour of a brother. The proposed army reforms of Selim III precipitated a full-scale rebellion. Selim was deposed, replaced by his reactionary brother Mustafa IV, and eventually murdered. But the Janissaries' hour had come. For Mustafa was not long on the throne, and his successor was Selim's cousin, a man whose life had been saved by a loyal harem slave (*see pp. 88–89*). He was to reign as Mahmut II, and in 1826 he crushed the Janissaries forever, bombarding their barracks at Aksaray and setting it on fire. Those who did not perish were beheaded. The corps was at an end.

Attempts at reform and the last years of the Ottoman Empire

Mahmut II (r. 1808–39) instituted an extensive programme of reform in all the basic institutions of the Ottoman Empire, remodelling them along Western lines. This programme continued for a time during the reigns of his immediate successors, Abdülmecit I (r. 1839–61) and Abdülaziz (r. 1861–76). The reform movement (in Turkish, *Tanzimat*) culminated in 1876 with the promulgation of the first Ottoman constitution and the establishment of a parliament, which convened on 19th March 1877. But the following year the constitution was revoked and the parliament dissolved by Abdülhamit II (r. 1876–1909), who ruled as an autocrat for the rest of his reign, trying to preserve the disintegrating Ottoman Empire.

The reform movement had came too late, and Abdülhamit's reactionary stance could not prevent the dismemberment of the Empire, which in the 19th century lost considerable territory as the subject peoples of the Balkans fought wars of national liberation. Between 1804 and 1878 five independent states came into being on what had been Ottoman territory in the Balkans: Serbia, Greece, Montenegro, Romania and Bulgaria. The Ottoman Empire was the Sick Man of Europe and it seemed to be just a matter of time before it would pass on.

1908 was the year of the 'Young Turk' revolution, led by a group of enthusiastic young intellectuals who promised freedom, socialism, economic liberalism, the emancipation of women, technological modernisation, democracy—all the buzzwords in the early 20th-century lexicon. In 1909 Sultan Abdülhamit was deposed and despatched by train to exile in Salonica. His chief eunuch was hanged, his harem dispersed and his family jewels sold. The Young Turks restored parliament and the constitution. But this second experiment in Ottoman democracy lasted little longer than the first, for the Young Turks, under the leadership of Enver Pasha, set up a military dictatorship in which neither the new sultan, Mehmet V (r. 1909–18), nor the people had any voice in the government. In 1912 the Greeks, Serbs and Bulgarians inflicted a severe defeat on the Turks in the First Balkan War, in which the Ottoman Empire lost virtually all of Macedonia and Thrace, its last remaining territories in Europe. In 1913 the Balkan allies fell to fighting among themselves, and in the process the Turks regained eastern Thrace.

In 1914 Enver Pasha brought the Ottoman Empire into the First World War on the German side, a decision that proved to be a fatal mistake. For when the war ended the Ottoman Empire was in ruins, its armies defeated in Palestine and the Caucasus, and Istanbul was occupied by Allied troops. A Greek army landed in Smyrna (modern İzmir) in May 1919 with the approval of the USA, France and Great Britain, and soon afterwards began advancing into western Asia Minor as far as the Sea of Marmara. The defeated Ottoman army was in no position to resist them, and so on 10th August 1919 Sultan Mehmet VI (r. 1918–22), a puppet of the Allies, was forced to agree to an armistice. In doing so he put his signature to the Treaty of Sèvres, by which the Ottoman Empire lost all of its territory except Istanbul and that part of Anatolia which was not occupied by the Greeks and the other Allies.

However, the great mass of the Turkish people in Anatolia refused to comply with the terms of the armistice or of the Treaty of Sèvres. They had found another rallying cry: nationalism. Under the Young Turks the people of Istanbul had begun to concern themselves with their ethnicity. Instead of thinking of themselves as Ottoman, which had been a supra-national concept, they began to call themselves Turkish. Now, under the leadership of Mustafa Kemal (1881–1938), a Gallipoli veteran born in Salonica, Turks embraced the idea of a nation state. Kemal (later to be known as Atatürk, 'Father of the Turks') called upon his fellow Turks to embark upon a war of national liberation. In the following year he presided over a meeting in Ankara of the new Turkish National Assembly, which formed a government in opposition to the sultan's puppet regime in Istanbul. The Turkish Nationalists then defeated the Greeks in several engagements, and by September 1922 the Greek army was forced to withdraw from Anatolia. During the following year about 1,400,000 Greeks were forced to leave Asia Minor and to resettle in mainland Greece, part of the notorious 'population exchange' which also saw some 400,000 Turks living in Greek territory being returned 'home'. This was one of the results of the Treaty of Versailles, signed in July 1923, which established the boundaries of Turkey as they are today except for the Hatay province, annexed in 1939.

Meanwhile, the Turkish National Assembly had, on 1st November 1922, declared that the Osmanlı sultanate no longer existed, whereupon Mehmet VI fled from Istanbul aboard a British warship. He died in San Remo in 1926. His younger brother Abdülmecit II succeeded him as Caliph only.

The climax of these developments came on 29th October 1923, when the Turkish National Assembly proclaimed the founding of the Turkish Republic, with Atatürk as its first President. At the same time the Assembly declared that Ankara was the capital of the new nation. Soon afterwards the embassies of the great European powers packed up and moved to new quarters in Ankara, leaving their old mansions along the Grande Rue de Péra in Istanbul. And so for the first time in 16 centuries Istanbul was no longer the capital of an empire.

Atatürk's reforms and modern Istanbul

The measures that were taken to transform a once-powerful empire into a new and energetic nation, capable of rising to a position of similar influence in world affairs, were drastic: Islam was confined to the private sphere with the abolition of the office of Şeyhülislam, the closure of religious schools, the unveiling of women and the dissolution of the dervish orders. Islamic time-keepers were dismissed and the Western calendar was adopted; the Ottoman script was replaced with the Latin alphabet and the Turkish language was purged of Persian and Arabic words. It was made illegal to wear the fez. The office of Caliph of Islam was abolished in 1924. The Caliph, 'Commander of the Faithful and Successor of the Prophet of the Lord of the Universe, Protector of the Holy Cities of Mecca, Medina and Jerusalem', had been the head of the Islamic world since Abu Bakr, father-in-law of the Prophet Mohammed. After 1517, when Selim I conquered the Mamluks of Egypt and assumed the title, the Caliph of Islam was always the Ottoman sultan. Abdülmecit II was the last holder of the title. After its abolition in 1924, he was forced to flee from Turkey: he and all members of the Ottoman dynasty received the order to leave forever. Abdülmecit II died in Paris in 1944.

Not surprisingly, the modern metropolis is a very different place from what it was in the days when was the capital of the Ottoman Empire. When the Republic of Turkey conducted its first census in 1924, the population of Istanbul was 1,165,866. Of those, 61 percent were Muslim Turks, 26 percent Greeks, seven percent Armenians, and seven percent Jews. The population is now 15 million, with all of the non-Muslim minorities together now making less than one per cent and Turkish virtually the only language that is heard on the streets. As Orhan Pamuk so succinctly puts it, in his *Istanbul: Memories and the City* (Tr. Maureen Freely), more Greeks, Armenians and Jews have left Istanbul in the past half century than did so in the 50 years after the Ottoman conquest.

The surface area of the city has increased by a factor of four under the Turkish Republic, creeping up the Bosphorus to within sight of the Black Sea and hungrily eating up the miles along both the European and Asian shores of the Marmara. The construction boom involved in this enormous expansion has destroyed most of the old Ottoman neighbourhoods and their beautiful old wooden houses, replacing them with concrete apartment blocks and commercial buildings. Skyscrapers bristle along the skyline of the hills on the lower European shore of the Bosphorus, whose seaside villages have now been amalgamated into a continuous sprawling metropolitan mass.

The water which encircles the city is underused, both as a feature of the landscape and as a transport opportunity: streets are jammed with traffic and the air is polluted. A third great Bosphorus road bridge is to be built, near to where the strait enters the Black Sea. There are now two international airports, the first named after Atatürk, the second after his adopted daughter, Sabiha Gökçen (1913–2001), the first female fighter pilot in the world. But urban renewal has not been entirely absent. There are now parks and playgrounds along the Bosphorus, the Marmara and the Golden Horn, as well as pedestrian malls and restored market areas in several parts of the city. The Turkish Touring and Automobile Club, under the direction of the late Çelik Gülersoy, restored a number of late Ottoman mansions and palaces and converted them into elegant hotels, thus not only preserving these monuments but bringing them back into city life.

The Turkish Republic, through Atatürk's urging, early on established a policy of preserving historical monuments, beginning with Topkapı Palace in 1927. Many of the Ottoman monuments that have been restored are once again in public use. Archaeological excavations have uncovered parts of the ancient city and some of its lost monuments, including the Forum of Theodosius in Beyazıt Meydanı, the Harbour of Theodosius at Yenikapı, and some fragments of the Great Palace of Byzantium.

Today's city has to face the challenges of overdevelopment, renewed Islamism and the tensions of Turkey's relationship with Europe, the latter a thorny question that is as present now as it was in the days of the greatest sultans and the most arrogant and overweening of Pera ambassadors. Europe has never wanted to let Istanbul go; Istanbul has thus far never wholeheartedly abandoned her origins. Time will tell what comes next. Those who love the city believe that she will survive, just as she has so many times in the past—though perhaps in yet another guise, and perhaps not in a way that any of us expects.

BYZANTINE ART & ARCHITECTURE

Byzantine churches

The oldest surviving church in Istanbul is St John the Baptist of Studius, built in 450. The church is a **basilica** (fig. 1), a plan that was developed in Roman times for civic purposes, and which in the Early Christian period was widely used for churches. The typical basilica is a long, rectangular building divided by two rows of columns into three parts, a wide central nave flanked by an aisle on either side, while at the eastern end of the nave a semicircular projection forms the apse. The entrance, at the end opposite the apse, is generally preceded by a vestibule, or narthex, and sometimes by an outer vestibule, the exonarthex, which in turn opens into a large arcaded courtyard, the atrium.

Early Byzantine basilicas had pitched roofs and flat ceilings. Later, most notably in the reign of Justinian, a major innovation was made by introducing a dome. Two outstanding examples of the **domed basilica** (fig. 2) survive in Istanbul, the churches of Haghia Eirene and Haghia Sophia, both completed in 537. In Haghia Eirene the nave is surmounted by a large dome with a smaller, slightly elliptical domical vault to its west. In Haghia Sophia the enormous central dome is supported to east and west by two semidomes of equal diameter, and there are other modifications to the standard plan, but in essence it is a basilica.

Another type of classical building sometimes used for early Byzantine churches was

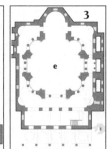

of a **centralised plan** (fig. 3), either circular or polygonal. In Istanbul the most famous and beautiful example of this type is the church of SS Sergius and Bacchus, built by Justinian in 527.

The Iconoclastic Period from the beginning of the 7th to the mid-9th century (*see p. 12*) may be called the Dark Ages of Byzantium. Little or no building of new churches was done, and virtually all the existing figurative mosaics and frescoes were destroyed. When Byzantine architecture began to revive in the second half of the 9th century, a new type of church building came into being,

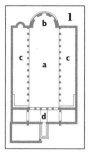
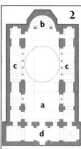

1: Early Christian basilica, with nave (a) ending in an apse (b). The nave is separated by lateral colonnades from the side aisles (c). In front of the church is the narthex (d). 2: Domed basilica (Haghia Eirene). Once again there is a nave (a) ending in an apse (b), two side aisles (c) and a narthex (d), but the centre of the nave is surmounted by a circular dome. 3: Church with a centralised plan (SS Sergius and Bacchus), where everything is centred architecturally on the central domed space (e).

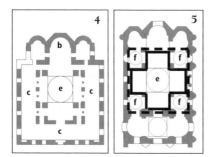

4: Cross-domed church, where the central domed space (e) is surrounded by barrel vaults, with aisles (c) on three sides. The central apse (b) is flanked by side apses. 5: Cross-in-square, inscribed-cross or quincunx church. The central dome (e) is flanked by four bays of equal size forming a Greek cross (black line). Beside each of these bays rises another bay surmounted by a smaller dome (f), forming a square (dotted line) around the cross.

one generally known as the **cross-domed church** (*fig. 4*). In this type, a central dome is surrounded on the axes of the building by four long barrel vaults resting on four strong corner piers, thus forming an internal cross; on three sides there are aisles and galleries, so that the exterior is rectangular. At the east end a wide central apse is flanked by two smaller side apses; thenceforth three apses became the rule. At the west end there is the usual narthex.

Another type is known as the **four-column church**, though it is not really a separate type but is more a development of the cross-domed design. The church of Constantine Lips (Fenari Isa Camii) is an example of this style, whose most striking internal features are the four columns that take the place of the corner piers of the earlier types as supports for the dome. Churches of this type tend to be small and tall, more or less square externally, but preserving the cruciform plan within. There are no galleries, except sometimes over the narthex, but the four corners of the cross are occupied by domed bays or by domical vaults on high drums; these, together with the central dome, form a **cross-in-square, inscribed cross or quincunx** (*fig. 5*), terms by which this type is often known. Such churches appeared in Constantinople in the 9th–10th centuries and thereafter became almost standard; their small size was suitable to the declining revenues of the shrinking Empire, while the internal form provided ample areas for mosaic and fresco decoration.

All the Byzantine churches in Constantinople were built of brick, including Haghia Sophia, and they were generally little adorned on the exterior, depending for their effect on the warm colour of the walls. Towards the end of the Empire, in the 13th–14th centuries, exteriors were often articulated by patterns in the brickwork and by the variation in colour between brick and stone.

Decoration in Byzantine churches

While the outsides of the churches may have been austere, the interiors blazed with colour and life. Here the whole majesty of heaven was replicated in precious marbles and shimmering mosaic. The lower parts of the walls up to the springing of the vaults were sheathed in marble. The most magnificent example of marble revetment is that in Haghia Sophia, where a dozen different kinds of rare and costly marbles are used, the thin slabs sawn in two and opened out to form symmetrical designs. Haghia Sophia is of course unique, but even the humbler and smaller churches of a later period had their revetment, largely of the common but attractive greyish-white marble from the nearby quarries on the island of Proconnesus in the Marmara. Most of the churches surviving in Istanbul have lost this decoration, but an excellent example survives almost intact in St Saviour in Chora (Kariye Müzesi).

The vaults, domes and upper walls of churches were covered in mosaic. Gold was often used in the tesserae, which were often stuck into the surface plaster at a slight angle, so that they would catch the candlelight and shimmer more effectively. The mosaics of the earlier Byzantine period seem to have consisted chiefly of a gold ground, round the edges of which, emphasising the architectural forms, were wide bands of floral decoration in naturalistic designs and colours; at appropriate places there would be a simple cross in outline. Large areas of this simple but effective decoration survive from Justinian's time in the dome and the aisle vaults of Haghia Sophia. It appears that in Haghia Sophia, at least, there were originally no pictorial mosaics. In the century following Justinian's death, however, picture mosaics became the vogue and an elaborate iconography was worked out which regulated which parts of the Holy Story should be represented and where the various pictures should be placed in the church building. The form of the church, a dome over a square, served as a symbol for the infinite sphere of the heavens rising above the earth. Thus the space in the dome was reserved for the divine: Christ, the Blessed Virgin, the hosts of angels. On the walls below appear scenes from the earthly lives of Christ, the Virgin and the saints. Between the two, in the pendentives that link the heavenly dome to the earthly body of the church, we traditionally find the four Evangelists, who spread the gospel of Christ to mankind.

After the hiatus of the Iconoclastic Age (*see p. 12*) there was a revival of pictorial art, still in the highly stylised and formal tradition of the earlier period, and all the great churches were again filled with holy pictures. The late 13th and 14th centuries were the time of the Palaeologue Revival, the last great flowering of Byzantine culture before the Ottoman Conquest in 1453, when art took on a more humanistic form. The fragmentary *Deësis* in Haghia Sophia in one example, but the most extensive and splendid mosaics from this time in Istanbul are the long cycles of the lives of Christ and the Virgin in the church of St Saviour in Chora, dating from the early 14th century and brilliantly restored by the Byzantine Institute. To this date also belong the glorious frescoes in the parecclesion of that church and the series of mosaics in the parecclesion of the church of the Pammakaristos (Fethiye Camii). The art of these pictures shows a decisive break away from the hieratic formalism of the earlier tradition: it has been suggested that the very poverty that had beleaguered Byzantium in the 13th century, meaning that wall painting took the place of expensive mosaic, meant that artists learned a new freedom of modelling which they then transposed back into mosaic in these 14th-century commissions. In Byzantium, sadly, this new freedom of expression had all too short a life.

OTTOMAN ART
& ARCHITECTURE

Mosques

The mosques of Istanbul fall into a small number of fairly distinct types. The simplest of all, found in all periods, takes the form of an oblong room covered by a tiled pitched roof; often there was an interior wooden dome but most of these have perished in fires and have been replaced by flat ceilings. The second type is the square room covered by a masonry dome resting directly on the walls. This was generally small and simple but could sometimes take on monumental proportions, as in the mosque of Selim I. Occasionally, as there, mosques had side rooms used as tabhanes, hospices for travelling dervishes. Later, in the 18th–19th centuries, a more elaborate form of this type was adopted for the Baroque mosques, usually with a small projecting apse for the mihrab, the niche that indicates the direction of Mecca.

The next two types of mosque both date from an earlier period and are rare in Istanbul. The two-domed type is essentially a large room divided by an open arch, each half being surmounted by a dome. It is derived from a style common in the Bursa period of Ottoman architecture, and hence is often known as the **Bursa type** (*see plan on p. 129*). A modification occurs when the second unit has only a semidome. Mosques of this type always have side chambers. A fourth type, of which a splendid example occurs in Istanbul (the mosque of Piyale Pasha), also derives from the earlier Seljuk and Ottoman periods: a rectangular room covered by a multiplicity of domes of equal size supported on pillars; this is often called the great-mosque or **Ulu Cami type**.

The **mosques of the classical period** (c. 1500–1650)—what most people think of as 'typical' Ottoman mosques—are more elaborate than their predecessors. They derive from a fusion of a native Turkish tradition with certain elements of the plan of Haghia Sophia. The great imperial mosques have a vast central dome supported to east and west by semidomes of equal diameter. (All mosques face in the direction of Mecca, which in Istanbul is approximately southeast, but for simplicity this book will follow the convention that they face east.) This strongly resembles the plan of Haghia Sophia, but there are significant differences, dictated partly by the native Turkish tradition, partly by the requirements of Islamic ritual.

Haghia Sophia is a domed basilica, divided into a nave and side aisles by a curtain of columns, both on the ground floor and at gallery level. The classical mosques suppress this division by getting rid of as many of the columns as possible, thus making the interior almost open and visible from all sides. Moreover, the galleries, which in Haghia Sophia are as wide as the aisles, are reduced to narrow balconies against the side walls. This is the plan of Beyazıt Camii and the Süleymaniye. Sometimes this centralisation and opening-up is carried even further by adding two extra semidomes to north and south, as at the mosques of the Şehzade, Sultanahmet and Yeni Cami. A further innovation is the attention paid to the exterior, which itself becomes monumental, in handsome grey stone, with the descending domes and semidomes balanced by the upward thrust of the minaret or minarets. The smaller mosques have a single minaret which is almost always on the right side of the entrance, while the larger imperial mosques may have two, four, or even six, in which case they rise from the corners of the building and/or the courtyard. These minarets often have elaborately sculptured şerefes, or müezzin's balconies.

Many mosques are provided with a **courtyard**, the *avlu*, surrounded on three sides by a domed arcade. In the centre of this courtyard there is usually a *şadırvan*, or ablution fountain, where the faithful perform their ritual *abdest* before going into the mosque to pray. Almost all mosques of whatever type are preceded by a **porch** of three or five domed bays. The stone platform under the porch is called the *son cemaat yeri*, literally the 'place of last assembly'. When the mosque is full, as it often is on the occasion of the Friday noon prayer, latecomers perform their devotions on this platform, which is strewn with rugs for the purpose.

The **interior furnishings** of all mosques are essentially the same. The most important element is the *mihrab*, the niche set into the centre of the east wall to show the direction of Mecca. In the imperial mosques of Istanbul the mihrab is invariably grand, with the niche itself made of finely carved marble and with the wall around it sheathed in ceramic tiles. To the right of the mihrab is the *mimber*, or pulpit. At the time of the noon prayer on Friday the *imam*, or preacher, mounts the steps of the mimber and gives the weekly sermon. To the left of the mihrab, often standing against the main pier on that side, is the *Kuran kursu*, where the imam sits cross-legged while he reads the Koran to the congregation. And to the right of the entrance in the larger mosques there is usually a raised platform, the *müezzin mahfili*, where the müezzins kneel when they are chanting the responses to the prayers of the imam.

In the imperial mosques there is always a *hünkar mahfili*, or imperial loggia, a chamber screened off by a gilded grille so that the sultan and his party would be shielded from the public gaze when they attended services. This royal enclosure is usually in the far left corner of the gallery as one faces the mihrab, and it often has its own entrance from outside the mosque.

The külliye

All imperial mosques and most of the grander non-imperial foundations form the centre of a *külliye*, a complex of religious and philanthropic institutions comprising a *vakıf*, or pious foundation, often endowed with great wealth. The founder invariably built his *türbe* (mausoleum) in the garden or graveyard behind the mosque; these are simple buildings, square or polygonal, covered by a dome and with a small entrance porch, sometimes beautifully decorated inside with tiles.

Of the utilitarian institutions, almost always built around four sides of a central arcaded and domed courtyard, the commonest is the *medrese*, or college. Originally these were for the study of the Islamic sciences: the Koran, the words and deeds of the prophet (*hadis*) and jurisprudence. Each student's cell, or *hücre*, had its dome and fireplace. The cells opened off the courtyard, which usually had a central fountain, and in the middle of one side of the portico was the large domed *dershane*, or lecture hall. Sometimes the medrese formed three sides of a mosque courtyard, while elsewhere it was an independent building, occasionally with an unusual shape, such as in the octagonal medrese of Rüstem Pasha. For much of the period of the Empire these medreses functioned at several academic levels, some being mere secondary schools, others teaching more advanced subjects, while still others were colleges for specialised studies: not only Arabic philology or the *hadis* but also subjects such as medicine. There were also primary schools, or *sibyan mektebi* (often simply called a *mektep*), which were usually small buildings with a single, domed classroom and sometimes an apartment for the teacher, or *hoca*.

The larger imperial foundations included a hospital (*darüşşifa*), a caravansaray and a public kitchen (*imaret*). Large institutions like the Süleymaniye also included a mental asylum (*timarhane*). The caravansaray was built to the same general plan as the medrese, with the domed rooms around the central courtyard serving to house and feed travellers. The imarets had vast domed kitchens with tall, stout chimneys and large vaulted refectories. They provided free food for all the people associated with the külliye, as well as for the poor of the neighbourhood. All the other institutions were free too, and in the great days of the Ottoman Empire they were very efficiently managed. In recent years many of them have been restored and are again serving the people of Istanbul, with Ottoman hospitals operating as clinics, schoolhouses functioning as children's libraries, and medreses being used as cultural centres or student dormitories.

The kütüphane and the tekke
Some pious foundations were not part of a mosque complex, but were independent institutions. One example was the Ottoman library, or *kütüphane*; another was the *tekke*, or dervish monastery, of which there were once more than 300, housing the members of the 17 different orders represented in Istanbul. All of these were closed when the dervish orders were banned in the early years of the Turkish Republic, and most of the buildings have since been destroyed or have fallen into ruins.

The han
Another important institution was the *han*, or inn, whose function was closely parallel that of the caravansaray. Like so many Ottoman structures, the han was built around one or more courtyards, but it consisted of two or three storeys, with the ground floor used as stables for the pack animals of the traders' caravans and the upper floors serving as guest-rooms for the merchants and as storage places for their wares. These hans were virtually self-sufficient institutions, complete with kitchens, dining-halls, baths, lavatories, a smithy and a mosque, and they were the mainstay of Istanbul's commercial life all through the Ottoman period. There are scores of them still extant in Istanbul, some of them as much as five centuries old. A large number of them, not surprisingly, are clustered around the Grand Bazaar.

Hamams
One of the most important of all the Ottoman foundations was the *hamam*, or public

bath, whose revenues were often used to pay for the upkeep of the other institutions in a külliye. Many are still functioning in Istanbul.

Turkish hamams are built to a similar general design to the baths of ancient Rome. Ordinarily, a hamam has three distinct sections. The first chamber that you enter is the *camekan*, the Roman apodyterium. This is usually the most monumental chamber in the hamam. It is typically a vast square room covered by a dome on pendentives or squinches, with an elaborate fountain in the centre. It is used as a reception hall and a place to relax and sip tea after bathing. It also sometimes doubles as the changing room: around the walls there is a raised platform where the bathers undress and leave their clothes. The first of the actual bathing chambers is the *soğukluk* or *ılıklık*, the equivalent of the tepidarium, a chamber of intermediate temperature that serves as an anteroom to the bath itself, keeping the cold air out on one side and the hot air in on the other. It is almost always a mere passageway, and usually contains the lavatories. The *hararet* is the steam room, the Roman caldarium. In the centre of it there is usually a large marble platform, the *göbektaşı*, or 'belly-stone', which is heated by a wood fire in the furnace room below, the *külhan*. The patrons lie on the belly-stone to sweat and to be massaged before bathing at one of the wall-fountains at the side. One important difference between Turkish baths and Roman baths is that hamams do not always have pools for immersion. The preference is for running water, and unless the hamam is fed by a spring, water will be supplied by taps. Bathers fill the basins provided and pour the water over themselves.

Fountains

Turkish fountains are ubiquitous; there are more than 700 in Istanbul dating from Ottoman times, and even one or two that may date from before the Turkish Conquest. The most monumental of these are the imperial street-fountains, such as the splendid fountain of Ahmet III beside the main entrance to Topkapı Palace. This huge structure is really a composite of the two basic types of fountain to be seen all over Istanbul. These are the *sebil*, or fountain house, and the *çeşme*, the founts of water themselves.

The sebil, which is often used to adorn the corner of a mosque precinct, is usually a domed structure with three or more barred openings in its façade. In Ottoman times these sebils were staffed with attendants who passed out cups of water free to thirsty passers-by. There are scores of them still standing in Istanbul, and many of them still serve refreshments to passers-by (with the difference that you have to pay for the snacks you want).

The most common type of Turkish fountain is the çeşme. In its most basic form it is merely a niche set into a wall, with water flowing from a spout into a marble basin. The water-spout is set into a marble tablet called the mirror-stone (*aynataşı*), which is often decorated with floral or geometric designs in low relief. The niche is usually framed in an arch, while the façade of the surrounding wall is decorated in the same design as the mirror-stone. At the top of this façade there is always a calligraphic inscription giving the name of the donor and the date of construction. The older inscriptions are often in the form of chronograms, in which the numerical values assigned to the Arabic letters spell out the date of foundation. These chronograms became a favourite artform for Ottoman poets, who vied with one another in composing clever and original epigrams, which would not only give the name of the donor and the date of foundation but would also advertise the poetic talents of the composer.

SINAN THE ARCHITECT

No discussion of Ottoman architecture would be complete without at least a brief biography of the great Sinan, who created most of the masterpieces commissioned by Süleyman and his immediate successors.

Sinan was born of Christian parents, probably Armenian, in the Anatolian province of Karaman in about 1492. At the age of about 20 he was taken up in the *devşirme*, the annual levy of Christian youths who were taken into the sultan's service. As was customary, he became a Muslim and was sent to one of the halls of the Palace School in Istanbul (*see p. 78*). He was then assigned to the Janissaries as a military engineer and served in four of Süleyman's campaigns.

Around 1538 Süleyman appointed him Chief Imperial Architect, a post he held for half a century, continuing to serve under Süleyman's two immediate successors, Selim II and Murat III. Sinan built his first mosque in 1538, in Aleppo, and the following year he erected his first mosque in Istanbul; this was Haseki Hürrem Camii, commissioned by Süleyman for his wife Roxelana. In the following half-century he was to adorn Istanbul and the other cities of the Empire with a vast number of mosques and other structures. The *Tezkere-ül Ebniye*, the official list of Sinan's accomplishments, credits him with 81 large mosques, including 42 in Istanbul, 50 smaller mosques, 55 medreses, seven Koran schools, 19 mausolea, 15 public kitchens, three hospitals, six aqueducts, 32 palaces, six storehouses, 22 public baths and two bridges, a total of 323 structures, of which 84 still remain standing in Istanbul alone. He was nearly 50 when he completed his first mosque, 65 when he completed the Süleymaniye, the crowning glory of Ottoman architecture in Istanbul, and 84 when the Selimiye mosque complex in Edirne was completed, a work that is generally agreed to be the supreme masterpiece in the history of Ottoman architecture. Sinan did not pause even then, but continued to work as Chief Architect, and built a half-dozen of Istanbul's finer mosques for the sultan's viziers.

Koca Mimar Sinan, or the 'Great Architect Sinan', as the Turks call him, died in 1588 at the age of 98 (100 according to the Islamic calendar) just a few days after completing his last project, a new gate in the Byzantine sea walls along the Golden Horn. He was buried in a mausoleum that he had constructed himself in the shadow of the Süleymaniye, his greatest work in Istanbul. Sinan was the architect of the golden age of the Ottoman Empire, and his monuments are the magnificent buildings with which he adorned its capital.

Western influences

At the end of the 18th century European influence begins to make itself felt in Istanbul, directing taste and fashion in all branches of art. Architects with names like Raimondo d'Aronco (1857–1932) and Gaspare Fossati (1809–83) begin to appear. Some of these were born in Europe; others were from families that had naturalised: Giulio Mongeri (1873–1953) and Alexander Vallaury (1850–1921) were both born in Istanbul. The architecture that they created is always eclectic, borrowing from European traditions and fusing those elements with Ottoman forms to create a distinctive and always interesting style. The Balyan dynasty of architects is especially notable. The *pater familias* was Krikor, who worked for Abdülhamit I and Selim III. He was succeeded by his son Karabet and grandsons Nikoğos and Sarkis. They built Dolmabahçe Palace, the Ortaköy mosque and many of the palaces and kiosks along both shores of the Bosphorus.

APPLIED ARTS

Turkish tiles

The finest fritware kilns were at İznik, the ancient Nicaea, but tiles and other ceramics were also made (and still are) at Kütahya and in Istanbul itself.

In the early period after the Conquest, tiles were extremely plain and without design. These early examples are usually hexagonal, coloured deep blue, green or turquoise, and sometimes overlaid with an unfired pattern in gold. At this period too we find tiles in the *cuerda seca* technique: instead of a painted design covered by a transparent glaze, the glazes themselves are coloured and the colours are prevented from running into each other by a thread-like dividing line of potassium permanganate (hence the name *cuerda seca*, dry cord); if visible at all this line is deep purple or black. The predominating colours of these tiles are applegreen and bright yellow with subordinate blues and mauves. They are very beautiful, and rare in Istanbul, and the only extensive examples are in the türbe of Prince Mehmet at the Şehzade Camii and in the porch of the Çinili Köşk.

About 1550 this technique gave place to the famous Iznik style, where the design is painted on the clay and covered with an absolutely transparent glaze. On

Left to right from top: Çintamani design; curving '*rumi*' design of the 15th century; blade-shaped leaf design ('*saz*') with stylised rosettes ('*hatais*') within it, a common 16th-century motif; semi-stylised carnation and tulip, also of the 16th century; a naturalistic rose design of the 18th century.

a pure white background the motifs appear in shades of blue and green and tomato red, made with a clay known as Armenian bole, found near Erzurum in eastern Anatolia. It has to be laid on very thickly so that it protrudes from the surface of the tile like sealing-wax. The technique of using it successfully is extremely tricky, to the extent that it was only completely mastered toward 1570 and forgotten again in about 1620, so that absolutely perfect tiles of this type are confined to this half-century. Typical designs include the *çintamani*, wavy lines and concentric circles, originally a Buddhist motif as well as symmetrical patterns of concave and convex curves, sinuous like a wave or a bird's wing. They are known as *rumis* and occur on tiles, carpets and in textiles. Semi-stylised leaves and flowers, notably tulips and carnations are also ubiquitous (*see illustrations opposite*).

In the 18th century, European influence can be seen in tile design. Floral motifs are naturalistic instead of stylised. Today fine imitations of traditional tiles and ceramics are made at Kütahya, some of them so fine that it is hard to distinguish, at first glance, between the modern and the original.

Woodwork, calligraphy and carpets

The Turks are not traditional seafarers: most of the great pirate captains of the Ottoman Empire were Greek, Croatian or Italian-born. Where Turks excel, however, is in woodwork and joinery, typically without the use of nails or adhesive. They are excellent carpenters, and are known throughout history not only for their fine ships and beautiful wooden mansions, but also for smaller objects such as window shutters, screens, armoires and other furnishings. Many beautiful examples survive in the city's mosques.

Calligraphy did not originate in Turkey but the Ottoman Empire produced many fine exponents of this most rarefied of arts. Traditionally there are seven writing styles: the geometric Kufic script, used for decorative work, and six cursive styles used for deeds and documents and for Korans. The imperial monograms of the sultans, or tuğras (*see p. 74*) are a peculiarly Ottoman artform. Also notable are 'mirror calligraphy', where the script replicates itself in two symmetrical halves (there is a good example of this above the Imperial Gate of Topkapı) and 'picture calligraphy', where the forms of the script are fashioned into figurative designs of birds or animals or—a modern favourite of Grand Bazaar stallholders—whirling dervishes.

Turkish carpets are justly famed. They were used by early nomadic tribes as floor coverings and hangings in tents, as mats for prayer, and as bags into which to pack belongings. The Ottoman Empire is situated on the trade routes between East and West and there were plentiful supplies of silk and calico, and of course of wool. It is beyond the scope of this book to discuss Turkish carpets in any detail. Important is the distinction between carpets and kilims. Kilims are flat-weave rugs, that is, they do not have a pile. Pile carpets, made of knotted wool or silk, first appeared in this region with the Seljuk Turks in the 11th century. Designs and techniques differ from area to area. There are noted carpet-weaving centres such as Hereke, east of Istanbul, which is famous for its silk carpets (Hereke rugs adorn the palaces of Dolmabahçe and Beylerbeyi). The motifs used on all carpets are more than just geometric designs. They are heavily stylised symbols of marriage, motherhood, childbirth, good fortune, strength and fertility.

GEOGRAPHY OF ISTANBUL

Istanbul is the only city in the world that is built across two continents. Its name is a corruption of the Greek *stin poli*, meaning 'in the city', or 'to the city', a phrase that is still used by Greeks when referring to the imperial capital once known as Constantinople, and before that as Byzantium.

The European part of the city, situated at the southeastern tip of the continent, is separated from the Asian part by the Bosphorus, the beautiful and historic strait that cuts through from the Black Sea to the Sea of Marmara, the ancient Pontus and Propontis. The European city is further divided by the Golden Horn, a narrow inlet that is fed by two streams known as the Sweet Waters of Europe. The oldest section of the European city, known to earlier travellers as Stamboul and now the municipal district of Fatih, lies on the right bank of the Golden Horn. It forms a roughly triangular promontory, bounded on the north by the Golden Horn, on the south by the Sea of Marmara and on its western, landward side by the Theodosian walls. On the lower left bank of the Golden Horn is the port quarter of Galata (Karaköy), with the district of Beyoğlu on the hillside above it, the historic Pera, which in Ottoman times is where all the foreigners lived and had their embassies and places of worship.

The Asian part of Istanbul includes the historic suburb of Üsküdar, formerly known as Scutari, where Florence Nightingale had her hospital; and Kadıköy, anciently Chalcedon, an earlier Greek colony even than Byzantium and scene of the Ecumenical Council of 451. Modern Istanbul extends far beyond the limits of the ancient city, including within its boundaries the European and Asian suburbs along the Marmara coast, as well as both shores of the Bosphorus out as far as the Black Sea.

Orientation: the view from the Galata Bridge

Istanbul not only stands athwart two continents but, like Rome and Jerusalem before it, it is built on seven hills, a fact reflected by the seven little triangles on the municipal coat of arms. The first six hills form an almost straight line from Topkapı Palace to Edirne Kapı gate. The seventh stands above the Marmara shore, in the southwest of the old city. The lie of the land is well seen from the Galata Bridge (*map p. 349, D1*), the busy crossing point from the historic peninsula to its former European suburbs. All day and for much of the night a steady stream of pedestrians and traffic pours across the bridge between Karaköy and Eminönü, the busy squares at its Galata and old city ends, and on holidays the pavements fill with fishermen, who stand all day by the parapets with their rods.

The bridge is on two levels, with cafés and tea shops on the lower level and vehicle traffic on the upper. The latter, with its wide pavement, is an excellent vantage-point from which to orientate yourself before setting out to explore.

Looking towards the eastern tip of the old city you see Saray Burnu (*pictured opposite*), the point where the Golden Horn and the Bosphorus meet and flow together into the Sea of Marmara, together forming what the Byzantine historian Procopius called the city's 'garland of waters'. Above Saray Burnu, on what was once the acropolis of ancient Byzantium, are the pavilions and gardens of Topkapı Palace, for four centuries the imperial residence of the Ottoman sultan and his court. To the right of Topkapı, on the summit of the so-called First Hill, is the majestic edifice of Haghia Sophia, the former cathedral of Byzantine Constantinople, now garlanded with minarets.

On the foreshore at the Eminönü end of the Galata Bridge stands Yeni Cami, the 'new mosque', the only endowment by a female member of the imperial household to be built right in the heart of town. Further to its right, in the midst of the market quarter, is the smaller mosque of Rüstem Pasha. Above these, on the Second Hill, is Nuruosmaniye Camii, a Baroque mosque framed by a pair of minarets, standing just outside the famous Kapalıçarşı or Grand Bazaar. The Third Hill is crowned by the Süleymaniye, the great mosque complex of Süleyman the Magnificent, which dominates the skyline of the old city from this and other vantage points.

The Fourth Hill is surmounted by Fatih Camii, the Mosque of the Conqueror, whose dome and two minarets can be seen in the middle distance, some way in from the Golden Horn. On the top of the Fifth Hill, on the edge of the ridge above the Golden Horn, stands the Mosque of Selim I, flanked by a pair of minarets. Just visible in the distance are the dome and two minarets of Mihrimah Camii; this marks the summit of the Sixth Hill, some 2km in from the Golden Horn and just inside the Theodosian walls. The Seventh Hill lies behind the ridge.

Across the Golden Horn in the other direction, the skyline is dominated by the conical-capped Galata Tower, originally a lighthouse.

View across the water to Saray Burnu, where the Bosphorus, Golden Horn and Sea of Marmara meet. The kitchens of Topkapı Palace can be seen on the right, the former church of Haghia Sophia in the centre, while the Blue Mosque, the Sultanahmet Camii, lies beyond it.

YENİ CAMİ
& THE SPICE BAZAAR

The south bank of the Golden Horn around the present Galata Bridge was in Byzantine times the principal port and commercial quarter of the city. During the latter period of the Byzantine Empire this part of town was given over to various Italian city-states. The area west of the Galata Bridge was the territory of the Venetians; the area to the east belonged to the Amalfitans; beyond that was the concession of the Pisans, followed by that of the Genoese, who also controlled the town of Galata.

The area at the Eminönü end of the Galata Bridge, where Yeni Cami now stands, was a Jewish quarter, inhabited by members of the schismatic Karaite sect, who broke off from the main body of Orthodox Jewry in the 8th century. The Karaites continued to live here until the end of the 16th century, when they were evicted to make way for the construction of Yeni Cami; they were resettled across the Golden Horn in Hasköy,

Eminönü is still a busy port, filled with people hurrying to catch a ferry or a tram, or queuing to buy a fried fish sandwich from one of the barge-kitchens that bob on the water here, gaudily decorated like Las Vegas versions of a sultan's *kayık*.

YENİ CAMİ

Yeni Cami, the 'New Mosque' (*map p. 349, D1*), is one of the most familiar landmarks in the old city, standing at the Eminönü end of the Galata Bridge. It was the last large mosque to be built during the classical period of Ottoman architecture. Its grandeur is enhanced by its dramatic setting beside the Golden Horn.

HISTORY OF YENİ CAMİ

The name of the building is an abbreviation of Yeni Valide Camii, the 'New Mosque of the Valide Sultan'. The first stage in its construction began in 1597, under the sponsorship of the Valide Sultan Safiye, mother of Mehmet III. The original architect was Davut Ağa, a former apprentice of the great Sinan. Davut Ağa died in 1599, however, and was replaced by Dalgıç Ahmet Çavuş. Dalgıç Ahmet Çavuş remained chief architect until 1603, when the death of Mehmet III halted construction, for his mother then lost her power in the palace. Half a century later, in 1660, the unfinished mosque was destroyed by fire and the charred ruins attracted the attention of another Valide Sultan, Turhan Hatice, mother of Mehmet IV (and nemesis of her predecessor as Valide; *see p. 107*), who decided to rebuild it as an act of piety. The architect Mustafa Ağa was placed in charge of the project, which was completed in 1663 according to the original design.

The two minarets of Yeni Cami, seen from the Galata Bridge.

EXTERIOR OF YENİ CAMİ

The avlu

Like all of the imperial mosques in Istanbul, Yeni Cami is preceded by a monumental courtyard (*avlu*) on its west side. The **ceremonial entrance** to the courtyard is at the centre of its west end, where a grand flight of steps leads up to an ornate portal. A calligraphic inscription over the gateway reads: 'Health be with you; should you be worthy, enter in for eternity.'

The courtyard is square in plan, measuring 39m on a side along its outer walls. Around its interior there is a portico carried by a peristyle of 20 columns, with a pretty octagonal **şadırvan**, or ablution fountain, in the centre. Its engaged columns have stalactite capitals. The **façade of the mosque** under the porch is decorated with tiles and faience inscriptions forming a frieze. The two centre columns of the portico that frame the entrance to the mosque are of a most unusual and beautiful grey-green marble not seen elsewhere in the city. The mosque is entered through a grand door with a gilded stalactite canopy.

The mosque

The external form of the mosque reflects its internal plan. The central dome is flanked by semidomes along both axes, with smaller domes at each corner and still smaller domes beside these, two each at the northeast and southeast corners and three each above the northwest and southwest corners. The north and south sides of the mosque have two storeys of porticoed galleries that produce a charming effect. Notice how the four great piers that support the dome are continued above the building as tall octagonal turrets. Smaller turrets rise in steps on either side of the semidomes, producing a symmetrical cascading impression. There are two minarets, with three şerefes each, with superbly sculptured stalactite parapets.

The kasır

At the northeast corner of Yeni Cami there is a very interesting and unusual building, through the centre of which a great arched portal allows you to pass around behind the mosque. This is a kasır, or royal pavilion, entered by the ramp beside the mosque. This ramp leads to a suite of rooms (*not open to the public*) built over the archway, and from there a door leads to the royal loggia within the mosque. The suite included a salon, a bedchamber and a toilet, with kitchens on the lower level, and served as a *pied-à-terre* for the imperial family when they attended services.

INTERIOR OF YENİ CAMİ

The floor plan of the mosque is a square, 41m on a side. On the sides and at the rear there is a colonnade of slender marble columns connected by alternating large and small arches, which vary in shape from ogee to pointed to round. This colonnade supports the upper gallery, which has a fine marble parapet.

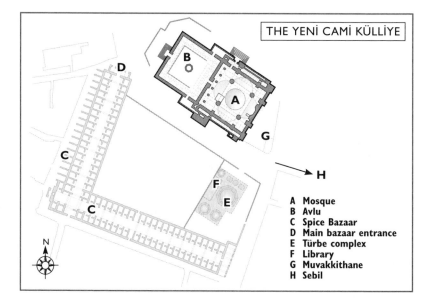

THE YENİ CAMİ KÜLLİYE

A Mosque
B Avlu
C Spice Bazaar
D Main bazaar entrance
E Türbe complex
F Library
G Muvakkithane
H Sebil

The central area of the interior is defined by the four huge piers that are the main support of the dome. From these piers rise four great arches, and between them four squinches make the transition from square to circle, upon which rests the dome, 17.5m in diameter and 36m above the floor at its crown. The interior space is extended by the semidomes along the east–west axis of the mosque, with smaller domes above each corner of the nave and still smaller domes above the corners of the galleries.

The imperial loggia is at the northeast corner of the gallery; this is screened off by a gilded grille to shield the sultan and his family from the public gaze when they attended services. This loggia is connected by a long passageway to the imperial pavilion at the northeast corner of the mosque.

The interior furnishings of the mosque are quite elegant in detail, particularly the mihrab, which is decorated with gilded stalactites, and the mimber, which is surmounted by a conical canopy carried on marble columns.

THE PRECINCTS

The original külliye of Turhan Hatice included the mosque **(A)**, a hospital, a primary school, a mausoleum, two fountains, a public bath, and a market, with the proceeds of the latter two institutions contributing to the support of the rest of the foundation. The hospital, the public bath and the primary school have been destroyed, but the other institutions remain, although only the market is now open to the public.

The market of the Yeni Cami complex is the handsome L-shaped building to the south and west of the mosque. It is called the Mısır Çarşısı, or Egyptian Market, because it was originally endowed with the Cairo imposts. In English it known as the **Spice Bazaar (C)**, because it was famous for selling spices and medicinal herbs. Spices and herbs are still sold here, but the bazaar now deals in a wide variety of other commodities making it, perhaps, the most popular market in the city. Unlike the very touristic Kapalıçarşı (Grand Bazaar) further to the south, the Spice Bazaar still caters to the ordinary, everyday needs of Istanbullus. There are 88 vaulted rooms in all, as well as chambers above each of the entryways at the ends of the two halls. The **main entrance (D)** is through the monumental gatehouse near the southwest corner of Yeni Cami, an impressive building that gives an imperial Ottoman touch to the busy market square outside. The Spice Bazaar is home to Istanbul's most famous coffee merchant, **Kurukahveci Mehmet Efendi Mahdumları**, who, as their advertising will tell you, have been 'purveyors to a discerning world since 1871'. The shop is in the west corner of the bazaar, on Tahmis Sk. (*map p. 349, D2*).

The domed building at the east end of the mosque garden is the **türbe complex (E)**, or mausoleum, of the Yeni Cami külliye. Turhan Hatice, foundress of the mosque, is buried there. Buried beside her is her son, Mehmet IV, the sultan of Orhan Pamuk's *The White Castle*, who famously failed to capture Vienna and was deposed when the Habsburg armies recaptured Hungary. Five later sultans are also interred here: Mustafa II, Ahmet III, Mahmut I, Osman III and Murat V.

The small building to the west of the türbe is the **library (F)**, built by Turhan Hatice's grandson, Ahmet III. Across the street from the türbe is a tiny polygonal building with a quaintly shaped dome. This was the **muvakkithane (G)**, the house and workshop of the *müneccim*, the mosque astronomer.

THE MÜNECCİM

Mankind has always been influenced by portents. Just as the ancient Romans consulted augurers to determine whether times were propitious, so did the Seljuk Turks and their Ottoman successors. But while the Romans analysed entrails, the Ottomans surveyed the stars. Mehmet the Conqueror is said to have followed the advice of his astronomer about when to besiege Constantinople in 1453. Following the success of his conquest, the status of the court stargazer was assured. The Chief Astronomer (*müneccimbaşı*), aided by is assistants and clerks, was responsible for regulating the times for the five occasions of daily prayer and for fixing the exact times of sunrise and sunset during Ramadan, beginning and ending the daily fast which is required during that period. It was also his duty to determine the day on which each month of the Muslim lunar calendar commenced, beginning with the appearance of the first sickle moon in the western sky just after sunset. In addition to all this, he and his office also earned a steady income from plotting horoscopes. The post of Chief Astronomer was abolished by Atatürk in 1924.

Heading eastwards from Yeni Cami on Bankacılar Cd., which at the first intersection becomes Hamidiye Cd., you will see, at the near corner on the right, the **sebil (H)**, or fountain-house, of the Yeni Cami külliye, now used for commercial purposes. In Ottoman times attendants in the sebil would have handed out cups of water free to passers-by. If you turn right past the sebil, up Şeyhülislam Hayri Efendi Cd., stop just beyond the narrow alleyway on the left. Looking up to your left you will see a building on whose façade there is a series of reliefs between the windows, the uppermost ones in the form of five-pointed stars. This is the **Yıldız Dede Tekkesi**, a former dervish lodge that also included a hamam. The tekke was founded shortly after the Turkish Conquest by Yıldız Dede, a Turkish holy man who was Fatih's court astrologer. This is evident in his name, for in Turkish *yıldız* means 'star', whereas Dede, or 'Grandfather', is one of the words used in Turkish to designate a saint, another being Baba, or 'Father'. According to Evliya Çelebi, the 17th-century Turkish chronicler, Yıldız Dede built his lodge on the site of an ancient synagogue, perhaps one belonging to the Karaite Jews, since this was their quarter before they were moved to Hasköy.

Retrace your steps as far as the alleyway, Zahire Borsası Sk. This is an L-shaped lane in the crook of which, on the right, is the **Ticaret Borsası**, the Istanbul Commodity Exchange. This is housed in part of the medrese, or school of higher studies, of Sultan Abdülhamit I (*see below*), which takes up the rest of that side of the alleyway and the block beyond it. The alley leads into Hamidiye Caddesi. On either corner as you emerge is a shop of the famous confectioner **Şekerci Hacı Bekir**, founded here in 1777. The founder, Hacı Bekir, was chief *şekerci*, or confectioner, in the reign of Abdülhamit I; he is renowned for his creation of *lokum*, or Turkish Delight, which was first sold in this shop and is still sold here today, in a variety of delicious flavours.

Turning right on Hamidiye Caddesi (the street takes its name from the medrese complex of Abdülhamit), the huge building that takes up the whole block on the opposite side is the **fourth Vakıf Hanı**, built by the architect Kemalettin Bey in 1911–26 on the site of the imaret, or public kitchen, of Abdülhamit's külliye, opposite the sultan's medrese. At the near corner on the right is the **türbe of Abdülhamit I** (r. 1774–89), adjoining the corner of his medrese. Buried alongside him is his son, Mustafa IV, whose short and reactionary reign ended in deposition and death on the orders of his ruthless, reform-minded brother, who succeeded him as Mahmut II. The külliye also included a sebil, which was displaced when Hamidiye Cd. was widened (*see p. 52*).

TURKISH DELIGHT

Turkish delight, *lokum*, is usually encountered in the form of a small cube dusted with icing sugar and flavoured with chopped nuts, rosewater, mint or mastic. It is a gelatinous, chewy confection of corn starch, sugar and cream of tartar, invented by an Ottoman pastrycook and popularised all over the Ottoman world: it is widely eaten today in Greece, Bosnia and Macedonia as well as in Turkey.

THE FIRST HILL
& HIPPODROME

The summit of the First Hill (*map p. 349, E3*) was, in the early centuries of the Byzantine Empire, the centre of the political and religious life of the city. Today it is dominated by two great religious buildings, the former church of Haghia Sophia and the Sultan Ahmet Camii (better known in English as the Blue Mosque). The area between the two, now a spacious park filled with pigeons, juice sellers and *simit* vendors, was the site of the Augustaeum (or, in Greek, Augustaion), the principal square of ancient Constantinople (*see map opposite*). West of the Blue Mosque, the long park of At Meydanı occupies the site of the Hippodrome, the huge circus that played such an important and dramatic role in the public life of Byzantine Constantinople.

On the site of the Augustaion
The Augustaion was a ceremonial square surrounded by public buildings (the church of Haghia Sophia, the senate house, the Baths of Zeuxippus, the Hippodrome) and by the imperial palace of ancient Constantinople. To the west of it stood the Milion Arch, beyond which stretched the Mese, the central street of the city.

The **Baths of Zeuxippus** was the largest public bathing establishment in the ancient city. It stood somewhat to the west of the present-day **Hamam of Roxelana**. This public hamam, with separate sections for men and women, was commissioned by Süleyman the Magnificent in the name of his wife, Hürrem, better known in the West as Roxelana. The building was designed by Sinan and was completed by him in 1556.

The street that runs past the east end of Haghia Sophia was known in Byzantium as the Embolos of the Holy Well. This was a porticoed way by which the emperor could walk from the **Chalke**, the Brazen House, the monumental vestibule of the imperial palace, to the Holy Well, a sacred spring that issued forth near the southeast corner of Haghia Sophia. From there the emperor could enter Haghia Sophia directly, passing through the large portal that can still be seen in the east bay of the south aisle. On or near the site of the sacred spring today stands the elaborate Ahmet III fountain (*see p. 70*). The area to the east of this street is now under excavation by the Archaeological Museum. Extensive **remains of the Great Palace of Byzantium** have been unearthed, as well as Ottoman, Roman and even earlier vestiges. Plans to open the site to the public had, at the time of writing, as yet come to nothing. The palace was first built by Constantine when he founded his new capital. Much of it was destroyed during the Nika Revolt in 532, but it was rebuilt and considerably enlarged by Justinian soon after. Several later emperors restored and extended it, adorning it with works of art, most notably Basil I (r. 867–86). It served as the imperial residence until the sack of Constantinople by the Crusaders in 1204. After the recapture of the city from the Latins in 1261 it was found to be in a state of advanced decay and was never afterwards restored. Instead, the emperors took up residence in the Palace of Blachernae, in the northwest corner of the city. At the time of the Turkish Conquest, the Great Palace was

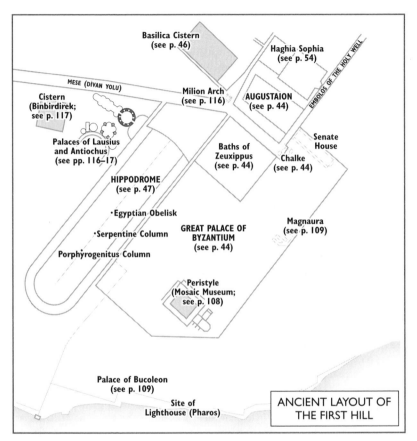

ANCIENT LAYOUT OF
THE FIRST HILL

completely in ruins. Shortly after he entered the city, Mehmet the Conqueror walked through its ruined halls and was so saddened that he recited a melancholy distich by the Persian poet Saadi: 'The spider is the curtain-holder in the Palace of the Caesars. The owl hoots its night call on the Towers of Aphrasiab.'

Opposite the Hamam of Roxelana are two restored Ottoman buildings. The first of these is the **Cedid Mehmed Efendi Medresesi**, founded in the 18th century by the Şeyhülislam Mehmet Efendi. The medrese has been beautifully restored and now houses the **Istanbul Handicrafts Centre**. Each of the chambers around the courtyard is occupied by an artisan practising old Ottoman crafts, including engraving, bookbinding, embroidery, carving on bone and doll-making. The restorations were carried out by the Turkish Touring Club, directed by the late Çelik Gülersoy, which now operates the splendidly rebuilt 19th-century konak next door as a luxurious hotel, the **Yeşil Ev**, 'Green House'. It has an extremely pleasant café-restaurant in its rear courtyard, centred on an elegant Ottoman *selsebil*, or cascade fountain. This is a perfect place to stop for lunch.

THE BASILICA CISTERN

From outside the entrance to Haghia Sophia, if you cross the tramline and go a short way up the left side of the street opposite, Yerebatansaray Cd., you will come to a small building that serves as the entrance to an enormous underground cistern called Yerebatan Sarnıcı, the 'Sunken Cistern', known in English as the Basilica Cistern because the space it occupies was once beneath the old Byzantine Stoa Basilike (*map p. 349, E3; open every day 9–5. There is a café*).

HISTORY OF THE BASILICA CISTERN

Close to the basilica of the Theotokos Chalkoprateia, the church of the 'Virgin in the Copper Market', was a great subterranean reservoir, rebuilt by Justinian after the Nika Revolt in 532, possibly as an enlargement of an earlier cistern constructed by Constantine the Great. Throughout the Byzantine period the Basilica Cistern was used to store water for the imperial palace and the other buildings on the First Hill. After the Conquest it served Topkapı Sarayı and the palace gardens. However, the Ottomans (and Muslims in general) always preferred running water to what they termed 'dead water', and gradually the cistern fell into disuse. All knowledge of its existence seems to have been lost until it was rediscovered c. 1547 by Petrus Gyllius. Inhabitants of this part of the city were found to be lowering buckets into 'wells' beneath their houses. Until very recently the only way to explore the cistern was by boat. The modern concrete walkways were constructed in the 1980s. The water is inhabited by enormous carp.

Yerebatan Sarnıcı, 138m long by 64.6m wide, is by far the largest of the many underground cisterns in the city remaining from Roman times. Its 336 columns, eight metres high, are arranged in twelve rows of 28 each. Ninety columns in the southeast corner of the cistern were walled off at the end of the 19th century and are not visible today. Most of the columns are topped by Byzantine Corinthian capitals; these have imposts above them that support little domes of brick constructed in a herring-bone pattern. One of the columns sports the distinctive lopped branch motif. In situ it is labelled the 'weeping column', and legends abound of its design being intended to resemble the tears of the slaves who built the cistern. This is fanciful nonsense. The column came from the Forum of Theodosius (*see p. 124*).

In the far left-hand corner of the cistern are two columns mounted on Classical bases supported by the heads of Gorgons, one of them upside down and the other on its side. The Gorgons in Greek mythology were three snake-haired sisters, one of whom, Medusa, was slain by Perseus. These Gorgon heads and the two that are now outside the Archaeological Museum were originally in the Forum of Constantine. The two heads here were probably put in place when Justinian rebuilt the Basilica Cistern in 532.

THE HIPPODROME

The long, rectangular space to the northwest of the Blue Mosque preserves in its layout the form of the ancient Hippodrome, the famous circus of Byzantine Constantinople. It was 480m long and 117.5m wide, and according to one estimate could seat 100,000 spectators. The royal enclosure, the *kathisma*, was probably at the middle of the east side, where the emperor and his party could enter directly from the imperial palace. The entrance to the arena was through vaulted passageways at the north end of the present park, where the charioteers and other performers would also wait in the *carceres*, or traps. The semicircular south end, the sphendone, is today concealed by buildings. At the top of the outer wall, an arcade of columns with a Classical epistyle ran around the structure. Many of its columns were still standing a century after the Turkish Conquest, but in 1550 they were pulled down and used for building material. The final destruction of the Hippodrome occurred in 1609, when what remained of it was demolished to make way for the mosque of Sultan Ahmet I. The site of the arena became a public square, as it still is today, and was given the appropriate name of At Meydanı, the 'Square of Horses'. Near the north end of it there is a domed structure known as the **German Fountain**. Kaiser Wilhelm II donated the funds to build it in 1895, on the occasion of his state visit to Abdülhamit II, and it was completed three years later.

Fourth-century relief on the base of the Egyptian obelisk in the Hippodrome. It shows the emperor Theodosius I in the imperial box, surrounded by his family and bodyguards. He holds a wreath with which to crown the winning charioteer.

HISTORY OF THE HIPPODROME

The original Hippodrome was constructed c. AD 200 by the emperor Septimius Severus, when he rebuilt the town of Byzantium. Constantine the Great reconstructed and enlarged it, adorning it with works of art from all over the Roman Empire. It has often been remarked that just as Haghia Sophia was the centre of the religious life of Constantinople, so the Hippodrome was the focal point of its civil activities. Many of the great events in the history of the Byzantine Empire took place here, beginning with the solemn inaugural rites of the new capital on 11th May 330. The triumphs of victorious generals and emperors were celebrated here, and on several occasions the remains of deposed rulers were exposed for public abuse in the arena. But the Hippodrome functioned primarily as a sports centre, where the regular programme of chariot races and circuses served as a diversion for the people of the city.

The turbulent mobs of the Hippodrome were originally divided into four factions: the Greens, Blues, Whites and Reds. In the early centuries of Constantinople the Blue and Green factions began to achieve dominance, and eventually the Whites and Reds were absorbed by the other two groups. Traditionally, the Blues were recruited from the upper and middle classes and were orthodox in religion and conservative in politics, while the Greens were lower class and radical both in their religious beliefs and in their politics. The social, religious and political polarisation between the two factions was the source of constant dissension during the early history of the Byzantine Empire. The worst of these disturbances was the Nika Revolt in 532, which ended when Justinian's general Belisarius trapped 30,000 partisans in the Hippodrome and slaughtered them there. This broke the political power of the popular factions in the Hippodrome, and they were never again a serious problem for the reigning emperor.

MONUMENTS IN THE HIPPODROME

Down the long central axis of the arena there was—as was true of all Roman circuses—a raised terrace called the *spina*, or spine, adorned with a line of statues and monuments. Three of those from the ancient Hippodrome are still standing *in situ*.

The Egyptian obelisk

The first of the ancient monuments on the spina, beginning at the north end of the Hippodrome, is the **Egyptian obelisk**. This was originally commissioned by the Pharaoh Thutmose III (r. 1549–1503 BC), who erected it at Deir-el Bahri in western Thebes in Upper Egypt to commemorate one of his campaigns in Syria and his crossing of the Euphrates river. The obelisk was originally about 60m tall and weighed some 800 tonnes, but it broke apart during shipment to Constantinople in the late 4th century AD and only the upper two-thirds survived. For some years this fragment lay where it was unloaded on the seashore, until it was finally erected on its present site by Theodosius I in 390.

The obelisk is mounted on four brazen blocks resting on a marble base with sculptured reliefs. The scenes on the four sides of the base represent Theodosius I and his family in the kathisma, as they look down at various events taking place in the circus below. On the north side of the base the emperor is shown supervising the erection of the obelisk, with the operations shown on the lower block. On the west he is depicted with his family as he receives homage from a group of kneeling captives; seated beside him is his nephew Valentinian II, ruler of the western part of the Roman Empire, and beside them are his two eldest sons, Honorius and Arcadius, who would themselves later become emperors of West and East, respectively. On the south side, the royal family is shown watching a chariot race (on the lower panel you can see the chariots speeding around the Hippodrome, where the obelisk is shown in place), and on the east side Theodosius is represented standing between Honorius and Arcadius, holding a laurel wreath in his hand as he prepares to crown the winner of a race. Below the kathisma, in this last scene, you can see the packed crowd in the Hippodrome; their faces, like those of the royal family, have been badly eroded by the elements. At the bottom of the panel there are dancing girls, in a line, accompanied by three musicians.

Inscriptions in Greek and Latin on the base praise Theodosius and his prefect Proclus for erecting the obelisk; the Latin inscription says that 30 days were required to do the job, while the one in Greek says that it took 32 days. The total height of the monument, including the base, is about 26m and its base represents the original level of the race-course, about 4.5m below the present surface of the ground.

The Serpentine Column

At the centre of the spina stands the so-called Serpentine Column, its shaft taking the form of three intertwined bronze serpents. This was the base of a trophy which once stood in the Temple of Apollo at Delphi, dedicated to the god by the 31 Greek cities who defeated the Persians at Plataea in 479 BC. The base of the column was uncovered in 1920, revealing the names of the cities inscribed on the lower coils of the serpents. The column was brought from Delphi by Constantine the Great; it seems to have stood at first in the courtyard of Haghia Sophia and was erected in the Hippodrome only at a later date. There are several stories about what became of the serpents' heads, but the most likely one is that they were chopped off by a drunken member of the Polish Embassy, one night in April 1700. The upper part of one of them was found in 1847 and is now in the Archaeological Museum.

The 'Column of Constantine Porphyrogenitus'

The third of the ancient monuments on the spina is a roughly built pillar of stone 32m high that stands near the south end of the Hippodrome. The 16th-century French traveller Petrus Gyllius called it the Colossus, but most modern writers refer to it, albeit incorrectly, as the Column of Constantine Porphyrogenitus. Both names stem from the Greek inscription on its base, where the pillar is compared to the Colossus of Rhodes, and where it is recorded that the pillar was restored and sheathed in bronze by the emperor Constantine VII Porphyrogenitus (r. 913–59). But the inscription also states that the pillar was decayed by time; thus it must date from an earlier period, perhaps to that of Theodosius I or Constantine the Great himself.

MINOR MONUMENTS ON THE FIRST HILL

The hectic, traffic-filled **Ankara Caddesi**, which leads uphill from the Golden Horn to the ridge that joins the First and Second hills, follows approximately the course of the defence walls that Septimius Severus built around Byzantium c. AD 200. Beyond is **Sirkeci Station**, the last stop for trains from Europe to Istanbul. The station was built by the German architect August Jachmund in 1887–89 as the terminus for the *Orient Express*, which made its first through run from Paris to Istanbul in 1889. Guests at the famous Pera Palace Hotel (*see p. 237*) would be conveyed from the station in sedan chairs.

THE CAĞALOĞLU HAMAMI

Map p. 349, D3. Open 8–10 (men), 8–8 (women); T: 212 522 2424; www.cagalogluhamami.com.tr.
This is the most famous and beautiful Turkish bath in Istanbul—and you are not alone in knowing this. The hamam features in Patricia Schultz's *1,000 Places to See Before You Die*, and fame has caught up with it. Prices are high and staff can be surly. This is a pity, because the building in splendid, and a working hamam is a sight worth seeing.

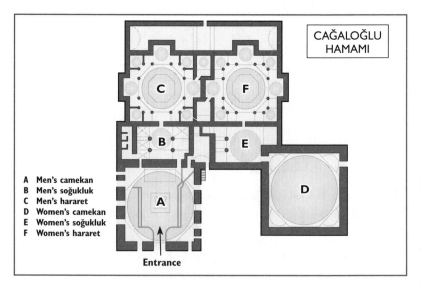

CAĞALOĞLU HAMAMI

A Men's camekan
B Men's soğukluk
C Men's hararet
D Women's camekan
E Women's soğukluk
F Women's hararet

Entrance

Architecture of the hamam

The hamam was built in 1741 by Mahmut I, who used the revenues from the baths to pay for the upkeep of the library that he endowed in the nave of Haghia Sophia. The layout of the men's bath is conventional, in that the bathers pass from the *camekan* (reception hall) through the narrower *soğukluk* (cool room) into the *hararet* (steam room), with all three chambers laid out in a straight line. In the women's baths the *camekan* is set off to the side, with one of its corners joining a corner of the soğukluk. As in most Turkish baths, the most elaborate chamber is the hararet, which has the same form in both the men's and women's sections: an open cruciform space with its central dome supported by a circlet of columns and with domed side chambers in the arms of the cross.

Using a hamam

The first part that you'll see on entering a hamam is the changing room, where you will undress, wrap a special towel (*peştamal*) around yourself, and slip on a pair of non-slip slippers (*terlik*). These are flat-soled today, but in the past women always wore tall pattens, the finer ones inlaid with mother of pearl (there are good examples in the Sadberk Hanım Museum). This kind of footwear not only protected clothing from the wet floors but also safeguarded the wearer against malevolent jinns, believed to lurk in dark, damp corners. Bathers are generally nude beneath the *peştamal*, but it is equally acceptable to wear swimming trunks. You may be offered soap, shampoo or a skin-scrubber. The quality of these varies from place to place, as does the price; if you prefer, you can always bring your own.

Once you're properly attired, you'll be led into the hamam proper, where you'll be asked if you'd like a massage or scrub. If you opt for it, be prepared for a little pain—the attendant's ministrations can verge on the sadistic, with all manner of limb-yanking, neck-clicking and skin-scraping taking place. If you choose not to undergo the full treatment, you'll be led to the hararet, where you can relax in the hot, humid air. In the centre of the room is a raised, heated stone dais (*göbektaşı*, literally 'belly stone') on which hamam-goers recline. On the walls are small basins, filled with hot or cold water from taps above, which are used for washing off sweat and dead skin, or simply to cool oneself down. Opening off the central space there are usually hot side-chambers known as halvets. The dome is typically pierced with small, glazed apertures through which shafts of light penetrate the steam. When the heat becomes too much, you can enter the soğukluk, which is also less humid than the main area; there are cold showers in order to prevent further sweating. On leaving the hamam, you will be swaddled in fresh, dry towels, and led into the main changing area, where you will be offered tea, coffee, tisanes, and possibly a *nargile*. Here, you can sit, chat, and relax for as long as like, until you are ready to put your clothes back on and leave.

Tipping is entirely at your discretion, although at some hamams (particularly tourist-heavy ones) the attendants can be quite insistent, even aggressive. Only pay what you think is deserved; ten percent for a good masseur should be acceptable.

Working hamams include Cağaloğlu and Çemberlitaş in the old town, and Galatasary in Beyoğlu. The Süleymaniye, also in the old town, is mixed sex.

BEŞİR AĞA CAMİİ

Beşir Ağa Camii (*map p. 349, E3*) is a small mosque complex on the corner of Alay Köşkü Cd. and Hükümet Cd. It was built in 1745 by Beşir Ağa, Chief Black Eunuch in the reign of Mahmut I. In addition to the mosque, the külliye consisted of some shops, housed in the vaults beneath the building, a medrese, and a dervish tekke. The tekke is no longer occupied by dervishes, since their various orders were disbanded in the early years of the Turkish Republic. The shops still exist. The pretty Baroque sebil on the corner, now the Antik Büfe, was also part of Beşir Ağa's foundation.

THE SUBLIME PORTE & ALAY KÖŞKÜ

On a bend in Alemdar Caddesi stands a large ornamental gateway with a projecting canopy in the Turkish Rococo style. This is the famous **Sublime Porte**, which in former times led to the palace and offices of the Grand Vizier, the first minister of the sultan. The first palace on this site was built by Sokollu Mehmet Pasha when he became Grand Vizier in 1564, during the last years of Süleyman's reign. From that time onwards most of the business of the Ottoman Empire was conducted here, behind the Sublime Porte. Hence the gateway came to stand for the government itself, and ambassadors were accredited to the Sublime Porte rather than to the Ottoman Empire, just as to this day ambassadors to the United Kingdom are accredited to the Court of St James. The present gateway was built early in the reign of Abdülmecit I, dating to about 1840. It now leads to various offices of the Vilayet, the headquarters of the governor of Istanbul Province.

Across the avenue from the Sublime Porte there is a large polygonal gazebo built into a defence tower of the old Topkapı Palace wall. This is the **Alay Köşkü**, the Review Pavilion, originally constructed in about 1565 and rebuilt in 1819. From its latticed windows the sultan, unobserved himself, could observe the comings and goings at the palace of his Grand Vizier across the way. The kiosk also served as a pavilion from which the sultan could review military parades or the fabulous Processions of the Guilds that were held from time to time in the earlier centuries of Ottoman rule. Alay Köşkü is now used as an exhibition hall. The interior consists of several rooms reached by a ramp rising from just inside the gate of Gülhane Park.

ALONG ALEMDAR CADDESİ

Alemdar Caddesi leads uphill from the Sublime Porte past the entrance to Gülhane Park (*see p. 102*). It passes a Neoclassical building that now houses a government office. This was built in 1875 as a Military College, housing the faculty of Forensic Medicine. Further up on the right is an elaborate **Rococo sebil**. Though it appears to belong to the mosque behind it, it is not an original part of the foundation. It was built in 1778 as part of the külliye of Abdülhamit I (*see p. 43*) and was moved to its present location when Hamidiye Caddesi was widened some years ago. The small Baroque mosque beyond, **Zeynep Sultan Camii**, was built in 1769 by Mehmet Tahir Ağa for Princess

Zeynep, a daughter of Ahmet III. It is a very simple building, in form being merely a square room covered by a dome, with a square apse projecting to the east and a porch with five bays to the west. The walls are of alternating courses of brick and stone, and the cornice of the dome undulates to follow the outlines of the round-arched windows, giving it the distinctive pie-crust roofline of a Byzantine church (Rüstem Paşa Camii is similar in this regard). The architect, Mehmet Tahir, built a number of more elaborate mosques, among them the famous Laleli Camii (*see p. 140*). Princess Zeynep's külliye also included a primary school, which stands at the corner of the street just below the mosque, and the picturesque little cemetery where the foundress and members of her family and household are buried.

After crossing the side street just beyond Zeynep Sultan Camii, if you look to your right, you will see a short stretch of crenellated wall, just visible over the building in front of it. This is the apse of the Byzantine church of the **Theotokos in Chalkoprateia**, of which only this and a short stretch of the north wall remain. Chalkoprateia means 'Copper Market', which is where the church was built c. 450 by the empress Pulcheria, sister of Theodosius II and wife of the emperor Marcian.

The handsome long building on the left side of the street, with its domes and chimney stacks at roof level and souvenir shops below, is the **Caferağa Medresesi**, a work of the great Ottoman architect Sinan. The medrese was commissioned by Cafer Ağa, Chief White Eunuch in the reign of Süleyman the Magnificent. After Cafer's death in 1557 the work was continued by his brother Gazanfer, and the medrese was completed by Sinan in 1559–60. The hillside slopes quite sharply here, so Sinan first erected a vaulted brick substructure to support the medrese and its courtyard. The entrance to the medrese is approached from the street running parallel to the west end of Haghia Sophia, where a little alleyway leads steeply down to the inner courtyard. The dershane, or lecture-hall, is the large domed chamber to the left as you enter (just beyond the bust of Sinan). The students' cells, each with its little fireplace, are laid out around the other three sides of the courtyard. The medrese has been converted into a centre for traditional Turkish arts and crafts, and there are items on sale outside the old cells, which are now used as workshops. It also operates a simple café-restaurant (*breakfast and lunch only; closes 6pm*), where you can eat either outside in the courtyard or under the portico, in a very pretty and relaxed setting.

HAGHIA SOPHIA

Haghia Sophia (in Turkish, Aya Sofya; *map p. 349, E3; open 9 or 9.30–4.30 every day except Mon*) is one of the most extraordinary buildings in the history of architecture. It was the cathedral of Byzantine Constantinople for more than a thousand years, and then for nearly five centuries after the Turkish Conquest it served as a mosque. It was deconsecrated and converted into a museum in 1934. Nevertheless, it retains a powerful religious, historic and symbolic significance for both Christians and Muslims, and recent rumours that it may be reopened for worship (Christian? Islamic? Both, on a share-and-share-alike basis?) have sparked debate, controversy, excitement and anxiety.

HISTORY & ARCHITECTURE OF THE CHURCH

The present edifice of Haghia Sophia is the third church of that name to stand upon this site. The first church was completed c. 360 in the reign of Constantius, son and successor of Constantine the Great, and was dedicated to Haghia Sophia, the Divine Wisdom, an attribute of Christ. This church was burnt down in 404 during a riot by supporters of the Archbishop St John Chrysostom, who had been removed from office by Eudoxia, wife of the emperor Arcadius: it is said that she had taken his diatribes against female extravagance as a personal gibe. A new church was built on the site by Theodosius II, son and successor of Arcadius, and dedicated in 415. This was destroyed in the reign of Justinian, on the first day of the Nika Revolt (*see p. 9*). After the end of the rebellion Justinian began work on a new church, appointing as head architects Anthemius of Tralles and Isidorus of Miletus, the former a professor of geometry, the latter a physicist and mathematician. Anthemius died during the first year of construction, but Isidorus carried the project through to completion late in 537 and the church was dedicated on 26th December of that year. On entering the church and beholding its splendour, Justinian is said to have exclaimed, 'Solomon, I have outdone thee!'

During the construction, a number of structural problems arose. The greatest challenge was how to support such a wide and shallow dome. In 558, five months after having been weakened by earthquake, the eastern part of the dome collapsed. Justinian entrusted the task of rebuilding it to a nephew of Isidorus, Isidorus the Younger, who decided to change the shape of the dome, making it higher so as to reduce the lateral stress. The reconstruction project was completed late in 563 and the church was rededicated on Christmas Eve of that year.

Schism, sack and conquest

It was in this church in 1054 that a cardinal of Rome delivered a sentence of excommunication against the Patriarch, Michael I, thus beginning the rift between Rome and By-

zantium which is known as the East-West Schism. A century and a half later, when the Latin armies sacked Constantinople in 1204, Haghia Sophia suffered great ignominy. It was stripped of its sacred relics and liturgical objects. According to the chronicler Nicetas Choniates: 'When the sacred vases and utensils of unsurpassable art and grace and rare material, and the fine silver, wrought with gold, which encircled the screen of the tribunal and the ambo, of admirable workmanship, and the door and many other ornaments, were to be borne away as booty, mules and saddled horses were led to the very sanctuary of the temple. Some of these which were unable to keep their footing on the splendid and slippery pavement, were stabbed when they fell, so that the sacred pavement was polluted with blood and filth…Nay more, a certain harlot, a sharer in their guilt, a minister of the furies, a servant of the demons, a worker of incantations and poisonings, insulting Christ, sat in the patriarch's seat, singing an obscene song and dancing frequently…'. During the subsequent Latin occupation of the city, Haghia Sophia served as the Roman Catholic cathedral.

Following the recapture of Constantinople by the Byzantines in 1261, Haghia Sophia was reconsecrated as a Greek Orthodox church and its interior was refurbished and redecorated. The dome suffered another partial collapse in 1346 and the church was closed for nine years until reconstruction was completed. During the last century of Byzantine rule, Haghia Sophia was allowed to fall into serious disrepair, sharing in the general decay of the ailing city, and travellers to Constantinople in that period report that the great church was partially in ruins.

The last Christian liturgy in Haghia Sophia began shortly after sunset on Monday, 28th May 1453. Constantine XI arrived an hour or so before midnight and prayed there silently for a time before returning to his post on the Theodosian walls, where he died the following morning when the city fell to the Ottoman besiegers. Within hours, the victorious Turkish soldiers broke into Haghia Sophia and carried off those they found there into bondage.

Conversion to a mosque

Mehmet II made his triumphal entry into the city on the afternoon of 29th May and rode directly to Haghia Sophia. After inspecting the building he ordered that it should be immediately converted into a mosque, and the following Friday he attended the first Muslim service to be held in Aya Sofya Camii, the Mosque of Haghia Sophia. Divine Wisdom being also an attribute of Allah, it was found unnecessary to change the name of this holy place.

A minaret was erected at the southeast corner, a mihrab and mimber were constructed at the east end, and the figurative mosaics were plastered over. Fatih and his successors continued to keep Haghia Sophia in good repair, for it was one of the principal imperial mosques of the city and was always held in great veneration. The last and most thorough of these restorations was commissioned by Abdülmecit I and was carried out in 1847–49 by the Swiss architects Gaspare and Giuseppe Fossati. In April 1932 Thomas Whittemore and other members of the Byzantine Institute began the task of uncovering and restoring the mosaics, and at that time Haghia Sophia was closed, in preparation for its reopening as a museum in 1934. Restoration of the mosaics was not completed until 1964, when the galleries of Haghia Sophia were also opened to the public.

Exterior of Haghia Sophia

The main ground plan of the building (*see overleaf*) is a rectangle, approximately 70m wide and 75m long. At the centre of the east wall there is a projecting apse, semicircular within and polygonal on the exterior, while to the west the church is preceded by a narthex and exonarthex. Above the central part of the rectangular area there is an enormous dome, with smaller semidomes to east and west and conches over the apse and the four corners. The nave is flanked by side aisles with galleries above them, extending also above the narthex.

Though majestic within, the exterior appearance of the building is somewhat hulking: earthquake damage over the centuries necessitated the erection of buttresses on all sides. The oldest of these are the two pairs of very tall buttresses built against the north and south walls. These were built during Justinian's reign, either in the latter part of the original construction or in the rebuilding of the dome in 558–63. The pillar-like outer parts of these buttresses were added in 1317 by Andronicus II to provide additional support. The four massive flying buttresses against the west gallery were added in the second half of the 9th century. The arch buttresses and retaining walls at the east side of the church were erected by Fatih soon after the Conquest.

Fatih also built the brick minaret at the southeast corner of the building; this replaced a temporary wooden minaret which had been erected over the southeast buttress when Haghia Sophia was converted into a mosque. Selim II built the stone minaret at the northeast corner in 1574, and the two stone minarets at the northwest and southwest corners were added a year or so later by his son and successor, Murat III. All three of these stone minarets are works of Sinan.

TOUR OF HAGHIA SOPHIA

Justinian's church was preceded by a porticoed atrium, nothing of which remains. The site of its eastern half is occupied by the present garden, café and shop. The columns and other ancient architectural fragments arrayed in the garden were unearthed in the past half-century. To the right after you pass through the security check is the **şadırvan of Aya Sofya Camii**, a Rococo structure built c. 1740 by Mahmut I.

The entrance to the building itself is on the middle of the west side. As you approach you see on the left an excavation pit, where you can look down upon the **remains of the Theodosian church**, excavated in 1935. Some fragments of reliefs, showing sheep and a palm tree, remain in the pit. What remains *in situ* are chiefly the foundations of a monumental entrance-porch: the Theodosian church was a basilica comparable in size to the present structure. It well deserved the name by which it was generally known and which it passed on to its successor: Megali Ecclesia, the 'Great Church'.

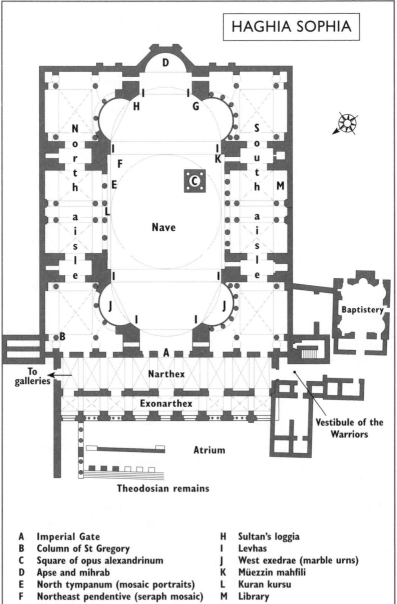

HAGHIA SOPHIA

A Imperial Gate	**H** Sultan's loggia
B Column of St Gregory	**I** Levhas
C Square of opus alexandrinum	**J** West exedrae (marble urns)
D Apse and mihrab	**K** Müezzin mahfili
E North tympanum (mosaic portraits)	**L** Kuran kursu
F Northeast pendentive (seraph mosaic)	**M** Library
G Mimber	

The exonarthex and narthex

Entering the church you find yourself in the **exonarthex**. This outer vestibule comprises nine cross-vaulted bays separated by arches, as does the narthex beyond. In the last bay of the exonarthex is a huge Byzantine sarcophagus in *verd antique*. Originally in the church of the Pantocrator, this contained the remains of the empress Eirene, wife of John II Comnenus (1118–43). Mosaic likenesses of the imperial pair can be seen in the gallery above (*see p. 65*).

Five doors in alternate bays lead from the exonarthex into the **narthex**, which is about twice as high and wide as the exonarthex. The piers and walls are revetted with superb marble panels. According to Paul the Silentiary, who wrote a long encomium on Haghia Sophia, 'The marbles are cut and joined like painted patterns and in stones formed into squares or eight-sided figures the veins meet to form devices; and the stones show also the forms of living creatures...'. In order to obtain the elaborate symmetrical patterns of each panel, thin blocks of marble were cut in two, sometimes two again, and opened out like a book so that the natural veining of the stone was duplicated and quadruplicated, giving the unique natural designs that add so much to the beauty of the interior.

Beneath the Turkish painted decoration on the vaults, both here and in the nave, can be seen portions of the original mosaic. This consists of large areas of plain gold ground adorned with bands of geometric or floral designs in various colours. Simple crosses in outline on the crowns of vaults and the soffits of arches are constantly repeated: according to the Silentiary, there was a cross of this kind on the crown of the great dome. It is clear from his description that in Justinian's time there were no figurative mosaics in the church. The figurative mosaics that have survived are all from after the Iconoclastic period, which ended in 843.

The doors into the nave

Doors open off from each bay of the narthex into the nave, with the largest one at the centre, flanked by a pair of somewhat smaller portals, and with two pairs of still smaller doors to either side. The monumental central door was known as the **Imperial Gate (A)**; this was reserved for the use of the emperor and the patriarch and those who accompanied them in processions. High up above the centre of the brass cornice there is an embossed decoration in very low relief showing a dove flying straight down above an open book, which rests upon a throne framed by two pillars and an arch. The book is inscribed with these words from the tenth chapter of the Gospel according to St John, in which Jesus addresses the Pharisees: 'Our Lord spoke: "I am the door; by me, if any man enter in he shall be saved, and shall go in and out, and shall find pasture" '.

In the lunette above the Imperial Gate there is a figurative mosaic, the second of those uncovered in 1932. The mosaic shows Christ seated upon a jewelled throne, his feet resting upon a stool. He raises his right hand in a gesture of blessing, and in his left hand he holds a book with this inscription: 'Peace be with you, I am the Light of the World'. Above, on either side of the throne, there are two roundels, the one on the left containing a bust of the Blessed Virgin and the other an angel carrying a staff or wand. On the left a crowned figure prostrates himself before the throne, his hands outstretched in supplication. It is thought to depict the emperor Leo VI, the Wise, and the mosaic is dated to the period of his reign, 886–912.

The nave: architecture and design
On entering the nave one inevitably pauses to look upon the vast interior of the church, particularly the fabled dome, which similarly impressed Paul the Silentiary:

Paul the Silentiary on Haghia Sophia

Above all rises into the immeasurable air the great helmet [of the dome], which, bending over like the radiant heavens, embraces the church...And wondrous it is to see how the dome gradually rises wide below, and growing less as it reaches higher. It does not however spring upwards to a sharp point, but is like the firmament which rests on air, though the dome is fixed on the strong backs of the arches...Everywhere the walls glitter with wondrous designs, the stone for which came from the quarries of seagirt Proconnesus. A thousand [lamps] within the temple show their gleaming light, hanging aloft by chains of many windings. Some are placed in the aisles, others in the centre or to east and west, or on the crowning walls, shedding the brightness of flame. Thus the night seems to flout the light of day, and be itself as rosy as the dawn...Thus through the spaces of the great church come rays of light, expelling clouds of care, and filling the mind with joy. The sacred light cheers all: even the sailor guiding his bark on the waves...does not guide his laden vessel by the light of Cynosure, or the circling Bear, but by the divine light of the church itself. Yet not only does it guide the merchant at night, like the rays from the Pharos on the coast of Africa, but it also shows the way to the living God.

From *Descriptio Sanctae Sophiae* (Tr. Swainson and Lethaby, 1894)

The main support for the dome is provided by four enormous and irregularly-shaped piers standing in a square approximately 31m on a side. From these piers rise four great arches, between which four pendentives make the transition from square to circle. Upon the cornice of this circle rests the slightly elliptical dome (the east–west diameter is about 31m and the north–south approximately 33m) with the crown soaring 56m above the floor, about the height of a 15-storey building.

The dome has 40 ribs which intersect at the crown, separated at the base by 40 windows. To east and west smaller pairs of subsidiary piers support the two great semi-domes, each pierced by five windows, which give the nave its vast length. The central arches to north and south are filled with tympanum walls each pierced by twelve windows, seven in the lower range, five in the upper.

Between the great piers on the north and south, four monolithic columns of *verd antique* support the galleries; above this six columns of the same marble carry the tympanum walls. At the four corners of the nave there are semicircular exedrae covered by conches, in each of which there are two massive columns of porphyry below and six of *verd antique* above. At the east, beyond the subsidiary piers, a semicircular apse projects beyond the east wall of the church, covered by a conch.

To the north and south of the main piers there are lateral piers, which are joined structurally with the four main buttresses on those sides, consolidating the fabric of the church. These divide the side aisles and the galleries above into six large compartments on each floor, three on either side, joined to one another by great arches springing between the piers. The north and south compartments on either side consist of a single bay and those at the centre have two bays each, all of them domical cross-vaults surrounded by half-barrel vaults. These vaults are supported internally by a double colonnade within each aisle, with pairs of rectangular pillars at the ends of each aisle and *verd antique* columns in between.

Columns, capitals and other marbles

The column capitals are unique and famous. They are all alike in having the surface decoration of acanthus leaves and palm foliage so deeply undercut that they produce an effect of white lace on a dark ground. Those in the nave and gallery arcades are of the bowl type: Ionic volutes support a decorated abacus, beneath which the bowl-shaped body of the capital is adorned with acanthus leaves. In the centre of the bowl, at both front and back, are the embossed imperial monograms of Justinian and Theodora. These are of several types, most often made up of the letters needed to spell out the words ΙΟΥCΤΙΝΙΑΝΟΥ (Justinian), ΘΕΟΔΩΡΑC (Theodora), or ΒΑCΙΛΕΩC (king).

The capitals in the aisles are of similar type but smaller in scale. Those of the eight pillars at the ends of the aisles are much the same, only there the bowl, instead of becoming circular towards its base, remains rectangular throughout.

From the Silentiary's description there can be little doubt that the *verd antique* columns in the nave and galleries were expressly hewn for Haghia Sophia from the famous quarries in Thessaly. There is a possibility that the eight porphyry columns in the exedrae, which differ from one another in height and diameter, may have been taken from an ancient building, but if so there is no evidence as to its identity.

The only other kind of marble used for columns in the church comes from the ancient quarries on the island of Proconnesus in the Marmara. This is a soft white stone streaked with grey or black, and is used for the 24 aisle columns of the gallery and the eight rectangular pillars at the ends of the ground-floor aisles. The pavement of the church, the frames of the doors and windows, and parts of the wall surfaces are also made of this marble.

Bowl capital from Haghia Sophia. In the centre of the acanthus-leaf decoration is the monogram of the emperor Justinian.

THE COLUMN OF ST GREGORY THE MIRACLE-WORKER

Sheathed in brass at the northwest corner of the north aisle **(B)**, is a pillar labelled as the 'sweating column'. It is the subject of a medieval legend that still has believers today. Antony of Novgorod, who visited Haghia Sophia in 1200, reports it thus: 'One sees at the side of the church the column of St Gregory the Miracle-Worker. St Gregory appeared near this column, and the people kiss it and rub their breasts and shoulders against it to be cured of their pains'. Credulous pilgrims have worn a hole in the brass plate and into the pillar itself, for the moisture contained in the cavity has always been considered a cure for eye diseases and a nostrum for fertility.

The great **square of opus alexandrinum (C)** in the pavement towards the southeast of the nave is made up mostly of circles of granite, red and green porphyry and *verd antique*. According to Antony of Novgorod, the emperor's throne stood upon this square at the time of his coronation, surrounded by a bronze enclosure.

There are also some interesting marble panels above the inner side of the Imperial Gate, in which slabs of *verd antique* alternate with inlaid panels of various marbles. At the top is an elaborate ciborium with drawn panels revealing a cross on an altar; lower down are other panels with ovals of porphyry, those at the bottom surrounded by pairs of stylised dolphins with foliate tails gobbling up tiny squid with waving tentacles. In the spandrels above the nave there is a superb frieze of sectile work with scrolls of trees, birds and flowers.

The mosaics in the nave

The largest and most beautiful of the surviving mosaics is in the conch of the apse. It depicts the **Virgin and Child (D)**. The Virgin is dressed in flowing robes of blue with a small star on her mantle over her head and one on each shoulder; her right hand rests upon her son's shoulder and her left upon his knee. Jesus is dressed in gold and wears sandals; his right hand is raised in blessing while his left hand holds a scroll. The Virgin sits on a throne inlaid with cabochon gems. Beneath her are two cushions, the lower one green, the upper one embroidered with spade shapes like those on playing-cards, while her feet rest upon a plinth-like stool, also bejewelled.

At the bottom of the arch that frames the apse there is a colossal figure of the **Archangel Gabriel**; he wears a *divitision*, an undergarment, over which is thrown a *chlamys*, a cloak of white silk; his great wings, reaching nearly to his feet, are of brightly-coloured feathers, mostly green, blue and white. In his right hand he holds a staff, in his left a translucent globe through which can be seen his thumb. Although the upper part of his left side and the top of his wings are lost, he is a fine and striking figure.

Opposite, on the north side of the arch, there are only a few feathers remaining from the **wings of the Archangel Michael**. On the face of the apse conch there remain the first three and the last nine letters of an inscription in Greek, of which the whole of the middle part is now missing. The inscription was an iambic distich that once read in full: 'These icons the deceivers once cast down the pious emperors have again restored'.

The apse mosaic was unveiled by the patriarch Photius on Easter Sunday 867; this was a most momentous occasion, for it signified the final triumph of the Orthodox party over the Iconoclasts and celebrated the permanent restoration of sacred images to the churches of Byzantium. The two 'pious emperors' referred to here are Michael III and his protégé, Basil I, whom Michael had made co-emperor the previous May and who would the following September murder his benefactor and usurp the throne for himself.

Three other **mosaic portraits (E)** are located in niches, high up at the base of the north tympanum wall (just visible from the nave). In the first niche from the west there is St Ignatius the Younger, who was twice patriarch of Constantinople (847–58 and 867–77); in the central niche is St John Chrysostom, Archbishop of Constantinople in 398–404; and in the fifth niche from the west is St Ignatius Theophorus of Antioch. All three of these mosaics are dated to the last quarter of the 9th century.

Recent restorations have revealed mosaics on the soffit of the great eastern arch that frames the apse. These have not yet been restored and are only faintly visible, although one of them can be identified as the Virgin. These were done immediately after the restoration of 1346–55.

The only other mosaic visible from the nave is the **six-winged seraph in the northeast pendentive (F)**, probably dating from the mid-14th century. Those in the west pendentives are imitations in paint done by the Fossatis in 1847–49. The Fossatis covered the seraphs' faces with gold star-medallions, still in place over the other three.

Mosque furnishings

When Haghia Sophia was converted into a mosque, the **mihrab (D)** and **mimber (G)** were orientated towards Mecca, which is some 10 degrees south of the main axis of the church. These undistinguished structures date from the Fossati restorations of 1847–49, as does the **Sultan's loggia (H)** against the northeast pier. The Fossatis were also responsible for the eight huge green **levhas (I)**, or painted wooden plaques, that hang from the piers at gallery level. These were done by the calligrapher Mustafa İzzet Efendi and bear in golden letters the Sacred Islamic Names: those of Allah and the Prophet Mohammed flanking the apse arch, and in the nave the first four Caliphs: Abu Bakr, Umar, Uthman and Ali; and two of the grandsons of Mohammed, Hussein and Hasan.

Levha of the Prophet Mohammed, placed at the side of the apse arch.

The inscription in the dome is also by Mustafa İzzet Efendi. This is a quotation from the Koran, reading: 'In the name of God the Merciful and Compassionate; God is the light of Heaven and Earth. His light is Himself, not that which shines through glass or gleams in the morning star or glows in the firebrand.'

The oldest objects now remaining in Haghia Sophia from the Ottoman period are the two beautiful **lustration urns (J)** of Proconnesian marble in the west exedrae. These are late classical or early Byzantine urns to which Turkish lids have been added. According to Evliya Çelebi, these were gifts of Murat III, who also built the large **müezzin mahfili (K)** beside the southeast pier and the smaller enclosures for chanters against the other three piers. The marble **Kuran kursu (L)** in the north arcade was presented to the mosque by Murat IV, and the very elegant **library (M)** in the south aisle was built by Mahmut I in 1739. The library, which was endowed with the revenues of the Çağaloğlu Hamamı (*see p. 51*), consists of several domed rooms revetted with superb Iznik tiles of the 16th century, which the sultan found stored in Topkapı.

THE GALLERIES

The public entrance to the galleries is at the north end of the narthex, where a door leads into the north vestibule. From there a ramp leads up to the northwest corner of the galleries. The north and south galleries have the same plan as the side aisles below them, with a series of four cross-vaulted bays in succession with smaller barrel-vaulted bays, while the west gallery, which is above the narthex, is a broad barrel-vaulted hall with nine windows on the west, framed by pillars.

West gallery

Paul the Silentiary and other contemporary sources write that the galleries in Haghia Sophia served as the gynaeceum, the women's area. The **throne of the Empress of Byzantium**, from where she observed services, was located just behind the balustrade at the centre of the west gallery; the spot is marked by a disc of green Thessalian marble set into the pavement, framed by a pair of coupled columns of green marble.

South gallery

There is reason to believe that the two eastern bays of the south gallery were reserved for the use of the royal family and, on occasion, for synods of the Greek Orthodox Church. This is the part screened off by two pairs of false doors of marble with elaborately ornamented panels, the so-called **Gates of Heaven and Hell**. Between them is the actual doorway, surmounted by a slab of Phrygian marble, above which a wooden beam carved with floral designs in low relief forms a cornice to the whole gateway. This gateway is certainly not an original part of the church but a later addition, and it was probably erected to close off the far end of the south gallery when it was used for Church synods.

Beyond this screen are preserved three mosaics. The latest in date is in the right-hand bay just beyond the screen. This is the **Deësis**, an iconographic type in which Christ is flanked by the Virgin and St John the Baptist, who are shown interceding with him on behalf of mankind. Although two-thirds of this superb mosaic are now lost, the features of the three figures are still completely unmarred. The mosaic is dated to the second half of the 13th century, and is one of the finest extant works of art from the Palaeologue Revival.

Set into the pavement just opposite the Deësis there is part of a **sarcophagus lid** inscribed with the name Henricus Dandolo. Dandolo, Doge of Venice, was one of the generals of the Fourth Crusade, and though nearly 90 years old and almost blind, he led the charge that broke through the Byzantine defences on 13th April 1204. Dandolo died in Constantinople on 16th June 1205, after which he was buried here in the gallery of Haghia Sophia.

Two further mosaics are located on the east wall at the far end of the last bay. The oldest of these, the so-called **Zoë mosaic**, is on the left, next to the apse. Christ is

The figure of Christ from the Deësis mosaic (13th century).

shown enthroned between an emperor and empress of Byzantium. His right hand raised in a gesture of benediction, his left holds the Gospels. The emperor is shown offering a money-bag. Above his head an inscription reads: 'Constantine, in Christ, the Lord Autocrat, faithful Emperor of the Romans, Monomachus'. The legend above the head of the empress reads: 'Zoë, the most pious Augusta'. The scroll in her right hand has the same legend as that over the emperor's head, save that the words Autocrat and Monomachus are omitted for want of space. It is evident that all three heads and the two inscriptions concerning Constantine have been altered. This has led to the identification of the imperial figures as Zoë, daughter of Constantine VIII and one of the few women to rule Byzantium in her own right (r. 1042), and her third husband, Constantine IX Monomachus (r. 1042–55). It has been suggested that the head of Constantine is a replacement for that of Zoë's her second husband, Michael IV (r. 1034–41), who in turn replaced her first husband, Romanus III Argyrus (r. 1028–34), with the identifying inscription also being changed on each accession. The mosaic in its present state is thus dated to 1042 or shortly afterwards.

The third of the mosaics, showing **John II and the empress Eirene**, is to the right of the Zoë mosaic, separated from it by a window. In the centre the Virgin is depicted holding the Christ Child; to the left an emperor is shown offering a bag of gold, while on the right a red-haired empress holds forth a scroll. The imperial figures are identified by inscriptions as: 'John, in Christ the Lord, faithful Comnenus', and 'Eirene, the most pious Augusta'. The mosaic extends onto the narrow panel of side wall, at right-angles to the main composition; here is the figure of a young prince, identified as 'Alexius, in Christ, faithful Emperor of the Romans, Porphyrogenitus'. These are portraits of

The old ablution taps of Aya Sofya Camii.

John II Comnenus (r. 1118–43), known as 'John the Good'; his wife Eirene, daughter of King Ladislaus of Hungary; and their eldest son Alexius. The main panel has been dated to 1118, the year of John's accession to the throne, and the portrait of Alexius to 1122, when at the age of 17 he became co-emperor with his father. Alexius did not live to succeed John, dying shortly after his coronation. The Byzantine historian Nicetas Choniates wrote of John that 'he was the best of all the emperors, from the family of the Comneni, who ever sat upon the Roman throne'. Eirene was noted for her piety and her kindness to the poor, for which she is revered as a saint in the Greek Orthodox Church.

North gallery

The fourth of the surviving mosaics in the galleries is located high on a pier above the balustrade, on the right as you walk towards the exit, facing east. It represents the emperor Alexander (r. 912–13), who ascended the throne in May 912, succeeding his elder brother Leo VI. 'Here comes the man of thirteen months', said Leo with his dying breath, as he saw his despised brother coming to pay his last respects. This cynical prophecy was fulfilled in June of the following year, when Alexander died of apoplexy during a drunken game of polo. The mosaic portrait of Alexander is dated to the brief period of his reign. He is depicted full-length, wearing the gorgeous ceremonial costume of a Byzantine emperor: crowned with a *camelaucum*, a conical, helmet-shaped coronet of gold with pendant pearls; draped in a *loros*, a long gold-embroidered scarf set with jewels; and shod in gem-studded crimson buskins. Four medallions flanking the imperial figure bear the legend: 'Lord help the servant, the orthodox and faithful Emperor Alexander'.

THE VESTIBULE OF THE WARRIORS

The official exit from Haghia Sophia is through the door at the south end of the narthex. This leads into a narrow chamber that was called the Vestibule of the Warriors, since the troops of the emperor's bodyguard waited here for him while he was in the church. The vestibule is roofed by three cross-vaults of unequal size that bear no relationship to the room below, a fact that has led some authorities to suggest that the vestibule was added after the original construction of the church. If so, the addition must have been made soon afterwards, perhaps during the reconstruction of 558–63, because the gold mosaics on the vault are from Justinian's reign. Look back the way you came, to the lunette over the doorway. The **mosaic panel** here was first figurative mosaic to be uncovered in the restoration project that began in 1932. It depicts the Virgin enthroned in a hieratic pose, holding the Christ Child in her lap, as she receives two crowned and haloed figures. The figure on the right, identified by inscription as 'Constantine, the great Emperor among the Saints', offers the Virgin a model of a walled town representing Constantinople. The figure on the left, identified as 'Justinian, the Illustrious Emperor', offers her a model of a church symbolising Haghia Sophia. The mosaic is dated to the last quarter of the 10th century. The exit is through a pair of magnificent **bronze doors**, extending to below current floor level. They belonged to the first rebuilding of Haghia Sophia and were brought from a 2nd-century BC temple in Tarsus by the emperor Theophilus (r. 829–42).

THE PRECINCTS OF HAGHIA SOPHIA

There are a number of minor monuments of interest in the precincts, some of them dating from Byzantine times and others from the Ottoman era. These precincts are open during the same hours as the museum, except for the buildings and grounds in the restricted area just to the north of the church.

On leaving the church through the Vestibule of the Warriors, you pass on your left a window that looks into the **former baptistery** (*not open to the public*). In 1623 it was converted into a mausoleum to house the remains of the mentally unstable Mustafa I, who died shortly after he was deposed by the Janissaries in September of that year. A quarter of a century later, in 1648, his nephew the mad Sultan İbrahim was interred here too, again in September, after he also had been deposed in a palace coup, sent back to the Cage (*see p. 82*) and then executed. Opposite the baptistery is a pretty wall fountain.

The other Ottoman structures in the courtyard of Haghia Sophia are of very minor importance. The building just to the right of the exit is a **mektep** built by Mahmut I in 1740. It is typical of the one-room schoolhouses of that period, consisting of a porch giving onto a square chamber covered by a dome. It was used for the education of the children of the clergy and staff of Aya Sofya Camii. To the left of the exit there is a little domed structure built by the Fossatis in 1847–49. This was the **muvakkithane**, the house and workshop of the mosque astronomer, whose sundial can still be seen on the façade of Haghia Sophia.

THE TÜRBE GARDEN

The domed buildings in the garden to the south of Haghia Sophia (*separate entrance and security check*) are all imperial Ottoman tombs. They are extremely beautiful and interesting and well worth a visit. At the time of writing entrance was free.

Türbe of Mehmet III
This is the latest in date of the türbes, the resting place of Mehmet III (r. 1596–1603), son and successor of Murat III. The türbe was completed by the architect Dalgıç Ahmet Çavuş in 1603, the year of the sultan's death. It is octagonal in plan, with a double dome, and is also revetted with superb Iznik tiles. Mehmet was the son of the strong-willed Safiye Sultan, a Venetian girl who had been captured in a pirate raid on Corfu, where her father was governor. Through her influence, Ottoman policy was pro-Venetian, though Mehmet's reign was otherwise racked with conflict, notably in Hungary, where his armies sustained heavy losses.

Türbe of Selim II
The earliest of the türbes, completed in 1577, is that of Selim II (r. 1566–74), son of Süleyman the Magnificent and Roxelana, who died of an accidental blow to the head sustained in the Harem baths. This türbe is important because it is a work of Sinan and also because both the exterior entrance façade and the whole of the interior are revetted with superb Iznik tiles. The building is square, with an outer dome resting directly on the exterior walls, while within, a circlet of columns supports the inner dome.

Türbe of Murat III
Murat III (r. 1574–95) was the son and successor of Selim II. His fine türbe was completed in 1599 by Davut Ağa, the successor to Sinan as Chief of the Imperial Archi-

Sixteenth-century Iznik tiles on the exterior of the türbe of Selim II.

tects. It is hexagonal in plan, also with a double dome, and is revetted with Iznik tiles comparable in quality to those in Selim's türbe. Built up against Murat's türbe is a little mausoleum called the **türbe of the Princes**, which contains the small cenotaphs of four sons and a daughter of Murat, who died during one of the many plagues that ravaged the Harem. Murat had been enthusiastic in his congress with his concubines and is recorded to have sired over a hundred children. On his accession, Mehmet III had a great many of them strangled.

ON SOĞUKÇEŞME SOKAK

The monumental **street-fountain of Ahmet III** stands just to the right of the outer entrance to Topkapı Sarayı. This is one of the most beautiful and elaborate of the monumental Ottoman fountains in Istanbul, and is a particularly fine example of Turkish Rococo architecture. It is a favourite subject of old prints and photographs. The dedicatory inscription gives the date of the fountain as 1728.

On the street that runs past the east end of Haghia Sophia, at the northeast corner of the church, there is a large **Turkish gateway** in the Rococo style. This is the rear entrance to the garden north of Haghia Sophia (*closed to the public*) and it leads to a building known in Byzantine days as the **Skeuophylakion**, the treasury of Haghia Sophia, where all the precious objects and sacred vessels of the church were kept. Standing just to the east of the northeast buttress, it is two storeys high, circular in plan and covered with a dome. There is a multi-domed Ottoman building south of it, built in between the two north buttresses. This dates to the 16th century and was an imaret, which served the clergy and staff of the Mosque of Haghia Sophia.

Soğukçeşme Sk., the 'Street of the Cold Fountain', leads off to the left at this point, passing between the precincts of Haghia Sophia and the outer defence walls of Topkapı Sarayı, leading downhill to the gateway of Gülhane Park. The old Ottoman houses that line the right side of the street, backing against the defence walls of the palace, have been completely restored and well decorated by the Turkish Touring and Automobile Club (TTOK), directed by the late Çelik Gülersoy. The houses now form the **Ayasofya Pansionlar**, a comfortably-appointed hotel complex operated by the TTOK. The largest of the buildings, an Ottoman konak dating from the early 19th century, now serves as the Istanbul Library of the Çelik Gülersoy Foundation, which houses a rich collection of books on Istanbul and old prints depicting the city in Ottoman times. During the course of the reconstruction of Soğukçeşme Sk., an ancient cistern of the late Roman period was discovered along the lower section of the street. The cistern is now the **Sarnıç Lokantası**, an atmospheric restaurant operated by the TTOK, where you can dine in Roman splendour in a most extraordinary setting (*evenings only; see p. 296*).

TOPKAPI SARAYI
& HAGHIA EIRENE

Map p. 349, F2. Open 9.30–5; Harem 10–4; closed Tues. The ticket office is in the First Court. A separate ticket must be purchased to gain admission to the Harem (ticket office beside the Harem entrance).

Topkapı Sarayı was for more than four centuries the imperial residence of the Ottoman sultans and the administrative heart of their Empire. In addition to its historical and architectural interest, it houses important collections of porcelain, armour, costumes and jewellery, as well as many precious objects and works of art. It also has in its safe-keeping a number of sacred relics of the Prophet Mohammed.

HISTORY OF TOPKAPI SARAYI

When Fatih Sultan Mehmet captured Constantinople in 1453, he found the palaces of the Byzantine emperor to be ruinous and uninhabitable. He chose a large plot of land on the broad peak of the Third Hill as the site of his first imperial residence, in the area where Istanbul University now stands. This came to be known as Eski Saray, the 'Old Palace', when a few years later he decided to build a new palace on the north side of the First Hill, on what had been the acropolis of ancient Byzantium.

He began by ringing the acropolis with a wall, long stretches of which still stand. The new palace took its name from the main sea gate, Topkapı, 'Cannon Gate', a twin-towered gateway flanked by two enormous cannon that threatened all shipping approaching Saray Burnu (the gate was destroyed in the 19th century).

Fatih constructed his palace buildings on the high ground, while on the hill slopes and along the shore he laid out parks and gardens. This was done during the period 1459–65. The Conqueror used Topkapı as his own residence and as the seat of government. The Old Palace became a residence for the harem and remained such until the reign of Süleyman the Magnificent, when Roxelana moved herself and her retinue into Topkapı. After that it was to the old 'Palace of Tears' that the women of a previous harem would be banished on the accession of a new sultan.

Topkapı also housed the largest and most select of the training schools for the imperial civil service. These various institutions each occupied their own buildings around the four main courtyards. The residential section of the palace extended along the west side of the three inner courts, with the Harem, the family quarters and domain of the women, to the south, and the Selamlık, the sultan's public reception suite, to the north. During the great days of the Ottoman Empire, the population of the palace is estimated to have been between three and four thousand.

Topkapı Sarayı continued as the principal imperial residence for nearly four centuries, until in 1853 Sultan Abdülmecit I moved into the new palace of Dolmabahçe on the Bosphorus. Topkapı was thereafter little used until 1924, when it was converted

Selim III on his Bayram Throne outside the Gate of Felicity (Bab-üs Saadet). Artist unknown.

into a museum. In the years since then the Saray has undergone a continuous process of renovation and restoration.

THE FIRST COURT

The main entrance to the palace grounds, now as in Ottoman times, is through Bab-ı Hümayün, the **Imperial Gate**, opposite the northeast corner of Haghia Sophia. This monumental gateway was erected by Fatih in 1478. Originally there was a second storey, demolished in 1867 when Sultan Abdülaziz surrounded the gate with the present marble frame and lined the niches on either side with marble. In Ottoman times these niches often displayed the severed heads of rebels or the ears and noses of those convicted of lesser crimes. The rooms in the gateway housed the *kapıcıs*, or guards, of whom 50 were on watch at all times of the day and night. Above the central part of the arch is a calligraphic inscription extolling Fatih and above that, in elaborate mirror-calligraphy, are the following verses from the Koran: 'Yea, the righteous shall dwell amongst gardens and fountains. Safely and in peace shall they enter therein; and all injury shall be lifted from their hearts; yea, they shall be like unto brothers facing each other upon thrones. No weariness shall come upon them, nor shall they ever be

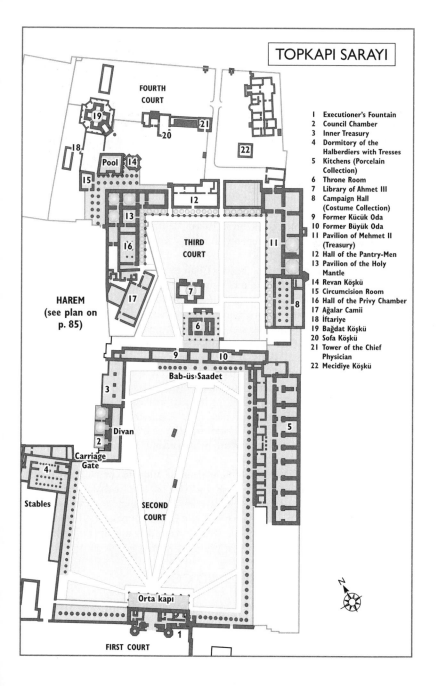

TOPKAPI SARAYI

FOURTH COURT

THIRD COURT

HAREM
(see plan on
p. 85)

Pool

Bab-üs› Saadet

Divan

Carriage
Gate

Stables

SECOND
COURT

Orta kapı

FIRST COURT

1 Executioner's Fountain
2 Council Chamber
3 Inner Treasury
4 Dormitory of the
  Halberdiers with Tresses
5 Kitchens (Porcelain
  Collection)
6 Throne Room
7 Library of Ahmet III
8 Campaign Hall
  (Costume Collection)
9 Former Kücük Oda
10 Former Büyük Oda
11 Pavilion of Mehmet II
  (Treasury)
12 Hall of the Pantry-Men
13 Pavilion of the Holy
  Mantle
14 Revan Köşkü
15 Circumcision Room
16 Hall of the Privy Chamber
17 Ağalar Camii
18 İftariye
19 Bağdat Köşkü
20 Sofa Köşkü
21 Tower of the Chief
  Physician
22 Mecidiye Köşkü

banished from that place.' The *tuğra*, or imperial monogram, is that of Mahmut II.

The Imperial Gate leads to the **First Court**, where the ticket office is. This was sometimes called the Courtyard of the Janissaries, as they assembled here when on duty in the palace, up until their destruction in 1826 by Mahmut II (*see p. 22*). The First Court formed the outer grounds of Topkapı Sarayı and was not considered to be part of the palace proper. To the left of the entrance stands the Byzantine church of Haghia Eirene (*see p. 89*). To the right stood the palace infirmary. Behind the ticket-office wall were the palace bakeries, famous for the superfine white bread baked for the sultan and the chosen few upon whom he bestowed it.

Tuğra of Mahmut II, reading 'Mahmut Khan, son of Abdülhamit, Victorious Always'.

Near the far right-hand corner of the First Court there is a fountain known as Cellad Çeşmesi, the **Executioner's Fountain (1)**, so named because the Chief Executioner of the palace cleaned his hands and sword there after performing his duties. The fountain is flanked by two truncated pillars called 'Example Stones'. The examples were the severed heads of executed criminals and rebels, which were placed upon these stones.

At the far end of the First Court is Bab-üs Selam, the Gate of Salutation, better known as **Orta Kapı**, 'Middle Gate'. This was the entryway to the Inner Palace, through which only authorised persons could pass, and only on foot. It is a much more impressive entryway than the Imperial Gate and it preserves its original appearance to a greater extent. The gateway is typical of the military architecture of Fatih's time, with its twin octagonal towers capped with conical roofs. The gatehouse itself is surmounted by a crenellated parapet, concealing a patrol-walk broad enough to hold several cannon. The double-arched doorway is closed by two pairs of splendid doors, the outer one of which bears the date 1524/5.

Above the inner arch is the **tuğra of Süleyman the Magnificent** and a calligraphic inscription giving the Islamic creed: 'There is no God but God, and Mohammed is his Prophet'. All who passed through this gate were required to dismount, with the exception of the sultan, who rode through on horseback. Foreign ambassadors hoping for an audience would wait in a chamber in one of the towers. There was also a cubicle for the Chief Executioner here and a tiny cell for prisoners awaiting execution.

THE SECOND COURT

The enormous Second Court, some 130m long and 110m wide at its south end, appears much as it did when it was first laid out in the time of Fatih. In Ottoman times this was known as the Court of the Divan, after the Imperial Council, which met in the domed chambers at the far left corner of the courtyard. A colonnade with antique marble columns and Turkish capitals runs around much of the courtyard. Beyond the colonnade the whole of the right side of the courtyard is occupied by the palace kitchens, while beyond the wall to the left are the royal stables, a mosque and some dormitories (*none of these were open to the public at the time of writing; some of the carriages from the stables are occasionally on view*).

The Divan

The Second Court seems to have been designed essentially for the pageantry connected with the transaction of the public business of the Empire. Here, four times a week, the Divan met to deliberate on administrative matters or to discharge its judicial functions. They came to the palace along Divan Yolu, the 'Divan Way', the former Mese, the main street of ancient Constantinople (*map p. 349, D3*). On such occasions the whole courtyard was filled with a vast throng of magnificently dressed officials and the corps of palace guards and Janissaries: at least 5,000 people on ordinary days, but more than twice that number when some special ceremony was being held. Even at such times an almost total silence prevailed throughout the courtyard, a fact commented upon with astonishment by the travellers who witnessed it.

The Divan building is dominated by a square tower with a conical roof, the **Tower of Justice**, a conspicuous landmark. The complex as a whole dates in essentials from the time of Fatih, though much altered in subsequent periods. The tower was originally lower and had a pyramidal roof; the present structure with its Corinthian columns was built for Mahmut II in 1820.

The **Divan buildings** consist of the Council Chamber, the Public Records Office and the Office of the Grand Vizier, all housed under a deeply projecting roof. The first two rooms, both of which are square and covered by a dome, open widely into one another under a great arch. Both chambers were badly damaged by fire in 1574, and were immediately afterwards restored by Murat III, probably under the supervision of Sinan. During the reign of Ahmet III they were redecorated in Rococo style, but in 1945 the **Council Chamber (2)** was re-restored to appear as it was after the repairs by Murat III. The lower walls are revetted in fine Iznik tiles while the upper sections, as well as the vaults and the domes, retain faded traces of their original arabesque painting. Around three sides of the room there is a low upholstered couch, the 'divan' from which the Council took its name. Here sat the members of the Council: the Grand Vizier in the centre opposite the door, the other viziers on either side of him in strict order of rank. Over the Grand Vizier's seat there is a barred window looking into a small room in the tower; this was called the **Eye of the Sultan** because from his hiding-place he could witness the proceedings of the Council without being observed.

The **Public Records Office**, which has retained its 18th-century décor, served as an archive for Divan records and for documents that might be needed at Council meetings. From here a door (*closed*) leads to the **Office of the Grand Vizier**.

The Inner Treasury

Adjacent to the Divan complex is the **Inner Treasury (3)**, a long chamber roofed with eight domes. This building dates from the late 15th or early 16th century. Here, and in the vaults below, were stored the tax receipts and tribute money as they arrived from all over the Empire. These funds were kept here until the quarterly pay-days for the use of the Council in meeting the expenses of government, and at the end of each quarter what remained unspent was transferred to the Imperial Treasury in the Third Court. The Inner Treasury is now used to display the palace's **collection of arms and armour**, with weapons and accoutrements spanning many centuries, including objects that belonged to the sultans themselves. Particularly exquisite is a round 16th-century shield of bound willow wands, painted with stylised tulips and carnations. It is an appealing idea to think of this lovely thing saving a man's life. It does not look like a weapon of war; from a distance it appears as innocuous as a dinner plate.

Around the corner from the Divan, directly under the south side of the Tower of Justice, is the **Carriage Gate**, one of the two main entrances to the Harem (*NB: The Harem ticket office is here; you can either visit it now or later; the Harem is described on pp. 83–89*). Just to the left of the Carriage Gate a doorway leads to the **dormitory of the Halberdiers with Tresses (4)** (*closed at the time of writing*), so called because they wore headdresses in which two tufts of horse-hair hung down before their eyes, designed to prevent them from getting a good look at the women when they delivered firewood to the Harem.

The Palace Kitchens

The palace kitchens, which produced an average of 5,000 meals a day, consist of a long series of ten spacious chambers with chimneys on the courtyard side and equally lofty domes on the Marmara side—a conspicuous feature of the Istanbul skyline. The two southernmost domes go back to Fatih's time, the other eight to that of Beyazıt II, while the cone-like chimneys in front of them are additions by Sinan, who reconstructed much of this area after the fire of 1574.

Today the kitchens house the **Porcelain Collection (5)**, an incomparable array of Chinese porcelain and other china and glassware. The Chinese collection boasts of being the finest outside China. The collection was begun by Beyazıt II, and augmented by Selim I and above all by Süleyman the Magnificent. Istanbul porcelain includes mid-19th-century items made in Beykoz on the Asian side of the Bosphorus and late 19th-century pieces from the Yıldız manufactory. The last two kitchens at the north end, the *helvahane*, where halva, mastic gum and other confectionery was made, have been restored to their original appearance and are used to display Turkish cooking utensils, including platters, bowls, ladles and *kazans* (bronze cauldrons of prodigious size), all of which were once used here.

The so-called Beverage Kitchen at the north end of the complex houses an interesting collection of **Turkish glass** from Beykoz (Paşabahçe; *see p. 275*) and other Istanbul factories of the 18th–19th centuries, some of it very lovely.

Bab-üs-Saadet

Bab-üs Saadet, the 'Gate of Felicity', is the entrance to the Third Court, the inner sanctum of the palace, also known as the Enderun Court. This was the strictly private and residential area of the palace, which in Ottoman times was called the House of Felicity. The gateway itself was originally built in Fatih's time, though it was reconstructed in the late 16th century and redecorated in the Rococo style in the 18th. At the time of his accession and on holidays, the sultan sat before the gate on his gold and emerald Bayram Throne to receive the homage of his subjects and officials.

THE THIRD COURT

The Throne Room

Just beyond the inner threshold of the Bab-üs Saadet stands the Arz Odası, the **Throne Room (6)**. Although situated in the Third Court, it belongs by function and use rather to the Second, for it is here that the last act of the ceremonies connected with the meetings of the Divan was performed. At the end of each session of the Council, the Grand Vizier and other high officials waited on the sultan here and reported to him upon the business transacted and the decisions taken, which could not be considered final until they had received the royal assent. Here also the ambassadors of foreign powers were presented to the sultan upon their arrival and departure. Whenever a session was in progress here, the palace fountains would all be made to play so that the sound of their waters would frustrate would-be eavesdroppers.

The Throne Room occupies a small building with a heavy and widely overhanging roof supported on a colonnade of antique marble columns. The foundations date from Fatih's time, but most of the superstructure dates to the reign of Selim I (r. 1512–20); inscriptions record restorations by Ahmet III (r. 1703–30) and Mahmut II (r. 1808–39). The room was restored yet again in more recent times, after having been badly damaged by fire in 1856.

The Library of Ahmet III

In the centre of the court, standing by itself, is the Library of Ahmet III **(7)**, erected in 1719 near the site of an older pavilion with a pool. It is an elegant little building of Proconnesian marble consisting of three domed areas flanked by three loggias with sofas and cupboards for books. Although 18th-century, the decoration is still largely classical, except for the windows, which almost anticipate Art Nouveau. The ceiling, also is entirely of its time. To understand the delicacy, frivolity and grace of the Tulip Era, just look upwards. Exquisite panels of vases of flowers and dwarf fruit trees, arranged nosegay-style, appear amongst more conventionally-inspired symmetrical floral compositions. The same thing occurs in stone on street fountains of the period (*see illustration on p. 226*).

The Imperial Costume Collection

The Campaign Hall **(8)** was the dormitory of a corps established by Murat IV in the 17th century. Not only did its members accompany the sultan on campaign, but they also performed the duties of launderers and turban-folders. Hence it is appropriate that today their quarters house the Imperial Wardrobe, a fascinating collection of costumes of the Ottoman sultans from Fatih's time onwards which includes a kaftan worn by the Conqueror himself and another, of Italian velvet, thought to have belonged to Süleyman the Magnificent. There are also several examples of talismanic shirts, decorated with verses from the Koran designed to protect the wearer. The later pieces in the collection include European-style military uniforms, adopted after reforms to the army in the 19th century.

THE PALACE SCHOOL

Many of the buildings in and around the Third Court were devoted to the various branches of the Palace School. This elaborately organised institution for the training of the Imperial Civil Service appears to be unique in the Islamic world. It was founded and its principles laid down by Fatih Mehmet, though later sultans added to and modified it. The pupils, recruited from among the Christian subjects of the Empire and promising youths captured in war, entered at various ages from 9 to 18 and received a vigorous training. This was designed specifically to prepare them for the administration of the Empire, and included the traditional Islamic studies (the Koran, the hadis, law, rhetoric) as well as the liberal arts (music, geography, arithmetic, history) and physical training (wrestling was particularly favoured).

The School was organised into six divisions, or Halls: the two introductory schools, **Küçük Oda** (Small Hall) **(9)** and **Büyük Oda** (Large Hall) **(10)**, occupied the entire south side, to left and right respectively, of the Bab-üs Saadet. The Büyük Oda burned down in 1856 but has since been reconstructed and is now used for museum offices. Here also were the quarters of the White Eunuchs, and their Ağa, who were in charge of administration and discipline.

If a boy was talented in any field, he would pass from this introductory school to one of the four vocational halls. These were the Seferli Koğuşu, or **Campaign Hall (8)**, the Hasine Koğuşu or **Hall of the Treasury (11)** and the Kilerli Koğuşu, the **Hall of the Pantry-Men (12)** on the east and north sides of the court and, the last and highest of the vocational schools, the Has Oda Koğuşu, the **Hall of the Privy Chamber (16)** on the west side. The Ağalar Camii **(17)** was the principal mosque of the School.

The Treasury

Next to the Campaign Hall, on a slightly lower level, is the pavilion of Mehmet II **(11)**, which served him and several later sultans as a suite of reception rooms. The vaults below were used as the Privy Treasury and gradually, from the 17th century onwards, the rooms themselves were turned into storerooms—a curious turn of events considering that these some of the finest apartments in the palace and with an unrivalled view. The rooms are now used for the display of the palace treasures; it is altogether an astonishing collection, admirably exhibited.

Highlights of the Treasury Collection

Room 1: The most notable object is an **ebony throne** inlaid with ivory and mother-of-pearl, made for Murat IV. There are several *nargiles*, or water-pipes, with cut-crystal bases and mouthpieces set with diamonds; little coffee-cup holders, including one set with small rose-coloured diamonds, and an enamelled gold pen-box encrusted with gems.

Room 2: The **Eve Throne** was used by the sultans, beginning with Ahmet I, in ceremonies that took place on the eve of festivals. The famous 18th-century **Topkapı Dagger**, made for Mahmut I, has three great emeralds on the sides and one on the top that opens to reveal a watch. Other highlights are a suit of armour that belonged to Murat IV; and robes, turbans and aigrettes belonging to various sultans, including one made for his own use by Süleyman, who was an accomplished goldsmith.

Room 3: The most notable exhibits include a throne presented by Nadir Shah of Iran to Mahmut I, an elaborate oval seat plated with gold and set with emeralds, rubies and pearls in an enamel base; a Koran case encrusted with gems, belonging to Mehmet III, with a floral design in diamonds on the cover; a gold-plated belt, armlet and goblet belonging to Shah İsmail, part of the loot taken by Selim I in his victorious Persian campaign of 1514; and a golden reliquary for the supposed hand of St John the Baptist.

Room 4: The golden Bayram Throne was first used by Murat III in 1579; the **Kaşıkçı Elması**, an 86-carat diamond, the fifth-largest in the world, was worn by Mehmet IV in his turban on his accession to the throne in 1648 at the age of six. Also on show are an 80-carat diamond that belonged to Ahmet I along with jewel-studded pendants, aigrettes and other precious objects belonging to various sultans.

The Pavilion of the Holy Mantle

A portal at the northwest corner of the Third Court gives entrance to Hırka-i Saadet Dairesi, the chambers where the relics of the Prophet Mohammed and other sacred objects are preserved **(13)**. These relics, of which the Prophet's mantle is the most sacred, were brought from Egypt by Selim I after his conquest of that country in 1517, when he assumed the title of Caliph (*see p. 24*). For centuries these relics were guarded here and displayed on state occasions only to the sultan, his family, and his immediate entourage; in 1962 the present exhibit was arranged and opened to the public. The mantle was traditionally used to make relics by contact, when muslin cloths were touched to it and thus sanctity was imparted to them. Also here is a hair from the Prophet's beard and a tooth from his head, as well as the sword of David, the rod of Moses and the prayer-mat of Fatima.

The Revan Köşkü and Circumcision Room

An open, L-shaped portico adjoins two sides of the Pavilion of the Holy Mantle, with kiosks opening off from both ends. The **Revan Köşkü (14)** was built in 1636 by Murat IV to commemorate his capture of Yerevan in the Caucasus. It is an octagonal building revetted in Iznik tiles and with beautiful woodwork with mother-of-pearl inlay. The kiosk at the west end of the portico is the Sünnet Odası, the **Circumcision Room (15)**, built for Sultan İbrahim in 1641. The circumcision rites of Ottoman princes began to be carried out here from the reign of Ahmet III. Both the interior and exterior are covered with ceramic tiles ranging in date from the earliest Iznik style in *cuerda seca* through to the great period in the second half of the 16th and the early 17th centuries. The overall effect is something of a patchwork, but individually the panels are fine and interesting.

The Hall of the Privy Chamber

Has Oda, the **Hall of the Privy Chamber (16)**, was the highest of the vocational divisions of the Palace School. It was limited to 40 pages in immediate attendance upon the sultan. An exhibition of sultans' portraits is now displayed here. Mehmet the Conqueror was the first sultan to sit for his portrait. His likeness, by the Venetian Gentile Bellini, remains the most accomplished and psychologically insightful. The original portrait (*see illustration on p. 158*) is now in the National Gallery in London. In the Topkapı collection is a copy of it by Fausto Zonaro, another Italian from the Veneto, who was court painter to Sultan Abdülhamit II. Portraiture is not a naturally Islamic art, and many of the sultans were in fact painted by Europeans.

The palace also has a superb collection of Islamic miniatures, displayed on a rotating basis. The oldest pieces in the collection are in the so-called *Fatih Album*, whose works, tentatively ascribed to Mohammed Siyah Kalem, are from Iran and dated variously from before the 13th to the second half of the 15th centuries. The oldest Ottoman works are by Matrakçı Nasuh, court painter of Süleyman. One of his miniatures shows Süleyman's fleet sailing down the Golden Horn, with both Istanbul and Galata represented in accurate detail. The portrait of Süleyman in his last years is by Nigari, the finest Ottoman portraitist in the reigns of Süleyman and Selim II. The latest in date of the imperial albums was made in 1720 to commemorate the circumcision feast of four sons of Ahmet III. The miniatures (*example illustrated on p. 216*) are by Levni (d. 1732), the greatest court painter of the Tulip Era.

The Ağalar Camii

Jutting out at an angle to the other buildings of the courtyard is the Mosque of the Ağas or Ağalar Camii **(17)**, the principal place of worship of the Palace School, used by the sultan, the pages of the School, and the White Eunuchs. Though dating in origin from the time of the Conqueror, it has been much remodelled.

Early 18th-century miniature by Levni showing a court page carrying a cup of coffee. Coffee first came to Istanbul in 1543 from the Yemen, where it had been introduced from Ethiopia. The sultan's Chief Coffee Maker (*kahvecibaşı*) was an important court official.

THE FOURTH COURT

The Fourth Court is not really a courtyard at all but a garden on several levels, adorned with a number of pavilions. The west side takes the form of a broad marble terrace overlooking the Golden Horn. The large marble **pool with a fountain** at its centre was once the scene of aquatic revels staged for Sultan İbrahim by the women of his harem.

CRAZY İBRAHİM & THE INMATES OF THE CAGE

İbrahim was of weak understanding. It was because of this that he had not been strangled when his brother took the throne in 1623, but was confined instead to the *Kafes* (*see below*). On his retrieval from it 18 years later, his understanding was yet further impaired. The unfortunate creature had no conception of affairs of state; instead his appetite was directed towards his women, and the fatter they were, the better he liked them. Mental instability plagued him. When rumours reached him that someone else had been taking liberties with his concubines, he is said to have had over 200 women tied in sacks and tossed into the Bosphorus. After losing important territory to Venice, he was deposed and strangled. His remains are interred in the former baptistery of Haghia Sophia.

The *Kafes* (Cage) was not always the selfsame room or rooms, but as an institution it fulfilled only one function: to keep potential rivals for the throne in close confinement. İbrahim was not the first to be shut away: the custom began with Prince Mustafa, imprisoned by the clemency of his brother Ahmet I, who could not bear to have his half-witted sibling strangled. After that the fate of all royal princes was to be shut away, without education or instructive entertainment, and with only slaves and barren concubines for company. Many went mad, and when they were plucked out and placed on the throne, were found inadequate to govern. The last sultan, Mehmet VI, spent over 40 years of his life in the Cage.

The terrace has a curving balustrade of white marble carved in openwork design. At its centre, hanging high out over the lower gardens, is a charming little balcony covered by a domed canopy in gilded bronze carried on four slim bronze pillars. On misty days it gleams from afar and is a noticeable feature as you cross by boat from Eminönü to Üsküdar. This is the **İftariye (18)**, made in 1640 for Sultan İbrahim. It takes its name from the *İftar,* the festive meal taken after sunset in the holy month of Ramadan, which ends the daily fast.

The **Bağdat Köşkü (19)** was built in 1638–40 by Murat IV to commemorate his capture of Baghdad the previous year. It thus forms a pair with the Revan Köşkü, built by the same sultan two years previously, also to celebrate a military victory. The wide overhanging eaves are carried by an arcade of slender marble columns. The walls inside and out are sheathed in ceramic tiles, chiefly blue and white. The interior is furnished with carved wooden cabinets and coffee tables inlaid with mother-of-pearl, and the window recesses on four sides are lined with embroidered divans. One of the eight walls is taken up with a splendid bronze chimney-piece. The dome is adorned with elaborate arabesques on a crimson ground, painted on leather.

A staircase beside the pool leads down into what was once the garden of Ahmet III, one of the sites of his fabulous Tulip Festivals. At its centre is a charming pavilion known as the **Sofa Köşkü (20)**, built in the late 17th century and restored for Ahmet III, probably as a *pied-à-terre* for his use during the festivals; in 1752 it was redecorated in the Rococo style by Mahmut I. Farther on there is a low tower called Hekimbaşı Kulesi, the **Tower of the Chief Physician (21)**.

The **Mecidiye Köşkü (22)** was the last building to be erected at Topkapı before it was abandoned as an imperial residence. Noticeably Western in style, it was built c. 1840 for Abdülmecit I by Sarkis Balyan, a member of the great Armenian architect dynasty that did so much to shape the idiom of imperial Ottoman architecture in the 19th century. In recent years the lower floor and terrace of the kiosk have been converted into a branch of the **Konyalı restaurant** (*closed evenings and Tues; see p. 296*), from which there is a panoramic view out across the Sea of Marmara.

THE HAREM

The Harem is entered from the Second Court. For opening times see p. 71. At the time of writing, about 20 rooms and courtyards were open to the public. These are described below.

The Harem was not an original part of the palace as laid out by Mehmet II. Fatih seems to have designed Topkapı Sarayı primarily as the administrative centre of his empire, reserving the Old Palace (*see p. 71*) for his court and harem. This arrangement was maintained by his three immediate successors: Beyazıt II (r. 1481–1512), Selim I (r. 1512–20) and Süleyman the Magnificent (r. 1520–66), at least during the early years of his reign. According to tradition, Süleyman allowed Roxelana to install herself in Topkapı Sarayı, but probably only in wooden pavilions, and his son Selim II (1566–74) seems to have followed his father's example. The first permanent structures of the Harem as we know it today appear to have been built during the reign of Selim's son Murat III (r. 1574–95). The Harem in its present state dates largely from the reign of Murat, with extensive reconstruction and additions made chiefly under Mehmet IV (r. 1648–87) and Osman III (r. 1754–57).

TOUR OF THE HAREM

The Harem is entered through the **Carriage Gate**, which takes its name from the fact that the Harem ladies entered their closed carriages here when they left the Harem on an excursion. Above the gateway is an inscription giving the date 1588. The gate opens into a small, dark vestibule called **Dolaplı Kubbe (1)**, the 'Dome with Cupboards', which is followed by a larger cobbled antechamber revetted with fine tiles, which served as a **guardroom (2)**. On the left a door (*closed*) gives access to a long ramp leading down to the stables; while on the right a door opens into the Tower of Justice. It is from here that the sultan would have entered the tower to listen in on the meetings of the Divan (*see p. 75*).

Service areas of the Harem
The long, narrow **Courtyard of the Black Eunuchs (3)** is bordered by an arcade of ten marble columns with lozenge capitals, above which hang wrought-iron brackets for the lamps that once lighted the way to the Carriage Gate. The building under the porch, which is revetted in ceramic tiles, was the **Dormitory of the Black Eunuchs (4)**; an inscription in the courtyard bears the date 1668–69, indicating that this part of the Harem was rebuilt by Mehmet IV after the great fire of 1665. It is in this area of the Harem that the young sons of the sultan received their primary education. Here also were the quarters of the palace dwarves.

At the far end of the Courtyard of the Black Eunuchs is the main gate, the **Cümle Kapısı (5)**, which opens into the Harem proper. This leads to a **second guardroom (6)**, from where you can look out into the spacious **Courtyard of the Valide Sultan (7)**. From here a long, narrow service corridor stretches to the open **Courtyard of the Cariyeler (8)**, or women servants. This was the domain of the chief women officials of the Harem, the Head Stewardess, the Treasurer and the Chief Laundress, and also of the wives and concubines. Before additional chambers for the favourites were built further to the north, this courtyard would also have housed the sultan's bedfellows and the mothers of his children. All but the most favoured had a rather small cubicle to sleep in, and only the superior rooms had fireplaces. It must have been a chilly life in winter, when the Bosphorus damps rose up from the water below.

Apartment of the Valide Sultan
A warren of passages brings you into the apartment of the Valide Sultan, the most powerful woman in the Ottoman world. Not only did she reign over the Harem but she frequently also dominated her son, the sultan, and through him the Empire. Her apartments occupy a large central area of the Harem, overlooking the gardens.

The principal room of the suite is the **Salon of the Valide Sultan (9)**. At the window end there is a raised alcove that has been restored and furnished with wax figures representing the Valide and her ladies in waiting. We must imagine that the wax Valide is either Nurbanu, mother of Murat III, for whom this chamber was first built in the 16th century, or Mihrişah, mother of Selim III, for whom the smaller suite on the upper floor was constructed. The Western-style landscape panels date from this time.

A corridor paved in marble leads from the Valide's apartment to the **Royal Baths (10)**, which was a double hamam used both by the Valide and by the sultan himself, who bathed here after visiting one of his favourites. Selim II died in these baths on 15th December 1574, after falling while drunk and hitting his head on the marble pavement. Note the fine mixer taps.

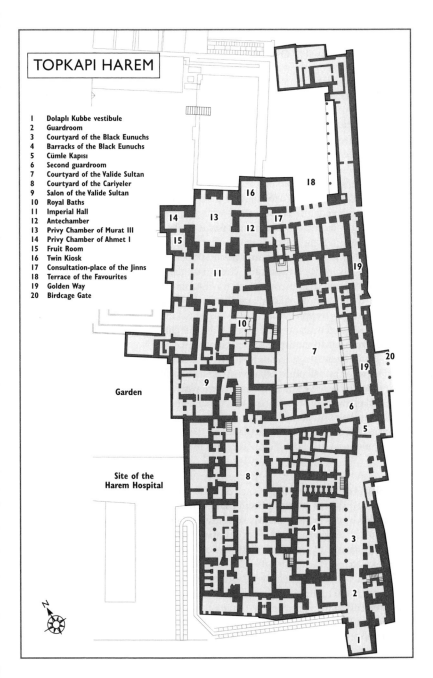

TOPKAPI HAREM

1   Dolaplı Kubbe vestibule
2   Guardroom
3   Courtyard of the Black Eunuchs
4   Barracks of the Black Eunuchs
5   Cümle Kapısı
6   Second guardroom
7   Courtyard of the Valide Sultan
8   Courtyard of the Cariyeler
9   Salon of the Valide Sultan
10 Royal Baths
11 Imperial Hall
12 Antechamber
13 Privy Chamber of Murat III
14 Privy Chamber of Ahmet I
15 Fruit Room
16 Twin Kiosk
17 Consultation-place of the Jinns
18 Terrace of the Favourites
19 Golden Way
20 Birdcage Gate

Garden

Site of the
Harem Hospital

THE ORGANISATION OF THE HAREM

The *haremlık* is the private, family section of an Islamic home where the women and children live secluded from the gaze of unauthorised males. In Topkapı Palace, the Harem of the sultan was also an efficiently controlled insemination parlour, dedicated to the perpetuation of the dynasty. Its population consisted of captive concubines and consorts, male children before the age of puberty and female children before marriage. All were watched over by castrated guards and waited on by other captive women. Every Harem lady began her life as a slave, either purchased in the markets of the Empire, captured in military conquest or in pirate raids, and presented to the sultan. These girls were well educated, beautiful, graceful and accomplished, and those who did not bear sons were sometimes set free to marry and make other lives outside the palace. A strict hierarchy obtained. On the bottom rung was the simple *cariye*, or maid of all work. Above her was the *kalfa*, a servant with a defined role and responsibility. Then came the *usta*, the 'mistress', in charge of a particular division or department. The *odalık* was at the head of her own *oda*, or 'court', a group of harem girls under training. The *gedik* was a lady-in-waiting to the sultan. Then came the *gözde*, a girl whom the sultan had noticed with approval, but had not yet summoned to his bed. After this came the privileged few, those whom the sultan had chosen as his bedfellows. These girls were assigned their own servants, and were given larger and better quarters. The *ikbals* (addressed as *hanımefendi*) were the favourite concubines. Above them were the *kadıns*, the official consorts who had borne children to the sultan, and who enjoyed a status similar to that of legal wives. At the top of the pyramid was the most powerful lady of all, the Valide Sultan, mother of the reigning monarch. This was the position that all mothers of boys aimed to hold—for a son who did not succeed to the throne would either be strangled with a bow-string by a deaf-mute or (after 1617) find himself confined to the Cage (*see p. 82*).

The imperial quarters

The Hünkar Sofası, or **Imperial Hall (11)**, is the most sumptuous room in the palace. It is divided by a great arch into two unequal sections: the larger section is domed and the smaller, slightly raised, had a balcony above. This splendid chamber is believed to have been constructed for Murat III (1574–95), in which case the architect would surely have been Sinan. The upper part—dome, pendentives and arches—has been restored to its original appearance. The lower part retains the Baroque decorations added by Osman III (1754–57). The hall was used by the sultan as a reception room and for giving entertainments to the women of the Harem: the balcony was used by the musicians.

A door at the northeast corner of the Imperial Hall leads into a small but lavishly tiled **antechamber (12)**. During a reconstruction in the late 16th or early 17th century, the room was cut in half right through the dome to make space for an adjacent apartment.

The antechamber leads into the **Privy Chamber of Murat III (13)**, the best-preserved room in the palace. It is dated by an inscription to 1578, and unlike the Imperial Hall it has retained the whole of its original decoration. The walls are sheathed in Iznik tiles from the greatest period of their manufacture; the panel of plum blossoms surrounding the elegant bronze chimney-piece is especially noteworthy, as is the calligraphic frieze which runs around the room. The text is the so-called Ayet el-Kürsi verse of the Koran: 'There is no deity but Allah, the Ever Living, Who sustains and protects all life…His throne extends over heaven and earth…He is the Most High, the Lord of all.' Opposite the fireplace there is an elegant cascade fountain of carved polychrome marble. The plash of the fountain was designed to mask the sound of human voices, and thus prevent eavesdropping on private conversations. The beauty of the decoration and the perfect and harmonious form of the room identify it as a work of Sinan.

The small **Privy Chamber of Ahmet I (14)**, built in 1608–09 and adorned with cabinets inlaid with turtle shell and mother-of-pearl, its walls revetted with blue and green tiles, is lighted by windows on two sides affording sweeping views across the Marmara and up the Bosphorus and the Golden Horn. A marble doorway in the south wall leads to the famous **Fruit Room (15)**, constructed almost a century later, in 1705–06. Its walls are decorated with naturalistic paintings of flowers in vases, of heaped bowls of fruit (grapes, figs, pomegranates, pears), and, in one corner, a group of yellow-feathered ducklings following their mother. These decorations are characteristic of the Tulip Era, when Rococo art and architecture made its first appearance in Istanbul. Relief carvings on fountains of the period are very similar. The street fountain on the terrace behind the Galata Tower (1732) features identical baskets of fruit.

The pair of handsome rooms known as the **Twin Kiosk (16)** dates from the early 17th century. It was used by the sons of the sultan. The first room has a dome magnificently painted on canvas, while the ceiling of the inner room is flat but also adorned with superb painted designs. The tiles are perhaps the most beautiful in the palace. On the side wall in one of the rooms are panels with three striking cypress trees in a vivid dark green against a swirling background of leaves and large mulberries. The cypress, symbol of the universe and immortality, may have offered consolation to the inmates of these rooms. Royal princes by tradition were sent out, accompanied by their mothers, to govern provinces of the Empire, never to return unless they took the throne. Later, however, these rooms and the apartments above functioned as little more than prisons: notions of immortality can have occurred only to those whose natures tended toward self-denial and asceticism. Genetic immortality through their own progeny was not an option offered to the royal males incarcerated here, for these rooms formed part of the terrible *Kafes*, the 'Cage', where brothers of the sultan were kept under house-arrest when the practice of strangulation was discontinued (*for more on the Kafes, see p. 82*).

The colonnaded corridor that runs past the Twin Kiosk, known as the **Consultation-Place of the Jinns (17)**, leads to a courtyard known as Gözdeler Taşlığı, the **Terrace of the Favourites (18)**, which overlooks the lower gardens. On the right side of the terrace is a long wooden building, two storeys high, which once housed the sultan's favourite women.

An Englishman spies on the women of the Harem

[My guide] pointed me to go to a grate in a wall, but made me a sign that he might not go thither himself. When I came to the grate the wall was very thick, and grated on both sides with iron very strongly; but through that grate I did see thirty of the Grand Signior's concubines that were playing with a ball in another court. At the first sight of them I had thought they had been young men, but when I saw the hair of their heads hang down on their backs, plaited together with a tassel of small pearls hanging in the lower end of it, and by other plain tokens, I did know them to be women, and very pretty ones indeed.

They wore upon their heads nothing but a little cap of cloth of gold, which did but cover the crown of the head; no bands about their necks, nor anything but fair chains of pearl and a jewel hanging on their breast, and jewels in their ears. Their coats were like a soldier's mandilion, some of red satin and some of blue and some of other colours; they wore breeches of scamatie, a fine cloth made of cotton wool, as white as snow and as fine as lawn, for I could discern the skin of their thighs through it. These breeches came down to their mid-leg; some of them did wear fine cordoban buskins, and some had their legs naked, with a gold ring on the small of their leg; on their feet a velvet pantouffle, four or five inches high. I stood so long looking upon them that he which had showed me all this kindness began to be very angry with me. He made a wry mouth and stamped with his foot to make me give over looking; the which I was very loth to do, for the sight did please me wondrous well.

Then I went away to the place where we left my dragoman or interpreter, and I told my interpreter that I had seen thirty of the Grand Signior's concubines; but my interpreter advised me that by no means I should speak of it whereby any Turk might hear of it; for if it were known to some Turks, it would present death to him that showed me them.

From the diary of the Lancashire organ-maker Thomas Dallam, 1599–1600

It is interesting to note the fate of Dallam's organ. It was a gift to Sultan Murat III from Queen Elizabeth I of England, and Dallam had been sent to Istanbul to install it. It was a wonder of its time, being not only a manual keyboard instrument but also an automaton: it could be set to play a number of melodies by itself and it also chimed the hours. The statuary that adorned its case was later smashed with a battleaxe by Ahmet I, because it mimicked the creation of Allah. The event forms a memorable scene in Orhan Pamuk's *My Name is Red*.

The route to the exit

The last part of the tour of the Harem brings you to Altın Yol, the **Golden Way** (**19**). It was in this corridor, after the murder of Selim III (1808), that the would-be murderers of his cousin Mahmut were thwarted in their fell designs by the resourcefulness of Cevri the servant girl, who threw hot ash in their faces. A mektep on Divan Yolu was built in her honour (*see p. 116*). The corridor brings you to Kuşhane Kapısı, the **Birdcage Gate (20)**, where in 1651 the Valide Sultan Kösem was dragged out of the cupboard where she was hiding and brutally strangled by the Chief Black Eunuch, Tall Süleyman, possibly on the orders of her rival, Turhan Hatice Sultan (who had heard of Kösem's plots to annihilate her son, Mehmet IV). On Kösem's death the people of Istanbul declared three days of public mourning.

The last word on Topkapı, perhaps, should go to Edmondo de Amicis, whose book *Constantinopoli*, published in 1877, inspired so many travellers with enthusiasm, awe and admiration for this extraordinary place:

Edmondo de Amicis on Topkapı

It is not for its architectural beauty that all eyes are drawn to these walls. The palace is not a great work of art like the Alhambra. The Patio of the Lions alone in the Arab palace is worth all the kiosks and all the turrets of the Turkish version. No, the value of the palace is its history, the fact that it interprets and illuminates virtually the entire life of the Ottoman dynasty, that the stones of its walls and the very trunks of its trees are inscribed with the most intimate, most secret story of the empire. Twenty-five sultans lived here. Here the dynasty entrenched itself; here it rose to the zenith of its power; here its decline began. It was at once a palace, a fortress and a sanctuary; it was the nerve centre of the empire and the heart of Islam; it was a city within a city, an august and magnificent stronghold inhabited by its own populace and guarded by an army, and which embraced within its walls an infinite variety of buildings, places of bliss and of horror, urban and rural, state rooms, arsenals, schools, offices, mosques; where festivals and murders, devout rituals and love trysts, ceremonial and madness alternated; where sultans were born, raised to the throne, deposed, imprisoned, strangled; where conspiracies began and the cry of revolt rang out; where the purest blood and gold of the empire flowed; where a firm hand was maintained on the hilt of that sword which threatened the heads of a hundred peoples; where for almost three centuries the eyes of anxious Europe, timorous Asia and affrighted Africa were fixed, as on a smoking volcano, which threatens all the world.

From *Constantinopoli*, 1877 (Tr. AB)

HAGHIA EIRENE

Haghia Eirene (*map p. 349, E3; only open for exhibitions or concerts*) is the second largest Byzantine church in the city, surpassed in size only by Haghia Sophia.

History of Haghia Eirene

According to tradition, the original church of Haghia Eirene was the cathedral of Byzantium before Constantine established his capital here. The church was dedicated to Haghia Eirene, the Divine Peace, an attribute of Christ (complementary to his personification of the Divine Wisdom; Haghia Sophia) and was rebuilt by the emperor Constantius (337–61). During the Nika Revolt of 532 (*see p. 9*) both Haghia Eirene and Haghia Sophia were totally destroyed by fire. After the revolt was put down, Justinian began a project to rebuild both churches; the new Haghia Eirene was probably completed at about the same time as Haghia Sophia, in 537. Thenceforth the two churches were closely linked and formed two parts of what was essentially one religious establishment, both of them administered by the Patriarchate and served by the same clergy. Haghia Eirene was almost destroyed in 564, when a fire ruined the atrium and part of the narthex, but it was immediately restored by Justinian, then in the last year of his life. In 740 the church was severely damaged by an earthquake, after which it was restored, either by Leo III or his son, Constantine V.

It appears that since that date no other major catastrophes have befallen the church, therefore the building you see today dates from Justinian's time, with the exception of 8th-century repairs and minor Turkish additions. After the Conquest, Haghia Eirene was enclosed within the outer walls of Topkapı Sarayı, serving as an arsenal for the Janissaries until they were annihilated in 1826 (*see p. 22*). In the late 19th century the building became a storehouse for antiquities, principally old Ottoman armaments. The building was restored in the 1980s and is now used for exhibitions and concerts.

The apse of Haghia Eirene with its mosaic cross. Scholars are unsure whether it dates from the Iconoclastic period of the 8th century or from the time of Justinian.

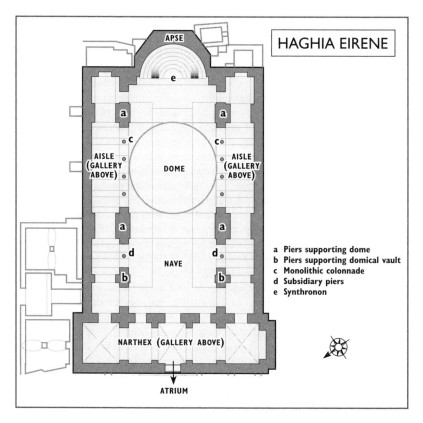

a Piers supporting dome
b Piers supporting domical vault
c Monolithic colonnade
d Subsidiary piers
e Synthronon

Exterior of Haghia Eirene

The church is rectangular in plan, 42.2m long and 36.7m wide, with a five-sided apse projecting from the east wall, and to the west a narthex preceded by an atrium. The central area of the nave is covered by a dome carried on a high drum, with peaked roofs to its north, east and south, and a lower domical vault to the west. The ancient architectural fragments arrayed around the building are from excavations on the First Hill. The ground around the church has risen some 5m above its original level and the present entry is through a Turkish porch and outbuildings outside the west end of the north aisle. From there a ramp leads down to the level of the interior.

Interior of Haghia Eirene

The church is a basilica of a very unusual type, as can be seen from an examination of its plan. The **nave** is flanked by a pair of **side aisles**, above which there is a gallery that also surmounts the narthex. The central area of the nave is covered by the great **dome**, some 15.5m in diameter, supported primarily by four huge **piers (a)** standing on the corners of a square. Between these piers there are four great arches; pendentives then make the transition to the circular base of the drum that carries the dome. Another pair of **piers at the west end of the nave (b)** support an elliptical domical vault. At the west end of the nave an attractive Turkish wooden staircase leads to the **galleries**.

The nave is separated from the side aisles by the usual colonnade: there are four **monolithic columns (c)** on either side between the main piers, and another one on either side between the west piers, and a pair of **subsidiary piers (d)** which help to support the west ends of the north and south galleries. Around the periphery of the semicircular apse there is a **synthronon (e)**, the only one in the city to have survived from the Byzantine period. This has six tiers of seats for the clergy, with doors at either side leading to an ambulatory which runs beneath the fifth tier.

In the **conch of the apse** a mosaic cross in black outline stands on a pedestal of three steps, against a gold ground with a geometric border. The inscription here is from Psalm LXV, 4 and 5: 'Blessed is the man whom thou choosest; and causest to approach unto thee, that he may dwell in thy courts: we shall be satisfied with the goodness of thy house, even of thy holy temple.' In both cases parts of the mosaic have fallen away and letters have been painted in by someone who was indifferent to both grammar and sense. There is some difference of opinion concerning the dating of these mosaics; one theory is that they date from the reconstruction after the earthquake of 740, the other, that they are from Justinian's reign (the decorative **mosaics in the narthex**, which are similar to those in Haghia Sophia, are almost certainly from Justinian's period).

The **atrium** has been rather drastically altered: the whole of the inner peristyle is Turkish, as well as a good many bays of the outer. However, most of the outer walls date from the Byzantine period: they are curiously irregular, the north portico is considerably longer than the south, thus the west wall of the atrium is not parallel to the narthex. The **two porphyry sarcophagi**, from the 4th–6th centuries AD, are from the imperial mausoleum in the Church of the Holy Apostles, destroyed at the time of the Turkish Conquest. They were brought here when Haghia Eirene became a storehouse for antiquities. Four others of the same type and period are now arrayed outside the Archaeological Museum. Two others, belonging to Constantine's mother Helena and his daughter Constantia, are in the Vatican. It is tempting to believe that one of the Istanbul sarcophagi once belonged to Constantine himself.

The ruins of the Hospice of Samson
The ruins to the south of Haghia Eirene, between the church and the outer walls of Topkapı (*not open to the public*) are the remains of the Hospice of Samson, partially excavated in 1946. Procopius, Justinian's court chronicler, writes that between Haghia Sophia and Haghia Eirene 'there was a certain hospice, devoted to those that were at once destitute and suffering from serious illness, namely those who had lost their property and their health. This was erected in early times by a certain pious man, Samson by name.' Procopius goes on to report that the Hospice of Samson was destroyed by fire during the Nika Revolt of 532—along with Haghia Sophia and Haghia Eirene—and that it was rebuilt and considerably enlarged by Justinian.

THE ARCHAEOLOGICAL
MUSEUM & GÜLHANE PARK

Map p. 349, E2–3. Open Tues–Sun 9–5, last tickets 4pm. Closed Mon. Audio guides available.
The Archaeological Museum can be approached from Gülhane Park or from the First
Court of Topkapı Palace. The approach path in either direction is flanked by ancient col-
umns, capitals, sarcophagi and architectural fragments, an overflow from the museum.

Beyond the ticket office stretches a wide courtyard and tea garden. Once part of the
gardens of Topkapı, it now houses three museums: the Archaeological Museum (Arke-
oloji Müzesi), Museum of the Ancient Orient (Eski Şark Eserleri Müzesi) and the Tiled
Pavilion (Çinili Köşk). Antiquities of all sorts are arrayed in the courtyard. The most
noteworthy of these are the four huge porphyry sarcophagi in front of the Archaeological Museum; they were originally in the imperial mausoleum of the Church of the
Holy Apostles. Also here is a fragment of one of the 'Hercules Club' columns from the
Arch of Theodosius (*see p. 124*) and two colossal Gorgon heads identical to those in
the Basilica Cistern (*see p. 46*); these are from the Forum of Constantine (*see p. 118*).

THE ARCHAEOLOGICAL MUSEUM

The Archaeological Museum has one of the world's richest collections of antiquities,
principally from Anatolia, the Near East and the eastern Mediterranean. The collection
is superbly displayed and captioned, and in some of the rooms the pieces are set off
by excellent photographs. This is one of the finest museums of its kind in the world.

HISTORY OF THE ARCHAEOLOGICAL MUSEUM

The first systematic attempt in the Ottoman Empire to collect and preserve its
antiquities began in 1846, during the reign of Abdülmecit I. The project was
initiated by Fethi Ahmet Pasha, son-in-law of Mahmut II, who contacted governors
all over the Empire and directed them to collect all the movable works of art in their
provinces and ship them to Istanbul. These antiquities were at first stored in Haghia
Eirene, and when that was full the Çinili Köşk was used, beginning in 1874. The
modern history of the museum dates from 1881, when the archaeologist Osman
Hamdi Bey was made director. The Archaeological Museum's main building, in the
Beaux Arts style, is the work of Istanbul-born Alexander Vallaury (who was also
the architect of the Pera Palace Hotel). The museum was first opened to the public
on 13th June 1891, and new wings were added in 1902 and 1908. A new museum
was added behind the old museum and was dedicated in 1991, with its newest
gallery, devoted to Istanbul Through the Ages, opened in 1994.

THE OLD BUILDING

Facing the door in the entrance lobby is a colossal Roman-era statue from Amathus, Cyprus (1st–3rd centuries AD) of the **Egyptian god Bes**, who is shown holding up the headless form of a lioness; the gaping hole in his loins was probably the site of a gigantic phallus. Bes was traditionally seen as a protector god and was often set up in entryways to ward off evil spirits and intruders. The Romans used the phallus as a talisman in much the same way.

Left-hand wing

Room 9: An excavation directed by Osman Hamdi Bey in 1887 in the royal necropolis at Sidon in Syria unearthed a number of extraordinary sarcophagi belonging to a succession of kings who ruled in Phoenicia between the mid-5th and latter half of the 4th century BC. The earliest is the **Tabnit Sarcophagus** (6th century BC), a so-called anthropoid sarcophagus, in the form of a diorite mummy-case. The Egyptian hieroglyphic inscription on the lid records that it originally belonged to an Egyptian commander named Peneptah. Another inscription, in the Phoenician alphabet, states that the second owner of the sarcophagus was Tabnit, King of Sidon, whose mummy is exposed in the glass case just beyond.

The **Lycian Sarcophagus** (end 5th century BC), from Lycia on the southwest coast of Asia Minor, is decorated on its sides with a lion hunt and a boar hunt, and on its ends with the figures of centaurs, griffins and sphinxes. The **Satrap Sarcophagus** (second half of the

Detail of a lion hunt, from the Alexander Sarcophagus (4th century BC).

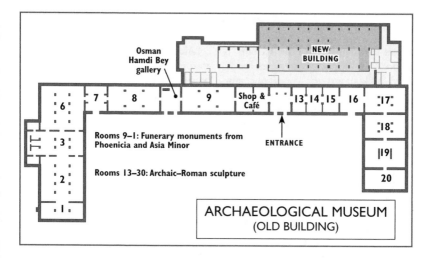

5th century BC) takes its name from the fact that it was the tomb of a satrap, or Persian viceroy, who is shown reclining on a couch on one end of the monument, while on the side he is shown in a hunting scene.

The next gallery is devoted to **Osman Hamdi Bey** (1842–1910), the founder of the Archaeological Museum, with photographs showing his life and highlights of his career.

Room 8: The most famous work of art in the museum, the so-called **Alexander Sarcophagus** (late 4th century BC), is the latest in date of the funerary monuments from the royal necropolis of Sidon. The sarcophagus, in Pentelic marble, once painted in vivid colours, was originally believed to have been that of Alexander the Great himself, for it is adorned with sculptures in deep, almost round relief, showing the hero in scenes of hunting and battle. But Alexander is known to have been buried in Alexandria. The sarcophagus has now been identified as belonging to Abdalonymos, who became

King of Sidon in 333 BC after Alexander defeated the Persians at the battle of Issus, which apparently inspired the Battle scenes in the reliefs.

The **Sarcophagus of Mourning Women** (mid-4th century BC) takes its name from the figures of the women framed between Ionic columns on its sides and ends. A funeral procession is shown on a frieze on the lid. The sarcophagus is thought to have belonged to King Straton of Sidon, who died in 360 BC.

Rooms 7–1: The **Meleager Sarcophagus** (Room 6), the **Sarcophagus of Phaedra and Hippolytus** (Room 6), and the **Sidamara Sarcophagus** (3rd century AD; Room 3) are all exceptionally fine. The two stone lions at the foot of the staircase in Room 3 once stood on the façade of the Palace of Bucoleon (*see p. 108*) on the Marmara shore. Other outstanding exhibits include reliefs from two **Hellenistic temples in Asia Minor** (Room 2): the temple of Hecate in Lagina and the temple of Artemis at Magnesia on the Maeander.

Right-hand wing

Room 13: Sculptures of the Archaic period (700–480 BC): Notable are the head of a kouros from Samos (6th century BC) and a legless kouros from Cyzicus (modern Erdek; c. 550–540 BC), There is a headless statue of a seated male figure (mid-6th century BC) from the Branchidae, the famous family of oracles at the temple of Apollo in Didyma, found in Miletus. Other sculptures are in the form of reliefs on funeral stelae and include a relief (6th century BC) showing a long-haired youth driving a chariot drawn by two horses, from Cyzicus.

Room 14: Sculptures from Persian rule in Anatolia: The two most notable examples are funerary stelae (5th century BC) from Daskyleion in Bithynia, both with reliefs showing funeral processions in which mourners are following a cart carrying a sarcophagus. A surviving lion from the famous Mausoleum at Halicarnassus is also on display.

Room 15: Attic grave stelae: The finest stelae are a relief of a young athlete from the Dodecanese island of Nisyros (c. 480–460 BC); a young warrior from Pella in Macedonia (c. 430–420 BC); and a man bidding farewell to his two sons, from Amisos (Samsun, on the Black Sea; end of 5th century BC). The two most notable sculptures in the round are the head of a horse (provenance unknown; second half of the 5th century BC); and a statuette of Athena from Leptis Magna in Libya, a Roman copy of an original from the end of the 5th century BC.

Room 16: Sculptures of the Hellenistic period (323–31 BC): The most famous are **representations of Alexander the Great**. There is a superb head of Alexander from Pergamon (first half of 2nd century BC after a 4th-century BC original by Lysippus). Beside it is an outstanding life-size statue of Alexander from Magnesia ad Sipylum (Manisa), an original work dating from the mid-3rd century BC. Other interesting works are a relief of a Dionysiac dancer from Pergamon (end of 3rd century BC); a statue of Hermaphroditus, the bisexual offspring of Hermes and Aphrodite, from Pergamon (3rd century BC); and a statue of Marsyas, from Tarsus, a Roman copy of an original from the 3rd century BC.

Room 17: Sculpture from Tralles and Magnesia on the Maeander: The most famous work here is the **Ephebus of Tralles**, representing a youth resting after exercise. He is shown standing in a relaxed attitude with a cape draped over his shoulders, a wistful smile on his face (late 1st century BC–early 1st century AD). Also notable is a **Caryatid from Tralles** (1st century AD); this is similar to those in the Erechtheion on the Athens Acropolis, where a kore serves as a column with her headdress as the capital. Notice also a statue of a matron named Baebia, from Magnesia (mid-1st century BC).

Room 18: Hellenistic and Roman sculpture: In the centre of the room is a colossal **head of the poetess Sappho**, from Smyrna (İzmir), a Roman copy of a Hellenistic original. Beside the door on the left is a herm from Pergamon (2nd century AD), a statue of the god Hermes in which only his head and genitals are represented on a stele. An inscription states that it is a copy of the famous Herm by Alkamenes, which stood just outside the Propylaia on the Athens Acropolis.

Head of Sappho from Smyrna (Roman period).

Roman portrait busts of the 1st–4th centuries AD include portraits of a number of emperors, including Augustus, Diocletian and Constantine. On the right side of the room is a relief honouring Euripides, from Smyrna (1st century BC–1st century AD); the dramatist is being presented with a tragic mask by Skene, the personification of the theatre, while Dionysus looks on with approval. There is a also a relief of a Muse playing the lyre (2nd century BC).

Room 19: Sculptures from Ephesus, Miletus and Aphrodisias: The principal work from Ephesus is a large reclining **statue of Oceanus** (2nd century AD). The sculptures from Miletus include statues of Apollo Kitharoidos (Apollo playing the lyre) and five Muses, all dating from the 2nd century AD (and presumably part of a group). The works

from Aphrodisias, exhibited in an area dedicated to the archaeologist Kenan Erim (1929–91), include statues of Valentinian II (late 4th century AD), a Roman judge (AD 425–450), a young matron (2nd century AD), a relief of a Gigantomachia (2nd century AD), and a pillar (2nd century AD) delightfully decorated with reliefs of animals and erotes among foliage.

Room 20: Sculpture of the Roman imperial period: To the left of the entryway is a colossal statue of Tyche, the Goddess of Fortune, who is shown holding the child Ploutos, the God of Wealth, while above them there is a profusion of fruits and flowers in a cornucopia, the horn of plenty (tentatively dated to the 2nd century AD). In the centre of the wall opposite the door is a colossal statue of Zeus, from Gaza (2nd century AD).

THE NEW BUILDING

Byzantium and its Neighbours (ground floor)

The exhibits come from archaeological sites in Thrace and Bithynia, the regions that bordered the lands of the ancient city of Byzantium in Europe and Asia. Nicomedia (İzmit) was capital of Bithynia in the Hellenistic era. The displays span the Archaic to the Byzantine periods.

A number of the exhibits are from tumuli, huge mounds of earth covering royal graves, many of which can still be seen in the Thracian countryside. The most distinctive of the objects found in these tombs are **reliefs of the heroic horseman cult**, representing a mounted warrior, perhaps a deified chieftain. One particularly striking object, found in the Vize Tumulus, is a superb **bronze head of a warrior**, with a tightly-fitted helmet and cheek-protectors elaborately carved in relief, dating from the 1st century AD.

The inner gallery is devoted to exhibits from the Byzantine period, most of them from Constantinople. This gallery is in fact built up against the wall of a Byzantine structure of the 5th century AD, discovered when the new wing of the museum was being erected; this has been left exposed so that you can see its brick and limestone construction. The most prominent exhibit is a **mosaic pavement from Jerusalem** dating from the late Roman period, with Orpheus as the central figure. Noteworthy exhibits from Byzantine Constantinople include two monuments originally erected in the Hippodrome in the late 5th century in honour of the famous charioteer Porphyrios; a large part of the architrave of the Baths of Constantine; two slabs of a parapet with reliefs of peacocks, the Byzantine symbol of incorruptibility; and a pair of reliefs of a fabulous beast called the Simurg, with the head of a wolf, the body of a lion, and the tail of a peacock.

The rest of the ground floor is devoted to the **Children's Museum** (its most prominent exhibit is a large model of the Trojan Horse) and to the **reconstructed front of the Archaic temple of Athena in Assos**. Completed c. 530 BC, this is the only Doric temple erected in Asia Minor during the Archaic period. It was first excavated in 1881–83 by J.T. Clarke and F.H. Bacon of the Antiquarian Society of Boston. The reliefs that they found are now in the Boston Museum of Fine Arts. The reliefs in the model are casts, along with a few of the original sculpture (the wall chart shows which is which).

Istanbul Through the Ages (first floor)

Prehistory: The exhibits show the very earliest sites of human habitation in the environs of Istanbul. The most notable site is the Yarımburgaz Cave on the European shore of the Marmara, where archaeologists have unearthed evidence of human settlement dating back some 350,000 years. A glass case contains the complete skeleton of a man from Pendik, on the Asian shore of the Marmara, dated to the 6th millennium BC. The oldest object found in Istanbul itself is a baked clay jar unearthed in the Hippodrome and dated to the 6th millennium BC.

Ancient Byzantium: The display is devoted to objects from the ancient Greek city-state of Byzantium, the oldest of them dating to the 7th century BC. These include a large number of tombstones from the early cemeteries of the city. There are striking sculptures from a Gigantomachia of the 2nd century AD excavated at Silahtarağa above the Golden Horn. The Olympians are in white marble, while the Giants, of whom only fragments survive, are in grey limestone.

Byzantine Constantinople: The displays are arranged topographically, covering the period 330–1453. Areas covered include ancient Chalcedon, now the suburb of Kadıköy; Constantinople's harbours; hydraulic works, including cisterns; the Theodosian Walls; the sea walls along the Golden Horn and the Marmara; the Augustaion; the churches of Haghia Sophia, Haghia Eirene and SS Sergius and Bacchus; the Great Palace of Byzantium; the Hippodrome (including the surviving upper jaw of one of the snakes from the Serpentine Column); the palaces of Antiochus and Lausus; the area within the walls of Topkapı Sarayı; the Forum of Theodosius; the Forum and Column of Constantine; churches of Constantinople; the Palace of Blachernae; Galata; the Princes' Islands; and the Bosphorus. In the last gallery is displayed a length of the huge chain that was used to close the Golden Horn in times of siege. There is also an exhibition of coins from ancient Byzantium and Byzantine Constantinople.

Anatolia and Troy through the Ages (second floor)

The display is arranged chronologically, beginning at the north end, where the exhibit explains the **topography of the site and the history of the excavations** by Schliemann, Dörpfeld, Blegen and Manfred Korfmann. The exhibition areas that follow on the right have **artefacts** from Troy I (3000–2500 BC) to Troy IX (350 BC–AD 400). The exhibition areas on the left have **objects from other sites in Anatolia**, ranging through the Upper Palaeolithic (350,000–12,000 BC) to the Archaic (700–480 BC) periods.

At the south end of the hall there is a gallery devoted to **Phrygia in the Archaic period**, with photographs of the extraordinary rock-carved sanctuaries and sculptures of the fertility goddess Cybele-Kubaba. A display case has antiquities from Phrygian sites in western Anatolia, most notably the huge bronze cauldrons that are the most distinctive works of this culture.

Cultures of Anatolia's Neighbours (third floor)

This display is devoted to antiquities from Cyprus, Syria and Palestine. The most striking exhibit, at the north end of the hall, is a **hypogeum from Palmyra** in Syria. This is modelled on an original hypogeum in the Valley of the Tombs built by the Yarhai family in AD 108; the sculptural portraits are original and came from different hypogea in Palmyra.

The route to the exit takes you through a room with clay votive figurines of the Classical and Hellenistic periods. In the centre of the room is a colossal **bronze statue of Hadrian** from Nicomedia (mid-2nd century AD). From the window you have an excellent view of the Çinili Köşk.

ÇİNİLİ KÖŞK

The Çinili Köşk, or Tiled Kiosk, was built by Fatih in 1472 as an outer pavilion of Topkapı Sarayı, serving as a *pied-à-terre* on occasions when he wanted to escape the crowded confines of the Inner Palace. A large level area was cleared in front of it so that the young princes and palace pages could play *cirit*, a form of polo, and enabling the sultan to look on from the elevated front porch. The pavilion continued in use until 1856, when the imperial residence was shifted to Dolmabahçe Palace. It was abandoned until 1874, when it was converted into a storehouse for antiquities. During the 1950s it was thoroughly restored to its original condition and converted into a museum.

Exterior of Çinili Köşk

The kiosk is laid out in two almost identical storeys (the lower one completely visible only at the rear), cruciform in plan with chambers in the corners of the cross. It has a deeply recessed entrance alcove on the main floor entirely revetted in tiles of various kinds, most of them tile mosaic in turquoise and dark blue. On the back wall these form simple geometric designs, but in the deep soffit of the arch there is an inscription in a geometricised form of Kufic calligraphy. On the three faces of the vault at the height of the lintel of the main door there is a long double Persian inscription in the beautiful *cuerda seca* technique. The main inscription is in white letters on a dark blue ground. Above and entwined with this is a subordinate inscription in yellow, with the tendrils of a vine meandering in and out between the letters, the whole encased in a frame of deep mauve with flowers of dark blue, turquoise and white.

Interior of Çinili Köşk

The interior consists of a central salon in the shape of an inverted Latin cross with a dome over the crossing. The cross is extended by a vestibule at the entrance end, an apse-like room at the far end, and two eyvans or open alcoves (now glassed in) at the ends of the shorter arms, with additional chambers at the corners of the cross. All of these rooms were once tiled and many of them still are, with triangular and hexagonal panels of turquoise and deepest blue, sometimes with superimposed gold designs.

The articles on display are mostly tiles of enamel and majolica, as well as ceramics, from the 12th–19th centuries. There are good examples of the finest Iznik ware as well as some of the later, European-influenced designs. The labelling is good.

Tile design (detail) from the upper-floor entrance of Çinili Köşk.

MUSEUM OF THE ANCIENT ORIENT

Flanking the entrance steps are two **basalt lions of the neo-Hittite period**, dated c. 800 BC; these were talismans to frighten enemies away from the gateway of the city. The collection is arranged by geographical area, and contains artefacts from Arabia and Nabataea, Egypt, Mesopotamia and Anatolia. Highlights are given below.

The Arabian collection: The objects are from the pre-Islamic period. Highlights include the torsos of two red sandstone statues of kilted male figures, one of which has retained its head (3rd–1st centuries BC); a superb relief with the heads of five bulls above a floral design, flanked by two giraffe heads (2nd century AD); and an Arabic inscription of the 6th century mentioning the name of Christ. One of the cases contains tombstones, funerary offerings, tomb furniture, and other objects, as well as statuettes of seated deities (1st century BC–1st century AD). Elsewhere in the room there are two reliefs, one of a robed warrior and the other of a mythological creature with the head of a bearded man and body of a lion, both dated 4th–1st centuries BC.

The ancient Egyptian collection: Objects range in date from the rise of the First Dynasty (c. 3200 BC) to the beginning of the Ptolemaic Dynasty (310 BC). These include sphinxes, stelae, tombstones, mummy cases, funerary pottery, tomb furnishings, votive offerings, statuary and architectural fragments. Three mummy cases bear inscriptions identifying the deceased as priests and priestesses of Amun. The small containers are canopic jars, with lids in the form of animal heads; these preserved the various internal organs of the deceased, the various heads symbolising the gods who protected these parts until they were reunited with the body in the next world.

The Mesopotamian collection: Some of the walls here sport colourful **tile panels from Babylon** with relief figures of lions and mythological beasts. These panels date from the reign of Nebuchadnezzar II (r. 605–562 BC) and formed part of the monumental processional way that led from the Ishtar Gate to the sanctuary where the New Year's festival was held. There is also a representation of Lamassu, a demon who guarded Assyrian doorways (9th century BC).

Important exhibits from Mesopotamia and the Urartian culture, which flourished in eastern Anatolia at the beginning of the 1st millennium BC, are several tiles with stamped inscriptions dating from the period 2334–2154 BC, the **oldest-known examples of printed writing**. There is also a bronze bar marked with various lengths and a basalt duck representing a standard weight; these are dated 13th and 15th century BC respectively and are the **oldest standard measures in existence**. The duck combines lovely naturalistic design with function. Other highlights are a series of bas-reliefs of genies from the palace of King Ashurnasirpal (883–859 BC).

Another room is devoted mostly to antiquities from the New Assyrian period, along with some of the oldest inscriptions in existence. The most historic is the famous **Code of Hammurabi**, dated

Composite creature, half lion-half man, from the gateway of ancient Sam'al in southeast Anatolia (Late Hittite; 9th century BC).

There are Assyrian reliefs from the palaces of Tiglath-Pileser III (r. 745–727 BC), Sennacherib (r. 705–688 BC) and Ashurbanipal (r. 669–629 BC) and objects of the Hatti and Hittite cultures of Anatolia. The earliest work of the Hatti, who preceded the Hittites in Anatolia, is a fragment of a vase with a relief of a monstrous fertility god, dated c. 3000 BC. Another Hatti work is a bronze standard in the form of a solar disc surmounted by two stags outlined in a braided halo, dating from early in the 3rd millennium BC. The famous **Treaty of Kadesh**, dated 1269 BC, records the end of a war between the forces of Ramesses II of Egypt and Hattusilas, the Hittite emperor (it is the earliest known peace treaty in the world). Other exhibits include works of the Chalcolithic era (c. 5500–3000 BC), as well as the Old Hittite Kingdom (c. 1700–1450 BC), Hittite Empire (1450–1200 BC), Late Hittite (1200–700 BC), and neo-Hittite (10th–9th centuries BC).

The most striking of the neo-Hittite works is the **Ivriz Kaya Relief**, a plaster copy of an 8th-century BC original showing a diminutive king offering gifts of grain and fruit to a gigantic god. Another interesting relief, from the palace of the Aramaean king Barrakab, shows four musicians in a procession, dated to the third quarter of the 8th century BC.

1750 BC, the world's oldest recorded set of laws. Also of great interest is a Babylonian tablet, dated c. 320 BC, recording astronomical observations, one of the earliest extant scientific records. The **world's earliest recorded love poem** is also among the exhibits.

GÜLHANE PARK & SARAY BURNU

Gülhane Park (*map p. 349, E2*) occupies part of the site of the ancient city of Byzantium, whose outer defence circuit followed much the same course as the outer walls of Topkapı Sarayı. Once part of the Topkapı gardens, it is now a public park.

The Museum of Science and Technology in Islam

This museum (*open 9–4.30*), to the west of the main path, was conceived by the Turkish historian of science Professor Fuat Sezgin. The display is devoted to the history of Islamic science and technology from the 9th–16th centuries. The instruments and other objects displayed here were made by the Institute for the History of Arabic-Islamic Science at the Goethe University in Frankfurt, based predominately on illustrations and descriptions found in original sources and, to a lesser extent, on surviving originals.

The Orphanage of St Paul and Goth's Column

Near the Golden Horn end of the park, above the main path to the right, behind railings, are a number of marble columns and other ancient architectural fragments. This has been identified as the **Orphanage of St Paul**, founded by Justin II (r. 564–78). It was rebuilt by Alexius I Comnenus (r. 1081–1118); then in the reign of Michael VIII Palaeologus (r. 1259–82) it was used to house the University of Constantinople.

A path leads past the vestiges of hospital to the top of the hill overlooking Saray Burnu. Here stands one of the very oldest but least known monuments in the city: the so-called **Goth's Column**, a granite monolith 15m high surmounted by a Corinthian capital. The name of the column comes from the laconic inscription in Latin on its base (on the side facing the water; barely legible): 'To Fortune, who returns by reason of the victory over the Goths'. Some scholars have ascribed this column to Claudius II Gothicus (r. 268–70) and others to Constantine the Great, both of whom won notable victories over the Goths, but there is no firm evidence either way. According to the Byzantine historian Nicephorus Gregoras, the column was once surmounted by a statue of Byzas the Megarian, the eponymous founder of Byzantium.

Beyond the column is a **tea garden** with a view of the Bosphorus and Golden Horn.

Saray Burnu

The main path leads northwards out of the park and crosses the railway line. There is a pedestrian crossing leading over the shore highway to Saray Burnu, 'Palace Point', the promontory at the confluence of the Bosphorus and the Golden Horn. From here there is a splendid view up the Bosphorus and across to the suburbs on the Asian shore. In the park here there is a large bronze statue of Atatürk (1881–1938), the father of modern Turkey and the first President of the Turkish Republic. This monument, made in 1926 by the Austrian sculptor Heinrich Krippel, was the first statue of a Turk ever to be erected in this country. (*NB: The park was closed at the time of writing because of work on the Marmaray rail tunnel under the Bosphorus to Üsküdar. When complete, it will be the world's deepest immersed tube tunnel. Work was delayed when important archaeological discoveries were made; see p. 192.*)

THE BLUE MOSQUE
& SULTANAHMET DISTRICT

THE BLUE MOSQUE

The Sultanahmet Camii, known as the Blue Mosque (*map p. 349, E4*), is one of the most prominent landmarks in Istanbul, with its graceful cascade of domes and semidomes, and its six slender minarets accentuating the corners of the mosque and its courtyard.

The mosque was founded by Ahmet I, who in 1609 directed the architect Sedefhar Mehmet Ağa to begin construction. The mosque and all of its associated pious foundations were completed in 1616, just a year before Amhet's death at the age of 27. For the next 250 years most reigning sultans chose to perform their Friday noon prayers at the Blue Mosque, because of its proximity to Topkapı Sarayı, and the imperial processions to and from the mosque were the high point of Istanbul life during that period. Even after Topkapı was abandoned as the imperial residence, Sultanahmet Camii continued to hold pride of place as one of the two supreme imperial mosques of the city, sharing that honour with the Süleymaniye.

Exterior of the Blue Mosque

Sultanahmet Camii is preceded by a **courtyard** (*avlu*) as large in area as the mosque itself, with monumental entrance portals at each of the three sides. The **gate at the centre of the west side** (the Hippodrome side) is the grandest of these; its outer façade is decorated with a calligraphic inscription by Derviş Mehmet, the father of the 17th-century traveller and writer Evliya Çelebi. The courtyard is in the classic style, bordered by a peristyle of 26 columns forming a portico covered by 30 small domes. At the centre of the courtyard stands a handsome octagonal **şadırvan**, which now serves only a decorative purpose. The ritual ablutions are actually performed at water taps in the outer courtyard, beneath the graceful arcade which forms part of the north and south walls of the avlu.

The six minarets are fluted and the şerefes have sculptured stalactite parapets. The two minarets at the outer corners of the avlu are less tall than those that at the corners of the mosque itself. This kind of display is typical of imperial Ottoman mosque architecture, for ruling sultans employed minarets for show as well as for their function. But the Blue Mosque was the first—and remains the only—mosque in Istanbul to boast six minarets. There is an often-repeated tale that this caused an uproar: the holiest mosque in Islam, that around the Ka'aba in Mecca, also had six minarets. Today, however, the Saudi mosque has nine: it has far surpassed Sultanahmet.

The central **dome** of the mosque is flanked by semidomes on all four sides, with those to north and south surrounded by three smaller semidomes and those to east and west by two each, and with small full domes above the four corners of the building. The four piers supporting the main dome continue above the building as tall

Sultanahmet Camii, the Blue Mosque, seen from across the ancient Hippodrome.

octagonal turrets capped with domes, while smaller round turrets flank each of the corner domes, all of which creates a harmonious succession from the main dome down through the clustering semidomes, turrets and smaller domes. The north and south façades of the building have two storeys of porticoed galleries.

NB: The main entrance to the mosque itself is through the east door, with smaller entrances from the outer courtyard beside the central minarets on the north and south sides. Visitors are asked to use one of the latter and are restricted to the rear half of the mosque, so as not to disturb the faithful at their prayers.

Interior of the Blue Mosque

The interior plan, like that of so many mosques in Istanbul, derives its inspiration from Haghia Sophia, though in this case there are important differences. It is very nearly a square (51m long by 53m wide) covered by a **dome** (23.5m in diameter and 43m high) resting on four pointed arches and four smooth pendentives. To east and west there are **semidomes (A)** which are themselves flanked by smaller semidomes. Thus far, the plan is not unlike that of Haghia Sophia. But in the Blue Mosque, instead of tympanic arches to north and south, there are **two more semidomes (B)**, making a quatrefoil design (*see plan overleaf*). The main support for the great dome comes from four colossal free-standing columns or **piers (C)**, 5m in diameter, which are divided

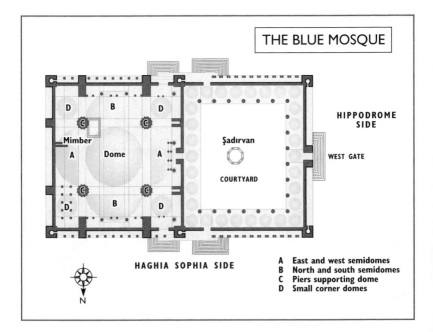

THE BLUE MOSQUE

HIPPODROME SIDE

WEST GATE

Şadırvan

COURTYARD

Mimber

Dome

HAGHIA SOPHIA SIDE

A East and west semidomes
B North and south semidomes
C Piers supporting dome
D Small corner domes

N

in the middle by a band and ribbed above and below with convex flutes. **Small full domes (D)** surmount the four corner bays.

The mosque has 260 **windows**. These were originally filled with stained glass, which would have muted the incoming sunlight. The original windows have been lost and are being replaced by modern imitations. The **painted arabesques** in the domes and the upper parts of the building also attempt to replicate 17th-century originals. The predominant colour is blue, from which the building derives its popular name of the Blue Mosque.

The lower part of the walls is clad in beautiful **Iznik tiles** featuring the traditional semi-stylised lily, carnation, tulip and rose motifs, as well as cypresses and other trees; these are all in exquisite colours, subtle blues and greens predominating. The **mihrab and mimber**, of white Proconnesian marble, are also original; they are fine examples of the carved stonework of the early 17th century. The **woodwork of the doors and window-shutters** is inlaid with ivory, mother-of-pearl and turtle shell.

PRECINCTS OF THE BLUE MOSQUE

The Blue Mosque and its courtyard were surrounded by an outer precinct wall, of which only part of the north section remains. This wall separated the mosque from its dependent buildings in the külliye, which included a medrese, türbe, hospital, caravansaray, mektep, public kitchen and a market (*arasta*). The rents from this last helped defray the expenses of the other pious foundations. Of these, what remain are the **mektep**, which is elevated above the north wall of the outer precinct of the mosque; the large **medrese**, just outside the precinct wall toward the northwest; and, near it, the large square **türbe**, where Ahmet I is buried along with his chief consort Kösem and three of his sons: Osman II, Murat IV and Prince Beyazıt. The türbe can be visited.

KÖSEM, OSMAN & MURAT, SUCCESSORS OF SULTAN AHMET

The Greek-born Kösem, whose palace name means 'leader', was the most powerful and fascinating woman in the history of the Ottoman Empire. She ruled in the Harem until Ahmet I's premature death in 1617, whereupon she was banished from Topkapı to the Eski Saray (Old Palace) in Beyazıt, the traditional fate of the women of departed sultans. She remained sequestered there until 1623, when her eldest son, Murat IV, became sultan, at which time she made her triumphant return to Topkapı as Valide Sultan. Her control over state affairs extended through Murat's reign and that of her other son İbrahim and grandson Mehmet IV, a period of 38 years. Her downfall was orchestrated by Mehmet's mother, who is said to have ordered her death. She was strangled in Topkapı palace at the age of about 62.

Osman II was the son of Ahmet by a different woman. His brief four-year reign (1618–22) saw defeat in battle by Poland and an attempt by the palace to curb the power of the Janissaries, which led to his overthrow and execution in Yedikule. He was only 17.

Murat IV, Kösem's son (r. 1623–40), was a very different character. Physically huge, and warlike by nature, he is known to have roamed the city in disguise, searching for people who disobeyed his bans on coffee and tobacco (the coffee houses where these articles were consumed were seen as meeting places where people could exchange ideas and foment rebellion). In war he was victorious, capturing Baghdad and Yerevan: he built pavilions at Topkapı to celebrate these successes. But Murat was not a great frequenter of the Harem, and he died without issue. Thus the throne passed to his feeble-minded brother İbrahim (*see p. 82*).

A ramp at the northeast corner of the mosque leads up to the **Hünkar Kasrı**, the imperial pavilion, a suite of rooms used by the sultan whenever he came here for services, with an internal passageway leading to the royal loggia within the mosque. The Hünkar Kasrı now houses the **Kilim Museum** (*open 9.30–12 & 1–4; closed Sun and Mon*), a remarkable collection of carpets from all over Turkey and covering all periods of Ottoman history, including a number that were made for use in the sultan's tent when he was on campaign.

Beneath the kible wall of the mosque there are huge vaulted structures that once served as storerooms and stables. They are now used as a **Rug Museum** (*open 9.30–12*

Tiger threatened by two young men with spears, detail of a floor in the Mosaic Museum.

&1–4; closed Sat and Sun), exhibiting works ranging from the 15th to the 19th centuries, including rare and beautiful examples. This museum has a separate entryway from the courtyard below the mosque.

The lower stretch of Kabasakal Sk., the 'Street of the Bushy Beard', just below the Blue Mosque, is now known as the **Arasta Bazaar**. It is the restored market street of the Sultanahmet külliye and its shops now serve the tourist trade.

THE MOSAIC MUSEUM &
PALACE OF BUCOLEON

The Mosaic Museum (*map p. 349, E4. Open 9–4.30; closed Tues; entrance on Torun Sk., signed from the Arasta Bazaar*) displays artefacts discovered during excavations made in 1935 to search for the remains of the Great Palace of Byzantium. The digs revealed extensive sections of mosaic pavement as well as columns, capitals and other architectural fragments. The ruins were identified as the northeast portico of the Mosaic Peristyle, a colonnaded walkway which may have led from the imperial apartments of the palace to the kathisma, the royal enclosure on the Hippodrome.

The mosaics, made of limestone, terracotta and glass tesserae, depict a variety of scenes: there are scenes of hunting such as the tiger hunt, men being chased by bears; scenes of animals in the wild (a fight between an elephant and a lion, leopards eating a deer and a wolf devouring its prey), domestic animals and farmyard scenes (a donkey throwing his rider, horses grazing, an old man milking goats); mythological scenes and scenes with children (a boy 'herding' geese; two children spinning hoops. The latter makes a reference to the two opposing factions in the Hippodrome: one boy's tunic is trimmed in green, the other's in blue). Around the whole mosaic ran a frieze bordered with a vine motif, with acanthus wreaths in the centre out of which spring wild animals and garlanded human faces. There has been considerable discussion about the date of these mosaics, but current opinion is that they were made during the reign of Justinian (r. 527–65). The wall panels (in Turkish and English) are excellent.

The old streets near the Mosaic Museum

The streets in this part of Sultanahmet are lined with old wooden houses, for the most part renovated and turned into hotels. On Tevkifhane Sk. (*map p. 349, E3*) is the **Four Seasons Hotel**, housed in the reconstructed Sultanahmet Prison. The prison was completed in 1917, probably by the architect Vedat Tek, and functioned until the 1970s. Between Kutlugün and Akbıyık streets is the site of the Byzantine **Magnaura Palace** (*map p. 349, E4*), currently being investigated.

İshakpaşa Cd. is a street lined with picturesque old houses built up against the outer defence walls of Topkapı Sarayı. At the point where the road veers round, following a bend in the walls with an old tower, you will see, on the opposite side, a mosque and hamam flanking the side street known as Akbıyık Cd., the 'Avenue of the White Moustache'. The mosque is **İshakpaşa Camii**, and the hamam across from it is part of the same complex, built in the late 15th century by İshak Pasha, who served as Grand Vizier under both Fatih and Beyazıt II. The mosque has been restored recently, and the hamam is now home to warehouses and workshops.

İshakpaşa Cd. leads down to **Ahır Kapı**, an old portal in the Byzantine sea walls. The Byzantine name of this gateway is unknown, but in Ottoman times it was called Ahır Kapı, 'Stable Gate', because it led to the Imperial mews in the lower gardens of Topkapı palace. The gateway is still in use.

THE PALACE OF BUCOLEON

About half a kilometre west of Ahır Kapı, on the Marmara highway beyond the Kalyon Hotel, you will see, behind a fence, the ruins of the Palace of Bucoleon (*map p. 349, D4*), once one of the seaside pavilions of the Great Palace of Byzantium, whose gardens covered the Marmara slopes of the First Hill. The Great Palace was divided into several different establishments: the Sacred Palace and the palaces of Daphne and Chalke

Pastoral scene (?6th century AD) of a man milking a goat while a young boy stands ready with a pitcher. This, like the scene opposite, is from the Mosaic Museum.

near the present site of the Blue Mosque; the palaces of Magnaura and Mangana to the southeast of Haghia Sophia, on the slope of the hill leading down to the Marmara; and the seaside Palace of Bucoleon. The remains of this last can be seen. It was entered from the sea by the Porta Leonis, the emperor's private harbour, which took its name from the two stone lions that flanked the Imperial Marine Gate. These are the lions now in the Archaeological Museum (*see p. 95*). The surviving remains are of the east loggia, with its three huge marble-framed windows and a vaulted room behind them. Below the windows some projecting corbels indicate that a balcony ran along the façade, suspended over a marble quay below. Notice the curious-looking row of large square marble slabs built into the lower part of the wall; these are the bottoms of Doric capitals of the 5th century BC, doubtless from some ancient temple that stood nearby.

The tower that forms the angle in the defence walls just to the east of the Palace of Bucoleon was once the **Pharos**, the lighthouse of Constantinople. In modern times the lighthouse has been relocated farther to the east along the sea walls.

HISTORY OF THE BYZANTINE SEA WALLS

The Byzantine sea walls along this part of the Marmara shore were originally constructed by Constantine the Great, ending where his land walls met the sea at Samatya (*map p. 346, B3*). When the Theodosian walls were built in the following century, the sea walls along the Marmara and the Golden Horn were extended to meet them. During the 9th century the Marmara walls were almost completely rebuilt by the emperor Theophilus, who sought to strengthen the city's maritime defences against the Arabs. The Marmara defences consisted of a single line of walls 12–15m high with 188 towers at regular intervals. These walls stretched from Saray Burnu to the terminus of the Theodosian walls on the Marmara, a total distance of 8km, and were pierced by 13 sea gates. Although much of the fortifications along the Marmara have been destroyed in modern times, particularly during the building of the railway in the 1870s, that which remains is still grand and impressive, particularly the walls and towers below the First Hill.

MUSEUM OF TURKISH & ISLAMIC ARTS

Opposite the Blue Mosque on the west side of the Hippodrome is the Palace of İbrahim Pasha, now home to the Museum of Turkish and Islamic Arts (*map p. 349, D3; open 10–4.30; closed Mon*).

The original palace here was acquired in 1524 by İbrahim Pasha, a Greek convert to Islam who became an intimate companion of Süleyman the Magnificent during the early years of the sultan's reign. In 1523 İbrahim was appointed Grand Vizier and the following year he married Süleyman's sister Hatice. Some idea of the enormous wealth and influence that İbrahim had at this time can be gained from even a casual glance at the palace, the grandest private residence ever built in the Ottoman Empire, far greater in size than any of the buildings of Topkapı Sarayı itself. When the Ottomans plundered the palace of Buda in Hungary after 1526, bronze statues of Hercules and Athena were brought back and placed outside this mansion. But ultimately İbrahim's great wealth and power lead to his downfall. In 1536 Süleyman had him executed and immediately afterwards all of İbrahim's wealth and possessions, including this palace, were confiscated by the state. The bronze statues were smashed as being un-Islamic.

By the beginning of the 20th century much of the palace was in ruins. The surviving parts of it have been restored and now house the Museum of Turkish and Islamic Arts. The most important part of the present structure is the great hall on the upper level. In İbrahim's time this would have been the Audience Room for the Grand Vizier, and afterwards it was probably the site of the High Court of Justice. Later it seems to have been used as a barracks for unmarried Janissaries and also as a prison. Now it is hung with magnificent and enormous carpets, including several with the distinctive çintamani design, a composition made up of two parallel wavy lines and three circles. Of Buddhist origin, it was used by the Ottomans as a symbol of good luck and virility.

The great central courtyard with its ancient plane tree (over 200 years old) has been attractively restored, with marble paving around a garden and with a terrace overlooking the Hippodrome. Next to the bookshop (which has a good selection) is a small café, decorated to look like an old-fashioned Istanbul coffee-house. It is a pleasant place to have a drink before or after seeing the exhibits; in fine weather you can sit outside.

The permanent collection includes works from all periods of the Turkish and Islamic world, from the Umayyad, Abbasid, Mamluk, Seljuk, Beylik and Ottoman periods, ranging in date from the 7th–19th centuries. As well as carpets, there are manuscripts and calligraphy, miniatures, woodwork, stonework, ceramics and glassware, metalwork and folk arts.

At the south end of the Hippodrome is the Neo-Ottoman Marmara University, with a **gallery of Turkish contemporary art**. From outside it, a narrow street named Şehit Mehmetpaşa Yokuşu leads off to the south, winding down towards the Marmara. At the second turning on the left, the street passes on the right the remains of **Helvacı Camii**, a mosque founded in 1546 by one İskender Ağa and now fallen into ruin. Şehit Mehmetpaşa Yokuşu continues downhill past a walled garden, after which it turns left to continue past the lower wall of the enclosure. Here is the entrance to Sokollu Mehmet Paşa Camii.

SOKOLLU MEHMET PAŞA CAMİİ

Sokollu Mehmet Paşa Camii (*map p. 349, D4*), one of the most beautiful of the smaller mosques in Istanbul, is a minor masterpiece by Sinan. It was built in 1571–72 for

Sokollu Mehmet Pasha, the son of a Bosnian priest who rose to be perhaps the ablest of all of Süleyman the Magnificent's Grand Viziers. Recruited into the Janissary corps as a youth, Mehmet was educated in the Palace School at Topkapı. His obvious abilities brought him early preferment and he rose rapidly in the Ottoman hierarchy, becoming Grand Vizier in 1565. He continued to hold the post under Süleyman's son and successor, Selim II, and married the Selim's daughter, Princess Esmahan, in whose honour he built this mosque (the mosque is officially named after her but it is more commonly associated with her more famous husband). After Selim's death in 1574, Sokollu Mehmet Pasha continued as Grand Vizier under Murat III until 1579, when he was murdered by a mad soldier in the Divan.

Exterior of Sokollu Mehmet Paşa Camii

The courtyard of the mosque is extremely pleasing. It served, as did many mosque courtyards, as a medrese, with the scholars living in the little domed cells under the portico (now glassed in). Each cell had a single window, a fireplace, and a recess for storing bedding, books and personal belongings. Instruction was given in the dershane, the large domed room over the staircase in the west wall. The fine şadırvan in the centre of the courtyard is still in use. Above the windows of the mosque porch are some elegant Koranic inscriptions in blue and white faience.

Interior of Sokollu Mehmet Paşa Camii

The mosque interior is extremely harmonious. In plan the space is a hexagon inscribed in an almost square rectangle, and the whole is covered by a dome, with small semidomes at the four corners. Around three sides runs a low gallery supported on slender marble columns with lozenge capitals. The polychrome of the arches, whose voussoirs are of alternate red and white marble, is characteristic of the period.

Koranic inscription fringed by leaves and flowers. Sixteenth-century calligraphic faience panel from the exterior of Sokollu Mehmet Paşa Camii.

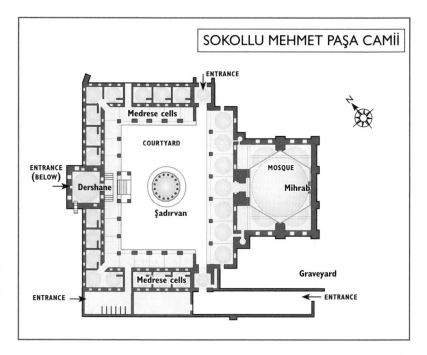

The tile decoration is used sparingly and to good effect. Only certain portions of the walls have been given revetment, most importantly the central section of the east wall. The mihrab is framed with tiles decorated with vine and floral motifs in turquoise on a background of pale green, interspersed with panels of fine calligraphy with white letters on a deep blue field. The mimber hood is clad in similar tiles. Above the mihrab, the framed arch is pierced by elegant stained glass windows, whose bright spectrum of colours complements the cool tones of the faience flowers around and below.

Above the entrance portal is a small surviving specimen of painted decoration. It consists of elaborate arabesque designs in rich and varied colours. Also above the door, surrounded by a design in gold, there is a fragment of black stone from the Ka'aba in Mecca; there are other fragments in the mihrab and mimber.

Environs of Sokollu Mehmet Paşa Camii

After leaving the mosque courtyard by the gateway under the dershane, turn left and then right at the next corner onto Kadırga Limanı Cd. (*map p. 349, D4*). This picturesque old street soon leads to a large open square, the heart of area known as **Kadırga Limanı**, 'Galley Harbour'. This was originally a seaport, long since silted up and built over, created by Julian the Apostate in 362. In about 570 Justin II redredged and enlarged it and named it after his wife Sophia. It had to be continually redredged but remained in use until after the Ottoman Conquest. By about 1550, when the French topographer Petrus Gyllius saw it, only a small part of the harbour remained, and now even this is gone.

In the centre of the square is the *namazgah* **of Esma Sultan**, daughter of Ahmet III, which was built in 1779. It takes the form of a rectangular block with fountains on two sides and a staircase leading to a platform on top. This is the only surviving example in old Istanbul of a *namazgah*, or outdoor place of prayer, in which the direction of Mecca is indicated by a niche.

KÜÇÜK AYASOFYA CAMİİ

Küçük Aya Sofya Camii, the former church of SS Sergius and Bacchus, is one of the loveliest small mosques in the city (*map p. 349, D4*). Its Turkish name, the 'Little Haghia Sophia Mosque', comes from its supposed resemblance to the Great Church. There is a pleasant tea garden in its precincts.

HISTORY OF SS SERGIUS & BACCHUS

The church was begun by Justinian in 527, the first year of his reign, and it was completed before 536. He dedicated the church to SS Sergius and Bacchus, two Roman soldiers martyred for their faith and later the patron saints of Christians in the Roman army. The church belongs to that extraordinary period of prolific and fruitful experiment in architectural forms which produced, in Constantinople, buildings so ambitious and so different as the present church, Haghia Sophia itself, and Haghia Eirene—to name only the surviving monuments—and in Ravenna, San Vitale, the Arian Baptistery and Sant' Apollinare in Classe. It is as if the architects were searching for new modes of expression suitable to a new age. The domes of this period are especially worthy of note: the great dome of Haghia Sophia is of course unique, but the dome of SS Sergius and Bacchus is no mere small-scale version of it, being quite different in design and very extraordinary on its own account.

The church was finally converted into a mosque in the first decade of the 16th century by the Chief Black Eunuch Hüseyin Ağa, who also built the nearby Çardaklı hamam and whose tomb can be seen in the garden to the north of the mosque.

Interior of Küçük Aya Sofya Camii

In plan the church is an irregular octagon crookedly inscribed in a very irregular rectangle. It is difficult to account for these irregularities, but they may be partly due to the fact that SS Sergius and Bacchus was one of a pair of contiguous churches and had perhaps to be slightly deformed to accommodate its neighbour. The neighbouring church is thought to have been that of SS Peter and Paul, which was probably located

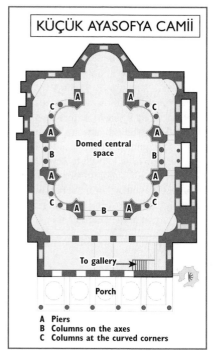

KÜÇÜK AYASOFYA CAMİİ

Domed central space

To gallery

Porch

A Piers
B Columns on the axes
C Columns at the curved corners

just to the south of the present building.

The method of transition from the octagon to the dome is astonishing: the dome is divided into 16 compartments, eight flat sections alternating with eight concave ones above the angles of the octagon. This gives the dome the oddly undulatory or corrugated effect that is so distinctive when the building is observed from the heights of the First Hill. The octagon has eight polygonal piers **(A)** with pairs of columns in between, alternately of *verd antique* and red Synnada marble, both above and below, arranged straight on the axes **(B)** but curved out into the exedrae at each corner **(C)**. The space between this brightly coloured, moving curtain of columns and the exterior walls of the rectangle becomes an ambulatory below and a spacious gallery above, reached by a staircase at the south end of the narthex.

The capitals and the classic entablature are exquisite specimens of the elaborately carved and deeply undercut style of the 6th century, similar to those in Haghia Sophia. On the ground floor the capitals are of the melon type, in the gallery pseudo-Ionic; a few of them still bear the monogram of Justinian and Theodora, though most of these have been effaced. In the gallery the epistyle is arcaded in a way that became traditional in later Byzantine architecture. On the ground floor, the entablature is still basically classical, trabeated instead of arched, with the traditional architrave, frieze and cornice, but it is very different in effect from anything classical, the impression is of lace. The frieze consists of a long and beautifully carved inscription in twelve Greek hexameters honouring Justinian and Theodora, the two founders, and also St Sergius (for some reason St Bacchus is not mentioned).

Nothing remains of the original interior decoration of the church. The walls, like those of Haghia Sophia, were revetted with veined and variegated marbles, while the vaults and domes glittered with mosaics. As described by Procopius, Justinian's court chronicler: 'By the sheen of its marbles it was more resplendent than the sun, and everywhere it was filled profusely with gold.'

DİVAN YOLU CADDESİ
& BEYAZIT CAMİİ

In Ottoman times the route of the ancient Mese, the Byzantine 'Middle Way', continued to be the principal artery of the city. It was known as Divan Yolu: 'Divan Way'. Four times a week the vast apparatus of Ottoman government, comprising thousands of individuals, would make their way along this street to Topkapı Sarayı, for meetings of the Divan, or Imperial Council. Consequently, the modern street is lined with monuments from the imperial Ottoman centuries, along with some ruined remnants of the Byzantine Empire. It is a busy road today, the route of the tram from Kabataş to Zeytinburnu. Local legend says that if you put your ear to any of the old buildings along the street, above the rattle of the tram and the noise of other traffic, you will hear the hollow clang of the Janissaries' rice kettles, which they banged in premonitory fury whenever a hapless sultan had the temerity to try to cut their pay or rein in their contumacy.

From the Milion Arch to Firuz Ağa Camii

At the beginning of Divanyolu Caddesi, on the right (*map p. 349, E3*), there is a ruined Ottoman *su terazi*, or water-control tower. The marble shaft at its foot was discovered during excavations in 1965. This was part of the Miliarium Aureum, the Golden Milestone, also known as the **Milion**. The Milion was a triumphal archway that stood at the beginning of the Mese, or Middle Way, the main thoroughfare of Byzantine Constantinople. It served as the reference point for the milestones on the Via Egnatia, the great Roman road that extended from Byzantium to Dyrrachium (medieval Durazzo, modern Dürres) on the Albanian coast of the Adriatic. During Byzantine times it was surmounted by statues of Constantine the Great and his mother Helena, who stood holding the True Cross between them.

The famous *köfte* restaurant at no. 12, beyond the Pudding House Lale, is the **Tarihi Köftecisi**, which has been in business since 1920 (*see p. 296*). The **former Cevri Kalfa Primary School** next door is named after the brave servant girl who saved the life of the future sultan Mahmut II (*see pp. 88–89*).

A little further along on the left is **Firuz Ağa Camii**, constructed in 1491 for Firuz Ağa, chief treasurer in the reign of Beyazıt II. It is an elegant little building, preceded by a little porch of three bays, with the minaret, unusually, on the left side. Inside, it consists merely of a square room covered by a windowless dome resting on the walls, the so-called single-unit type of mosque. Though altered after a fire in 1823, it is one of the few examples in Istanbul of a mosque of the 'pre-classical' period, that is, of those built before 1500 in the architectural style that flourished principally in Bursa when it was the capital of the Ottoman Empire, in the century before the Conquest. The tomb of the founder, in the form of a marble sarcophagus, is on the terrace outside.

Just beyond Firuz Ağa Camii a little park borders an open area excavated in the 1950s. The ruins are fragmentary and there is little to see *in situ*, but it is thought that these are the ruins of the **palaces of Antiochus and Lausus** (*see plan on p. 45*), noblemen of the early 5th century AD. The grander of the two was the Palace of Antiochus, a hexagonal building with five deep semicircular apses, between each pair of which there were circular rooms. It is now used as an open-air stage. Early in the 7th century it was converted into a martyrium for the body of St Euphemia of Chalcedon, who was martyred for her faith c. 300. The martyrium was decorated with late 13th-century frescoes of scenes from the life of St Euphemia, along with a striking depiction of the Forty Martyrs of Sebaste, 40 Christian soldiers in the Roman army who died in the persecutions of Constantine's rival Licinius. The silver-plated casket of St Euphemia's relics is preserved in the church of St George in the Greek Orthodox Patriarchate in Fener (*see p. 210*).

The Binbirdirek and Theodosius cisterns

Outside the park, opposite the Palais de Justice (the large pink building) on the cobbled İmran Öktem Cd., is the entrance to the **Binbirdirek Sarnıcı**, the Cistern of a 'Thousand-and-One Columns' (*map p. 349, D3; open 9–4.30*). It has been restored (rather tastelessly) and is open as a tourist attraction. This is the second largest underground cistern in the city, but still only about a third of the area of Yerebatan Sarnıcı. It is thought to have been built by Philoxenus, a Roman senator who came to the city with Constantine the Great, although there is evidence that some of the structure dates to the 5th–6th centuries. It has been dry at least since the 17th century, when silk-weavers had their workshops in it. There were originally 224 double columns in 16 rows of 14 each, but twelve of these were walled in not long after the cistern was completed. The impost capitals are plain except that some of them are inscribed with the monograms of the stonemasons. The vaults are of herring-bone brick.

The **Theodosius Cistern** (Şerefiye Sarnıcı; *map p. 349, D3; closed at the time of writing*) is on Piyer Loti Cd., not far down from the Divan Yolu end on the right, in a plot that at the time of writing was being redeveloped. Very little was visible while work was still in progress. The cistern is believed to have been built during the reign of Theodosius II (r. 408–50) by his sister Pulcheria, who would later marry her brother's successor Marcian (r. 450–57). The brick roof is supported by 32 columns of white marble, with capitals mainly of a simplified, rather crudely carved Corinthian order.

The türbe of Mahmut II and the Köprülü külliyesi

The **türbe of Mahmut II** (r. 1808–39), enclosed by a long garden wall (*map p. 349, D3; open 9–5*), was completed in 1840. It was designed in the Empire style then popular in Europe, in keeping with the tastes of Mahmut, the most ruthless of all the reforming 19th-century sultans. Mahmut's son and grandson, sultans Abdülaziz and Abdülhamit II, together with a large number of princes and imperial consorts, are also buried here, as is Ziya Gökalp (d. 1924), the great writer and opinion-shaper of post-imperial Istanbul, hailed by many as the 'father of Turkish nationalism'. His anti-Ottoman stance makes him an unlikely tenant of this most imperial of burial grounds.

Directly opposite the türbe, on the left side of Divanyolu Cd., is an elegant brick and stone Ottoman library. This is one of the buildings of the **Köprülü külliyesi**, whose other institutions are scattered about in the immediate neighbourhood. These buildings were erected in 1659–60 by two members of the illustrious Köprülü family, Mehmet Pasha and his son Fazıl Ahmet Pasha. The Köprülüs, of Albanian origin, were perhaps the most distinguished family ever to serve the Ottoman Empire. During the second half of the 17th and the early years of the 18th century, they supplied five grand viziers, some of them among the most able of those that ever held that post—although one of them, Kara Mustafa, went down in history for failing to take Vienna in 1683 (*see p. 120*). The library of the Köprülü külliye is a handsome little building with a columned porch and a domed reading-room. It contains an important collection of books and manuscripts, many of which are state papers and other documents belonging to the two founders.

One block beyond the library on the same side are two other institutions belonging to the külliye; these are the **mosque and the türbe of Mehmet Pasha**. The türbe is surmounted by a metal grille. The octagonal mosque is a few steps beyond, projecting out onto the pavement. It was once the lecture hall of the Köprülü medresesi, most of which has now disappeared. Opposite these monuments is the Column of Constantine.

The Column of Constantine and Çemberlitaş Hamamı

The **Column of Constantine** (*map p. 349, D3*), known as Çemberlitaş, the 'Hooped Column' (a name that it has given to the adjacent bath and the surrounding neighbourhood), was erected by Constantine to commemorate the dedication of the city as capital of the Roman Empire on 11th May 330. It stood at the centre of the Forum of Constantine, a colonnaded oval portico adorned with statues of pagan deities, Roman emperors and Christian saints, and thought to have been the inspiration for what Bernini later built in front of St Peter's in Rome. Around it stood several large public buildings, temples and churches. All that remains of this grandeur now lies buried beneath 3m of earth, with only the battered column itself surviving, standing to a height of almost 35m.

The column originally had a square pedestal standing on five steps; above this there was a porphyry plinth and column base supporting a shaft of seven porphyry drums. In 416 the column was damaged during an earthquake. As it seemed in imminent danger of collapse, iron hoops were bound around the junctions of the drums to stabilise the shaft. At the summit there was a large capital, presumably Corinthian, upon which stood a colossal statue of Constantine as Sol Invictus, the Unconquerable Sun, with the orb of the world in his hand and a crown of brazen sun-rays glittering in his helmet. The statue fell down and was destroyed during a hurricane in 1106, and some 50 years later Manuel I Comnenus replaced the capital with the present masonry courses and marble block, with a large cross above, which was removed after the Ottoman Conquest. In 1779 the column was damaged during a great fire that destroyed most of the surrounding neighbourhood, leaving the black scars that you see today. The column was soon afterwards repaired by Abdülhamit I, who enclosed its base in the present masonry casing, which conceals the lowest porphyry drum. The column was restored during the 1970s, when the ancient iron hoops were replaced. It has recently been restored once again.

Behind the column is the entrance to the **Çemberlitaş Hamamı** (*map p. 349, D3*), one of the finest extant examples of a classical Turkish bath. It was founded some time before her death in 1583 by the Valide Sultan Nurbanu, consort of Selim II and mother of Murat III. Its revenue was put towards her mosque in Üsküdar. The bath was originally double, but the women's section was destroyed when the avenue was widened. Nevertheless, it still has sections for both men and women and is one of the best of the working hamams in the city. (*For information about visiting a hamam, see p. 51.*)

Vezir Hanı and Atik Ali Paşa Camii

Vezir Hanı (*map p. 349, D3*) was erected in 1659–60 by Mehmet Pasha and his son Fazıl Ahmet Pasha and thus was another of the buildings in the Köprülü külliyesi (*see opposite*). It served as a hostel for travelling merchants and was equipped with stables for their animals as well as shops and storerooms for their goods. It was also the principal slave market of Istanbul, until the abolition of slavery in the Ottoman Empire in 1855.

Just beyond the Column of Constantine, on the same side of the street (now called Yeniçeriler Cd.), is **Atik Ali Paşa Camii**, one of the oldest mosques in the city, built in 1496 by Hadım (Eunuch) Atik Ali Pasha, Grand Vizier of Beyazıt II. It is an attractive little building, particularly from the outside. Inside it consists of a rectangular room divided into two unequal parts by an arch. The larger west section is covered by a dome, the east by a semidome under which is the mihrab, as if in a sort of great apse. The west section is also flanked to north and south by two rooms with smaller domes. The semidome and the four small domes have stalactite pendentives, a common feature in Ottoman mosques of early date.

Atik Ali Paşa Camii originally had several dependencies: a tekke, an imaret and a medrese. Of these only a part of the **medrese** remains, across Yeniçeriler Cd. from the mosque. It is one of the very few surviving medreses of the pre-classical period.

The külliye of Koca Sinan Pasha

The **külliye of Koca Sinan Pasha** (*map p. 348, C3*), enclosed by a picturesque marble wall with iron grilles, consists of a medrese, a sebil and the türbe of the founder, who died in 1595. Koca Sinan was Grand Vizier under both Murat III and Mehmet III, and was the conqueror of the Yemen. His türbe is a fine structure with 16 sides, built of polychrome stonework, white and rose-coloured, and with a rich cornice of stalactites and handsome window mouldings. The medrese, which is entered through a gate in the alley alongside, has a charming courtyard with a portico in ogive arches. The sebil, too, is an elegant structure with bronze grilles separated by little columns and surmounted by a hanging roof. The külliye was built in 1593 by Davut Ağa, the successor to Mimar Sinan as Chief Architect of the Empire.

The foundations of two luckless Grand Viziers

On the other side of the alley across from the sebil, a marble wall with grilles encloses another complex of buildings, the **külliye of Ali Pasha of Çorlu** (*map p. 348, C3*). Ali Pasha was a son-in-law of Mustafa II and served as Grand Vizier under Ahmet III. He fell from favour after becoming embroiled in failed diplomatic talks between Sweden and Russia and was exiled to the Aegean island of Lesbos. Ahmet III later ordered his execution and he was beheaded in 1711. His head was brought back to Istanbul and buried in the cemetery of his külliye, which had been completed three years earlier. The külliye, consisting of a small mosque and a medrese, belongs to the transitional period between the classical and Baroque styles, though in spirit it is still essentially classical. The only truly Baroque features are the capitals of the porch columns. A large market is now encroaching on the complex.

Directly across the avenue stands the octagonal **mosque of Kara Mustafa Pasha of Merzifon** (*map p. 348, C3*). Though a Turk by birth, 'Black Mustafa' married into the great Köprülü dynasty (his wife was the daughter of Fazıl Ahmet), but his career was never as illustrious as that of the greatest members of that family. After the second unsuccessful siege of Vienna in 1683, he was executed by strangulation on the orders of Mehmet IV. The buildings of his külliye were begun in 1669 and finished by his son in 1690. The mosque is of the transitional type between classical and Baroque. The medrese has been converted into a research institute commemorating the poet Yahya Kemal, who died in 1958.

Gedikpaşa Hamamı

The street beyond this little külliye is called Gedikpaşa Cd. It leads to a **hamam** of the same name, on Hamam Cd. (*map p. 348, C3; open 6am–midnight for men and women*), which is one of the very oldest baths in the city (c. 1475). Its founder was Gedik Ahmet Pasha, one of Mehmet the Conqueror's grand viziers, commander of the Ottoman fleet at Azov and conqueror of Otranto. This hamam has an unusually spacious and monumental soğukluk, consisting of a large domed area flanked by alcoves and cubicles; the one on the right has a very elaborate stalactited vault. The hararet is cruciform except that the lower arm of the cross has been cut off and made part of the soğukluk; the corners of the cross form domed cubicles. The bath has recently been restored and now glistens with bright new marble; it is still very much in use. After steaming yourself, you can take a dip in its immersion pool.

BEYAZIT CAMİİ

On Beyazıt Meydanı (*map p. 348, C3*), one of the busiest intersections in the old city, stands the second great mosque complex to be erected in Istanbul after the Conquest, the first being that of Mehmet II himself (*see p. 155*). Since the first Fatih Camii was destroyed by an earthquake in the 18th century, Beyazıt Camii, built by Mehmet's son Beyazıt II, remains the earliest extant example of the great imperial mosques of Istanbul.

Built between 1501 and 1506, the külliye consists of the great mosque itself along with a medrese, primary school, public kitchen, public bath and several türbes. Until now the architect's name has variously been given as Hayrettin or Kemalettin, but a recent study has shown that the külliye is due to a certain Yakub-şah bin Sultan-şah, who also built a caravansaray at Bursa. His background is unknown and his origin uncertain, but he may have been a Turk. Whatever his origin, he created a work of the very greatest importance, both in its excellence as a building and in its historic significance in the development of Ottoman architecture.

The Beyazıt mosque marks the beginning of the great classical period that continued for more than two centuries. Before this time Ottoman architects had been experimenting with various styles and had often produced buildings of great beauty, as in Yeşil Cami at Bursa or Üç Şerefeli Cami at Edirne; but no definite style had been evolved that could produce the vast mosques demanded by the capital of a world empire.

Exterior of Beyazıt Camii

The two minarets are very fine, their shafts picked out with geometric designs in terracotta; they stand far beyond the main part of the building, positioned in a way that gives a very grand effect. The mosque is entered through a particularly charming courtyard, with three magnificent entrance portals. A peristyle of 20 ancient columns—porphyry, *verd antique* and Syenitic granite—supports an arcade with red-and-white or black-and-white marble voussoirs, a standard alternating pattern. The colonnade is roofed with 24 small domes. The pavement is of polychrome marble and in the centre stands a beautifully decorated şadırvan (the surrounding colonnade of stumpy *verd antique* columns supporting a dome is probably a restoration). Capitals, cornices and niches are elaborately decorated with stalactite mouldings. The harmony of proportions, the rich but restrained decoration and the brilliance of the variegated marbles, give this courtyard a special charm.

Interior of Beyazıt Camii

An exceptionally fine portal leads into the mosque, which in plan is a greatly simplified and much smaller version of Haghia Sophia. As there, the great **central dome (a)** and the **semidomes (b)** to east and west form a kind of nave, beyond which to north and south are **side aisles (c)**. The arches supporting the dome spring from four huge **rectangular piers (d)**; the dome has smooth pendentives but rests on a cornice of stalactite mouldings. There are no galleries over the aisles, which open wide into the nave, separated only by the piers and by a single antique granite column between them. This is an essential break with the plan of Haghia Sophia: in one way or another the mosque architects all tried to centralise their plans as much as possible, so that the entire area would be visible from any point. At the west side a broad **corridor (e)**, divided into domed or vaulted bays and extending considerably beyond the main body of the mosque, creates the effect of a narthex. This is a transitional feature, retained from an older style of mosque; it appears only rarely later on.

At the end of the south arm of the corridor, a small **library (f)** was added in the 18th century by the Şeyhülislam Veliyüttin Efendi. An unusual feature of the interior of the mosque is that the **Sultan's loggia** is to the right of the mimber instead of to the left. The loggia is supported on columns of very rich and rare marbles. The central area of the building is approximately 40m square, and the diameter of the dome is about 17m.

THE PRECINCTS OF BEYAZIT CAMİİ

NB: The description below reflects the status quo before extensive renovation and repair work was begun on the külliye, which was still in progress at the time of writing.

Behind the mosque is the **türbe garden**; Beyazıt II is buried here in a simple, well-proportioned türbe of limestone picked out in *verd antique*. The even simpler türbe of his daughter Selçuk Hatun is nearby. Behind these a third türbe, in a highly ornate Empire style, is that of the Grand Vizier Koca Reşit Pasha, the distinguished leader of the Tanzimat Movement (*see p. 23*), who died in 1857. Below the east side of the türbe garden facing the street is an arcade of shops originally erected by Sinan in 1580; it had almost disappeared by the time it was restored during the 1960s.

Just beside these shops is the large double **mektep** with two domes and a porch; this is the oldest surviving primary school in the city. It now houses the hakkı tarık us Research Library (hakkı tarık us was a journalist who, like the poet e.e. cummings, had an aversion to capital letters).

The imaret

Almost opposite the north minaret stands the extremely impressive imaret of the külliye. In addition to serving as a public kitchen, it seems also to have been used as a caravansaray. Its various rooms line three sides of the courtyard (now roofed in), with

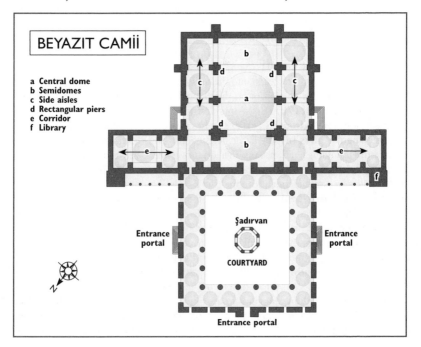

BEYAZIT CAMİİ

a Central dome
b Semidomes
c Side aisles
d Rectangular piers
e Corridor
f Library

Şadırvan

Entrance portal

Entrance portal

COURTYARD

Entrance portal

the fourth side pierced by the monumental entrance portal. The first room on the right housed an olive press, the second was a grain storeroom, and the third, in the right-hand corner, was the bakery, equipped with two huge ovens. The large domed chamber at the far corner of the courtyard was the kitchen and dining-room. The even larger domed chamber beside it, forming the left third of the complex, served as a stable for the horses and camels of the travellers who were guests at the imaret, while the chamber between the stable and the courtyard was used as a dormitory. The imaret was converted into a library by Abdülhamit II in 1882; it now houses the State Library. This library is an important one, with 120,000 volumes and more than 7,000 manuscripts, and the imaret makes a fine home for it.

The medrese (Museum of Calligraphic Art)

It is appropriate that the Museum of Calligraphic Art should be situated here, in the medrese of Beyazıt II's mosque at the far west end of the square. Beyazıt gave sanction to the Sephardic Jews of Spain in Istanbul, and it was one of those refugees who set up the first printing press in the Ottoman Empire (in 1493, the year after their expulsion from Iberia). In the succeeding centuries, following the Jewish example, the Greeks and Armenians also set up their own presses. But Sultan Beyazıt was a champion of calligraphy. He himself was an accomplished calligrapher, a student of the great master Şeyh Hamdullah, who had copied over 40 Korans and who allowed his sultan the honour of holding his inkwell while he wrote. Beyazıt banned the use of printing for Arabic and Osmanlı texts, and it was not until 1729 that a Hungarian Christian convert, İbrahim Müteferrika, at last introduced movable type to the Ottoman world.

The medrese of the Beyazıt mosque is of the standard form; the cells where the students lived and studied are ranged around four sides of a porticoed courtyard, while the lecture-hall is opposite the entrance portal. This building now serves as the Municipality Library; unfortunately, the restoration and conversion were rather badly done, a lot of cement having been used instead of stone, and with the portico very crudely glassed in. Nevertheless, the proportions of the building are so good and the garden in the courtyard is so attractive that the general effect is still charming.

The Museum of Calligraphic Art (Hat Sanatlar Müzesi; *closed at the time of writing*) has collections organised into sections specialising in the different types of calligraphic script, including Kufic (geometrical) and the cursive styles, Naskh, Thuluth, Nastaliq and Muhaqqaq. Depending on their complexity, these types are used in Korans, panels, wooden cut-outs, collages, mirror-writing, representations of the Holy Relics, tuğras, hilyes (descriptions of the features and qualities of the Prophet), as well as in embroidered inscriptions. One of the chambers in the medrese has been set up with life-sized wax models showing a calligrapher instructing his students in this quintessentially Islamic art form.

The hamam

Beyond the medrese, facing the main road (which here takes the name Ordu Cd.), are the splendid remains of Beyazıt's hamam. It was a double hamam; the two sections were almost identical, except that the women's bath was slightly smaller than the men's. Notice the ancient reliefs built into the lower part of the façade near the street corner, including a line of marching soldiers placed upside down in the wall. These are fragments of the triumphal arch that stood in the centre of the Forum of Theodosius (*see below*).

On the north side of Beyazıt Meydanı is the ornate entranceway to the **University of Istanbul**. The main buildings of the university are the former Seraskerat or Ministry of War, constructed by the French architect Marie-Auguste Antoine Bourgeois in 1866. The buildings stand on the site of Mehmet the Conqueror's first palace, the Eski Saray, of which no trace remains.

In the courtyard of the University is the **Beyazıt Tower** (*no public access*), built in 1828 by Mahmut II as a fire-watch station. It is some 50m high and is made largely of Proconnesian marble.

THE FORUM OF THEODOSIUS

At the beginning of Ordu Cd., flanking both sides of the avenue as it leaves Beyazıt Meydanı, are some huge architectural fragments of the Forum of Theodosius, unearthed when this area was redesigned in the 1950s. This was the site of the ancient Forum Tauri, remodelled in 393 by Theodosius I, after which it was called the Forum of Theodosius. This was the largest of the great public squares of Byzantine Constantinople. It contained, among other things, a gigantic triumphal arch in the Roman fashion, and a commemorative column with reliefs showing the victories of Theodosius I, like that of Trajan in Rome. Colossal **fragments of the triumphal arch** can be seen just opposite the hamam of Sultan Beyazıt. Notice the columns curiously decorated with the lopped branch design. These once gigantic monoliths were fashioned to look like clubs of Hercules, and were clutched at the top by giant carved fists. Fragments of them crop up in different places all over the old city.

Fragment of 'lopped banch' column in the Forum of Theodosius.

THE MARKET QUARTER
& SÜLEYMANİYE

The busy, bustling area between Beyazıt Meydanı and the Golden Horn, the old Second Hill, is the old market quarter of Istanbul. Shops and stalls, workshops and ateliers, warehouses and storage cellars all rub shoulders here, many of them housed in old Turkish hans, some of which are excellent examples of Ottoman civic architecture. A large number of the streets are named after the artisans, tradesmen and merchants who carried on their activities here—and in some cases still do. If you want to explore rather than to shop, the best time to come is in the early morning, before the Grand Bazaar opens its doors (before 8am in summer, 8.30 in winter). At this hour no one will badger you to make a purchase as everyone is too busy setting up their stalls. The narrow streets are filled with porters, bent double under enormous bundles of merchandise, and tea-sellers scurry to and fro with trays of refreshment.

Sahaflar Çarşısı

Nestling against the Beyazıt mosque to the east is a small square with a gateway at either end. This is Sahaflar Çarşısı, the 'Market of the Secondhand Booksellers', which has been located here since the early 18th century. It is lined with bookshops and stalls, and in the centre is a bronze bust of İbrahim Müteferrika (1674–1745), an ethnic Hungarian Unitarian from Transylvania who was captured by the Turks and became a Muslim, entering the Sultan's service and setting up the first Ottoman printing press for texts in the Arabic, Persian or Osmanlı scripts.

KAPALIÇARŞI

The Kapalıçarşı or 'Covered Market' (*map p. 348, C3; open 8–8 April–Oct, 8.30–7 Nov–March; closed Sun*), known in English as the Grand Bazaar, grew up around a large commercial hall established by Fatih to provide revenue for Haghia Sophia after the latter's conversion into a mosque. This hall, the İç Bedesten, is still the focal point of the bazaar. Market streets, or arastas, began to cluster around the bedesten, along with workshops and hans to accommodate travelling merchants with their wares and their pack animals. Members of the various tradesmen's guilds set up their shops and stalls close together, which also made it easy for shoppers to find that they were looking for and to compare prices. Still today, shops selling the same kind of merchandise tend to be congregated together and thus there is a street of rug-merchants, a street of goldsmiths, a street of coppersmiths, etc. Kapalıçarşı has been destroyed several times by fire and earthquake, and much of the fabled Oriental atmosphere has vanished. It is one of the main tourist sights of Istanbul and coach parties often fill it to bursting, particularly when there is a cruise ship in the Bosphorus. Though the variety of goods is much narrower now than it was in the market's heyday, there are thousands of shops

THE GRAND BAZAAR

FROM THE GOLDEN HORN

N

FABRIC
&
TEXTILES

Çukur
Han

Kalcılar
Han

Cebeci
Han

FABRIC
&
TEXTILES

JEWELLERY

Zincirli
Han

Kaşıkçı
Han

CARPETS

SOUVENIRS

CARPETS

JEWELLERY

DENIM
&
LEATHER

Şark Café

İç Bedesten

SOUVENIRS

Sandal
Bedesten

CARPETS

Bodrum
Han

DENIM
&
LEATHER

SOUVENIRS

JEWELLERY

LEATHER

LEATHER

FROM NURUOSMANIYE

FROM ÇEMBERLİTAŞ

FROM BEYAZIT MOSQUE

FROM BEYAZIT MOSQUE

here, and there are bargains to be had if you enjoy haggling and can withstand the importunities of the vendors. Most of the shops now cater to the tourist trade, but not all. This a good place to find souvenirs such as evil-eye charms or a set of tulip-shaped tea glasses. Some of the stallholders have developed a witty patter: 'Good afternoon. Can I sell you something you don't need?'. There are plenty of snack bars and cafés too, and waiters bustle from shop to shop with their lovely old hanging trays, suspended on three arms so that perfect equilibrium is maintained and not a drop of tea is ever spilled.

The bedestens

In the centre of the Bazaar is the great domed hall known as **İç Bedesten**, the Inner Market Hall. This is one of the original structures surviving from Fatih's time and then, as now, it was used to house the most precious wares—beautiful silver, great ropes of pearls, turquoise and coral—for it can be securely locked and guarded at night. The east portal of the Bedesten is known as Kuyumcu Kapışı, the 'Gate of the Goldsmiths'. Above its outer face is a relief of a single-headed Byzantine eagle, the date and origin of which are unknown. The single-headed eagle was the imperial emblem of the Comnenus dynasty, who ruled over Byzantium in the 11th–12th centuries.

The other great hall, the **Sandal Bedesten**, dates from 1461. The design of the great brick domes is the same as in the İç Bedesten.

The hans

Narrow streets lead in all directions out of Kapalıçarşı. Many of them have picturesque names: Kılıççılar Sk. ('Street of the Sword-Makers'), Yağlıkçılar ('Kerchief-Makers'), Yorgancılar ('Blanket-Makers'). All were once bazaar streets and they are still filled with shops and bustle, though modern signage and shopfronts, as well as the mountains of discarded packaging everywhere, create an insalubrious atmosphere sometimes. The streets are lined with old hans. Evliya Çelebi, writing in the mid-17th century, mentions more than 25, and many others were built during the following century. Some of the oldest go back to the time of the Conquest and many are built on Byzantine foundations. The hans functioned as inns, where merchants could be housed with their wares and their animals. Typically they consist of one or more arcaded storeys built around a central courtyard or courtyards. Warehouses and storerooms were on the ground floor, with stabling below and sleeping quarters above.

A good street for hans is Çakmakçılar Yokuşu (*map p. 348, C2*), a steep cobbled lane with brick gutters on either side. One one side (the right as you walk uphill) is the **Büyük Valide Han**, built by the Valide Sultan Kösem shortly before her murder in 1651, apparently on the site of an older Ottoman palace. A tall gateway leads into the first courtyard, which is small and irregularly shaped because of the alignment of the han relative to the street outside. From here another arched passage leads into the main court, a vast area 55m square, surrounded by shops and the remainder of an upstairs arcade. A vaulted tunnel leads from the far left-hand corner of the main courtyard into the inner court, which doglegs to the right, from where steps descend to a lower level. From the balustrade of the steps you can look over the well of the courtyard to see, at on corner, the remains of a Byzantine tower, traditionally called the Tower of Eirene. It appears as a prominent feature of the city skyline in a drawing made by Melchior Lorichs in 1559; it is much taller in the drawing than it is today.

Just beside the steps an archway leads to an open area to the rear of the han. Just opposite stands the large **mosque of İbrahim Pasha**, one of the most ancient in the city. This mosque was founded in 1478 by Çandarlı İbrahim Pasha, Grand Vizier under Beyazıt II, who was killed during the siege of Lepanto (the Battle of Zonchio) in 1499. The mosque was in ruins for many years and was restored in the 1970s, in such a way that one would never guess at its antiquity.

Also on Çakmakçılar, on the corner of Sandalyeciler (on the opposite side to Büyük Valide Han) is the **Büyük Yeni Han**, with a fine old façade. The courtyard follows the typical layout of a han, with upstairs arcades in the main courtyard and a further courtyard beyond. It was built in 1764 by Sultan Mustafa III. Just beyond it is another han of about the same date, the **Küçük Yeni Han**, or the 'Small New Han', also commissioned by Mustafa III. Look up and you will see a small minaret perched on the roof. It belongs to the mosque of Sultan Mustafa, used by the merchants and workers in the market quarter.

NURUOSMANİYE CAMİİ

The Nuruosmaniye Camii (*map p. 349, D3; under restoration at the time of writing*) stands in one of the most picturesque mosque courtyards in the city, shaded by plane trees and horse chestnuts, with the mosque on the left and the various buildings of the külliye—the medrese, library, türbe and sebil—scattered here and there. The mosque itself was begun in 1748 by Mahmut I and completed in 1755 by his brother and successor, Osman III, from whom it takes its name, the 'Mosque of the Sacred Light of Osman'. It is an extremely unusual building. It has a certain perverse genius and much charm, but its proportions are awkward and its constituent parts seem to have no organic unity. The architect seems to have been a Greek by the name of Simeon, who had probably studied in Europe: Nuruosmaniye Camii is the first large and ambitious Ottoman building to exemplify the new Baroque architectural style then prevalent in the West.

The whole structure is erected on a low terrace to which irregularly placed flights of steps give access. On the west the mosque is preceded by a porch with five bays, and this is enclosed by a very unusual horseshoe-shaped courtyard with nine domed bays. The two minarets rise from outside the ends of the porch. At the northeast corner, an oddly shaped ramp supported on wide round arches leads to the sultan's loggia.

Inside, the mosque consists essentially of a square room covered by a large dome rising above four wide-arched tympana. The form of these is strongly emphasised (on the exterior their great wheel-shaped arches constitute the most characteristic feature of the building). There is a semicircular apse for the mihrab at the centre of the east wall and side chambers at the northeast and southeast corners. The sultan's loggia, which is screened off by a gilded metal grille, is in the gallery above the northeast corner.

MAHMUT PAŞA CAMİİ & KÜLLİYE

The large and venerable mosque known as Mahmut Paşa Camii, built in 1463, was the first large mosque to be erected in Istanbul (*map p. 349, D3; from the top of Mahmutpaşa Yokuşu, where it meets Kapalıçarşı, set off away from the market and take the first right, then right again*). The founder was a Greek from an aristocratic Byzantine family who converted to Islam and joined the Ottoman army, rising to become Grand Vizier under Fatih. Mahmut Pasha proved to be an extremely capable administrator, but when his army suffered a severe defeat in Anatolia in 1474, Fatih beheaded him.

The mosque is a fine example of the so-called Bursa style, of which very few examples survive in Istanbul. To the west it is preceded by a porch of five bays. Unfortunate-

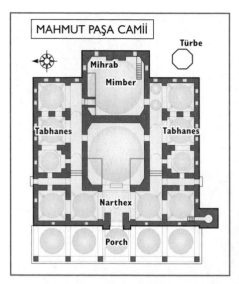

MAHMUT PAŞA CAMİİ

Türbe

Mihrab

Mimber

Tabhanes

Tabhanes

Narthex

Porch

Mahmutpaşa Camii is built in the 'Bursa style' of an inverted capital T. An entrance vestibule flanked by smaller chambers (effectively a kind of narthex) leads into a central hall beyond which opens a further hall with mihrab niche.

ly the original columns have been replaced by, or encased in, much newer octagonal piers. Over and beside the entrance portal there are several calligraphic inscriptions in Arabic and Osmanlı verse giving the date of foundation and of two restorations, one in 1755 and the second in 1828. The piers undoubtedly belong to the latter restoration. The entrance portal is restoration work of the 19th century.

Interior of Mahmut Paşa Camii

The main door leads into a vestibule flanked by domed chambers, a feature which in Istanbul mosques is found only here and in Beyazıt Camii. The central vestibule has a square vault heavily adorned with stalactites. In the first two bays on either side smooth pendentives support domes with 24 ribs; while in the two end bays the domes are not supported by pendentives at all, but by a very curious arrangement of juxtaposed triangles so that the dome rests on a regular sixteen-sided polygon. Other examples of this odd and not unattractive expedient are found in Istanbul only in the west dome of Murat Paşa Camii (*see p. 183*) and in one or two other mosques that belong to the same early period.

The mosque itself consists of a long rectangular room divided in the middle by an arch, thus forming two square chambers each covered by a dome of equal size. On each side of the main hall there is a narrow barrel-vaulted passage that communicates both with the hall and with three small rooms on either side. The two large domes of the great hall of the mosque have smooth pendentives, rather than the stalactited ones usually found in these early mosques. The mihrab and mimber are inferior works of the 18th century or later, as are most of the other decorations and mosque furniture. This is a pity, since it makes it difficult to recapture the original charm of the interior. In the small side chambers some of the domes have smooth pendentives while others are stalactited. Side chambers of this type are known as tabhanes, and were used as hostels by travelling dervishes, a feature found only in early Ottoman mosques.

The külliye of Mahmut Pasha

Of the külliye of Mahmut Pasha, only the hamam, han and the founder's türbe survive.

The türbe of Mahmut Pasha, with its distinctive tile revetment of interlocking circles.

The **türbe** is just behind the mosque, in a little graveyard (*no access but you can see it through a fence from the street on the south side*). This magnificent and unique tomb is dated to 1474, the year Mahmut Pasha was executed. It is a tall octagonal building with a blind dome and two tiers of windows. The upper part is entirely encased in a mosaic of tilework, in circular geometric patterns, with blue and turquoise predominating (though much of the turquoise has fallen out). There is nothing else exactly like them in Istanbul.

The **hamam** is downhill from the mosque on Mahmutpaşa Yokuşu. It is an imposing domed building standing off a little to the left as you walk away from Grand Bazaar (opposite Yıldız Han). The inscription over the entrance portal records the date 1476, two years after the Grand Vizier's death. Now disused, there are shops in the camekan (the wooden changing cubicles on the upper floor are still *in situ*) and a café in the soğukluk, with light filtering down through the perforations in the dome. The soğukluk is far larger than in most baths, a truly monumental room covered by a dome with spiral ribs and a huge semidome in the form of a scallop shell.

The han (**Kürkçü Hanı**, the 'Han of the Furriers') is also on Mahmutpaşa Yokuşu, further downhill from the old hamam, on the same side. Signs at roof level announce 'Tarihi Kürkçü Han'. It was built at about the same time as the mosque, making it the oldest surviving han in the city. The architect is thought to have been Atik Sinan, who built Fatih Camii. Originally it consisted of two large courtyards. The first, nearly square, has a great modern market hall in the centre and orange-painted arcades on the upper floor. The second courtyard to the north was smaller and very irregularly shaped because of the layout of the adjacent streets. It had about 30 rooms on each floor and must have been very attractive; unfortunately it has now been replaced by modern buildings.

The medrese of Rüstem Pasha

This fine building (*map p. 349, D2*) was designed by Sinan, and an inscription records that it was completed in 1550. It has a unique plan for a medrese. The courtyard is octagonal, with a şadırvan in the centre and a colonnaded portico of 24 domes. Behind the portico the cells are also arranged in an octagonal plan, but the building is made into a square on the exterior by filling in the corners with auxiliary rooms, which served as baths and lavatories. One side of the octagon is occupied by the lecture-hall, a large domed room that projects from the square on the outside like a great apse. The medrese is now a community services centre.

ON & AROUND UZUNÇARŞI CADDESİ

Uzunçarşı Caddesi, the 'Avenue of the Long Market' (*map p. 348, C2*), follows the course of the ancient Byzantine street called Makros Embolos, which led from the Forum of Constantine to the Golden Horn, down the valley between the Second and Third Hills. The Greek name means 'Great Colonnade', and the street was indeed lined with porticoes on both sides. Today this is the place to come for suitcases, guns or nargiles. The street known as Nargileci Sk. is appropriately named.

On the east side of the street (on the right as you go downhill) is a little mosque known as **Yavaşca Şahin Camii**. This is one of several very early mosques to be found in this neighbourhood, which, apparently, was the first Turkish quarter to be established after the Conquest. Yavaşca Şahin Pasha was a captain in the fleet of Mehmet II; he built this mosque soon after the Conquest, but the exact date is unknown.

At the lower end of the street on the left is a cavernous former bath house, the **Tahtakale Hamamı**, which also dates from the reign of Fatih. The hamam's various rooms are now filled with shops. The most impressive chamber is the camekan (entrance hall), which is almost square in plan, 16.7m by 16.25m, covered by a huge dome on a low drum, with an elaborate central fountain.

Straight ahead as you look down to the bottom of Uzunçarşı Cd. is the great dome of Rüstem Paşa Camii.

RÜSTEM PAŞA CAMİİ

Rüstem Paşa Camii (*map p. 348, C1; closed to visitors during prayer hours*) is an exquisite mosque, built by Sinan in 1561 for Rüstem Pasha, twice Grand Vizier under Süleyman and husband of the Sultan's much-loved daughter, the Princess Mihrimah. It stands huddled amid busy market stalls in an area that is more authentic than either the Grand Bazaar or the Spice Bazaar. The shops above which the mosque stands origi-

Detail of the famous 16th-century Iznik tiles of Rüstem Paşa Camii.

nally provided rents that maintained the entire külliye. Interior flights of steps lead up from Hasırcılar Cd. to a spacious terrace courtyard. The mosque is preceded by a curious double porch: first the usual type of porch consisting of five domed bays, and then, projecting from this, a deep and low-slung pent roof, its outer edge resting on a row of columns. Rüstem Paşa Camii is especially famous for its tiles, both on the exterior and inside. They are from the kilns of Iznik in its greatest period (c. 1555–1620), and they show the tomato-red or 'Armenian bole' which is characteristic of that period.

Interior of Rüstem Paşa Camii

The plan of the mosque consists of an octagon inscribed in a rectangle. The dome is flanked by four small semidomes in the diagonals of the building. The arches of the dome spring from four octagonal pillars, two on the north, two on the south, and from piers projecting from the east and west walls. To the north and south there are galleries supported by pillars and by small marble columns between them.

Exquisite tiles, in a wide variety of floral and geometric designs, cover not only the walls, but also the columns, the mihrab, and the mimber. Altogether they make this one of the most beautiful and striking mosque interiors in the city. You should also climb to the galleries to see the tiles there, which are of a different pattern.

THE MARKET DISTRICT AROUND RÜSTEM PAŞA CAMİİ

The streets near Rüstem Paşa Camii, Hasırcılar Cd. ('Street of the Mat-Makers'), Kutucular Cd. (Tinsmiths) and Kantarcılar Cd. (Scale-Makers) are bazaar streets catering to local people. Here you'll find shops devoted to aluminium pots and pans, or to cast-iron stoves. Grocers' shops are filled with great sacks of dried fruit and nuts or herbs and linden blossom. Granaries and storage warehouses are known to have existed here since the 4th–5th centuries and the streets are still lined with old hans, such as **Hurmalı Han** (*map p. 348, C1*), the 'Han for Dates', which has been ascribed to early Byzantine times, perhaps the 6th–7th century, and **Balkapanı Han**, the 'Han of the Honey-Store', on Balkapanı Sk. off Hasırcılar Cd. (*map p. 348, C2*). In Evliya Çelebi's day it was the storehouse used by the Egyptian honey-dealers, hence its current name.

Close to Atatürk Blv., where the market stalls have petered out, is an unremarkable mosque with a remarkable history. This is **Yavuz Ersinan Camii**, also known as

Sağrıcılar Camii, the 'Mosque of the Leather-Workers' (*map p. 348, B1*). It is probably the oldest mosque in the city, founded in 1455 by Yavuz Ersinan, standard-bearer in the Conqueror's army. He was an ancestor of Evliya Çelebi and his family remained in possession of the mosque for at least two centuries, living in a house just beside it. Evliya Çelebi was born in that house in 1611, and 21 years later he began to write his *Narrative of Travels* there, much of it devoted to a description of Istanbul and its daily life. The founder is buried in the little graveyard beside the mosque. Beside him is buried one of his comrades-in-arms, Horoz Dede, one of the folk-saints of Istanbul. Horoz Dede, or 'Grandfather Rooster', received his name during the siege of 1453, when he made his rounds each morning and woke the troops with his loud rooster call. He was killed in the final assault on the walls, and after the city fell he was buried here, with the Conqueror himself among the mourners.

THE ZİNDANKAPI QUARTER

Zindan Hanı (*map p. 3348, C1*), a large late 19th-century commercial building beside Eminönü bus station on the shore of the Golden Horn, took its name from the ancient tower adjoining it to the rear, originally part of the Byzantine defence walls along the Golden Horn, which in both Byzantine and Ottoman times served as a prison (in Turkish, *zindan*). Its ground floor contains the türbe of a Muslim saint named Cafer Baba, whose grave has been a place of pilgrimage since the time of the Conquest. According to tradition, he came to Constantinople as the envoy of Haroun al-Rashid but was imprisoned here and died. His grave was rediscovered and restored after the Conquest, along with that of his former gaoler, Zindancı Ali Baba, a Greek who was executed after he was converted to Islam by Cafer Baba.

Just west of the tower in a small garden, are the scant remains of an arched gateway dating from the medieval Byzantine period. This is known in Turkish as **Zindan Kapı**, the 'Prison Gate', because of its proximity to the tower. This whole area was also known as Zindankapı and from Ottoman times right up until the 1980s this was the principal fish and produce market. Then, in a grandiose programme to beautify the shores of the Golden Horn, the Istanbul Municipality demolished the entire quarter. Beautification, it must be said, is yet to follow.

A short distance beyond the gateway is **Ahi Çelebi Camii** (*map p. 348, C1*), founded in the early 16th century by Ahi Çelebi ibni Kemal, who was chief physician at the hospital attached to Fatih Camii. He died in 1523 while returning from a pilgrimage to Mecca and the mosque can thus be dated to before that time. Ahi Çelebi Camii figures prominently in the life of Evliya Çelebi, for in a dream he had on his 21st birthday, 25th February 1632, he met the Prophet Mohammed here, and instead of asking the Prophet to intercede for him (*şefa'at*) asked for travel (*seyahat*). The Prophet granted his wish, assuring him that he would become a great traveller and would write a chronicle of his times, as indeed he did: his ten-volume *Book of Travels* or *Seyahatname* (excerpts from which are now available in English translation, published by Eland).

THE SÜLEYMANİYE

The Süleymaniye (*map p. 348, B2*), the great mosque complex of Süleyman the Magnificent, is the finest of Istanbul's imperial mosque complexes. It is a fitting monument to its founder, the great sultan who did so much to extend the Ottoman Empire, and is a master work of Sinan, the greatest of all Ottoman architects.

Construction began in 1550 and the mosque itself was completed in 1557. It stands in the centre of a large rectangular precinct surrounded on three sides by a wall, with the other buildings of the külliye arranged outside it. From the north side, where the land slopes down to the Golden Horn, there is a superb view of the water.

The avlu and exterior of the mosque

The porticoed **avlu** in front of the mosque is very fine. Its **west portal** is flanked by two storeys of rooms which once contained the house and workshop of the mosque astronomer or müneccim (*see p. 42*). The columns of the courtyard are of marble, porphyry and granite. At its four corners rise the four great **minarets**, traditionally said to signify that Süleyman was the fourth sultan to rule in Istanbul. The ten şerefes denote that he was the tenth monarch of the imperial Ottoman line.

The four piers that support the central dome are strengthened by huge external buttresses, concealed on the north and south sides by arcaded galleries built between them. On the east and west façades the buttresses are smaller, since here the weight of the dome is distributed by the semidomes. On the east face the buttresses are wholly outside the building, where they serve to articulate an otherwise blank façade. On the west side, in order to preserve the unity of the courtyard, Sinan once again decided to mask the buttresses with galleries, but in this case the device was less successful. The great west portal seems squeezed between them and is somewhat overshadowed.

Interior of the mosque

The interior of the mosque takes the form of a vast, square room, surmounted by a huge dome, 27.5m in diameter (the dome of Haghia Sophia is 31–33m across; that of Pantheon in Rome is 43m). To east and west it is flanked by semidomes, and to north and south by tympanum arches pierced by windows. The dome arches rise from four irregularly-shaped piers. Up to this point the plan follows that of Haghia Sophia, but beyond this all is different. Between the north and south piers, triple arcades on two monolithic porphyry columns support the tympana. There are no galleries, nor can there really be said to be aisles, since the porphyry columns are so high and so far apart that they do not form any real divide between the central area and the walls. Thus the immense space is centralised and continuous.

The general effect is of a severe and simple grandeur, enlivened by the red carpet with its individual prayer-mat design and by the stained glass windows at the east end. The tiles, used sparingly, are the earliest known examples of the new Iznik techniques, leaf and flower motifs in turquoise, deep blue and red on a pure white ground. The mihrab and mimber, in Proconnesian marble, are simple and very fine, as is the woodwork of the doors, window shutters and preacher's chair, inlaid with ivory and mother-of-pearl. Throughout the building the inscriptions are by the famous calligraphers, Ahmet Karahisarı and his pupil Hasan Çelebi.

SÜLEYMAN & ROXELANA

Sometime around the middle of the 16th century, when the great Padishah and Caliph of Islam Süleyman the Magnificent, conqueror of the Magyars and of Belgrade, married one of his harem concubines, the Ukrainian-born Roxelana, who went under the palace name of Hürrem, he was taking an unprecedented step. No other Ottoman sultan had confined himself to a single woman; neither was it any longer the custom for them to contract legal marriages, not even with the women who bore them sons. But Roxelana was different. She was beautiful (one must suppose), she was intelligent, she was cunning and—fortunately for her, because in her position she had to be—she was ruthless. Süleyman's favour was a great thing to have gained, but it was not enough. In order to secure the

Roxelana, the Ruthenian concubine who enslaved her master's heart.

succession of her son Selim, who was not Süleyman's first born, Roxelana had to remove the able and popular Prince Mustafa, son of his former First Kadın Gülbahar. Gülbahar had not come to the harem as a captured slave, and had mocked Roxelana as 'bought meat' when she came to the attention of Süleyman. Roxelana contrived to have her sent, with her son, to the town of Manisa.

Roxelana had succeeded in clearing rival women from her path, but there were other obstacles. Her competitor for Süleyman's attention was his Grand Vizier, İbrahim Pasha, a Greek convert to Islam who had been the sultan's intimate companion since the early years of his reign. Roxelana set out to eliminate him, persuading Süleyman that his wealthy and powerful minister was taking on airs of royalty and had designs on the throne. In the year 1536, after an intimate supper in the palace with his beloved friend, Süleyman gave orders to his mutes to strangle İbrahim in his sleep. Roxelana then plotted with her son-in-law, the Grand Vizier Rüstem Pasha, to convince Süleyman that Prince Mustafa was planning to overthrow him and usurp the throne. In 1553 Süleyman had Mustafa strangled too, while he himself looked on through a screen. Mustafa's luckless mother was banished to Bursa.

Roxelana never lived to be Valide Sultan. She died in 1558 aged about 60. Süleyman died in Hungary at the age of 71, of an apoplexy while besieging the castle of Szigetvár—a siege which his army subsequently went on to win.

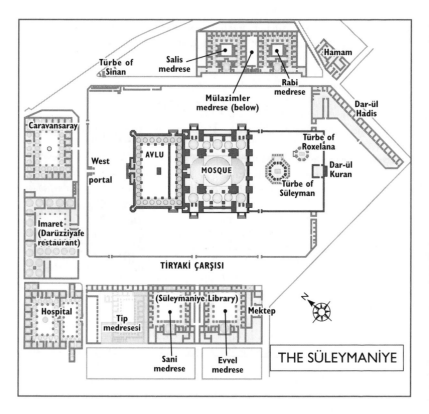

THE SÜLEYMANIYE

The türbes

The **türbe of Süleyman** is in the walled garden behind the mosque. Süleyman's türbe is the largest and grandest of all the mausolea built by Sinan. It is dated 1566, the year of Süleyman's death. Octagonal in form, with triple lancet windows in all eight faces, it is surrounded by a porch supported on slender columns. The walls of the interior are covered with Iznik tiles. The cenotaphs include that of Süleyman himself, his daughter, the Princess Mihrimah, and two later sultans, Süleyman II and Ahmet II.

The **türbe of Roxelana**, built eight years before Süleyman's, is smaller and simpler but decorated with even finer Iznik tiles. The cylindrical drum of the dome, slightly recessed from the octagonal cornice, is decorated with a long inscription forming a kind of sculptured frieze.

THE KÜLLIYE OF THE SÜLEYMANIYE

The Dar-ül Kuran

Behind the türbe garden is a large, triangular-shaped open space where weekly wrestling matches were held in early Ottoman times (wrestling has always been an honoured sport in Islam, because the Prophet himself enjoyed wrestling with his companions). At the western end of the area, set into the middle of the türbe garden wall, is the handsome former Dar-ül Kuran, or school for the study of the Koran. Such schools were usually small buildings, sometimes directly attached to a mosque and without accompanying living quarters for students, since the course in Koran reading was ancillary to more general studies. This example consists of a large, handsomely-proportioned domed chamber beneath which there is a small Byzantine cistern.

The Dar-ül Hadis and hamam

The **Dar-ül Hadis**, or 'School of Tradition', runs off at an angle to the north terrace, following the line of the street below. This is a medrese, consisting of 22 cells arranged in a straight line rather than around a courtyard. Opposite them is a plain wall with barred openings enclosing a long, narrow garden. At the end of the line of cells nearest the mosque a staircase leads up to a sort of open loggia, which appears to have served as the dershane. It must have been for summer use only since it would have been too cold in winter.

From the outer edge of the terrace you can look down onto the street that borders the north wall of the outer precincts. This was once an **arasta**, or market street, with shops built into the retaining wall of the terrace and also opposite. Revenue from these shops would have been used to fund the pious foundations of the külliye.

The **hamam** of the Süleymaniye is a fine building, of an original design and once elegantly decorated. It is still a fully functioning bath house (*mixed sex; open 10–midnight; www.suleymaniyehamami.com.tr*).

The Salis, Rabi and Mülazimler medreses

The medreses to the north of the mosque (*closed to the public at the time of writing; they can best be viewed from the terrace*) are the most elaborate, original and picturesque of all Sinan's medreses. The one to the west is called Salis (Third), while that to the east is known as Rabi (Fourth). They form a group

Building the türbe of Süleyman, by the miniaturist Nakkaş Osman. The figure on the left is thought to be Sinan.

with another pair that stand opposite, the Evvel (First) and Sani (Second). Each medrese served as a college in one of the four orthodox schools of Islamic law.

Salis and Rabi are absolutely identical; between them there is a small court from whose lower level two staircases lead to the courtyard of another medrese, the Mülazimler (for preparatory students). This medrese consists of 18 barrel-vaulted cells under the north side of the upper medreses. Because of the precipitous nature of the site, two expedients were necessary. The north side of the courtyard was raised on high superstructures, beneath which lies the Mülazimler medrese. Even so, the courtyard itself slopes downhill fairly sharply, and the cells along the sides are built on five different levels connected by flights of shallow steps. On each level outside the cells there is a verandah with a low parapet. The dershane occupies most of the upper side of the courtyard, but since it is at the highest level it is entered from the sides rather than from the façade on the court. As a display of architectural virtuosity these medreses surely have no rival.

Tiryaki Çarşısı

The long and broad esplanade on the south side of the mosque, outside the precinct walls, is called Tiryaki Çarşısı, the 'Market of the Addicts', because in Ottoman times the cafés here used to serve opium as well as the usual tea, coffee and tobacco. At its east end stands the **mektep**, where the children of the clergy, faculty and staff of the Süleymaniye received their elementary education.

The twin **Evvel and Sani medreses** form a group with the other two schools of Islamic law on the north side of the mosque. They now house the celebrated **Süleymaniye Library**, one of the most important in the city, with more than 32,000 manuscripts. The buildings are mirror-images of one another, and although the arrangement is typical enough—cells around a porticoed courtyard——there are interesting variations. For example, there is no portico on the north side, but, instead, the three cells are open, forming a kind of loggia; the portico on the south side is cut by the dershane. All of the porticoes have been glassed in to accommodate the library; this has been done well and attractively, and there is a charming garden in the courtyard itself.

Just beyond the Sani medrese stood the **Tip Medresesi**, or Medical College, once the foremost in the Empire. All that remains of it now is the row of cells along the Tiryaki Çarşısı; the other three sides have long since disappeared.

The hospital, imaret and caravansaray

The vast former **hospital** (darüşşifa), like most of the larger Ottoman hospitals, had a special section for the care of the insane. The **imaret**, or public kitchen, is enormous—as well it might be, for it had to supply food not only for the poor of the district but also for the several thousand people directly dependent on the Süleymaniye: the clergy of the mosque, the faculty and students of the several medreses, the staff and patients of the hospital, and the travellers staying at the caravansaray. The courtyard is charming, with its ancient plane trees and young palms and a lovely marble fountain in the centre. It now houses the **Darüzziyafe**, a well-known restaurant specialising in Ottoman cuisine (*see p. 296*).

Beyond the imaret is the building that was once the **caravansaray**, which included a kitchen, bakery, olive-press, sleeping quarters for travellers, stables for their horses and camels, and storage rooms for their belongings. According to Turkish tradition, all accredited travellers to the city were given free food and shelter for three days at this and other caravansarays.

The türbe of Sinan

The türbe of Sinan, the architect of the Süleymaniye complex, stands in a little triangular garden on the corner just beyond the caravansaray. Sinan apparently built a house here when he began construction of the Süleymaniye, and he lived in it until his death in 1588; he was then buried in his garden, in a türbe that he had designed and built himself. At the apex of the triangle is a sebil, from which radiate the garden walls that enclose the marble türbe. An arcade with six ogive arches supports the marble roof with a tiny dome that rises over Sinan's marble sarcophagus, with a turbaned tombstone at its head.

Around the türbe there are other tombstones, presumably marking the graves of members of Sinan's family. On the south wall of the türbe garden there is a long inscription by Sinan's friend, the poet Mustafa Sa'i, commemorating the achievements of his long life (he died at the age of 98). There could be no more appropriate place for the great architect's tomb, looking out toward the mosque complex of the greatest of all the sultans, and which is turn is Sinan's finest achievement in all Istanbul.

ORDU CADDESİ & THE ŞEHZADE CAMİİ

The area that was the Third Hill of Constantinople, sawn in half by Atatürk Bulvarı, is not always an easy part of town to like. On wet and windy days it yields its charms extremely grudgingly. Even though the broad flat summit has been laid out as a park, the noise of the road is tremendous, and crossing it can be an ordeal. If you want to buy a bicycle, however, this is the place to come: the underpass beneath the highway is thick with cycle shops. And on the credit side, the Şehzade Camii is one of the loveliest of all the larger mosques in the city.

ON & AROUND ORDU CADDESİ

The closest stops on the Kabataş–Zeytinburnu tram are Beyazıt or Aksaray.

Bodrum Camii

The Bodrum Camii (*map p. 348, A3*), or 'Subterranean Mosque', is so called because of the crypt that lies beneath it. The Byzantine church and monastery on this site were founded by Romanus I Lecapenus (919–44), in an area known as the Myrelaion, the 'place of the myrrh-oil'. Next to the church Romanus also built a palace, above a late Roman circular substructure known as the Rotunda. When his wife Theodora died in 922 she was buried in the crypt beneath the church. The church was converted into a mosque late in the 15th century by Mesih Pasha, a descendant of the Palaeologues, who led the Ottoman forces in their first and unsuccessful attack on Rhodes in 1479.

Studies have shown that the church and its crypt were built during the period 919–23, and that both were of the same design, namely the four-column type so common in the 10th–11th centuries. The church now serves as a mosque, but the crypt below is closed to the public. The Rotunda was built in the 5th century AD as the reception hall of a great palace, which apparently was never finished. When Romanus built his palace here, he roofed it over and used it as a cistern. It is now a subterranean mall. The restoration has been very successful, and it makes an extremely atmospheric place to go shopping.

Laleli Camii

The hemispherical dome of Laleli Camii, the 'Tulip Mosque' (*map p. 348, A3*), flanked by two slender minarets, bursts from its massive rectangular base giving a sense of upward thrust to the whole building. It was founded by Mustafa III and built between 1759 and 1763 by Mehmet Tahir Ağa, the greatest of the Turkish Baroque architects. He placed the mosque on a high terrace, beneath which were shops and a great hall supported by eight enormous piers, with a fountain in the centre. It has been suggested that this underground arcade was the architect's *tour de force*, designed to show that he could support his mosque virtually on thin air.

Inside the walls are heavily revetted in variegated marbles—yellow, red, blue and other colours. In the west wall of the gallery there are medallions of opus sectile which incorporate not only rare marbles but also semi-precious stones such as onyx, jasper and lapis lazuli. The mihrab and mimber are made of sumptuous marbles. The Kuran kursu is a rich work of carved wood heavily inlaid with mother-of-pearl.

Outside the mosque on Ordu Cd. is the pretty **sebil** and the austere octagonal **türbe of Mustafa III**, his mother Mihrişah, and his son, the murdered Selim III (*see p. 22*). Mustafa's own reign was not without its troubles. His attemtpts at Janissary reform were frustrated and his Russian policy led to humiliating defeat and annexation of the Crimea by Catherine the Great. He was advised by his Grand Vizier Ragip Pasha, whose battered library stands on the other side of Ordu Cd. (*map p. 348, B3*).

The street just to the east of the mosque, Fethi Bey Cd., leads at the second turning on the left to the **Büyük Taş Hanı**, or 'Han of the Big Stone', which probably belonged to the Laleli complex. The large central courtyard has two tiers of rounded arches and a ramp descending into what were once the stables. The han now houses shops, cafés and a restaurant.

Pertevniyal Valide Sultan Camii

Aksaray Square (*map p. 348, A3*), today a traffic-blighted intersection, occupies the site of the ancient Roman cattle market, the Forum Bovis. Here the ancient Mese divided into two branches, one leading off to the northwest along the route of the modern Millet Cd., the other going to the southwest, following approximately the course of Cerrahpaşa Cd. All trace of the market square of ancient times has been obliterated by today's massive clover-leaf intersection.

But there is a consolation. For just to the north of the overpass stands one of the most confidently exuberant of all the East-meets-West architectural creations of the 19th century. This is the Pertevniyal Valide Sultan Camii (*map p. 348, A3*), the last imperial mosque to be erected in Istanbul. It is generally ascribed to the Italian architect Pietro Montani, and was built in 1871 for Pertevniyal, mother of Sultan Abdülaziz. The foundress was a veritable Cinderella, for she was elevated in a single day from the palace kitchens to the bed of Sultan Mahmut II. Her mosque combines elements of Moorish, Turkish, Gothic, Renaissance and Empire styles, and one can see at a glance that it was built by an Italian. Inside, the predominant colour is a bright mauve, which by 1871 had become a fashionable hue, worn by Queen Victoria at the Royal Exhibition in London, and favoured by two empresses famed for their taste and their beauty, Eugénie of France and Elisabeth of Austria. Those who censure this mosque for its vulgarity have failed to understand the spirit of its times. It contains the tomb of Pertevniyal.

KALENDERHANE CAMİİ

Kalenderhane Camii (*map p. 348, B2*) occupies a large and handsome former Byzantine church, which was converted into a mosque by Fatih soon after the Conquest. Since it was used as a tekke by the dervishes of the Kalender order, it came to be known as Kalenderhane Camii. It was formerly the church of the Theotokos Kyriotissa (an attribute of the Virgin meaning 'Mother of God in Majesty'; icons of the Kyriotissa show her enthroned); this identification and the detailed architectural study of the building were the work of the Dumbarton Oaks Society and Istanbul Technical University, directed by Professor C. Lee Striker of the Pennsylvania State University. Professor Striker's work has shown that the present structure dates from the late 12th century, built on the ruins of earlier Byzantine and late Roman structures.

Interior of the Kalenderhane

The door through into the narthex has columns with melon capitals rather squashed now by a modern, lower doorway. In the ceiling, beneath the whitewash, the figure of a painted saint can be seen. The body of the church is cruciform, with deep barrel vaults over the arms of the cross and a ribbed dome. It still preserves some of its marble revetment and traces of sculptured decoration.

During restoration a series of wall-paintings was discovered in a small chapel to the right of the apse (bricked up). These proved to be a fresco cycle of the life of St Francis of Assisi painted during the Latin occupation of Constantinople. The frescoes are dated c. 1250, just a quarter of a century after the death of St Francis in 1226. This is the earliest known fresco cycle of St Francis. It shows the standing figure of the saint with ten scenes from his life, anticipating in many elements the frescoes of the Upper Church at Assisi. Other discoveries include a mosaic of the Presentation of Christ, dated to the 7th century, the only pre-Iconoclastic figurative mosaic ever found in the city. A late Byzantine mosaic of the Theotokos Kyriotissa came to light over the main door to the narthex, and another much earlier fresco of the Kyriotissa was found in the side chapel. The paintings and mosaics are now in the Archaeological Museum.

Precincts of the Kalenderhane

Excavations under and to the north of Kalenderhane Camii have revealed remains of a Roman bath of the late 4th or early 5th century, including evidence of a hypocaust. This was succeeded in the mid-6th century by a Byzantine basilica built up against the Aqueduct of Valens, using its arches as its north aisle. Finally, at some time prior to the Iconoclastic Period (which begain in 743), another church was built on the site, part of its sanctuary and apse being later incorporated into the present building.

ŞEHZADE CAMİİ

Şehzade Camii, the 'Mosque of the Prince' (*map p. 347, C2; under restoration at the time of writing*), was built by Süleyman the Magnificent in memory of Prince Mehmet, his first son by Roxelana, who died of smallpox in 1543 at the age of 21. Süleyman was heartbroken, and sat beside Mehmet's body for three days before he would permit burial to take place—most unusual in Islam, where bodies are usually buried with all speed.

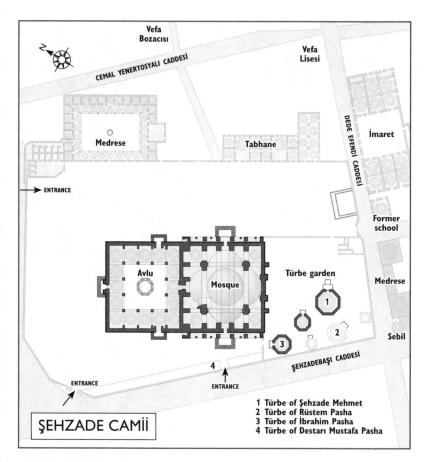

ŞEHZADE CAMİİ

1 Türbe of Şehzade Mehmet
2 Türbe of Rüstem Pasha
3 Türbe of İbrahim Pasha
4 Türbe of Destarı Mustafa Pasha

When Süleyman recovered from his grief he decided to erect a great mosque dedicated to his son's memory. Sinan was commissioned to design and build the külliye, which was completed in 1548. It was his first imperial mosque on a monumental scale.

The mosque

The mosque is preceded by a spacious porticoed avlu, equal in area to the mosque itself. In the centre is a şadırvan which, according to Evliya Çelebi, was a gift of Murat IV. The two minarets are exceptionally beautiful, with relief sculpture up their entire length picked out with terracotta inlay. It was here that Sinan first had the idea of placing colonnaded galleries along the north and south façades of the mosque in order to conceal the buttresses. This is one of the finest exteriors that Sinan ever created.

The interior of the mosque, austere in its simplicity, is unusual in that it has not a single column, nor are there any galleries.

Interior of the Şehzade türbe by the artist and archaeologist Osman Hamdi Bey (1842–1910).

The türbes

Behind the mosque there is the usual walled garden. The türbes within it boast some of the finest tile revetment in Istanbul (*the türbes were under restoration at the time of writing; it is to be hoped they will be open to the public when restoration is complete*). The buildings are of different dates and span the whole of the great age of Iznik tile-making.

The largest türbe is the **türbe of Şehzade Mehmet** himself **(1)**. It is octagonal, the faces separated by slender engaged columns; the stonework is polychrome, panels of *verd antique* being inset here and there in the façades, while the window frames and arches are picked out in terracotta. The dome, which is double and carried on a fluted drum, is itself fluted. The small entrance porch has a fine pavement of opus sectile. Altogether it is a very handsome building in the ornately decorated style of the mosque itself. The inscription in Persian verse over the entrance portal, which gives the date of the prince's death (1543), suggests that the interior of the türbe is like a garden in Paradise. It is sheathed in tiles from the floor to the cornice of the dome, all apple-green and vivid lemon-yellow. These are almost the last and by far the most beautiful flowering of the middle period of Iznik tiles, done in the *cuerda seca* technique. Tiles in this technique and in these colours are extremely rare. They were first manufactured at Iznik in about 1514, when Selim I brought back a group of Persian craftsmen after his conquest of Tabriz, while the latest known examples date from 1555. Thus the türbe of the Şehzade contains the most extensive and beautiful collection of tiles of this rare and beautiful type.

Just to the left and behind the türbe of the Şehzade is the **türbe of Rüstem Pasha (2)**, another work of Sinan, completed soon after the Grand Vizier's death in 1561. Just opposite the southwest precinct gate is the **türbe of the Grand Vizier İbrahim Pasha (3)**, son-in-law of Murat III. İbrahim Pasha died in 1601 and his türbe was completed early in 1603, designed and built by the architect Dalgıç Ahmet Çavuş. This türbe almost equals that of Şehzade Mehmet in splendour.

There are three other türbes in the garden: those of Prince Mahmut, son of Mehmet III; Hatice Sultan, daughter of Murat III; and Fatma Sultan, granddaughter of Prince Mehmet, but these are unadorned. Outside the türbe garden by the main entrance to the mosque precincts is the **türbe of Destarı Mustafa Pasha (4)**, dated by inscription to 1611. It is rectangular and roofed with a low central dome.

PRECINCTS & ENVIRONS OF THE ŞEHZADE

The **medrese** is at the far side of the precincts, near the northwest corner of the outer courtyard wall. It is a handsome building of the usual form. The south side, facing the mosque, has a portico but no cells. Opposite the entrance, instead of the usual dershane, there is an open loggia. The lecture-hall itself stands in the centre of the east side. The building has been well restored and is now a residence for university students.

In line with the medrese but farther east is the **tabhane**, which now belongs to the adjacent secondary school, Vefa Lisesi. This building is probably not by Sinan, although it is obviously contemporary with the rest of the complex. The structure is

L-shaped, with the bottom stroke of the L consisting of a long, wide hall, roofed with eight domes supported on three columns down its length; perpendicular to this is a block of eight cubicles, with two spacious halls providing access to them.

To the east of the türbe garden, in Dede Efendi Cd. (named after a famous composer of the age of Selim III), are the **former primary school and public kitchen** (imaret) of the complex. The primary school is of the usual type. The public kitchen consists of a spacious courtyard, on one side of which there were three double kitchens and a small domed refectory. Beyond the school is the very pretty old **medrese**. This was built by the Grand Vizier Nevşehirli İbrahim Pasha, and is dated by its inscription to 1720. It thus comes just between the end of the classical period and the beginning of the Baroque, so that it has pleasing characteristics of both eras. At the ends of the façade stand two large domed chambers surrounded by an attractive raised portico, with the entrance portal in the centre between them. The chamber to the left served as the library (it is now the Turkmenistan Cultural Centre). Beyond was the lecture-hall of the Dar-ül Hadis, or School of Sacred Tradition, which at a later date was turned into a small mosque (Damat İbrahimpaşa Camii), and a minaret was added.

Outside, at the street corner, is the extremely handsome **sebil**, a favourite among painters and etchers. Behind it is a little graveyard in which the founder of this fine small külliye is buried. İbrahim Pasha, *damat* or son-in-law of Ahmet III, served as Grand Vizier from 1718 until 1730, during the golden years of the Tulip Era. That epoch ended on 20th September 1730, when the Janissaries deposed the Tulip Sultan and strangled İbrahim Pasha. Ahmet ceded the throne without a fight and retired to seclusion in Topkapı palace. He died there six years later. He is buried by Yeni Cami.

Vefa Lisesi

Farther north on Dede Efendi Cd., just past the precinct wall of the Şehzade complex, is the Vefa Lisesi, built during the 1920s by the architect Kemalettin Bey. In its precincts stands the **library of Damat Şehit Ali Pasha**, built early in the 18th century. The founder, Ali Pasha, was called Damat (son-in-law) because he married Fatma Sultan, a daughter of Ahmet III, and Şehit (martyr), because he was killed in the battle of Peterwaredin in 1716. Fatma did not grieve long for Ali; shortly after she received news of his death she married Nevşehirli İbrahim Pasha.

The street beyond the school, Cemal Yenertosyalı Cd., follows the line of the Aqueduct of Valens (*see opposite*). At the street's northwest corner there is another ancient Ottoman building. This is the handsome medrese, built sometime before his death in 1618, by **Ekmekçizade Ahmet Pasha**, son of an Edirne baker, who rose to the rank of *defterdar* (first lord of the Treasury) and vizier, and died one of the richest men in the Empire.

Other sights of the Vefa district

Turn left on Cemal Yenertosyalı Cd. and then right at the next corner into Katip Çelebi Cd., where, just inside on the left, is the famous **Vefa Bozacısı** (*boza* is a drink made from millet, once a favourite of the Janissaries). Notice the silver cup in a glass case on the wall inside the shop; it is preserved there because Atatürk once drank from it.

Just beyond the Vefa Bozacısı, on the same side of the street, there is a little mosque called **Mimar Mehmet Ağa Mescidi**, built in 1514 by a certain Revani Şuccağ Efendi, who was an official escort of the annual embassy to Mecca.

At the next corner the street divides, with the right branch taking the name of Vefa Cd. A short way along on the left is **Vefa Camii**, the mosque from which the street and the surrounding neighbourhood take their name. This is a modern mosque erected on the site of the late 15th-century original, all that remains of which is the türbe of the founder, Şeyh Muslihiddin Vefa, who died in 1491. The türbe is a popular place of pilgrimage, for he is one of the most popular folk-saints in Istanbul.

Just beyond Vefa Camii, and on the same side of the street, is the **Library of Atıf Efendi**. Founded in 1741–42 and constructed of stone and brick in the Baroque style, it consists of two parts, a block of houses for the staff and the library itself. The former faces the street and its upper storey projects *en cremaillère*, that is, in five zigzags supported on corbels. The library itself is on the inner courtyard.

The street just opposite the library entrance is called Tirendaz Sk., the 'Street of the Archer'. At its far end, on the left, is the handsome **Kilise Cami** with its fluted minaret. The name, literally 'Church Mosque', alludes to its former function: it was identified by Gyllius as the church of St Theodore, but nothing is known of its history other than the fact that it was converted into a mosque soon after the Conquest. The most attractive part of the building is the outer narthex with its façade. Constructed of stone, brick and marble, its elaborate design and decoration identify it at once as belonging to the last great flowering of Byzantine architecture in the early 14th century. The narthexes contain some handsome columns, capitals and door-frames which appear to be spolia from an earlier sanctuary, probably of the 6th century.

SARAÇHANE & FATİH PARKS

Between Şehzade Camii and Atatürk Blv. stretches a grassy park (*map p. 347, C2*), scattered with ancient column stumps, and straddled by the great Aqueduct of Valens. This is the site of the ancient Forum Amastrianum, one of the main squares in Byzantine Constantinople. The little mosque just to the west of the Şehzade Camii precincts is **Burmalı Cami**, built c. 1540. It takes its name from its brick minaret with spiral ribs (*burma* means spiral); this is unique in Istanbul and is a late survival of an older tradition, of which a few examples survive in Anatolia. The porch is also unique: its roof is pitched, not domed, and is supported by four columns with Byzantine Corinthian capitals.

The Aqueduct of Valens

The Aqueduct of Valens, with its two tiers of arches marching across the valley between the Third and Fourth hills, gives an imperial Roman aspect to the skyline of this part of the old city. It was built by the emperor Valens in about AD 375 as part of a new water-supply system. The water, tapped from streams and lakes outside the city, appears to have entered through subterranean pipes near the Adrianople Gate (Edirne Kapı; *map*

Masonry fragment from the church of St Polyeuctus, now in the courtyard of the Archaeological Museum. The design incorporates the popular Christian motif of vines and, in the niche, where ancient Roman art would have had a scallop shell, we see peacock feathers, used in Christian iconography as symbols of immortality.

p. 342, C2) and to have passed underground along the ridges of the Sixth, Fifth and Fourth Hills to a point near the present site of Fatih Camii. From there it was carried by the aqueduct across the deep valley that divides the Fourth from the Third Hill.

Near the present site of Beyazıt Meydanı, the water was received in a huge cistern, the Nymphaeum Maximum, from which it was distributed to the various parts of the city. This ancient cistern seems to have been near the present *taksim*, the modern water-distribution centre, which is supplied from Lake Terkoz, some 60km northwest of Istanbul, near the Black Sea. The aqueduct was damaged at various times but was kept in good repair by both the Byzantine emperors and the Ottoman sultans, the last important restoration being that of Mustafa II in 1697. The aqueduct continued in use until the late 19th century, when it was replaced by the modern water-distribution system.

The aqueduct was originally about 1km long, of which some 625m remain; its maximum height, where it crosses Atatürk Blv., is 18.5m. A portion of the eastern side was demolished by Süleyman to give a clear view of the Şehzade mosque after it was built.

Fatih Park

On the south side of the aqueduct, on İtfaiye Cd., is the headquarters of the Istanbul Fire Department. One of the buildings has been converted into the **Fire Brigade Museum** (İtfaiye Müzesi; *open 9.30–5, closed Mon*).

Built up against the aqueduct is the **medrese of Gazanfer Ağa**, which now serves as the Caricature and Humour Museum (Karikatür ve Mizah Müzesi; *map p. 347, C2; under restoration at the time of writing*) with exhibitions of work by leading Turkish artists and cartoonists. The külliye to which this medrese belonged was founded in 1599 by the Venetian-born Gazanfer Ağa, Chief White Eunuch to Murat III. Gazanfer Ağa was the last of the Chief White Eunuchs to head the civil hierarchy in the Inner Palace, for after his time the Chief Black Eunuch, who had access to the Harem, became the dominant figure. Gazanfer was executed in 1603 by Murat's successor Mehmet III, who allowed him to die to appease his rebellious janissaries. The külliye includes a small medrese, a charming sebil with handsome grilled windows, and the türbe of the founder, in the form of a marble sarcophagus.

Fatih Park itself boasts a large sculpture of the Conqueror flying through the air on a charging horse. It was erected in 1987. In the southern section of the park, behind netting, are the remains of an ancient church. When the ground was being cleared for the Atatürk Blv. underpass in the mid-1960s these extensive ruins were discovered, and after excavation by Dumbarton Oaks were identified as the **church of St Polyeuctus** (*map p. 347, B2*). It was built between 524 and 527 for the princess Anicia Juliana, who dedicated it to St Polyeuctus, an early martyr. It is thus one of the earliest sanctuaries erected in Justinian's reign. It was an enormous building, some 52m square (compare the Süleymaniye mosque, which is about 58m square); it was essentially basilican in its ground plan, but very probably domed. The fragments of columns, capitals, an elaborately carved entablature, and parts of a long and beautifully written inscription, by which the building was identified, are very impressive indeed.

The külliye of Amcazade Hüseyin Pasha

Just to the west of the ruins of St Polyeuctus is the fine külliye of Amcazade Hüseyin Pasha (*map p. 347, B2*), a foundation of the illustrious Köprülü family. Hüseyin Pasha was a cousin (*amcazade*) of Fazıl Ahmet Pasha and was the fourth member of the Köprülü family to serve as Grand Vizier, from 1697–1702. The külliye now houses the **Museum of Turkish Architectural Works and Construction Elements** (*not normally open to the public, but the custodian can sometimes be persuaded to allow you in*). On display are architectural fragments, sculptured stonework, calligraphic inscriptions, and old tombstones. Many of these were formerly stored in the Second Court of Topkapı Palace, where they had been placed for safekeeping after the buildings to which they belonged were either ruined or demolished.

The complex includes an octagonal dershane, which also served as a mosque; a medrese; a library; a large primary school; two little graveyards with open türbes; a şadırvan; a sebil and a çeşme. The street façade consists first of the open walls of the small **graveyards**, divided by the projecting curve of the **sebil**. Beyond the entrance gate, with an Arabic inscription giving the date 1698, is the **çeşme**, with its reservoir behind, a somewhat later addition, for its inscription records that it was built in 1739 for the Şeyhülislam Mustafa Efendi.

On entering the courtyard, the first **open türbe** on the left has very handsome grilles, exceptionally beautiful specimens of early 17th-century grille-work. The columned portico of the **mosque** runs around seven of the building's eight sides, framing it in a rectangle. The mosque itself is without a minaret; its primary function was clearly as the lecture hall for the medrese. It is severely simple; its dome adorned only with some rather pale stencilled designs probably later than the building itself.

The far side of the courtyard is formed by the medrese cells with their domed and colonnaded portico. Occupying the main part of the right-hand side is the **library**. The upper floor is reached by a flight of outside steps, leading to a little domed entrance porch on the first floor. The medallion inscription on the front of the library records a restoration in 1755 by Hüseyin Pasha's daughter.

The right-hand corner of the courtyard is occupied by shops with the **mektep** above them: note the amusing little bird houses on the façade overlooking the entrance gate (*see box on p. 243*). A columned **şadırvan** stands in the middle of the courtyard.

THE COLUMN OF MARCIAN

On the south side of Macarkardeşler Cd. stands an ancient little mosque called **Dülger-zade Camii**, built by one of Fatih's officials, Şemsettin Habib Efendi, some time before his death in 1482. The side street beyond it leads to a monument known locally as **Kız Taşı**, the 'Maiden's Stone' (*map p. 347, B2*). This is actually the ancient Column of Marcian (*see box below*), one of three late Roman honorific columns in the city. The Turkish name of the column is undoubtedly due to the figure of Nike on the base, which has led travellers to confuse this column with the famous Column of Venus, which also stood in this neighbourhood and which reputedly possessed the power of being able to distinguish true virgins from false ones.

THE COLUMN OF MARCIAN

This column, though known to Evliya Çelebi and described by him in his *Narrative of Travels*, escaped even the penetrating eyes of Gyllius and remained unknown to the West until rediscovered in 1675 by Spon and Wheler. The reason for its obscurity was that it stood in the garden of a tall house, which, together with its neighbours, hid it from view. However, in 1908 a fire destroyed the houses and opened up the column to view, and now it stands in the centre of a small square. The base is formed by a marble pedestal on three steps; above this stands a monolithic column of Syenitic granite 10m high, surmounted by a battered Corinthian capital and a plinth with eagles at the corners; this once supported a seated statue of the emperor Marcian (r. 450–57). On the base fragments of sculpture remain, including a Nike, or Winged Victory, in high relief, as well as chi-rho symbols. There is also on the base an elegiac couplet in Latin which records that the column was erected by the prefect Tatianus in honour of Marcian.

Mid-19th-century engraving of the Column of Marcian, after a watercolour by W.H. Bartlett.

FATİH CAMİİ & THE ZEYREK DISTRICT

The great mosque of Mehmet the Conqueror, Fatih Camii, stands on the summit of what was the Fourth Hill of Constantinople. The district of Zeyrek, between the mosque and the roaring Atatürk Bulvarı, is home to the former Byzantine church of the Pantocrator.

THE DISTRICT OF ZEYREK

Prominent on the south side of Atatürk Bulvarı, the busy, noisy thoroughfare that runs along the valley between the old Third and Fourth Hills, is a handsome brick-and-stone mosque, **Şepsefa Hatun Camii** (*map p. 347, C1*), founded in 1787 by Fatma Şepsefa, one of the consorts of Abdülhamit I, in honour of her son Mehmet. Opposite it, on the other side of Atatürk Blv., a steep cobbled road leads into the district of Zeyrek. A short distance uphill, take a steep turning on the right, onto a path that looks like a terrace wall. At the corner on the left, with fine views of the Süleymaniye, is a small Ottoman building in a walled garden, the **former mektep of Zembilli Ali Efendi** (*map p. 347, C1*) scholar, cleric and Şeyhülislam. He died in 1526, so his mektep can be dated to some time prior to that year. The founder is buried beneath a marble sarcophagus in the garden.

Keeping the little graveyard on your left, continue along the road, which takes you into the heart of Zeyrek. This is a ramshackle quarter of narrow streets where hens and roosters scratch in the dirt, old wooden houses, some of them restored but most in a tragic condition of neglect and decay, and battered monuments. In the winter old tin stovepipes still emit curls of brown-coal smoke into the air, scarcely above eye level. All the women wear headscarves and all the men dress in uniform black and grey.

On İtfaiye Cd., opposite a butcher's shop where recently-flayed carcasses hang in the window, is the historic **Çinili Hamam**, the Tiled Bath (*map p. 347, C2; closed at the time of writing*), an early work of Sinan. It was built c. 1545 for Süleyman's great admiral Hayrettin Pasha, or Kheir-ed Din or Barbarossa, to provide funds for his tomb on the Bosphorus (*see p. 250*). The famous tiles that gave the bath its name have largely disappeared. Ferzan Özpetek's 1997 film *Hamam* was shot here.

ZEYREK CAMİİ

The former church of the Pantocrator (*map p. 347, C1; closed for restoration at the time of writing*) is an irregularly-shaped building, originally two churches linked by a chapel in a process of agglutination that is typical of Byzantine church architecture. The churches were attached to an adjoining monastery and the whole complex was built between 1120 and 1136. The monastery and south church were founded by the empress Eirene, wife of John II Comnenus, and dedicated to the Holy Saviour Pantocrator,

Christ the Almighty. After Eirene's death in 1124, John erected the second church a short distance to the north, and dedicated it to the Virgin Eleousa, the Merciful. John then decided to join the two churches by means of a third, dedicated to the Archangel Michael. This was designed as a funerary chapel for the imperial Comnenus dynasty. The empress Eirene was reinterred there after its completion. John II was also buried there (in 1143), as was his son Manuel I (in 1180), the last of the Comneni.

In the early 15th century it was taken over as a funerary chapel by the Palaeologus family, the last dynasty to rule Byzantium. Two of the last three emperors were buried here: Manuel II in 1425 and John VIII in 1448. Buried alongside John was his wife, Maria of Trebizond, the last Empress of Byzantium (Constantine XI, the last emperor, was a widower when he succeeded to the throne, and he did not marry again).

During the Latin period (1204–61) the Pantocrator was in the hands of the Venetians. Immediately after the recapture of the city by the Byzantines, the Genoese crossed over from Galata and stormed the Pantocrator, where some of the Venetians were still holding out, and in the course of the fighting the monastery burned to the ground. It was soon afterwards rebuilt, and during the latter Byzantine period it resumed its role as one of the most important religious centres in the city.

The church was converted into a medrese shortly after the Conquest, and following that, when the scholars moved to Fatih's new mosque on the summit of the Fourth Hill, it became a mosque. It is named after Molla Zeyrek, one of the teachers from the medrese.

GENNADIUS THE PATRIARCH

The most famous resident of the monastery during the last years of Byzantine rule was Georgios Scholarios, better known by his monastic name of Gennadius. Gennadius accompanied John VIII Palaeologus and the patriarch Joseph II to the Council of Ferrara-Florence in 1438, when the Greek and Roman churches were officially reconciled. Gennadius bitterly opposed the union, however, and when he returned to Constantinople he vehemently denounced it; his view was shared by most people in the capital. After that Gennadius retired to his cell in the Pantocrator, emerging only after the city fell to the Turks. Shortly after the Conquest, Gennadius was invited to meet Mehmet II, who needed the support of the Eastern Christians and who believed that an anti-Roman Catholic would not appeal to the West for liberation. After several cordial conversations, Mehmet appointed Gennadius ethnarch, a post which, under Turkish rule, made him head of the entire Orthodox population in the Ottoman Empire.

Interior of Zeyrek Camii

NB: This description reflects the status quo before restoration work began; at the time of writing the mosque was closed and inaccessible.

The **south church** (the earlier) is of the four-column type (the columns were removed in Ottoman times and replaced by piers), with a central dome, a triple apse, and a narthex with a gallery overlooking the nave. It preserves the original narthex door-frames and the almost complete marble revetment of the apse. For Islamic liturgical reasons the floor is covered by a carpet; underneath is a magnificent pavement in opus sectile, arranged in great squares and circles of coloured marbles with figures in the borders. The mimber is made from Byzantine fragments, including the canopy of a ciborium.

The **north church** is somewhat smaller but essentially of the same plan. Here again the columns have been replaced by piers, but all the original decoration has been lost. The **chapel** that joins the two churches is an aisleless structure with a single apse, covered by two domes. It is highly irregular in form in order to make it fit between the two churches, which are not of exactly the same size. John added an outer narthex which must once have extended in front of all three structures, but which now ends in the middle of the chapel.

Behind the mosque is the **Zeyrekhane restaurant**, a good place for lunch (*see p. 296*).

Şeyh Süleyman Mescidi

The monastery of the Pantocrator was an extensive foundation, including a hospice for old men, an insane asylum and a famous hospital. Nothing remains of it today, though there are widespread ruins and substructures in the area. The ancient building known as Şeyh Süleyman Mescidi on the corner of Zeyrek Cd. and Atpazarı Sk., the 'Street of the Horse Market' (*map p. 347, C1*), and which is clearly Byzantine in construction, may possibly have belonged to it. It has never been seriously investigated, so that neither its identity nor its date are known. At the time of writing it was falling into ruin.

ESKİ İMARET CAMİİ

Eski İmaret Camii (*map p. 347, C1*) or İmaret-i Atik Cami, has been identified as the church of the Holy Saviour Pantepoptes, the 'All-Seeing', which was founded c. 1185 by Anna Dalassena, mother of Alexius I Comnenus, the first member of the Comnenus dynasty. Anna was the power behind the throne for the first two decades of her son's reign. She retired in 1100 to the convent of the Pantepoptes and was buried here in 1105. The church was converted into a mosque almost immediately after the Conquest. For a time it served as the imaret of Fatih Camii, hence its name, 'Old Imaret Mosque'.

The exterior is very attractive and characteristically Byzantine, with its twelve-windowed dome and its decorative brickwork. Inside it is a perfect example of a church of the four-column type, with three apses and a double narthex, where many of the doors retain their magnificent red marble frames. Over the inner narthex there is a gallery that opens into the nave by a charming triple arcade on two rose-coloured marble columns. The side apses retain their original windows and their beautiful marble cornice. The dome rests on a cornice which still preserves its original decoration, a meander pattern of palmettes and flowers.

FATİH CAMİİ

The huge mosque complex built by Mehmet the Conqueror (*map p. 347, B1*), known in Turkish as Fatih, was the most extensive in the whole of the Ottoman Empire. The main entrance is on İslambol Cd. There you are confronted by the imposing edifice of the mosque, flanked on either side by its great medreses.

HISTORY OF FATİH CAMİİ

The architect of the original mosque, built in 1463–70, was Atik Sinan. Little is known of this Sinan, but he is believed to have been a Greek, trained in an Ottoman school of architecture. The mosque and its külliye stood on the site of the famous Church of the Holy Apostles, in whose funerary chapel most of the earlier emperors of Byzantium were buried, including Constantine himself. The church and its attendant buildings, which were already in ruins at the time of the Ottoman siege, served as a quarry to supply building material for Fatih's triumphant foundation, and today not a trace of them remains.

The original mosque was destroyed by an earthquake in 1766. Mustafa III immediately undertook its reconstruction, and the present mosque, designed on a wholly different plan by Mehmet Tahir Ağa, was completed in 1771. What remains of the original complex is, most probably, the courtyard, the main entrance portal of the mosque, the mihrab, the minarets up to the first şerefe, the south wall of the türbe garden and the adjoining gate.

There has been much speculation about the original plan of Fatih Camii, the first imperial Ottoman mosque to be erected in Istanbul. It is believed to have had a very large central dome, some 26m in diameter (compare Haghia Sophia, where the average diameter is 32m), with a semidome of the same diameter to the east; these were supported by two rectangular piers on the east and by two enormous porphyry columns on the west. To north and south there were side aisles, each surmounted by three small domes. Those who saw and described it, Turks and foreigners alike, compared it to Haghia Sophia. There is a persistent tradition, repeated by Evliya Çelebi and other writers, that the architect was executed by the Conqueror soon after the mosque was completed, because Fatih was enraged that the dome was smaller than that of the Great Church.

The mosque courtyards

Adjoining the **outer courtyard** to the west were a small library (kütüphane) and a primary school (mektep), both since demolished. Still extant are the remains of the **Boyacı Kapısı**, the 'Painter's Gate'. There was a similar portal to the south of this called Çörekçi Kapısı, the 'Gate of the Çörek-Maker' (*çörek* are coiled, plaited or ring-shaped pastries eaten on holy days).

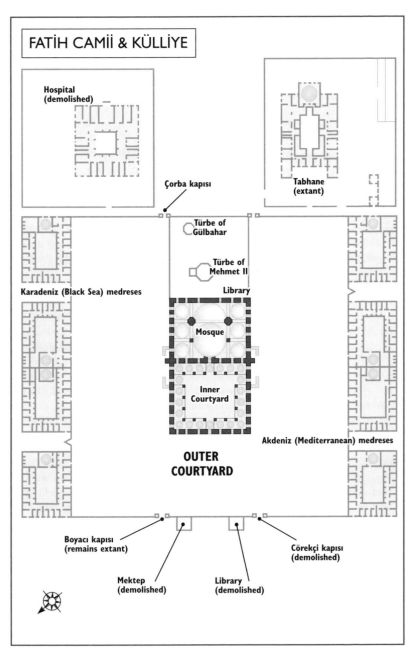

FATİH CAMİİ & KÜLLİYE

Hospital
(demolished)

Çorba kapısı

Tabhane
(extant)

Türbe of
Gülbahar

Türbe of
Mehmet II

Karadeniz (Black Sea) medreses

Library

Mosque

Inner
Courtyard

Akdeniz (Mediterranean) medreses

OUTER
COURTYARD

Boyacı kapısı
(remains extant)

Mektep
(demolished)

Library
(demolished)

Çörekçi kapısı
(demolished)

The **inner courtyard**, with its monumental entrance portal, is the original from Fatih's time. In the **lunettes of the six west windows** of the courtyard wall, the first sura of the Koran is written in white marble letters on a ground of *verd antique*: 'In the name of Allah, the merciful, the compassionate; Praise be to Allah, Lord of all Worlds; the merciful, the compassionate; Lord of the Judgment Day; Thee alone do we worship, to Thee alone do we pray for aid; Guide us along the straight path; The path of those who have found favour with Thee; Not of those who have incurred Thy wrath, nor of those who have gone astray.' The calligrapher was Yahya Sufi, whose son Ali made the inscriptions over the main portal of the mosque (and also over the Imperial Gate at Topkapı). The portal itself has engaged columns at the corners, whose convex ribs become interlaced to form an intertwined snake pattern, with a sort of hour-glass-shaped capital and base at top and bottom, a style unique to this külliye.

In the centre of the courtyard, surrounded by cypress trees, stands the **şadırvan**, with a conical witch's hat roof resting on eight marble columns. In essentials it is original—even to the cypresses, which are frequently mentioned by travellers. The marble columns of the portico are antique, with Ottoman stalactite capitals. At either end of the **mosque porch** are two exquisite faience inscriptions in the lunettes, in a combination of yellow, blue, green and white in the *cuerda seca* technique typical of this early period.

The mosque

The entrance portal of the mosque is also original. It has the same engaged columns as the courtyard gate and is surmounted by a stalactite hood. On the sides and over the door are historical inscriptions in bold calligraphy, giving the names of the founder and the architect and the date of completion of the mosque. The interior side of the portal is even more remarkable; its canopy is a finely carved scallop shell supported on a double cornice of stalactites. Unfortunately, it is masked by a later Baroque balcony built in front of it.

The interior of the mosque, dating mostly from Mustafa III's 18th-century reconstruction, is a copy of the type in which the central dome is flanked by four semidomes on the axes, a design developed by Sinan for the Şehzade and used again for the Blue Mosque and Yeni Cami. The **mihrab** is a survival from the original building, and it resembles the entrance portal, though the gilt-framed panels in the lower part are probably Baroque additions. The **mimber** and sultan's loggia are from the Baroque rebuilding.

The türbes

In the graveyard behind the mosque stand the türbes of Mehmet II and his senior consort, Gülbahar (d. 1492), the stepmother of Beyazıt II (she acted as Valide Sultan on his accession). Both of these türbes were completely reconstructed after the earthquake, though on the old foundations. Fatih's türbe is plain on the outside except for its extraordinary Baroque porch, a kind of crinkled canopy reminiscent of a tablecloth shaken in the wind. The interior is very sumptuous, and the cenotaph of the great conqueror is surmounted by a large turban. The türbe of Gülbahar is simple and classical and probably resembles the original. The little library in the southwest corner of the graveyard beside the mosque was built by Mahmut I and dates from 1742.

MEHMET II

'Son of Sultan Murat, son of Sultan Mehmet Khan, the sultan of the lands and the emperor of the seas, the shadow of God extending over men and jinns, the deputy of God in the East and in the West, the champion of the water and the land, the conqueror of Constantinople and father of that conquest Sultan Mehmet, may God make his reign eternal and exalt his abode above that of the highest stars in the firmament.' So wrote the great calligrapher Ali Sufi, on the outer face of the Imperial Gate of Topkapı Palace. Mehmet was 21 years old when he conquered Constantinople. Less than a decade later he took the Peloponnese and Trebizond, thus bringing the Byzantine world to an end. His sights, however, were always set on Rome, and his troops sacked Otranto in southern Italy in 1480. By 1481, however, the great conqueror was dead, at the age of only 49. Mehmet was fluent in many languages, including Hebrew, Greek and Latin. He was a noted patron of art and science, a founder of universities, an able administrator, a tolerant autocrat and, above all, a devout Muslim and warrior.

Contemporary portrait of Sultan Mehmet the Conqueror by the Venetian artist Gentile Bellini (National Gallery, London).

THE MOSQUE PRECINCTS

To north and south of the mosque precincts stand eight great medreses, survivals of Fatih's original construction. Those to the north were known as the **Karadeniz Medreseleri**, the 'Medreses of the Black Sea', while those to the south were called the **Akdeniz Medreseleri**, the 'Medreses of the White Sea', or Mediterranean. The buildings are severely symmetrical and almost identical in plan. Behind each medrese there was originally an annexe about half as large; these have totally disappeared.

Altogether there must have been about 255 students' cells, each housing perhaps four youths. Thus the establishment must have provided for about a thousand students in all, making it a huge foundation.

The gateway known as the **Çorba Kapısı**, 'Soup Gate', was so called because of the proximity of the imaret (soup kitchen). It is part of the Conqueror's original külliye; notice the elaborate designs in porphyry and *verd antique* let into the stonework of the canopy, and also the 'panache' at the top in *verd antique*.

The tabhane

The tabhane, or hospice for travelling dervishes, outside the southeast corner of the mosque precincts, has a very beautiful courtyard, its 20 domes supported on 16 lovely columns of *verd antique* and Syenitic granite (doubtless spolia from the Church of the Holy Apostles). The large square room at the east end served as the *mescit-zaviye*, the room where the dervish ceremonies were performed. On either side of it are two rooms opening out into unenclosed eyvans, whose domes are supported on engaged columns with the same twined ribs and hour-glass capital and base as those on the mosque entrance itself. It is thought that these eyvans were used for meetings and prayers in summer, the two rooms adjoining the mescit-zaviye for the same purpose in winter, and that the two farther rooms in the corner were depositories for the guests' baggage.

The imaret, which was adjacent to the tabhane, has perished. Evliya Çelebi writes that it had 70 domes—and one can well believe it. As it had to supply two meals a day to the thousand students of the medreses, along with the vast corps of clergy and professors of the foundation, to the patients and staff of the hospital, the guests at the tabhane and the caravansaray, as well as to the poor of the district, it is clear that it must have been enormous. The caravansaray has also disappeared, but it too must have been very big: Evliya Çelebi claims that it could hold 3,000 pack animals.

The only trace of the old hospital is in a surviving street name, Şifahane Sk., which recalls its site. Parts of its wall can be seen built into modern houses there.

The türbe of Nakşidil

The street that runs along the east side of the Fatih complex is called Aslanhane Sk., the 'Street of the Lion House', which suggests that the Conqueror may have had a menagerie near here. On the corner opposite the tabhane is a türbe complex built in 1817–18 for the Valide Sultan Nakşidil, consort of Abdülhamit I and mother of Mahmut II. Persistent legends that she was a Frenchwoman named Aimée, a cousin of the Empress Josephine, should be ignored; there is no truth in them—though it is true that she may have been French, and her son certainly had a penchant for fine French wines. Nakşidil's enormous türbe has 14 sides separated by slender columns which have, on top of their capitals, tall, flame-like acanthus leaves carved almost in the round, giving a fine bravura effect. The wall stretching along the street contains a gate and a grand sebil in the same flamboyant style. The gate leads into an attractive courtyard, which contains another türbe, round and severely plain. It is the burial place of the Valide Sultan Gülüstü, one of the numerous consorts of Abdülmecit I and mother of Mehmet VI Vahdettin, the last sultan of the Ottoman Empire, along with other members of the imperial family.

THE GRAVE OF ATİK SİNAN &
NİŞANCI MEHMET PAŞA CAMİİ

To see the grave of Atik Sinan, architect of the original Fatih Camii, follow Fatih Cd. north for about 500m until it intersects Yavuz Selim Cd. Turn right and then left. A short way along Nişanca Cd. is a mosque known as **Kumrulu Mescit**, the 'Mosque of the Turtle-Dove' (*map p. 347, A1*). It takes its name from a Byzantine relief fragment of two doves drinking from the Fountain of Life, incorporated in the adjoining çeşme. The founder of this mosque was Atik Sinan. He is buried in the garden and on his tombstone is an inscription recording that he was executed by the Conqueror in 1471 (*for the legend about this, see p. 155*).

Continuing along the same street, you will soon see, on the left, the beautiful mosque of Nişancı Mehmet Pasha.

Nişancı Mehmet Paşa Camii

This mosque (*map p. 347, A1*) was built between 1584 and 1588 for Mehmet Pasha the 'Marksman' (*Nişancı*) in the reign of Murat III. Though many sources attribute it to Sinan, it does not appear in the list of his works and is likely to have been completed by his follower Davut Ağa. The entrance courtyard with its ogive portico giving onto medrese cells and a şadırvan is very attractive. Under the entrance porch, the tuğra of Mustafa III records a restoration in 1766, presumably after the earthquake which felled the first Fatih Camii. Later restoration has been very successful, creating a soaring and light interior with the pattern combination of dome and semidomes as you look up appearing like a repeating design seen through a kaleidoscope. Nişancı Mehmet Pasha's türbe stands in the garden behind the mosque.

THE YENİ BAHÇE DISTRICT

Adnan Menderes Bulvarı runs along the ancient course of the Lycus River through a district called Yeni Bahçe, the 'New Garden'. Until recently this was indeed mostly garden land, though now the district is rapidly being covered with apartment buildings.

Fenari İsa Camii

On the corner of Adnan Menderes Cd. and Halıcılar Cd. stands the large former Byzantine church of Constantine Lips, now Fenari İsa Camii, the 'Mosque of the Lamp of Jesus' (*map p. 347, A2*). Constantine Lips was an official in the reign of Leo VI and later in that of Constantine VII Porphyrogenitus. In 907 he built a convent and church here, dedicated to the Theotokos Panachrantos, the Immaculate Mother of God. During the Latin occupation (1204–61) the convent seems to have been disused. When the Byzantines returned, it was refounded by Theodora, wife of Michael VIII Palaeologus. She added another church to the south, a chapel of St John the Baptist to the south of that, and linked the two churches by a narthex.

The chapel of St John was designed as a funerary chapel, and several members of the Palaeologus family were interred here, beginning with Empress Theodora herself in 1304. Others buried there include Theodora's sons, Prince Constantine and the emperor Andronicus II (r. 1282–1328), as well as the Princess Anna, first wife of John VIII (r. 1425–48). Contemporary accounts tell how Anna was buried at dead of night, in a city stricken by plague.

The church was converted into a mosque in 1496 and the monastery was given to a community of dervishes. The first head of the tekke was called İsa (Jesus), and the mosque thereafter was known as Fenari İsa Camii. The building has been completely restored by the Byzantine Institute of America.

The patterned brickwork of the exterior is very beautiful, particularly on the apses. with their blind niches and running swastika motif. Almost no trace of the original decoration survives in the interior, which is tall and sombre, with its bare brick walls and empty domes.

The medrese of Selim I and türbe of Şah Huban

West of Fenari İsa Camii, on the other side of Adnan Menderes Blv., is the large and handsome **medrese of Selim I** (*map p. 347, A2*), founded in 1562–63 by Süleyman and dedicated to the memory of his father; the architect was Sinan. Just west of it, across a side street, there is a small külliye consisting of a mektep and a türbe in a walled garden. This is the **türbe of Şah Huban Kadın**, a daughter of Selim I, who died in 1572. Both the mektep and the türbe are works of Sinan, dated to the year of Şah Huban's death.

Hüsrev Pasha türbe

The handsome octagonal **türbe of Hüsrev Pasha** (*map p. 347, A1*), with its eight sides separated by slender columns, was built by Sinan in 1545–46. Hüsrev Pasha was a grandson of Beyazıt II and had been one of the leading generals at the Battle of Mohács in 1526, when the Ottoman army defeated Hungary. After that victory Hüsrev Pasha governed Bosnia for a decade with great pomp and severe justice. Later he became governor of Syria, and in 1536–37 he commissioned Sinan to build a mosque for him in Aleppo; this is the earliest dated building by the great architect and it is still in existence. While governor of Rumelia (the Turkish Balkan region) in 1544, Hüsrev Pasha fell into disgrace through his complicity in a plot against the Grand Vizier Süleyman Pasha. He took his own life by starving himself to death, a rare case of suicide among the Ottomans.

Hırka-i Şerif Camii

Hırka-i Şerif Camii (*map p. 347, A1*), the 'Mosque of the Holy Mantle', was built in 1851 by Abdülmecit I to house the second of the two mantles of the Prophet that are among his chief relics in Istanbul (the other is in Topkapı; *see p. 79*). The mosque is in the purest Ottoman Empire style and has much verve and charm. A monumental gateway leads to a spacious paved courtyard, at the corners of which are the two tall, slender minarets with balconies in the form of Corinthian capitals. This is not the only feature that the mosque has in common with the Dolmabahçe Camii, built around the same time, and probably by the same architects, from the Armenian Balyan family. Here, as there, the façade is more like a palace than a mosque.

In the interior, part of the decoration consists of inscriptions by the famous calligrapher Mustafa İzzet Efendi; others are by Sultan Abdülmecit I, who was himself an able calligrapher. The sacred mantle is only on public display during the month of Ramadan.

YAVUZ SELİM CAMİİ & THE OLD FIFTH HILL

THE MOSQUE OF SELİM I

The imperial mosque of Sultan Selim I (*map p. 343, B4*) stands on a high terrace overlooking the Golden Horn. It was completed in 1522 under Selim's son and successor Süleyman the Magnificent. In all probability it had been begun two or three years earlier by Selim himself. The identity of the architect is not known.

The exterior aspect of the mosque, with its dark grey roof and pale stone walls, is impressive. The courtyard is extremely attractive, surrounded by a marble and granite colonnade, and with Iznik tiles in the lunettes above the windows. This is perhaps the least known of all the imperial mosques of the city, but in many ways it is the finest.

Interior of the mosque

The plan of the mosque is very simple: a square room covered by a high dome (32.5m at the crown), with the cornice resting on the outer walls through smooth pendentives. The dome is shallow: like that of Haghia Sophia but unlike that of most Ottoman mosques, it is significantly less than a hemisphere. This gives a very spacious and grand effect, in some ways reminiscent of the interior of the Pantheon in Rome. The room itself is vast and empty, the furnishings sparse. It is an appropriate atmosphere for a sultan who earned himself the epithet Yavuz, the 'Stern'. Selim was a brave and enthusiastic warrior, a severe and sometimes cruel overlord and—a combination that occurs so often in men of the sword of the late Middle Ages—an accomplished and tender poet.

The border of the ceiling under the sultan's loggia is a superb example of the painted and gilded woodwork of the early 16th century; notice the deep, rich colours and the varieties of floral and leaf motifs in the five separate borders. At either side of the great central area are passages leading to small domed rooms. These served as hospices for travelling dervishes.

The türbes

In the garden behind the mosque is the **grand türbe of Selim I**, with two beautiful panels of tilework, unique in colour and design, on either side of the door. The interior is impressive in its solitude, with the huge cenotaph of the sultan standing alone in the centre, covered with a velvet pall and with Selim's enormous turban at its head.

Facing Selim's türbe is another in which **four children of Süleyman the Magnificent** are buried. It was built in 1556, probably by Sinan.

The third mausoleum is the **türbe of Sultan Abdülmecit I**, built in 1855 by Karabet Balyan. Abdülmecit chose to be buried here because of his admiration for his ancestor,

though Abdülmecit himself was no warrior. He was known for his reforms of the army, the penal code and of financial matters (he introduced the first paper banknotes), for his extravagance and for his love of women. By the time he died, of tuberculosis at the age of only 38, he had fathered a great many children by over 20 consorts and concubines.

Environs of the Sultan Selim mosque
The mosque of Selim I was surrounded by the usual buildings of a külliye, of which only the **mektep** remains, a little domed building just outside the outer courtyard.

Next to the mosque precincts to the southwest are the remains of an enormous Roman reservoir, identified as the **Cistern of Aspar**, constructed by a Gothic general put to death in 471 by the emperor Leo I. This is the second largest of the three Roman reservoirs in the city, exceeded in size only by the St Mocius Cistern on the Seventh Hill; it is square, 152m on a side, and was originally 10m deep.

The street that borders the Cistern of Aspar to the south is called Yavuz Selim Cd. As you approach the far end of the cistern, make a short detour left into Ali Naki Sk. and stop at the second building from the corner on the right, an ancient structure with barred windows. If you peer through the windows you will see a superb **Roman basement** (*map p. 343, B4*), with a colonnade of marble columns consisting of four rows of seven monoliths topped with Corinthian capitals and imposts. It is thought to have been built by the empress Pulcheria, sister of Theodosius II (r. 408–50) and wife of the emperor Marcian (r. 450–57).

CİBALİ & AYA KAPI

Below the mosque of Selim I, on the shores of the Golden Horn, are the areas of Cibali and Aya Kapı (*map p. 343, C4*). The huge **Kadir Has University** on the shore road, a private institution founded in 2002, is housed in the former Cibali Tobacco Factory, one of the first factories in the Ottoman Empire, built in 1884 by the Armenian architect Hovsep Aznavur. Above the university is one of the surviving gates of the Byzantine sea wall, the Porta Puteae, known in Turkish as **Cibali Kapısı**. A Turkish inscription commemorates the fact that it was breached on 29th May 1453, the day on which Constantinople fell to the Turks.

The church of Haghios Nikolaos
The Greek church of Haghios Nikolaos (Aya Nikola; *map p. 343, C4*) is first recorded in 1573 by the German traveller Stefan Gerlach, though the present structure dates from a rebuilding in 1837. The date of the rebuilding is significant: many Greek churches in Istanbul were rebuilt around this time. In 1821, during reprisals following Constantinopolitan Greek support for the Greek War of Independence, the Patriarch Gregory V had been hanged from the gates of the Patriarchate in nearby Fener, and scores of Greek churches had been sacked and looted. For many years Greeks had feared to walk the streets, and many had fled the city. After 1830, however, the atmosphere changed.

Mahmut II issued a decree promising that Greeks need no longer fear punishment, and their places of worship were rebuilt.

Haghios Nikolaos was originally a metochion (dependency) of the Vathopedi Monastery on Mount Athos. Built into a wall of the courtyard there is an ancient Graeco-Roman tombstone with a relief of the deceased bidding farewell to his wife. Notice also in the narthex the model of an ancient galleon hanging from the ceiling. Ship models such as this are to be found in many of the waterfront churches of the city, placed there by sailors in gratitude for salvation from the perils of the sea. In the exonarthex there is an aghiasma dedicated to St Charalambos.

Aya Kapı and Gül Camii

Aya Kapı, the 'Holy Gate', a small portal in the sea walls (*map p. 343, C4*), was known in Byzantium as the Gate of St Theodosia since it led to the famous church of that name, now Gül Camii. This tall, imposing Byzantine edifice is believed to date from the 12th century. It was originally dedicated to St Euphemia of the Petrion, but when the popular iconodule, St Theodosia, was later buried here it came to be known by her name instead. The church was renowned for its collection of sacred relics, to which were attributed a host of miraculous cures. They were looted by the Crusaders when they sacked the city in 1204, and many still exist in the churches of Western Europe.

The church figured prominently in the final hours of Byzantine history, for the emperor Constantine XI stopped to pray here after his last visit to Haghia Sophia. At the time the church was adorned with roses in honour of St Theodosia, whose feast day is 29th May (the same day as the fateful siege). When the emperor arrived, accompanied by the Patriarch and the Senate, he found the church packed with women, children and old men, all of them praying to Theodosia to intercede with Christ and the Virgin to spare their city. When the emperor and his entourage left, the congregation remained, and were captured when the city fell to the Turks the following morning. The Turkish soldiers who stormed the church were evidently moved by the garlands of roses they found festooned here, for the tale became one of the enduring traditions of the Conquest.

After the Conquest the church basement became a storehouse for the Ottoman navy. It was converted into a mosque in 1490 and is known today as Gül Camii, the 'Rose Mosque'. The upper parts of the church were considerably altered in Ottoman times, a reconstruction that gives it the appearance of a medieval fortress. The two side apses, nonetheless, are worthy of note, with their three tiers of niches and their elaborate brick corbels. The handsome minaret dates from an early 17th-century rebuilding.

The interior is laid out on a cross-domed plan with side aisles surmounted by galleries; the piers supporting the dome are disengaged from the walls and the corners behind them form alcoves of two storeys. The central dome and the arches that support it are Ottoman reconstructions, as are most of the windows.

Küçük Mustafa Paşa Hamamı

Küçük (Little) Mustafa Paşa Hamamı (*map p. 343, C4; not in use at the time of writing*) is one of the oldest Turkish baths in the city, probably founded by Koca Mustafa Pasha, Grand Vizier to Beyazıt II, who built it some time before his death in 1512. The design of the hararet is particularly fine, with a deep cornice of carved stalactites. Each of the three cross-arms is covered with a different kind of vault, including one in the form of a scallop shell, a type also seen in the earlier hamam of Mahmut Pasha near the Grand Bazaar (*see p. 130*).

THE ÇARŞAMBA DISTRICT

Perhaps because of its proximity to Fatih Camii, the great mosque of the Conqueror, the area known as Çarşamba (*map p. 343, B4*) is one of the heartlands of conservative Islam in the city—just as in the early days of Byzantium its proximity to the church of the Holy Apostles meant that it was rich in Byzantine ecclesiastical foundations. The greatest of those that remain is Fethiye Camii, the former church of the Pammakaristos, once the seat of the Orthodox Patriarch.

Çarşamba, which in Turkish means Wednesday, is named after the picturesque market that throngs its streets on that day each week, as it has for centuries past. This is a travelling market that sets up its stalls and barrows in various parts of the city on different days; there are street markets in Istanbul named after all the days of the week except Sunday, the official day of rest in secular Turkey (even though the Turkish word for Sunday, *Pazar*, means market).

FETHİYE CAMİİ

Fethiye Camii (*map p. 343, B3; open 9.30–4.30, closed Wed*) is the name given to the mosque built into the former church of the Theotokos Pammakaristos, the 'Joyous Mother of God'. The exterior presents one of the best examples in the city of the fine stone and brickwork of the Palaeologue Revival. It takes the form of a three-storey cube articulated by blind arches and windows, some wider, some slenderer, with a number of domes poking above the roofline.

The church is in fact a complicated building (*see diagram opposite*), consisting of a central bay with a narthex; a small chapel, or parecclesion, to the south; and a kind of perambulatory forming a side aisle to the north. There is an exonarthex to the west and two bays of an aisle to the south in front of the parecclesion. Each of these three sections was radically altered when the building was converted into a mosque. The parecclesion is now separated from the mosque and is open as the Fethiye Museum.

History of the building

The main church is thought to have been built in the 12th century by an otherwise unknown John Comnenus and his wife Anna Ducaina, whose names indicate that they were related to the royal family. In form this church was of the ambulatory type, a triple arcade in the north, west and south dividing the central domed area from the

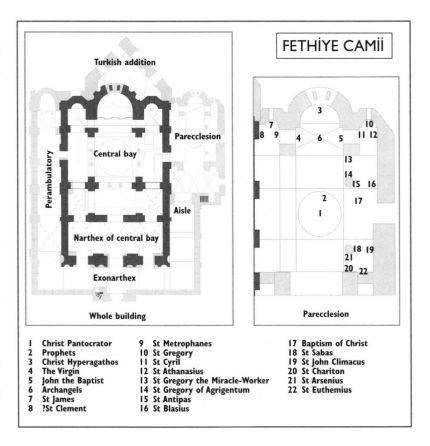

FETHIYE CAMİİ

Turkish addition

Parecclesion

Central bay

Perambulatory

Aisle

Narthex of central bay

Exonarthex

Whole building

Parecclesion

1 Christ Pantocrator	9 St Metrophanes	17 Baptism of Christ
2 Prophets	10 St Gregory	18 St Sabas
3 Christ Hyperagathos	11 St Cyril	19 St John Climacus
4 The Virgin	12 St Athanasius	20 St Chariton
5 John the Baptist	13 St Gregory the Miracle-Worker	21 St Arsenius
6 Archangels	14 St Gregory of Agrigentum	22 St Euthemius
7 St James	15 St Antipas	
8 ?St Clement	16 St Blasius	

ambulatory; at the east end there were the usual three apses, and at the west a single narthex.

Towards the end of the 13th century the church was reconstructed by a prominent general named Michael Ducas Glabas Tarchaniotes. Then, in about 1310, a parecclesion was added on the south side of the church by Michael's widow, Maria Ducaina Comnena Palaeologina Blachena, who used it as a funerary chapel for her husband. This chapel was of the four-column type and was preceded by a two-storey narthex covered by a tiny dome. In the second half of the 14th century the north, west and south sides were surrounded by a perambulatory, which ran into and partly obliterated the south chapel.

The church remained in the hands of the Greeks after the Ottoman Conquest and in 1456 it was made the seat of the Greek Orthodox Patriarchate, after the patriarch Gennadius was ejected from the Pantocrator. It was in the parecclesion of the Pammakaristos that Fatih came to discuss questions on religion and politics

Mosaic of Christ Pantocrator, surrounded by twelve prophets, in the dome of the parecclesion of the church of the Theotokos Pammakaristos, now Fethiye Camii.

with Gennadius. The Pammakaristos continued as the site of the Patriarchate until 1586, when Murat III converted it into a mosque. He then called it Fethiye Camii, the 'Mosque of Victory', to commemorate his conquest of Georgia and Azerbaijan.

When the building was converted into a mosque the main concern seems to have been increasing the available space. Most of the interior walls were demolished, including the arches of the ambulatory; the three apses were replaced by the present domed triangular projection; and the parecclesion was made part of the mosque by removing the wall and suppressing its two north columns. As a result, the main area of the church became a seemingly planless cavern of hulks of masonry joined by low, crooked arches. After the restoration by the Byzantine Institute, the main section was divided off from the parecclesion and reconsecrated as a mosque while the parecclesion itself was converted into a museum to exhibit the surviving mosaics.

The parecclesion

The parecclesion has been beautifully restored by the Byzantine Institute, its missing columns replaced and its surviving mosaics cleaned. The mosaics (*NB: numbering refers to the plan on the previous page*) are dated to the early 14th century and are thus contemporary with those at Kariye Müzesi. Though far fewer in number and less various than those, they are, nevertheless, an extremely precious addition to our knowledge of the art of the Palaeologue Revival.

In the crown of the dome is **Christ Pantocrator (1)**, surrounded by twelve **prophets**. In a clockwise direction beginning with **(2)**, they are Moses, Jeremiah, Zephaniah, Micah, Joel, Zachariah, Obadiah, Habakkuk, Jonah, Malachi, Ezekiel and Isaiah.

In the conch of the main apse is **Christ Hyperagathos (3)**, 'Good Beyond Goodness'; on the left wall of the bema is the **Virgin (4)**; on the right wall is **St John the Baptist (5)**. Together the triad forms a Deësis (*see Glossary*), watched from on high by the four **archangels (6)** in the dome: clockwise from the east quadrant they are Michael, Raphael, Gabriel and Uriel.

The mosaics in the side apses are all **portraits of saints** (*see plan on previous page*). Other mosaics of saints survive around the southeast and southwest piers and at the west end of the south aisle. The **only surviving scene mosaic** is the *Baptism of Christ* **(17)** in the south aisle.

Between the marble facing on the lower part of the south wall and the mosaics on the upper part there is a long inscription in gold letters on a blue ground. This is a threnody written by the Byzantine poet Philes to commemorate the love which Maria, the founder of the funerary chapel, bore her departed husband Michael Tarchaniotes.

AHMET PAŞA MESCİDİ

Fethiye Cd. bends to the south and becomes Manyasizade Cd. Just inside the bend is a small Byzantine church in the angle between two streets: this is the former church of St John the Baptist in Trullo, now **Ahmet Paşa Mescidi** (*map p. 343, B3–4*). In 1456, when Gennadius transferred the Greek Patriarchate to the Pammakaristos, he rehoused the nuns of the Pammakaristos here. Here they remained until about 1586, when the church was converted into a mosque by Hırami Ahmet Pasha, a former captain of the Janissaries, from whom it takes its name.

The little building is a typical example of a 12th-century four-column church, with a narthex and central semicircular apse flanked by two smaller ones. Nothing remains of the frescoes under the whitewash. Nor are the four columns the originals. The little building had fallen into ruins by the early 20th century and was only reopened to worship after restoration in the early 1960s. Its interest lies in its claim to be the smallest Byzantine church still extant in Istanbul, and in the fact that no academic study has ever been conducted on it. Its history in Byzantine times remains unknown.

KARİYE MÜZESİ & ITS DISTRICT

Kariye Müzesi (*map p. 343, A3; open 9.30–4.30; closed Wed*), the former church of St Saviour in Chora, is, after Haghia Sophia, the most interesting Byzantine church in the city. This is not due to the building itself, pretty as it is, but because of the superb mosaics and frescoes that it contains, a magnificent heritage of Byzantine art that has no equal in the world. You are fortunate if you find the church uncrowded. No longer a functioning mosque, it has been given over to tourism and is often filled to bursting with coach parties, cruise-ship groups, tour guides and security guards bellowing at everyone not to use flash. There are fears that the crowds and the humidity they cause are endangering the frescoes. Outside the church are souvenir stalls and tea houses—and usually a handful of conveniently waiting taxis.

HISTORY OF KARİYE MÜZESİ

The name of the Byzantine church, St Saviour in Chora means the Holy Saviour 'in the country', because the original church and monastery on this site were outside the walls of Constantine. Later, when the area was included within the Theodosian walls, the name remained (compare St Martin in the Fields, London) but was given a symbolic sense: Christ as the 'country' or 'land' of the Living, and the Blessed Virgin as the 'dwelling-place' of the Uncontainable, as they are referred to in inscriptions on mosaics in the church.

No trace remains of the original ancient church, nor is anything certain known about its origin. The present building in its first form dates only from the late 11th century. This church was founded by Maria Ducaina, mother-in-law of Alexius I Comnenus, between the years 1077 and 1081; it was probably of the four-column type so popular at that time. However, this church did not last long in its original form; the foundations at the east end appear to have slipped, causing the apses to fall in, and so the opportunity was taken to remodel the building. The present wide central apse with its deep barrel-vault was erected, and though the walls of the nave were retained, piers were added in the corners as supports for the arches of a much larger dome. A narrow side passage was added to the south, traces of which remain in the passages and gallery between the nave and the present parecclesion, which dates from a still later reconstruction. This elaborate remodelling was apparently carried out early in the 12th century by Maria Ducaina's grandson, the Sebastocrator Isaac Comnenus, third son of Alexius I Comnenus.

A third period of building activity some two centuries later created the present church. At this time the nave area was left essentially unchanged except for redecoration. But the inner narthex was rebuilt, the outer narthex and the parecclesion were added, the small side apses were reconstructed and the northern passage with its gallery was built in its present form. In addition to all these structural alterations, the church was completely redecorated and the interior was adorned with the superb marble revetment, mosaics and frescoes that we see today. All of this rebuilding and decoration was carried out in the period 1315–21.

The man responsible for all of this was Theodore Metochites, who served as both prime minister and first lord of the Treasury during the reign of Andronicus II Palaeologus. Metochites was one of the greatest men of his age: a diplomat and high government official, theologian, philosopher, astronomer, poet and patron of the arts, a leader in the artistic and intellectual renaissance of the late Byzantine era. The peak of his career came in 1321, when he was appointed as grand logothete, the highest-ranking official in the Byzantine Empire, an honour which was accorded him just weeks after he presided at the opening of the newly restored and redecorated church here. But his career ended just seven years later, when Andronicus III usurped the throne. Metochites was stripped of his power and possessions and sent into exile, along with most other officials of the old regime. He was allowed to return to the capital in 1330, on condition that he retire as a monk to the monastery of the Chora, where he died on 13th March 1332.

At the time of the Ottoman siege, St Saviour in Chora's proximity to the Theodosian walls placed it virtually in the front line. At that time it was used to house the famous icon of the Virgin Hodegetria, the Guide. This icon, which according to tradition was painted by St Luke, was the legendary protectress of the city, and during times of siege it was carried in procession along the Theodosian walls. When the Turks broke through the walls on the morning of 29th May 1453, the Chora was pillaged and the icon of the Hodegetria disappeared, never to be seen again.

Early in the 16th century the Chora was converted into a mosque by the eunuch Atik Ali Pasha, Grand Vizier in the reign of Beyazıt II. The mosaics and frescoes were never wholly obliterated, though in the course of time most were obscured by plaster, paint and dirt, and many were shaken down by earthquakes. The church and its extraordinary works of art were unknown to the scholarly world until 1860, when the Greek architect Pelopidas Kouppas brought them to the attention of Byzantinists. In 1948 the Byzantine Institute of America, under the direction of Paul A. Underwood, began a project to uncover the surviving mosaics and frescoes and to restore them and the fabric of the church to their original condition. After a series of eleven annual campaigns the project was carried through to completion in 1958, and today the church of St Saviour in Chora stands as one of the greatest monuments of Byzantine art in existence. Towards the end of his life, Theodore Metochites had written of his hope that the church of St Saviour in Chora would secure for him 'a glorious memory among posterity till the end of the world.' Thus far, he has had his wish.

The narthexes

The **exonarthex** extends across the entire width of the church in six bays, with a seventh bay extending at right angles to the east, so as to go around the south end of the narthex and open into the west end of the parecclesion. In order to provide illumination for the **narthex**, the two end bays were covered by domes carried on high drums, the sides of which were pierced by circlets of windows. It is in the narthexes that catechumens, those preparing for baptism, would traditionally have attended services and the iconographical scheme of the decoration reflects this: as they processed around these two spaces, they would have encountered the entire history of Christianity in pictorial form, in the following order:

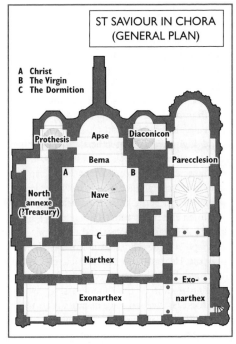

ST SAVIOUR IN CHORA (GENERAL PLAN)

A Christ
B The Virgin
C The Dormition

Prothesis
Apse
Diaconicon
Bema
Parecclesion
A
B
North annexe (?Treasury)
Nave
C
Narthex
Exo-
Exonarthex
narthex

I: Dedicatory and devotional panels, in the exonarthex and narthex;
II: The genealogy of Christ, in the two domes of the narthex;
III: The life of the Virgin, in the first three bays of the narthex;
IV: The infancy of Christ, in the lunettes of the exonarthex;
V: Christ's Ministry, in the vaults of the exonarthex and one bay of the narthex;
VI: Portraits of saints.

To view the mosaics as they were intended to be viewed, you need to follow this order. The genealogy in the domes serves as a prelude to the narrative cycles of the lives of the Christ and the Virgin in the narthexes. These cycles are closely linked and form one continuous narrative, for the cycle in the exonarthex takes up the account at the precise point in Mary's life, as narrated in the apocryphal Protoevangelium of James, where the Gospel accounts begin. Scenes depicting the Passion of Christ, now lost, would almost certainly have adorned the sanctuary.

The mosaics are the crowning glory of the art of the so-called Palaeologue Revival. The graphic depictions of motion and emotion are splendid, and many scenes are endowed with intimate details which give them life and interest. Art historians have compared them to the work of Giotto, but this is misleading. With their combination of spiritual grandeur and delight in the little things of this world, they are closer to the art of Siena.

I. Dedicatory and devotional panels (exonarthex and narthex)

(1) Christ Pantocrator: The inscription reads ICXC H XΩPA TΩN ZΩNTΩN: 'Jesus Christ, the Land (Chora) of the Living', a play on the name of the church.

(2) The Virgin Blachernitissa: The Virgin is shown praying (*orans*) with uplifted hands. The roundel of the Christ Child on her chest makes this an icon of the Platytera type (*see Glossary*), which was the type of the Theotokos Blachernitissa, venerated at a sacred spring near the Palace of Blachernae (*see p. 216*). The inscription reads MHP ΘY H XΩPA TOY AXΩPHTOY: 'Mother of God, the Dwelling-Place (Chora) of the Uncontainable', with the same play on the name of the church and a reference to the mystery of the Incarnation.

(3) Christ Enthroned with Donor: In the lunette over door into the nave, Metochites offers a model of his church to the enthroned Christ. He is dressed in his official robes, wearing the voluminous headdress of a Byzantine court official, the *skeiadon*. Christ has the same inscription as in the outer narthex, while the figure of the donor is thus identified: 'The Founder, Logothete of the Genikon (First Lord of the Treasury) Theodore Metochites'.

(4–5) St Peter and St Paul: To left and right of the door into the nave, between beautiful marble revetment arranged like a four-petalled rosette, St Peter (4) and St Paul (5) are represented in standing, full-length poses as the two 'Princes of the Apostles'; in this context they too, as it were, assume the character of 'founders', in as much as they, more than any of the other Apostles, were most influential in bringing Christ's Church into existence. St Peter is shown with the keys of Heaven dangling from his left hand. St Paul holds his right hand in a gesture of blessing while his left clasps a book, symbol of his Epistles.

(6) Deësis: Here Christ is of the type known as Chalkites, from the famous icon over the Chalke gate to the Great Palace of Byzantium. Below are the figures of two donors (very unusual in a Deësis). At the Virgin's right stands 'the son of the most high Emperor Alexius Comnenus, Isaac Porphyrogenitus'; this is Isaac Comnenus, third son of Alexius I, who was probably responsible for the rebuilding of the church in the 12th century. The inscription of the other figure is partly lost; what remains reads: '... of Andronicus Palaeologus, the Lady of the Mongols, Melane the nun'. This was either Maria, half-sister of Andronicus II, known as the Despoina ('Lady') of the Mongols, who founded the still-extant church of St Mary of the Mongols; or else another Maria, an illegitimate daughter of Andronicus II, who also married a Mongol Khan. To add to the confusion, both of these women took the name of Melane when they became nuns, making it impossible to say which of them is represented in the mosaic.

II. The genealogy of Christ (domes of the narthex)

(7) South dome: In the crown of the dome is a medallion of Christ Pantocrator and in the flutes two rows of his ancestors, from Adam to Jacob in the upper zone, and in the lower the twelve sons of Jacob (Reuben, Simeon, Levi, Judah, Zebulun, Issachar, Dan, Gad, Asher, Naphtali, Joseph, Benjamin) and some others. All are named.

(8) North dome: In the crown is a medallion of the Virgin and Child. The stars on her cloak, on her forehead and shoulders, here as in all other icons, symbolise her immaculate purity and virginity. In the flutes are 16 kings of the House of David (upper zone) and other ancestors of Christ (lower zone).

III. The life of the Virgin (narthex bays 1–3)

The cycle is based mainly on the Apocryphal Gospel of St James, better known as the Protoevangelium, which dates back to at least the 2nd century. This gives an account of her birth and life from the rejection of the offerings of Joachim, her father, to the birth of Jesus, her son. It was very popular in the Middle Ages and is the source of many cycles of pictures both in the East and the West. The scenes are as follows:

(9) Joachim's Offerings Rejected: Zacharias, the High Priest before the altar, raises his hands in a gesture of refusal. The rest of the scene is lost; it must have shown Joachim and his wife Anne bearing offerings. Their offerings were rejected because they had no children.

(10) Joachim in the Wilderness: Ashamed at the rejection of his offerings, Joachim goes into the wilderness to pray for offspring.

(11) Annunciation of St Anne: The right half of the scene shows the angel of the Lord announcing to Anne that her prayer for a child has been heard.

(12) The Meeting at the Golden Gate: Anne informs Joachim on his return from the wilderness of the annunciation of the angel. The scene is inscribed: 'The conception of the Theotokos'.

(13) The Birth of the Virgin.

(14) The First Seven Steps of the Virgin: She took her first seven steps when she was six months old.

(15) The Virgin Blessed by the Priests.

(16) The Virgin Caressed by her Parents: Note the two magnificent peacocks, representing incorruptibility, in the two pendentives.

(17) The Presentation of the Virgin in the Temple: The scene is inscribed 'The Holy of Holies'. At the age of three the Virgin was presented as an attendant at the Temple, where she remained until she was about twelve.

(18) The Virgin Receiving Bread from an Angel: While the Virgin remained in the Temple she was miraculously fed by an angel.

(19) Instruction of the Virgin in the Temple: The central figures of the scene, unfortunately, have been destroyed.

(20) The Virgin Receiving the Skein of Purple Wool: The priests decided to have the attendant maidens weave a veil for the Temple; the royal colours, purple, blue and scarlet, fell to Mary by lot.

(21) Zacharias Praying before the Rods of the Suitors: When the time came for the Virgin to be married, the High Priest Zacharias called all the widowers together and placed their rods on the altar, praying for a sign showing to whom she should be given.

(22) The Virgin Betrothed to Joseph: When the rods were returned to the

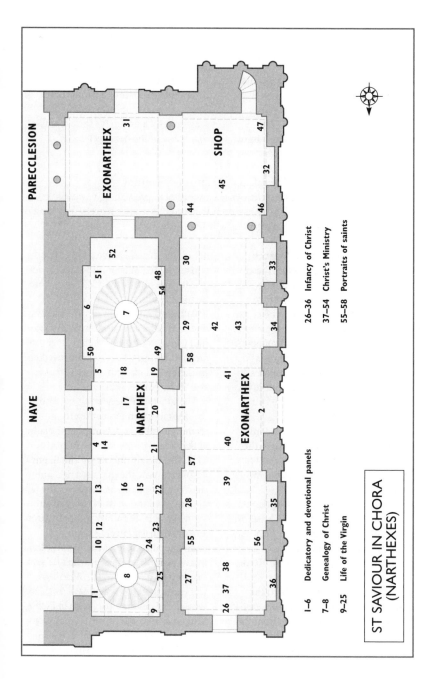

ST SAVIOUR IN CHORA
(NARTHEXES)

1–6   Dedicatory and devotional panels
7–8   Genealogy of Christ
9–25 Life of the Virgin

26–36 Infancy of Christ
37–54 Christ's Ministry
55–58 Portraits of saints

NAVE

PARECCLESION

EXONARTHEX

NARTHEX

EXONARTHEX

SHOP

widowers, Joseph's rod began to sprout with green leaves and the Virgin was awarded to him.

(23) Joseph taking the Virgin to his House: They are shown just leaving the Temple; the youth is one of Joseph's sons by his former wife.

(24) The Annunciation of the Virgin: The Angel Gabriel appears to Mary as she is fetching water from a well.

(25) Joseph taking leave of the Virgin; Joseph reproaching the Virgin: Joseph had to go away for six months on business; when he returned he found the Virgin pregnant and was angry (until reassured by a dream, as shown in the first scene of the next cycle).

IV. The infancy of Christ (exonarthex)

Each of the scenes occupies a lunette of the exonarthex, proceeding clockwise round all seven bays. The cycle is largely based on the accounts in the Gospels, and most of the scenes are inscribed with quotations which identify them.

(26) Joseph's Dream; the Journey to Bethlehem: The inscriptions read 'Behold, the angel of the Lord appeared to him in a dream, saying: "Joseph, thou son of David, fear not to take unto thee Mary thy wife: for that which is conceived in her is of the Holy Ghost"'. (Matt. 1:20); second scene uninscribed; third scene inscribed: 'And Joseph also went up from Galilee...unto the city of David, which is called Bethlehem...' (Luke 2:4).

(27) The Enrolment for Taxation: Inscription: '...(because he was of the House of David) to be taxed with Mary, his espoused wife, being great with child'. (Luke 2:4–5).

(28) The Nativity: The inscription is simply the title 'The Birth of Christ'. To the shepherds the angel says: 'Fear not; for behold, I bring you tidings of great joy, which shall be to all people'. (Luke 2:10).

(29) The Journey of the Magi; the Magi before Herod: Inscription: 'And behold, there came wise men from the East to Jerusalem, saying: "Where is he that is born King of the Jews?"' (Matt.

1:12). The second scene shows Herod consulting the Magi for information regarding the birthplace of Christ, whom he secretly wishes to destroy.

(30) Herod enquiring of the Priests and Scribes: Partly destroyed; inscription (mutilated): 'And when he had gathered all the priests and scribes together he demanded of them where Christ should be born'. (Matt. 2:4).

The lunette in the seventh bay above the door to the inner narthex, now blank, probably contained the Adoration of the Magi.

(31) The Flight into Egypt: Main scene destroyed, only the title remains. To the right of the window is a scene of the fall of idols from the walls of an Egyptian town as the Holy Family passes by (from an apocryphal source).

(32) The Massacre of the Innocents: Inscription: 'Then Herod, when he saw that he was mocked of the Wise Men, was exceeding wroth, and sent forth and slew all the children that were in Bethlehem, and in all the coasts thereof, from two years and under'. (Matt. 2:16).

(33) Mothers Mourning their Chil-

dren: Inscription: 'In Rama was there a voice heard, lamentation and weeping, and great mourning'. (Matt. 2:18).

(34) The Flight of Elizabeth: The inscription is the title. The scene, from the Protoevangelium, depicts Elizabeth with her baby son, John the Baptist, born about the same time as Christ, seeking refuge from the massacre in the mountains, which open up to receive her.

(35) The Return of the Holy Family from Egypt: Inscription: 'Being warned of God in a dream, he (Joseph) turned aside into the parts of Galilee: and he came and dwelt in a city called Nazareth'. (Matt. 2:22–23).

(36) Christ Taken to Jerusalem for the Passover: Inscription: 'Now his parents went to Jerusalem every year at the Passover'. (Luke 2:41).

V. Christ's Ministry (exonarthex and narthex)

This cycle occupies the domical vaults of each bay of the exonarthex as well as parts of the south bay of the narthex. Many scenes have been lost or reduced to mere fragments.

(37) Christ among the Doctors.

(38) John the Baptist Bearing Witness of Christ: Inscription: 'This was he of whom I spake, he that cometh after me is preferred before me: for he was before me'. (John 1:15).

(39) Temptation of Christ: The four scenes are accompanied by a running dialogue between Christ and the Devil (Matt. 4:3–10): 1. Devil: 'If thou be the Son of God, command that these stones be made bread'. Christ: 'It is written, Man shall not live by bread alone, but by every word that proceedeth out of the mouth of God'; 2. Devil: 'All these things will I give thee, if thou wilt fall down and worship me'. Christ: 'Get thee behind me, Satan' (the Devil has offered 'all the kingdoms of the world', represented by six kings in a walled town); 3. 'Then the Devil taketh him up to the holy city (and setteth him on a pinnacle of the temple)'; 4. Devil: 'If thou be the Son of God, cast thyself down'. Christ: 'It is written, thou shalt not tempt the Lord thy God'.

(40) The Miracle at Cana.

(41) The Multiplication of the Loaves.

(42) Christ Healing a Leper.

(43) Christ walking on the Water.

(44) Christ Healing the Paralytic at the Pool at Bethesda.

(45) Christ Healing the Paralytic at Capernaum.

(46) Christ and the Samaritan Woman at the Well.

(47) Christ Healing the Blind Man.

(48) Christ Healing the Blind and Dumb Man.

(49) Christ Healing the two Blind Men.

(50) Christ Healing Peter's Mother-in-Law.

(51) Christ healing the Woman with the Issue of Blood.

(52) Christ healing the Man with the Withered Hand.

(53) Christ Healing the Leper.

(54) Christ Healing a Multitude.

VI. Portraits of saints (exonarthex)

The soffits of the arches in the exonarthex are decorated with the portraits of martyr-saints; there were originally 50, of which 37 still exist in whole or in part. The portraits were of two kinds: busts in medallions, and full-length standing figures. In addition to these there were also a dozen portraits of saints on the pilasters that receive the transverse arches in the exonarthex, of which only battered fragments of six have survived.

The six panels in the first, second and third bays would seem to have been devoted to portraits of those who, by divine intervention, were precursors of the Incarnation. Facing one another across the exonarthex between the first and second bays are **St Anne (55)** with the infant Mary in her arms and her husband **Joachim (56)**. Between the second and third bays is the **Virgin and Child (57)**; facing this there was in all probability the figure of Joseph. On the east pilaster between the third and fourth bays is a small fragment of **St John the Baptist (58)**; across from this there would have been a portrait of either John's father Zacharias or his mother Elizabeth.

The nave

The nave is well lit by great triple-arched windows in the apse and in two of the tympanum walls (that on the north has been blocked). The dome is Turkish, made with wood and covered with plaster. The drum is from the reconstruction of 1315–21. It has 16 flutes, each pierced by a window. Three mosaics of great beauty survive:

(A) Christ: On the left of the bema arch (*see plan on p. 172*). Christ holds the Gospels open to Matthew 11:28: 'Come unto me, all ye that labour and are heavy laden, and I will give you rest'.

(B) The Virgin Hodegetria: On the right of the bema arch, with fragments of an inscription reading: 'The Mother of God, the Dwelling-place of the Uncontainable'.

(C) The Dormition of the Virgin: On the west wall, above the entrance door, the Virgin is shown laid out on her bier. Behind her Christ holds her soul, represented as a babe in swaddling clothes, while over his head hovers a six-winged seraph. Around the bier stand the Apostles, Evangelists and early bishops. The theme is taken from an apocryphal work ascribed to St John the Divine.

The parecclesion

The parecclesion was also a construction of Metochites, designed to serve as a funerary chapel. The north and south walls are articulated into bays by pilasters. Four recessed niches (arcosolia) are built within the thickness of the walls, one on each side of each of the two bays; these were designed to serve as sepulchral monuments for Metochites and other important persons.

The superb fresco decoration was the last part of Metochites's work of redecoration, carried out probably in 1320–21. The great but unknown master artist of these frescoes also, probably, created the mosaics in the rest of the church. The decoration of the chapel is designed to illustrate its purpose as a place of burial. Above the level of the cornice the paintings represent the Resurrection and the Life, the Last Judgement, Heaven and Hell, and The Mother of God as the bridge between Earth and Heaven. Below the cornice, there is a procession of saints and martyrs. A door on the north side leads into the diaconicon, which probably served as the sacristy for the chapel.

The *Anastasis*. Christ breaks down the gates of Hell and raises Adam and Eve from the grave.

I. Scenes of Resurrection

(59) The *Anastasis*: This scene, from the Greek for 'raising up', is known in English as the *Harrowing of Hell*. The central figure is Christ, who has just broken down the gates of Hell, which lie beneath his feet, while Satan lies bound before him. With his right hand Christ pulls Adam out of his tomb; behind Adam stand St John the Baptist, David, Solomon, and other righteous kings. With his left hand he pulls Eve out of her tomb; standing in it is Abel and behind him another group of the righteous. This is surely one of the greatest paintings in the world, and the apogee of Byzantine art in its last renaissance.

(60) Christ raising the Widow's Son.
(61) Christ raising Jairus' Daughter.

II. The Last Judgement

(62) The Second Coming of Christ: This vast scene occupies the whole domical vault; the title is inscribed at the centre. It represents the Doctrine of the Four Last Things: death, judgement, immortality in Heaven or damnation in Hell. In the crown is the Scroll of Heaven (Revelation 6:14). In the east half sits Christ in Judgement. To the souls of the saved on his right he says: 'Come, ye blessed of my Father, inherit the kingdom prepared for you from the foundation of the world'. To the condemned souls on his left he says: 'Depart from me, ye cursed, into everlasting fire, prepared for the Devil and his angels'. (Matt. 25). Below to the left, a river of fire broadens into a lake in which are the damned. Below Christ is the empty throne prepared for the Second Coming, with Adam and Eve prostrate before it. Below this is depicted the Weighing and Condemnation of Souls. The west half of the vault is occupied by the Choirs of the Elect in clouds.

(63) The Land and the Sea giving up their Dead.

(64) An Angel conducts the Soul of Lazarus to Heaven.

(65) Lazarus the Beggar in Abraham's Bosom.

(66) The Rich Man in Hell.

(67) The Torments of the Damned: The scenes in the east half of the lunette are identified as: (upper left) the Gnashing of Teeth; (upper right) the Outer Darkness; (lower left) the Worm that Sleepeth Not; (lower right) the Unquenchable Fire.

(68) The Entry of the Elect into Paradise: The Elect are led by St Peter toward the Gate of Paradise, guarded by a Cherub; the Good Thief welcomes them and points to the enthroned Mother of God.

III. The Mother of God and her Prefigurations

This cycle, in the west dome and bay, represents the Blessed Virgin in a series of five episodes from the Old Testament, which came to be symbolically interpreted as prefigurations or 'types' of the Mother of God and the Incarnation. The **Virgin and Child (69)** in the crown are surrounded by the **heavenly court of angels** in the spaces between the ribs. Four hymnographers are shown in the pendentives. These poets were chosen because in their hymns, verses of which are inscribed on their scrolls, they referred to the prefigurations of the Virgin depicted below. They are **St John Damascene (70), St Cosmas the Poet (71), St Joseph the Poet (72), St Theophanes (73).** Other scenes are as follows:

(74) Jacob's Ladder: Jacob wrestling with the Angel (west half of north lunette). The ladder or bridge to heaven is a prefiguration of the Virgin. The inscription reads: 'And Jacob took one of the stones of the place, and put it at his head, and dreamed; and behold, a ladder fixed on the earth, whose top reached to heaven, and the angels of God ascended and descended on it. And the Lord stood upon it.' (Genesis 28:11–13). Note that the Lord, here and elsewhere, is represented by the Virgin and Child.

(75) Moses and the Burning Bush: The story is represented in a scene in the east half of the north lunette and another on the soffit of the adjacent arch: *Moses before the Bush*; *Moses removes his Sandals*; *Moses hides his Face*. The burning bush

that was not consumed was another prefiguration of the Virgin. The first scene is inscribed: 'Now Moses came to the mountain of God, even to Horeb. And the angel of the Lord appeared unto him in a flame of fire out of the bush…saying "Put off thy shoes from off thy feet, for the place whereon thou standest is holy ground"'. (Exodus 3:1–5). The second scene, on the arch, is inscribed: 'And Moses hid his face; for he was afraid to look upon God'. (Exodus 3:6).

(76) The Dedication of Solomon's Temple: This event is depicted in four scenes on the south wall: *The Bearing of the Ark of the Covenant*; *The Bearing of the Sacred Vessels*; *Solomon and all Israel*; *The Installation of the Ark in the Holy of Holies.* The Ark of the Covenant is here symbolised as a prefiguration of the Virgin. The first scene, in the west half of the south lunette, is inscribed: 'And it came to pass when Solomon was finished building the house of the Lord, that he assembled all the elders of Israel in Sion, to bring the Ark of the Covenant of the Lord out of the City of David, that is Sion, and the priests took up the Ark of the Covenant and the tabernacle of the testimony'. (I Kings 8:1–4). The inscription on the second scene, on the soffit of the arch, is lost, but it was probably a continuation of verse 4: 'and the holy vessels that were in the tabernacle of testimony'. The third scene, on the east half of the south lunette, is inscribed: 'And the King and all Israel were assembled before the Ark.' (v. 5). The fourth scene, on the west half of the south lunette, is inscribed: 'And the priests bring in the Ark of the Covenant into its place, into the oracle of the house, even into the holy of holies, under the wings of the cherubim.' (I Kings 8:6).

(77) The Angels Smiting the Assyrians before Jerusalem: Here (south soffit of the west arch), the inviolable city is a prefiguration of the Virgin. The inscription on Isaiah's scroll is almost illegible, but probably reads: 'Thus saith the Lord concerning the King of Assyria: "He shall not come into this city"'. (Isaiah 37:33).

(78) Aaron and his Sons before the Altar: Here (north soffit of the west arch)the altar is a prefiguration of the Virgin. The inscription, almost illegible, is perhaps: 'They draw nigh to the altar and offer their sin-offerings and their whole burnt-offerings.' (Leviticus 9:7).

(79) The Souls of the Righteous in the

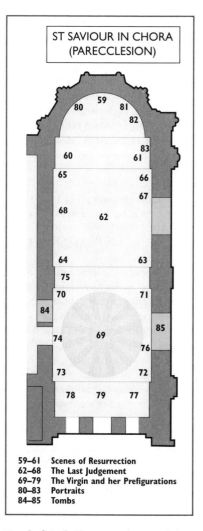

ST SAVIOUR IN CHORA
(PARECCLESION)

59–61	Scenes of Resurrection	
62–68	The Last Judgement	
69–79	The Virgin and her Prefigurations	
80–83	Portraits	
84–85	Tombs	

Hand of God: This scene (crown of the west arch) is almost entirely lost, but you can make out part of the hand of God holding the souls of the righteous, represented as infants in swaddling bands.

Portraits on the walls

A long frieze of portraits encircles the chapel walls. In the **apse** are full-length figures of six **Doctors of the Church**. The central three are St John Chrysostom **(80)**, St Basil **(81)** and St Gregory the Theologian **(82)**, whose relics are preserved in the church of the Ecumenical Patriarchate (*see p. 210*). In the rectangular panel on the south pier of the bema arch is a life-size depiction of the **Virgin and Child (83)** of the type called Eleousa, the Compassionate. There would originally have been a likeness of Christ on the opposite panel on the north side.

The **frieze** in the main body of the parecclesion consists mainly of depictions of martyrs and warrior-saints, the most prominent of them military figures in full armour.

The **site of Theodore Metochites' tomb (84)** is the first recess in the north wall. Opposite it is the **arcosolium of Michael Tornikes (85)**, a general who was a close friend of Metochites.

The **Asitane restaurant** just beside the Kariye museum is a good place for lunch after viewing the mosaics and frescoes (*see p. 295*).

ALONG DRAMAN CADDESİ

On Draman Cd., which leads between Kariye Müzesi and Fethiye Camii, there are two ancient Byzantine buildings, more or less opposite one another. **Kefeli Camii** (or Kefevi Camii; *map p. 343, A3*), a long narrow building now used as a mosque, may have been the refectory of the Monastery of the Prodromos (St John the Baptist), which is known to have been in this area. It has been dated variously from the 9th to the 12th century.

A short way farther east, turn left into a ramshackle yard. At the back, a gate leads into a further yard where you can see the fragmentary apse of a tiny Byzantine building. This is known as **Boğdan Saray**, the 'Moldavian Palace', because from the 16th–18th centuries it served as a private chapel attached to the palace of the Hospodars of Moldavia. In origin it appears to date from the 12th–13th century and it is thought to have been a funerary chapel dedicated to St Nicholas. At the beginning of the 20th century it had an upper storey with a dome, but the owner plundered it for building material and now all that remains is this small ruin.

Draman Camii

Draman Camii (*map p. 343, A3*) is a small mosque standing on a high terrace, reached by a double staircase from the street. It is a minor work of Sinan. Inscriptions show that the külliye was founded in 1541 by Yunus Bey, the famous interpreter (in Turkish, *drağman*, or dragoman) of Süleyman the Magnificent. According to Bassano da Zara, Venetian ambassador to the Sublime Porte, Yunus Bey was a Greek from Modon and 'possessed the Turkish, Greek and Italian languages to perfection'. In collaboration with Alvise Gritti, bastard son of the Doge of Venice, he wrote in the Venetian dialect a brief but very important account of the organisation of the Ottoman government. He also seems to have served on at least two occasions as the representative to the Venetian Republic of the Grand Vizier İbrahim Pasha.

THE SEVENTH HILL

The first six hills of old Constantinople are strung out in an almost straight line above the right bank of the Golden Horn. The Seventh Hill stands by itself toward the Marmara shore, comprising most of the southwest area of the old city. One of its two peaks is at Top Kapı (*map p. 342, A4*), from where it slopes north toward the valley which divides it from the Sixth, Fifth and Fourth hills. To the south it runs down to the Marmara shore. Though today this topography is largely hidden by high-rise constructions, the underlying features of the landscape are apparent from the heights, especially facing down onto the sea.

Two busy highways traverse the area. Millet Cd. runs up the back of the Seventh Hill to Top Kapı, once the Gate of Romanus in the Theodosian walls. Adnan Menderes Blv. follows the ancient course of the Lycus River, which is canalised beneath it.

Murat Paşa Camii

In the angle between Millet Cd. and Adnan Menderes Blv. stands the brick and stone Murat Paşa Camii (*map p. 347, B3*), one of the oldest vizieral mosques in the city. Murat Pasha was a convert to Islam from the imperial Palaeologus family; he became one of the Conqueror's viziers and died in battle as a relatively young man. The date of construction of his mosque is given on a stone plaque over the gate as 1473.

This is the later of the two mosques of the Bursa type that survive in Istanbul (the other is Mahmut Paşa Camii, built seven years before; *see p. 128*). The porch has handsome ancient columns, two of Syenitic granite, four of *verd antique*, with pairs of capitals arranged symmetrically. The rectangular inner space is divided by an arch into two square areas each covered by a dome. The two small side chambers were used as hostels for travelling dervishes. The eastern dome rests on pendentives while the western one has the same arrangement of triangles as the smaller domes at Mahmut Paşa Camii.

THE CERRAHPAŞA DISTRICT

Cerrah Paşa Camii (*map p. 347, A3*), a fine mosque standing in a walled garden, lends its name to the whole surrounding neighbourhood. Its founder, Cerrah Mehmet Pasha, was a barber and surgeon (*cerrah*) who rose in the favour of Murat III after performing the circumcision of his son, the future Mehmet III. The latter appointed him Grand Vizier in 1598 and wrote him a letter warning that he would be drawn and quartered if he did not do his duty. He was dismissed after about six months—without being drawn and quartered—after the failure of a military campaign against Hungary.

An Arabic inscription over the mosque door gives the date as 1593; the architect was Davut Ağa, Sinan's successor as Chief Imperial Architect. The plan is an interesting modification of the hexagon-in-rectangle type. The four domes that flank the central

The hexagon-in-rectangle ceiling of Cerrah Paşa Camii.

dome at the corners, instead of being oriented along the diagonals of the rectangle, are parallel with the cross axis. Such a plan is seen elsewhere only in Hekimoğlu Ali Paşa Camii, which is a little farther west (*see overleaf*).

Immediately across the street there is an interesting **medrese**, built in the second half of the 16th century by Gevher Sultan, daughter of Selim II and wife of the great admiral Piyale Pasha (*see p. 207*).

The Column of Arcadius

Haseki Kadın Sk. leads between Cerrahpaşa Cd. and Haseki Hürrem Cd. (*map p. 347, A3*). A few metres up the street on the right, are the weather-beaten remains of a massive column base wedged between two buildings. This is all that is left of the Column of Arcadius, erected by that emperor in 402 to commemorate his military triumphs. It stood in the centre of the Forum of Arcadius and was decorated with spiral bands of sculpture in bas relief representing the emperor's victories, like Trajan's column in Rome. At the top of the column, which was more than 50m high, there was an enormous statue of Arcadius, placed there in 421 by his son and successor, Theodosius II. This statue was eventually toppled from the column and destroyed during an earthquake in 704.

The column itself remained standing for more than another thousand years until it was deliberately demolished in 1715, when it appeared to be in imminent danger of collapsing on the neighbouring houses. Now all that remains are the mutilated base (*in situ*) and some fragments of sculpture in the Archaeological Museum.

The külliye of Bayram Pasha

On the corner of Haseki Kadın Sk. and Haseki Cd. is the külliye of Bayram Pasha, now undergoing restoration as the Bayrampaşa Cultural Centre. On the right are the medrese and mektep. When the külliye was built (1634), Bayram Pasha was governor of Istanbul. Two years later he became Grand Vizier under Murat IV and soon afterwards he died on the sultan's expedition against Baghdad.

On the left is the sebil and behind it Bayram Pasha's grand **türbe**. At the far end of the enclosed garden and graveyard stands the **mescit**, which is flanked on two sides by the porticoed cells of the dervish **tekke**. The mescit is a large octagonal building which served also as the room where the dervishes performed their mystical ceremonies. The whole complex is finely built of ashlar in the high classical manner.

THE KÜLLİYE OF HASEKİ HÜRREM

The külliye of Haseki Hürrem (*map p. 347, A3; under restoration at the time of writing*), built by Süleyman the Magnificent for his wife, Haseki Hürrem, the famous Roxelana (*see p. 135*), is surpassed in magnificence only by the mosque complexes of Fatih Sultan Mehmet and Süleyman the Magnificent himself. It was designed by Sinan and completed in 1539, making this the earliest known külliye by the great architect in Istanbul. According to tradition, Süleyman kept the project secret from Roxelana while it was being built, and brought her to the site only on the day it was dedicated in her honour.

> My own queen, my everything, my all, my shining moon;
> My boon companion, beloved, sovereign beauty, my sultan,
> My life, my gift, my raison d'être…
> I stand at your door to honour you, to sing your praises, on and on…
> *Lines from a poem written by Süleyman to Roxelana*

The buildings of the külliye

The mosque itself, preceded by its little porch, is quite modest. The other buildings of the complex, however, are magnificent. The **medrese**, on the other side of Haseki Cd., is truly imperial in its dimensions and handsome in detail. The columns of its portico are of granite, Proconnesian marble and *verd antique*; their lozenge capitals are decorated with small rosettes and medallions, as well as here and there a sort of snaky garland motif—a unique design. Also unique are the two pairs of lotus flower capitals, their leaves spreading out at the top to support a sort of abacus. Two carved hemispherical bosses in the spandrels of the arcade show the location of the dershane. Next to the medrese is the **mektep**, two storeys high with wide projecting eaves.

The **imaret**, beyond the mektep, is centred on a long rectangular courtyard, shaded with trees. The kitchens with their large domes and cluster of chimneys are best seen from the outside, in Özbek Sk. The **hospital** is also entered from Özbek Sk. It is built around an octagonal courtyard, off which open two large corner eyvans, with which all the other wards in the hospital communicated.

THE DAVUTPAŞA & ALTIMERMER DISTRICTS

On Hekimoğlu Ali Paşa Cd., set back from the road and partly concealed by trees and houses, is the fine old mosque that has given its name to this quarter. This is **Davut Paşa Camii** (*map p. 346, C2*), built in 1485. Davut Pasha, the founder, was Grand Vizier under Beyazıt II. The mosque is a very simple square chamber covered by a dome and with quite an elaborate mihrab in the form of a five-sided apse projecting from the east wall. The small rooms at the sides were used as hostels for travelling dervishes. The shallow dome rests on beautiful pendentives, magnificent examples of stalactite carving reaching some way down the corners of the walls. The founder's türbe is in the graveyard behind the mosque. The medrese of the külliye stands across the street to the north.

Hekimoğlu Ali Paşa Camii

This is a grand and interesting mosque (*map p. 346, C2*). Its founder, Ali Pasha, was an Ottoman nobleman who was the son (*oğlu*) of the court physician (*hekim*), and was himself Grand Vizier for 15 years under Mahmut I (he endowed the street-fountain Fındıklı; *see p. 235*). A long inscription in Turkish verse over the door to the mosque gives the date of construction as 1734–35; the architect was Ömer Ağa.

This complex may be said either to be the last of the great classical buildings or the first in the new Baroque style, for it has characteristics of both. At the corner of the precinct wall beside the north entrance is a lovely marble **sebil** with five bronze grilles. Above it is an elaborate **frieze** with a long inscription and carvings of vines, flowers and rosettes in the new Rococo style that had recently been introduced from France.

The façade of the **türbe** along the street is clad in marble, corbelled out toward the top and with a çeşme at the far end. It is a large rectangular building with two domes dividing it into two equal square areas, a rare form for this period. Farther along the precinct wall stands the monumental gateway with a domed chamber above; this was the **library** of the foundation and is still a library today, the Turkish-Islamic Arts Library. From the columned porch at the top of the steps leading to it there is a good view of the whole complex, with its garden full of tall cypresses and aged plane trees and opposite, the stately porch and slender minaret of the mosque.

The whole complex within the precinct wall has been well restored. The mosque itself is built in the classical Ottoman imperial style, and in its basic form is an almost exact copy of the Cerrah Paşa Camii (*see p. 183*). It is less successful overall, though possessing its own charm.

THE ALTIMERMER DISTRICT

The name of this district is a direct translation from the Greek *Exi Marmara*, meaning 'Six Marble Columns'. On Sırrı Paşa Sk. is a Greek Orthodox church surrounded by a garden. This is the church of the **Panaghia Gorgoepikoös** (*map p. 346, C2*), the Virgin 'Swift to Hear'. The church is referred to as early as 1342, and the first mention of it after the Conquest is in Tryphon's list of 1583. The epithet Panaghia Gorgoepikoös seems to be a survival of the ancient cult of Athena. Ancient architectural fragments found nearby suggest that a temple of Heracles or Zeus may have stood here. The eponymous six marble columns were part of its fabric.

The enormous open reservoir known as the **Cistern of St Mocius** (*map p. 246, C1*) is situated on an eminence that in Byzantine times was called Xerolophos, 'Dry Hill'. The name of the reservoir came from a church which stood nearby. It was constructed during the reign of Anastasius I (r. 491–518) and like the two other surviving Roman reservoirs, it fell into disuse in the later Byzantine period. It has now been converted into a recreation area known as the Fatih Educational Park. The cistern is a vast rectangle measuring 170m by 147m on the inside, with walls 6m thick; the present depth is about 10–15m. On the east and south sides the wall emerges, between 2m to 4m, from the surrounding earth. The walls are of good late Roman construction, they are composed of brick, alternating both inside and out with beds of dressed stone, 15cm to 20cm high. The interior of the cistern is most easily reached on the north side.

Ramazan Efendi Camii

This mosque, also known as Hüsrev Çelebi Camii (*map p. 346, B2*), is small but charming, with a pretty garden courtyard in front. It was founded by an official in the Ottoman court named Hoca Hüsrev; Ramazan Efendi Camii was the first *şeyh* of the dervish tekke that was part of the original külliye. The mosque was designed and built by

Detail of the late 16th-century Iznik tiles in Ramazan Efendi Camii.

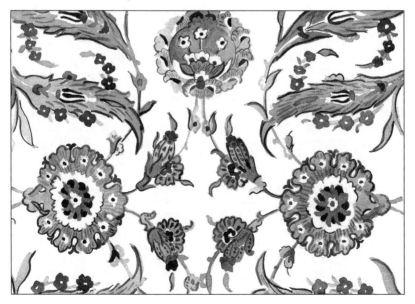

Sinan, and a long inscription over the inner door by his friend, the poet Mustafa Sa'i, gives the date as 1586, when the great architect was well into his nineties.

The plan is extremely simple: a small rectangular room with a wooden roof and porch. It is thought that it was originally covered by a wooden dome; the present wooden ceiling dates from a restoration after an earthquake. The minaret is an elegant structure both in proportion and detail, while the small şadırvan in the courtyard is exquisitely carved. The great fame of the mosque, however, comes from the magnificent panels of faience with which it is adorned. These are from the Iznik kilns at the height of their artistic production, and are some of the finest tiles in existence; the borders of red Armenian bole are especially celebrated.

KOCAMUSTAFAPAŞA & SAMATYA

Sancaktar Hayrettin Mescidi

The octagonal Byzantine building known as Sancaktar Hayrettin Mescidi (*map p. 346, C2*) is identified by some as one of the buildings of the Monastery of Gastria, said to have been founded in the 4th century by St Helena, mother of Constantine the Great, and which derived its name of Gastria, meaning 'vases', from the vases of aromatic plants she brought back from Calvary, where she had discovered the True Cross. There are no records of the monastery before the 9th century, and the identification with St Helena's foundation is likely to be fanciful.

The present building is octagonal on the exterior with a projecting apse at the east end; the interior takes the form of a domed cross. It is thought that it was once a funerary chapel, and has been dated variously from the 11th century to the 14th.

KOCA MUSTAFA PAŞA CAMİİ

Koca Mustafa Paşa Camii (*map p. 346, B2*), the mosque after which the avenue and the surrounding neighbourhood are named, was originally a Byzantine church, though its history is obscure. Some Byzantinists identify it with the church dedicated to St Andrew of Crete c. 1284 by Princess Theodora Raoulaina, which in turn may have been built on the foundations of an earlier church dedicated to St Andrew the Apostle. It certainly makes use of early spolia, especially capitals. What is certain is that the church was converted into a mosque by Koca Mustafa Pasha, Grand Vizier in the reign of Selim I (r. 1512–20).

When the church was converted, the interior arrangements were re-orientated by 90° because of the direction in which the building was laid out. Thus the mihrab and mimber are under the semidome against the south wall and the entrance is in the north wall. To get a view of the whole interior, make your way to the central bay of the narthex. This bay has a small dome supported by columns with beautiful 6th-century capitals of the pseudo-Ionic type. From here the central portal opens into a sort of inner narthex or aisle, separated from the nave by only two *verd antique* columns. The triple arcade supported by two columns on the west side probably originally continued to north and south as well, forming an ambulatory. Even in its greatly altered form it is an extremely attractive building.

The türbe of Sümbül Efendi

This is one of the most popular Muslim shrines in the city, for in one of the türbes in the courtyard the famous Istanbul folk-saint Sümbül Efendi (d. 1529) is buried. Sümbül Efendi was the first *şeyh* of the dervish tekke established here in the early 16th century, and ever since people have called on him in their prayers to help with personal problems. In the other türbe, according to legend, lie two daughters of Hussein, the grandson of Mohammed, who were allegedly brought to Byzantium as slaves. The ancient cypress above their türbe is said to possess miraculous powers.

SAMATYA

The district of Samatya derives its name from the Greek village which originally stood in this area, known as Psamatheia. As one of the independent walled settlements which existed within the city walls during the late Byzantine period, this village negotiated a surrender to Fatih's forces in 1453. Because it surrendered and was not taken by force, it was allowed to keep its churches, maintaining its position as a centre for Greek (and later Armenian) communities for another 500 years. When Selim I (r. 1512–20) tried to annexe all the surviving churches in the city, the Orthodox Patriarch managed to find three ancient Janissaries to testify that Mehmet II had allocated certain areas (including Samatya) to the Christians. In the 19th century Greeks began to make way for Armenians, who weathered the massacres of 1915–18, and whose numbers in this area perhaps even increased after the emergence of an independent Armenia in the 1990s. Recently, the area has seen an influx of migrants from central and eastern Anatolia.

Sulu Monastir

On Marmara Cd., a wide avenue that runs along the heights parallel to the sea, stands the large Armenian church of Surp Kevork (St George), in Turkish **Sulu Monastir** (*map p. 346, B2*). The present church is built on the site of an ancient Byzantine monastery dedicated to the Panaghia Peribleptos, the 'All-Seeing' Virgin. Excavation that began in 1998 revealed part of its structure. It was founded by the emperor Romanus III Argyrus (r. 1028–34), and after the recapture of Constantinople by the Byzantines in 1261 it was restored by Michael VIII Palaeologus (r. 1259–82). It remained in the hands of the Greeks after the Conquest, but then in 1458 Fatih gave it to the Armenians. The church served as the Patriarchate of the Armenian Gregorian Church until 1643–44, when it was supplanted by the church of Surp Asdvadzadzin in Kumkapı (*see p. 192*).

Canbaziye Sk. leads steeply downhill towards the Marmara. As you go down it, you see below you and to the left the domes of a large double bath known as **Ağa Hamamı** (*map p. 346, C2*), a work of Sinan, now used for commercial purposes and undergoing restoration. A number of Greek churches can be found in the area nearby, mostly 19th-century rebuildings of earlier structures.

İMRAHOR CAMİİ

Standing in a walled courtyard (*map p. 346, B3; no access at the time of writing*), the former Byzantine monastic church of St John the Baptist of Studius, known in Turkish as İmrahor Camii, is the oldest surviving Christian sanctuary in the city. Though in ruins, it is still one of the greatest monuments remaining from the days of Byzantium.

HISTORY OF ST JOHN THE BAPTIST OF STUDIUS

The church and monastery of St John the Baptist were built in the mid-5th century, endowed by the Roman patrician Studius, who served as consul during the reign of the emperor Marcian. The first monks in the Studion, as the monastery was called, were from an order known as the Akoimatoi ('the Unresting'), so called because they performed divine service day and night throughout the year, praying in shifts around the clock.

In its early years the Studion housed a thousand monks and was one of the richest and most populous monasteries in Byzantium. Together with all other monasteries in the Empire, it was suppressed during the Iconoclastic Period and did not resume life until 787, after the first restoration of icons by the empress Eirene, mother of Constantine VI.

The golden age in the history of the Studion began in 799, with the arrival of the great abbot Theodore, under whom the Studion became the most influential monastery in the Empire. Theodore was also an outspoken critic of court morals, and fell foul as a result of four emperors in turn. He died in exile on the island of Prinkipo (Büyükada; *see p. 282*) in 826, but was reburied in the garden of the Studion in 843, after the final restoration of icons under Michael III. Today he is venerated in the Greek Orthodox Church as St Theodore the Studite.

Under the direction of Theodore and his successors, the Studion flourished. Many monks won renown as hymnographers, icon painters and illuminators. The monastery was also noted for its scholarship and was one of the centres for the preservation and copying of ancient manuscripts, many of which would be carried to Europe by Byzantine scholars during the western Renaissance in the 14th–15th centuries.

On 15th August 1261, when the Byzantines recaptured Constantinople from the Latins, Michael VIII Palaeologus came in procession to the Studion, following the sacred icon of the Hodegetria. After reaching the Studion the icon was placed on the main altar of the church, and the emperor joined the Patriarch in a ceremony of thanksgiving. Then the emperor left the church, mounted his white charger in the square outside, and rode off to Haghia Sophia for his formal recoronation.

The Studion continued as one of the spiritual and intellectual centres of the Empire right up to the Conquest. During the first half of the 15th century the

University of Constantinople was located here; among its students and teachers were some of the greatest scholars in the history of Byzantium, men who would later be influential figures in the Italian Renaissance of the 15th century.

The Studion survived the fall of Byzantium and continued to function for nearly half a century after the Conquest, until, at the end of the 15th century, its church was converted into a mosque, founded by İlyas Bey, Master of the Horse (İmrahor) under Beyazıt II. What was left of the monastery in modern times was utterly destroyed in the earthquake of 1894. The church/mosque was also badly damaged, and from that time on it was abandoned and allowed to fall into ruins. At the time of writing, restoration was taking place.

The church

The church was basilican in plan, with a wide nave and narrow side aisles separated from each other by two rows of seven columns each. Its silhouette is well seen from the air (or Google Earth). Originally it was preceded by an atrium, or courtyard, whose site is now occupied by a walled garden. The narthex is divided into three bays; the wider central bay has a very beautiful portal consisting of four columns in antis, with magnificent Corinthian capitals supporting an elaborate, richly sculptured entablature. Two of the marble door-frames still stand between the columns. From the narthex five doors lead into the church. Six of the columns on the north side still stand; they are of *verd antique*, with capitals and an entablature as in the narthex. An upper row of columns above the aisle colonnades would have supported the wooden roof. The nave ends in a single semicircular apse, which would have been occupied by the synthronon. The interior was revetted with marble below and mosaics above.

NARLI KAPI & THE SEA WALLS

The ancient portal called **Narlı Kapı**, the 'Pomegranate Gate' (*map p. 346, B3*), was used in Byzantine times by the emperor when he went from the Great Palace to the Studion by sea. The imperial visit occurred annually on 28th August, the feast day of the Decapitation of St John, titular saint of the church. The emperor was received on the quay by the abbot, and the two then processed to the church between two files of monks holding lighted tapers. At the end of the service the emperor was served refreshments in the monastery gardens, after which he returned to the royal barge, passing once again through the portal, which even then was known as the Pomegranate Gate. A malodorous underpass now leads beneath the railway line and out to the sea walls.

Outside Narlı Kapı you come to a church built up against the sea walls. This is the Armenian Catholic church of **Surp Hovhannes Mıgırdıç** (St John the Baptist). It has been suggested (since the dedication is the same) that the original church here (though the location was moved slightly when the coastal highway was constructed) was Byzantine in foundation, and that it was a dependency of the Studion monastery.

The coastal highway, laid out on infilled land, was completed in 1959. Before that time the sea came right up to the Byzantine walls. Stretches of these survive, with the remains of some of their defence towers. They were built in the 9th century by the emperor Theophilus.

To explore the ancient Golden Gate, Yedikule and the land walls, see p. 194.

YENİKAPI & KUMKAPI

The present ferry station of Yenikapı (*map p. 348, A4*) occupies the **site of the ancient Harbour of Theodosius**. The area, in fact, had been a harbour since Constantine founded the city in AD 330. In 2004, during the construction of a new public transport facility, ancient remains were found and a team of archaeologists discovered the vestiges of more than 30 ships, along with the remnants of piers, warehouses and other structures, including parts of the city walls built by Constantine. The most spectacular find was made in 2008, when the skeletons of two adults and two children were unearthed along with the remains of a small Neolithic settlement dating from between 6400 BC and 5800 BC.

Kumkapı fishing harbour

The site of the ancient Kontoskalion Harbour is now known as Kumkapı, the 'Sand Gate' (*map p. 348, B4*). The harbour was originally built by Julian the Apostate (r. 361–63), and it was dredged and its fortifications strengthened and repaired by several later emperors. After the reconquest of the city from the Latins in 1261, Michael VIII Palaeologus made the Kontoskalion the main base for the Byzantine navy. The harbour silted up in Ottoman times and fell out of use. The lines of Çifte Genliner Cd. and Tavası Çeşmesi Sk., which form an arc some way inland, preserve the memory of the old harbour. A new harbour has now been created here for the local fishing fleet, which sells its catch in a market around the port. Kumkapı is the largest and busiest fishing harbour in the city. It is always filled with picturesque caiques and the quayside is often carpeted with brilliantly dyed fishing-nets spread there to be dried and mended by the fishermen and their families.

The old Armenian quarter

The area of Kumkapı inside the walls and railway line was once the Armenian quarter of the city, home also to a large number of Greeks. This is still a district of picturesque streets of pastel-wash houses with upper stories projecting out over the pavement. The main square of the area, **Kumkapı Meydanı**, is lively and picturesque and lined with fish restaurants.

The **Armenian Patriarchate** is located within the precinct of the Gregorian church of Surp Asdvadzadzin (the Immaculate Conception; *map p. 348, B4*). This was originally a Greek church, bequeathed to the Armenians after the Turkish Conquest and becoming the cathedral of the Armenian Patriarchate in 1641. The present church dates to a rebuilding in 1828 after a fire that destroyed the earlier building. Beneath the church there is an aghiasma dedicated to St Theodore.

ARMENIANS IN THE OTTOMAN EMPIRE

According to Edmondo de Amicis, in his 1877 travelogue *Constantinopoli*, the Ottoman Armenians were known as the 'camels of the Empire', which is to say they enjoyed a reputation for being hard-working, placid, pliable and not rebelliously ambitious. Like the Greeks and the Jews of Constantinople, the Armenians were principally traders and businessmen; some rose to positions of great power and influence within the imperial administration. During the later years of the Empire, Armenians found favour as architects, notably the Balyan family, who built mosques and palaces for all the sultans from Abdülhamit I to Abdülaziz. Among their best-known works are the famous landmarks of Dolmabahçe Palace, Beylerbeyi Palace and the mosque at Ortaköy.

After the Ottoman conquest in 1453, Mehmet II granted concessions to the Armenians, allowing them to build churches and to practise their religion. They have a patriarch, at the time of writing His Beatitude Mesrob II, who has been in office since 1998. As it does also for the Greek Patriarch, the Turkish government stipulates that the head of the Armenian Church in Istanbul must be a Turkish citizen. Most Istanbul Armenians belong to the Armenian Orthodox Church but there is also a small minority of Armenian Catholics, who recognise the pope as their spiritual leader.

At the beginning of the 20th century Armenians represented slightly under ten percent of the population of Istanbul. Since then numbers have dwindled greatly, an exodus precipitated by the terrible genocide of 1915–18, when over a million Ottoman Armenians were massacred.

The mosque known as **Tavası Süleyman Ağa Camii** (*map p. 348, B4–C4*) was founded early in the 17th century by Süleyman Ağa, a *tavası*, or black slave, who was castrated and sold to Topkapı Sarayı, where he rose to the rank of Chief Black Eunuch. The only part of the mosque remaining from the original foundation (the rest is a 19th-century rebuilding) is the ten-sided wooden minaret, a charming example of Ottoman wood-work.

THE LAND WALLS

The Byzantine land walls stretch for 6.5km from the Sea of Marmara to the Golden Horn. These fortifications protected Byzantium from its enemies for more than a thousand years, until the fateful day in late May 1453 when they were breached by Mehmet II and his army using a colossal cannon cast by a Hungarian. Today the walls are in ruins, the districts around them prey to dereliction and stray dogs. Nevertheless, they are still an impressive and evocative sight, with their tower-studded battlements marching across what were once the empty plains of Thrace.

HISTORY OF THE LAND WALLS

The land walls were largely built in the first half of the 5th century, during the reign of Theodosius II. The first phase of this Theodosian wall, completed in 413, consisted of a single wall with defence towers set at regular intervals. However, in 447 an earthquake destroyed much of this wall, throwing down 57 towers. This happened at a critical time, for Attila the Hun was then advancing on Constantinople. Reconstruction began immediately, and all the rival factions of the Hippodrome worked together, each of them assigned a certain stretch of the circuit. Within two months the walls had been rebuilt, stronger and better than before. Not only was the original wall consolidated, but an outer wall and moat were added, making the city virtually impregnable to assault by land. The new walls saved the city from Attila, Scourge of God, who turned back to ravage the western regions of the Roman Empire. In succeeding centuries the walls kept back other marauding armies: of Avars, of Arabs (a number of those who fell were buried here and in today's Islamic city they have martyrs' status) and of Bulgars. It was only with the invention of gunpowder that the walls met their match, finally to be stormed and broken down in 1453.

Design of the walls

The main element in the defence system (*see plan opposite*) was the **inner wall (A)**, about 5m thick at the base and rising to a height of 12m. This wall was guarded by 96 square or polygonal **towers (B)**, 18m to 20m high, at an average interval of 55m. Each tower was generally divided into two floors, which did not communicate with one another. The bottom storeys, used either for storage or as guard-houses, were entered from inside the city. The upper rooms were entered from the parapet walk, which was connected by staircases to the ground and to the tops of the towers.

Between the inner and outer walls there was a terrace, called the **peribolos (C)**, between 15m and 20m wide and standing about 5m above the level of the inner city. The

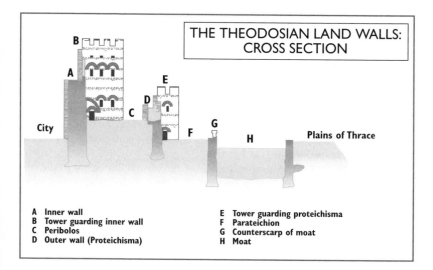

THE THEODOSIAN LAND WALLS:
CROSS SECTION

City

Plains of Thrace

A Inner wall
B Tower guarding inner wall
C Peribolos
D Outer wall (Proteichisma)

E Tower guarding proteichisma
F Parateichion
G Counterscarp of moat
H Moat

outer wall, the **proteichisma (D)**, was about 2m thick and 8.5m high. This wall also had 96 **towers (E)**, alternating in position with those of the inner wall. Beyond this there was an outer terrace called the **parateichion (F)**, bounded on the outside by the **counterscarp of the moat (G)**, which was a battlement nearly 2m high.

The **moat** itself **(H)** was originally about 10m deep and 20m wide, and was flooded when the city was threatened.

Most of the inner wall and nearly all of its towers are still standing, though many of the towers are in a tumbledown state. The outer walls have completely disappeared in many places, though sections of them have been reconstructed, particularly in the stretch near the Top Kapı, where you can see the whole cross-section of the defence-works from the inner ramparts to the outer works, including the ditch that extended along their outer periphery.

There are still 30 legible inscriptions recording imperial repairs on the towers, gates and ramparts between the Marmara and the Golden Horn; they range over a period of more than a thousand years, evidence of how carefully the Byzantines maintained the great walls that stood between them and their assailants.

The sea walls along the Marmara joined the land walls at the southwest corner of the city; they were anchored by the **Marble Tower** (map p. 346, A4), a tall square structure now isolated from the rest of the walls by the Marmara highway. It stands alone in the shoreside park. This tower is unlike any other structure in the whole defence system. It is thought that it may have been designed as a sea pavilion for the emperor and his party when they came by sea from the Great Palace to visit the shrine of the Zoödochos Pigi (the Balıklı Kilisesi; see p. 197). The tower also seems to have served, for a time, as a prison, and you can still see the chute down which the bodies of those executed were thrown into the sea.

YEDİKULE & THE GOLDEN GATE

Yedikule (*map p. 346, A4; open 9.30–5; closed Mon; metro to Yedikule or train from Sirkeci to Yedikule*), the Heptapyrgion or 'Castle of the Seven Towers', is a partly Byzantine and partly Turkish construction. The seven eponymous towers consist of four in the Theodosian wall itself, plus three additional towers built inside the walls by Fatih. The three inner towers are connected by a curtain wall, forming a five-sided enclosure. The two central towers in the Theodosian wall are marble pylons flanking the Golden Gate (*see below*) and are actually older than the walls themselves. Yedikule gained notoriety in Ottoman times when it was used as a prison.

The main entrance to Yedikule is by a gate near the east tower, sometimes called the **Tower of the Ambassadors** since in Ottoman times foreign envoys were often incarcerated here. Many of them carved their names upon the walls of the tower, and many of these inscriptions survive. The floors of the tower have fallen out but a staircase in the wall (no proper balustrade) leads up to the top. When at the top it is worth while walking around the *chemin de ronde* as far as the Golden Gate, for there is a fine view of the castle and of the Theodosian walls down to the sea.

The pylon to the left of the Golden Gate was also used as a prison in Ottoman times, and served as a place of execution. On display are the instruments of torture and execution that were used as well as the infamous 'well of blood', down which the heads of those executed in the tower were supposed to have been thrown to be flushed into the sea. Sultan Osman II was one of the many executed here, strangled with a bowstring after he was deposed on 22nd May 1622. He was only 17 years old.

The Golden Gate

The Golden Gate was a Roman triumphal arch erected c. 390 by Theodosius I at a point on the Via Egnatia which at that time was about 2km outside the city walls of Constantine (the present 'Theodosian walls' were built by Theodosius II). The arch was tripartite, consisting of a large central aperture flanked by two smaller ones. Their outlines can still be seen, although they were bricked up in later Byzantine times. The gates themselves were covered with gold plate—hence the name—and the façade was decorated with sculptures, the most famous of which was a group of four elephants, placed there to commemorate Theodosius' triumphal entry into the city after his victory over Maximus.

When Theodosius II decided to extend the city walls two decades later, he incorporated the Golden Gate within his new system of fortification, and it continued to be the scene of triumphal entries into the city by Byzantine emperors: Heraclius in 629 after he saved the Empire by defeating the Persians; Constantine V, Basil I and Basil II after their victories over the Bulgars; John I Tzimiskes after his defeat of the Russians; Theophilus and his son Michael III after their victories over the Arabs. Perhaps the most emotional of all these triumphal entries was that which took place on 15th August 1261, when Michael VIII Palaeologus rode through the Golden Gate on a white charger after Constantinople was recaptured from the Latins. This was also the last time an emperor of Byzantium rode in triumph through the Golden Gate. In its last two centuries, the history of the Empire was one of repeated defeat, and by that time the Golden Gate had been walled up for defence, never again to open. The next man to ride victorious into the city on a white horse would be Mehmet II in 1453.

Yedikule Kapı

Beyond the northernmost tower of Yedikule is Yedikule Kapı, a small portal which was the public entryway to this part of the city in Byzantine times, the Golden Gate being reserved for ceremonial occasions. In the interior above the archway there is an imperial Byzantine eagle in white marble.

THE CITY GATES

A number of gates, both civilian and military, pierced the land walls, with smaller posterns let into the fortifications as well. The original Byzantine names of the gates is still uncertain in some cases. At varying times in their history, gates were blocked up and unblocked again. Some have now been torn down altogether. The main gates that exist today, and the ones with the most interesting histories, are as follows:

Belgrat Kapı

Belgrat Kapı (*map p. 346, A3*) was known in Byzantium as the Second Military Gate or Porta tou Deuterou. Its Turkish name dates from after the conquest of Belgrade in 1521 by Süleyman the Magnificent, when he settled many of the artisans he brought back with him here. The stretch of walls just beyond it is in good condition, with all 13 towers still standing in the inner wall and only one missing in the outer. The third and fourth towers of the inner walls both bear 8th-century inscriptions of Leo III and Constantine V.

SİLİVRİ KAPI & BALIKLI KİLİSESİ

Silivri Kapı was known in Byzantium as the Porta tou Pigi because it was near the famous shrine of Zoödochos Pigi (*see below*). Like all of the larger gates, it is double, piercing both the inner and outer walls. The most memorable day in its history was 25th July 1261. On that day a small body of Greek troops, led by Alexius Strategopoulos, overpowered the Latin guards and forced their way inside, thus opening the way to the restoration of the Byzantine Empire in its ancient capital.

Just inside the gate is the attractive, recently restored **mosque of Hadım İbrahim Pasha** ('İbrahim Pasha the Eunuch'; *map p. 346, A2*), built in 1551. At the time İbrahim Pasha was Grand Vizier under Süleyman the Magnificent. The mosque has a fine porch with five domed bays, painted orange in their upper sections, and a portal surmounted by an elaborate stalactited hood. The open türbe of the founder stands in the garden.

The shrine of the Zoödochos Pigi (Balıklı Kilisesi)

The ancient shrine of Zoödochos Pigi, the Life-Giving Spring, is some 500m outside the walls in the vicinity of the Silivri Gate. It is approached by walking out from the gate along Seyitnizam Cd. for a short distance and veering right along Silivrikapı Balıklı Cd. The shrine, which stands to the left of this road just before the first crossroads, is known locally as Balıklı Kilisesi, the 'Church of the Fish', because of the carp that have swum in its sacred spring since Byzantine times.

According to tradition, the emperor Justinian, when on a hunting expedition nearby, met a crowd of women at the sacred spring who told him that its waters had been given healing powers by the Blessed Virgin. The emperor built a larger sanctuary to enclose the spring, using surplus materials from Haghia Sophia. This church remained in Greek hands after the Conquest. The present building dates from 1833.

The **outer courtyard** is particularly interesting for its tombstones, many of which have inscriptions in the Karamanlı script, i.e., Turkish written in the Greek alphabet. This was the script used by Turkish-speaking Anatolian Christians, whose clergy used Greek only in the liturgy. Many of the tombstones are carved with emblems representing the trade of the deceased: scissors for a tailor, scales for a grocer, a barrel for a tavern-keeper, etc. The **inner courtyard** has several elaborate tombs of bishops and patriarchs of the Greek Orthodox Church.

The **entrance to the shrine** is in the corner between the inner and outer courtyards. From there a long flight of steps leads down to a small chapel enclosing the sacred spring.

THE LEGEND OF THE FISH

The carp that swim in the aghiasma pool are the subject of legend. It is said that during the siege of Constantinople a monk was frying fish here when he was told that the city had fallen to the Turks. He claimed that he would only believe it if the fish jumped out of his pan and back into the water. They promptly did so, browned on one side and still gold on the other, though the fish that swim here today have reverted to their normal colour. It is considered great good fortune to see a fish in the pool (they do not always show themselves), and stories abound of people being healed of ailments here. The waters are said to be particularly efficacious against afflictions of the eyes.

Mevlana Kapı

In Byzantium the Mevlana Kapı (*map p. 346, A1*) was called the Gate of Rhegion, and sometimes also the Gate of the Reds, after the circus faction that built it. It is remarkable for the number of inscriptions preserved upon it: one of them indeed mentions the Red faction. The completion of the walls in 447 is commemorated in two inscriptions on the south corbel of the outer gate, one in Greek and the other in Latin. The Greek inscription merely gives the facts; the Latin one is more boastful, reading: 'By the command of Theodosius, Constantine erected these strong walls in less than two months. Scarcely could Pallas herself have built so strong a citadel in so short a span'.

The gate's Turkish name comes from the tekke of Mevlevi dervishes, **Yenikapı Mevlevihanesi**, that stands outside it. It burned down in 1961 but is now rebuilt and is used for *sema* performances (*for up-to-date information and news of events, see www. mevlanafoundation.com*).

There is an interesting Muslim shrine here too, approached by turning off from Mevlevihane Cd. to the right on Merkez Efendi Cd. (also accessible from the Topkapı tram stop). This is the **Merkez Efendi Tekkesi**, a 16th-century dervish lodge, founded by Şeyh Muslihiddin Merkez Musa Efendi, whose monumental türbe was reconstructed in 1837 by Şah Sultan, daughter of Selim III. According to Evliya Çelebi, Merkez Efendi built the tekke after he discovered here a miraculous aghiasma, which is still a popular shrine.

AROUND TOP KAPI

Top Kapı, the Cannon Gate (*map p. 342, A4*), was known in Byzantium as the Gate of St Romanus, because of its proximity to a church of that name. Its Turkish name stems from the siege in 1453, when the gate faced the largest cannon (*top*) in the Turkish arsenal, the famous Urban. This enormous weapon was named after the Hungarian engineer who made it for Mehmet II; it was 8m long, 20cm in diameter, and could fire a 1200-pound cannon ball a distance of one mile. This cannon caused considerable damage during the final days of the siege.

Panorama 1453 Museum

This museum, just outside Top Kapı (*open 9.30–5; take the tram to the Top Kapı stop*), celebrates the Ottoman conquest of Constantinople. The armies of Mehmet II breached the walls just north of Top Kapı and the Conqueror made his triumphal entry into the vanquished city through Edirne Kapı. The museum stands on the site where he pitched his tent. The circular hall, its roof painted to resemble the sky, represents in a fabulous 3D panoply the events of that great or calamitous day, 29th May 1453, when the armies of the 21-year-old Mehmet brought a crushing end to over a millennium of Christian rule and (barring the Latin interlude) to over two millennia of Greek control of the city, since the first colonists arrived in the 7th century BC. The information panels are in Turkish only (this is not a place intended to gladden the hearts of the conquered), but audio guides are available. Piped Janissary marches and simulated cannon fire, together with model cannon balls and other battle paraphernalia, aim to create a synaesthetic experience.

Takkeci İbrahim Ağa Camii

A short distance outside Top Kapı (*take the tram to the Top Kapı stop*) is Takkeci İbrahim Ağa Camii, recognisable immediately by its high wooden porch. The mosque was founded in 1592 by a certain İbrahim Ağa, who was a maker of the felt hats called *takke*, the most distinctive of which were the tall conical headdresses worn by the dervishes. Takkeci İbrahim Ağa Camii is the only ancient wooden mosque in Istanbul to have retained its porch and dome, spared by its remote location outside the walls from the many fires that destroyed or damaged all of the other structures of its type that once stood in the city.

The deeply projecting tiled roof of the porch is supported by a double row of wooden pillars. Since the porch extends halfway round both sides of the mosque, the pillars give the effect of a little copse of trees, the more so since the paint has long since worn off. The roof itself has three dashing gables along the façade; a very quaint and pretty arrangement. On the right rises the fine minaret with a beautiful stalactited şerefe.

Inside the mosque, the walls are revetted with tiles from the greatest Iznik period. There are some very elegant scrolling vine motifs in the mihrab.

Kara Ahmet Paşa Camii

Just opposite the end of Topkapı Cd., inside the walls, is Kara Ahmet Paşa Camii (*map p. 342, B3*), one of the most masterful of all Sinan's works. It was built in 1554 for Kara Ahmet Pasha, who at that time served as Grand Vizier under Süleyman the Magnificent.

Above the niches in the mosque porch are some exceptional tiles, in apple-green and vivid yellow, in the *cuerda seca* technique. They are the latest recorded examples of the second period of the Iznik potteries, the only other important examples being those in the türbe of the Şehzade and the fine series of panels in the mosque of Selim I.

Inside the mosque, the wooden ceilings under the west galleries, painted with elaborate arabesques, are original features. This is perhaps the most extensive and best-preserved example of this kind of painting in the city. The ceiling on the left is a partial restoration, the one on the right is original.

Outside the courtyard wall, towards the west, is the founder's türbe. Beyond it stands the large double mektep, of a very interesting design: a long rectangular building with a wooden roof. It is still in use as a primary school, one of the very few Ottoman mekteps that continues to serve its original purpose.

TOP KAPI TO EDİRNE KAPI

The stretch of fortifications between Top Kapı and Edirne Kapı, known in Byzantium as the Mesoteichion ('Middle Wall'), was the most vulnerable in the whole defence system, since here the fortifications descend into the valley of the Lycus, the river which entered the city midway between the two gates, where Adnan Menderes Blv. now runs. During the last siege, the defenders on the Mesoteichion were at a serious disadvantage, being below the level of the Turkish guns on either side of the valley. Thus it is that this is the most badly damaged stretch of the fortifications and in fact it was this section of the walls that was finally breached by the Turks on the morning of 29th May 1453. The final charge was led by a giant Janissary named Hasan, who fought his way up onto one of the outer towers. Though Hasan himself was slain, his companions managed to force their way across the peribolos and over the inner wall into the city. Within hours Constantinople had fallen.

The Entry of Mehmet II into Constantinople (1903). From the leafy fastness of Yıldız Palace, from
where he seldom ventured into old Stamboul, the reactionary and autocratic sultan Abdülhamit II
commissioned his court painter, the Venetian-born Orientalist Fausto Zonaro, to produce a series of
scenes from the life of Mehmt the Conqueror. This is one of the most famous.

Just inside the walls between Adnan Menderes Blv. and the former Fifth Military Gate, about 400m to the north, around Kaleboyu Cd., is the area called Sulukule ('Water Tower'; *map p. 342, B3*). From late Byzantine times until the summer of 2009, this was the Roma quarter of the city. They were evicted to make way for redevelopment.

According to tradition it was on this part of the walls that Constantine XI had his command post during the final siege. He was last seen there just before the walls were breached, fighting valiantly beside his cousins Theophilus Palaeologus and Don Francisco of Toledo and his faithful comrade John Dalmata, none of whom survived. The Fifth Military Gate is known in Turkish as Hücum Kapısı, the 'Gate of the Assault', preserving the memory of that last battle.

Edirne Kapı

Edirne Kapı (*map p. 342, C2*) stands at the highest point in the old city, 77m above sea-level. This gate has preserved in Turkish form one of its ancient names, Porta Adrianopoleos, as this was the beginning of the main road to Adrianople, Turkish Edirne. It was also known in Byzantium as the Gate of Charisius, or sometimes as the Porta Polyandriou, the Gate of the Polyandrion, or cemetery. This latter name came from the large necropolis outside the walls in this area; this still exists with large Turkish, Greek and Armenian burial-grounds. It was through Edirne Kapı that Mehmet II made his triumphal entry after his capture of Constantinople, early in the afternoon of 29th May 1453, and a plaque on the south side of the gate commemorates that historic event. Depictions of his entry into the city have become iconic. A painting by Fausto Zonaro shows him astride a white horse, green and red standards flying in his wake, with a turmoil of fallen Christians, horses and valiant gazis at his feet (*illustrated on previous page*).

MİHRİMAH SULTAN CAMİİ

Just inside Edirne Kapı to the south stands the splendid Mihrimah Sultan Camii (*map p. 342, C2*), one of the great imperial mosques of Istanbul. Built on the peak of the old Sixth Hill, it adorns the view from many parts of the old city.

This is one of the architectural masterpieces of Sinan, built by him for the Princess Mihrimah, the daughter of Süleyman the Magnificent. The külliye was built between 1562 and 1565 and includes a medrese, mektep, türbe, a double hamam and a long row of shops in the substructure of the mosque terrace.

Exterior of the mosque

Externally the building is strong and dominant, as befits its position at the highest point of the city. The square of the dome base with its multi-windowed tympana, identical on all sides, is given solidity and boldness by the four great weight-towers at the corners, prolongations of the piers that support the dome arches. Above this square rises the dome itself on a circular drum pierced by windows.

The mosque is preceded by an oblong courtyard with a large şadırvan in the centre. Around three sides are the porticoes and cells of the **medrese**.

The mosque **porch** was originally double, as evidenced by the column bases in the ground, which would originally have supported the outer portico. This type of double porch was a favourite of Sinan's; he used it in his earlier mosque for Mihrimah at Üsküdar (*for a charming legend about the two mosques, see p. 264*) and in many others.

Interior of the mosque

The central area of the interior is square, covered by a great dome 20m in diameter and 37m high under the crown, resting on smooth pendentives. To north and south, high triple arcades supported on granite columns open into side aisles with galleries above; each of these has three domed bays, reaching only to the springing of the dome arches. The tympana of all four dome arches are filled with three rows of windows, flooding the mosque with light.

The interior stencil decoration is modern. The **mimber** is a fine original work of white marble with a beautiful medallion perforated like an iron grille. The voussoirs of the gallery arches are fretted polychrome of *verd antique* and Proconnesian marble.

The church of St George and Cistern of Aetius

Just inside Edirne Kapı is the church of **Haghios Georgios** (Aya Yorgi). The original church of St George by the Adrianople Gate was built by Constantine V (r. 741–75) on the present site of Mihrimah Camii, and there is a reference to it as late as 1438. This building was demolished in 1562 to make way for the mosque, after which an imperial edict was issued giving the Greeks a plot of land on which they could build a new church of St George. The present church was built in 1836 and restored in 1922–24.

The huge **open cistern** on the eastern side of Fevzi Paşa Cd. (*map p. 342, C2*), now used as a football stadium, is one of three ancient Roman reservoirs in the city. It has been identified as the reservoir constructed c. 421 by Aetius, Prefect of Constantinople in the reign of Theodosius II. Huge as it is, it is the smallest of the three surviving reservoirs, measuring 224m by 85m; its original depth was probably about 15m. Like the others, it was already dry in later Byzantine times and was used as a kitchen garden.

TEKFUR SARAYI

Just beyond Edirne Kapı, the walls are broken by the broad Fevzi Paşa Cd. To the north of it, near the walls, is the Byzantine church of St Saviour in Chora, with its splendid mosaics and frescoes (*see p. 170*). The Theodosian walls continue on for about 600m beyond Edirne Kapı, at which point they give way to a stretch of walls constructed in later times. The inner wall is well preserved.

At the end of the existing Theodosian walls stand the evocative remains of an imperial Byzantine palace. The Turkish name of the building is Tekfur Sarayı, the 'Palace of the Sovereign' (*map p. 342, C1; closed for restoration at the time of writing*). In English it is known as the Palace of the Porphyrogenitus.

HISTORY OF TEKFUR SARAYI

The palace was probably built in the late 13th or early 14th century and was used as an imperial residence during the last two centuries of Byzantine rule. It may have been an annexe of the nearby Palace of Blachernae. Its proximity to the walls caused it to be badly damaged in the siege of 1453, but it was subsequently repaired and used for a variety of purposes. During the 16th–17th centuries it served as an imperial menagerie, particularly for larger and tamer animals such as elephants and giraffes.

Before the end of the 17th century the animals were moved elsewhere and the palace was turned into a brothel. It was redeemed from this indignity in 1719, when the famous Tekfursarayı pottery was set up here. When that ceased production in the 18th century, the palace went into its final decline. During the first half of the 19th century it was a poorhouse for Jews and in the 20th century it housed a bottle factory, before finally being abandoned.

The palace ruins

The palace is a three-storey building with arcades or window apertures of diminishing width on all three floors of the courtyard façade. At ground level there is an arcade of four wide arches. Above that are five arched windows, with seven narrower windows on the top level. The entire façade is articulated by the alternating use of red brick and white marble, typical of later Byzantine architecture.

Around the palace

Just beyond Tekfur Sarayı the Theodosian walls come to an abrupt end and the fortifications are continued by walls of later construction. There has been much discussion about the original course of the Theodosian walls from Tekfur Sarayı down to the Golden Horn. It would appear that they turned almost due north and followed a more or less straight line down to the water, whereas the present walls first bend in a westward arc before heading northeast again. **Stretches of the original Theodosian walls** can be seen at Tekfur Sarayı and also along Mumhane Cd., where their remains are quite impressive and picturesque.

TEKFUR SARAYI TO THE GOLDEN HORN

Eğri Kapı

Most authorities identify Eğri Kapı (*map p. 342, C1*) with the ancient Gate of the Kaligaria. It was here that Constantine XI was last seen alive by his friend George Sphrantzes, who would later write a history of the Fall of Byzantium. On the night of 28th May 1453 the emperor, accompanied by Sphrantzes, stopped briefly at the Palace of Blachernae after returning from his last visit to Haghia Sophia. According to Sphrantzes,

Constantine assembled the members of his household and said goodbye to each of them in turn, asking their forgiveness for any unkindness he might ever have shown them. 'Who could describe the tears and groans in the palace?' Sphrantzes wrote, 'Even a man of wood or stone could not have stayed from weeping'. The emperor then left the palace and rode with Sphrantzes down to the Gate of the Kaligaria. They dismounted there and Sphrantzes waited while Constantine ascended one of the towers nearby, from where he could hear the Turkish army preparing for the final assault. Soon after he returned and mounted his horse once again. Sphrantzes said goodbye to him for the last time and watched as the emperor rode off to his command post further south (*see p. 202*). He was never seen again. Poor Constantine. His realm was so impoverished that he had been unable to afford the pay stipulated by the Hungarian gunsmith who had cast the great cannon that finally breached the walls (*see p. 199*). According to the historian Jason Goodwin, in *Lords of the Horizons: A History of the Ottoman Empire*, the ever-flexible Urban promptly offered the behemoth to Sultan Mehmet. It was so heavy that it needed a team of 30 oxen to drag it along. Its baleful bronze barrel changed the course of history.

Eğri Kapı in Turkish means the 'Crooked Gate', because the narrow road that leaves the city here makes a detour around a türbe that stands almost directly in front of the portal. This is the supposed **tomb of Hazrat Hafir**, a companion of the Prophet, who, according to tradition, was killed on this spot during the first Arab siege of the city in 674–78.

The walls continue past Eğri Kapı to the point where they join the retaining wall of the Blachernae terrace. Most of the final section appears to be of later construction (*for Blachernae, see pp. 216–17*).

GREEK FIRE

The incendiary mixture known as Greek Fire, used with devastating effect against enemy armies and particularly against shipping, was a combustible liquid compound invented in the 7th century AD by a Greek from Heliopolis in Egypt. Since then the recipe for the mixture has been lost and scientists can only conjecture what it may have contained. It was projected onto its target through a kind of siphon (old illustrations show this being done) and on contact would ignite into a terrible fire unquenchable by water alone. Greek Fire was used by the defenders of Constantinople against the Arabs in the 7th century and against the Bulgars in the 10th. By the time of the Fourth Crusade in 1203–04, however, it appears already to have disappeared from the Byzantine arsenal.

THE GOLDEN HORN

Golden Horn ferries leave from Üsküdar via Eminönü, stopping at Kasımpaşa (10mins from Eminönü), Fener (15mins), Hasköy (20mins), Ayvansaray (25mins), Sütlüce (30mins) and Eyüp (35mins). Boats run approx. every hour, with no early morning services on Sun and holidays. The ferry landing at Eminönü is quite hard to find, tucked away behind the fenced car park beyond the bus station (map p. 348, C1). Bus no. 99 goes up the south shore of the Golden Horn from Eminönü and Karaköy (Galata). For timetables, see www.sehirhatlari.com.tr.

The Golden Horn (in Turkish, Haliç) is a scimitar-shaped inlet of the Bosphorus, its English name a direct translation of the Greek, *Chrysokeras*. It is some 7.5km long, and at its broadest part, near Kasımpaşa, it is 750m wide.

On the water's edge just east of the Galata Bridge stands a prominent Ottoman structure, **Sepetçiler Kasrı**, the 'Pavilion of the Basket-Weavers', built by their guild in 1647 for Sultan İbrahim. It served as a boat-house where the sultan and his entourage would board their *kayık* to be rowed up the Golden Horn for a day's outing. The kiosk was reconstructed in the 1980s and now serves as the International Press Centre. Boat trips up the Golden Horn today begin on the other side of the Galata Bridge, to its west.

KASIMPAŞA

In Evliya Çelebi's famous dream, when he met the Prophet Mohammed and was promised a life of travel, the scene took place in Ahi Çelebi Camii, just beside the modern Golden Horn ferry landing (*see p. 133*). The morning after the dream, Evliya went across the water to Kasımpaşa (*map p. 344, A3*) to consult two wise men: İbrahim Efendi, an interpreter of dreams, and Abdullah Dede, a Mevlevi dervish. Both confirmed that Evliya would travel greatly, see wonderful things and converse with kings. It seems almost churlish in the face of this to say that there is not much te see in Kasımpaşa today. For its history is strong. As the ferry approaches, you get a good view of the shipyard just above the Atatürk Bridge. This is the site of the famous Tersane, or **Ottoman Naval Arsenal**, founded by Fatih soon after the Conquest. In the 16th–17th centuries the Tersane made a great impression on foreign travellers, for it could accommodate 120 ships at one time. Today it is one of the largest shipyards in Turkey, extending well up the Golden Horn. Just in from the water's edge, on the landward side of the main highway, you can see the **Kalyoncu Kışlası** (*map p. 344, B3*), the barracks of the galleymen. This was built by Cezayirli (the Algerian) Gazi (Warrior for the Faith) Hasan Pasha in 1785 as a barracks for the marines of the Ottoman Navy, with a mosque at its centre. On the water's edge just upstream from the ferry landing is a faintly Moorish-looking Ottoman palace called **Bahriye Nezareti**, now used by the Turkish navy. It dates from the reign of Abdülaziz (r. 1861–76).

Pushbike, tractor, Porsche 928? This man has tyres for all. Single-focus shops like his are still a common sight in Fener, Balat, Galata and the other districts fringing the Golden Horn..

Just downstream from the ferry landing there is a **park** named after Cezayirli Gazi Hasan Pasha, who served as admiral of the Ottoman fleet under Mustafa III (r. 1757–74) and then Grand Vizier under Abdülhamit I (r. 1774–89). A large bronze statue shows him with the pet lion that he led on a leash when he strolled around the Tersane.

Piyale Paşa Camii

The principal monument accessible from Kasımpaşa is Piyale Paşa Camii (*map p. 344, A1; bus 77Ç from Eminönü or Kasımpaşa*), one of the most pleasing of the classical mosques. Standing in a picturesque grove of cypresses and plane trees, it was completed in 1573 by an unknown architect, though many sources ascribe it to Sinan. Piyale Pasha, the founder, began life as a Christian, the son of a Croatian shoe-maker. He was taken up in the *devşirme*, educated in the Palace School, and rose to the rank of Kaptan Pasha under Süleyman the Magnificent. While in command of the Ottoman fleet he terrorised the eastern Mediterranean, raiding as far as the coast of southern Italy, and captured Chios. Under Selim II, in 1571, he captured Cyprus. He crowned his career by marrying one of the sultan's daughters, Hace Guheri Mülük Sultan. He died in 1578.

Piyale Paşa Camii is the only classical mosque to revert to the Ulu Cami or multi-domed type common in the Seljuk and early Ottoman periods. It has six domes of equal size, arranged in two rows of three each, flanked by tympana pierced by windows. Round three sides of the building there is an arcaded porch with upper loggias to north and south, supported on slender columns. On the main west façade there is a second, outer arcaded porch in alternate courses of brick and stone. The founder's octagonal türbe behind the mosque also has a colonnaded porch. Around and behind it there are a number of gravestones.

The mosque interior is lighted by numerous windows, both small round oculi and lancets. Under the top tier of windows runs a wide frieze of blue faience with inscriptions from the Koran in white. These are by the hand of the famous calligrapher Karahisarı, who wrote the inscriptions in the Süleymaniye. The mihrab is also a very beautiful work, with Iznik tiles of the best period. The whole interior is unusual and charming.

FENER

The famous Fener Kapısı, the ancient Porta Phanarion or 'Gate of the Lighthouse', gave its name to the Fener district, so famous in the history of Istanbul. The gate has long vanished, but its site is easy to determine, with a modern mosque on one side and the faint spring of an arch on the other (*map p. 343, B3*). Though the immediate waterfront has been laid out as parkland and playgrounds, and though many old quarters were demolished in the process, many buildings of historic value have been preserved. Among these are massive stone and brick structures known as 'meta-Byzantine', i.e., erected after the Conquest in the Byzantine style. Here and there also are surviving stretches of the Byzantine sea walls. Even though only a couple of the gateways survive, the location of the others is easy to work out since the modern streets still converge where they once opened, following ancient routes that have long since lost their meaning.

Carved and gilt Byzantine eagle in the narthex of the Ecumenical Patriarchate church. Its two heads symbolise East and West. In many versions of this symbol the bird holds an orb in one claw and a cross in the other, signifying spiritual and temporal dominion. Here the grape motif is prominent: 'I am the true vine and my Father is the husbandman.'

HISTORY OF FENER

Beginning in the early 16th century, Greeks of this quarter, the Phanariots, amassed considerable wealth in trade and commerce under the protective mantle of the Ottoman sultan. Members of many Phanariot families—Ypsilantis, Mavrocordatos, Ghykas—achieved positions of great eminence in the imperial civil service, and some gained control of the Danube principalities of Moldavia and Wallachia, client states of the Ottomans. The Phanariots ruled there as hospodars, or princes, a position that allowed them to acquire enormous wealth. Much of this wealth was brought back to the Fener, where the hospodars and other members of their family and court built magnificent mansions and palaces. The palaces have all vanished, but a few of the mansions have survived, although in a very dilapidated condition. They can be seen here and there along the Golden Horn road, identified by their massive stone walls and their upper storeys projecting out on corbels.

Relations between the Constantinopolitan Greeks and their Ottoman overlords were not always harmonious. In retaliation for Phanariot support for the Greek War of Independence (1821), many churches were looted and destroyed, Greek businesses were ransacked and Greeks were attacked in the streets. Under the terms of the Treaty of Lausanne (1923), the Republic of Turkey is obliged to protect its Greeks, but tensions have arisen, and violent anti-Greek riots in the 1950s caused large numbers of what was already a depleted population to leave. Greeks now account for a tiny percentage of the city's population, although recently a reverse trend is being reported, with recession-hit Greeks finding work and congenial living standards in the city they once called their own.

THE GREEK ORTHODOX PATRIARCHATE

The main entrance gate to the Greek Orthodox Patriarchate (*map p. 343, B3*), the famous Orta Kapı, the Central Gate, is welded shut and painted black, a symbol of Greek-Turkish deadlock: it was here that Gregory V, Patriarch of Constantinople, was hanged for treason on 22nd April 1821, at the outbreak of the Greek War of Independence.

The patriarchal church of St George

The church of Haghios Georgios is, like almost all of the post-Conquest sanctuaries in the city, a small basilica. This form was adopted partly because of its simplicity, but largely because the Christians in Istanbul were forbidden to build churches with domes or masonry roofs, so that the basilica with its timbered roof, a traditional early Christian edifice derived from Roman models, was the obvious solution.

At the **east end** of the church is a richly carved and gilded iconostasis and two very fine cantor's music stands inlaid with ivory. In the **nave** stands the beautiful patriarchal throne, of 16th-century Athenian make, with ivory and mother-of-pearl inlay. The walnut-wood pulpit opposite, dating from the following century, is inlaid in the same manner. In the **north aisle** are two small marble caskets containing the relics of two revered former bishops of Constantinople and early patriarchs, St John Chrysostom and St Gregory of Nazianzus, returned from Rome in 2004, 800 years after they had been looted by Crusaders. These represent the last mortal remains of two out of the three Hierarchs, the Fathers of the Eastern Church (the third Hierarch is St Basil). In the **south aisle** is a fragment of the Column of the Flagellation and the relics of three female saints: St Solomone, St Theophano (wife of the emperor Leo the Wise), and St Euphemia of Chalcedon, whose remains were brought here after her martyrium near the Hippodrome was destroyed c. 1524 (*see p. 117*). Also in the south aisle is a beautiful mosaic of the Virgin Hodegetria, dating from the 11th century. It was the patronal icon of the church of the Theotokos Pammakaristos.

HISTORY OF THE GREEK ORTHODOX PATRIARCHATE

The Ecumenical Patriarch and Archbishop of New Rome is to Orthodox Christians what the Pope is to Roman Catholics. Indeed, he is more perhaps even than that, for by his description as ecumenical, he claims to be patriarch 'of the whole inhabited world'. The Church of Constantinople was founded, according to tradition, by St Andrew the Apostle, who always appears on lists as the first patriarch. In the earliest years the head of the church here styled himself Bishop of Constantinople. The title of patriarch first appeared in the 5th century, and that of Ecumenical Patriarch in the 6th century. During the period of Latin rule in Constantinople (1206–61), the Patriarchate was transferred to Nicaea.

After the conquest of 1453, in a bid to bring all the Eastern Christian churches together under the Ottoman aegis and prevent their reallying with Rome, Mehmet II appointed the patriarch Gennadius II 'ethnarch' of the Eastern Roman (*Rum*) peoples. Gennadius established his headquarters at the church of the Pammakaristos (*see p. 167*) and the Patriarchate remained there until 1586, after which it was moved to several other places before being established on its present site in 1599. Throughout the Ottoman period the Ecumenical Patriarch, under the suzerainty of the sultan, was the religious leader of all Christians in the Empire.

Today the Ecumenical Patriarch is subject to the authority of the Turkish Republic (which recognises him only as Greek Orthodox Patriarch of Fener) and must be a Turkish citizen to be eligible for the post.

Precincts of the church

The other buildings of the Patriarchate, with the exception of the library and an aghiasma dedicated to St Charalambos, are all modern structures erected after the fire of 1951. It was fortunate that the library was spared, because it houses an important collection of Byzantine manuscripts and documents.

> **Eating in Fener:** Close to the Ecumenical Patriarchate, built right against the old sea walls at Abdülezel Paşa Cd. 331, is the Fener Köşkü, which does a respectable lunch (*T: 212 621 9025/26; www.fenerkosku.com*). Alternatively, further south, is the Cibalikapı Balıkçısı, a fish restaurant with good mezes (*Kadir Has Cd. 5; T: 212 533 2846, www.cibalikapibalikcisi.com*).

OTHER SIGHTS & MONUMENTS IN FENER

The Metochion of the Holy Sepulchre

Continuing for a few steps past the site of Fener Kapısı, take the first left and then almost immediately turn right into the next street, Vodina Cd. At the next corner turn left and then right at the next turning. At the end of this street is a stepped lane that leads up past a high wall that encloses a large open area extending up the side of the hill (*map p. 343, B3*). This is the **Metochion of the Holy Sepulchre**, since the mid-17th-century the Istanbul dependency of the Greek Orthodox Patriarchate of Jerusalem. Halfway up the stepped path is the locked gate of the enclosure. Dimitrie Cantemir, son of a governor of Moldavia, lived here as an Ottoman hostage until 1710, when he became Prince of Wallachia. He is noted as the author of a work dedicated to Ahmet III, the *Book of the Science of Music as Explained in Letters*, in which he transcribed 351 Turkish, Persian and Arabic tunes according to his own system of notation. The former **residence of Cantemir** (a pink building) is at the top of the steps to the right. Recordings have been made of Cantemir's music, available on CD.

Within the walled compound is the church of **Haghios Georgios Metochi**, founded in the 12th century. The first mention of it after the Turkish Conquest is by Tryphon Karabeinikov, who in 1583 came to Istanbul as a representative of Tsar Ivan IV, the Terrible. The present very simple pitched-roof basilica dates from c. 1730. In 1906, among the church manuscripts, was found a perfect and complete 10th-century copy in palimpsest of a lost work of Archimedes: the 'Method of Treating Mechanical Problems, Dedicated to Eratosthenes', written in Alexandria c. 250 BC.

At the top of the steps on the left are the ruins of the church of the **Panaghia Paramythia** (St Mary the 'Consoler'). From 1586 until 1597 it served as the church of the Ecumenical Patriarcahte, after its removal from the Pammakaristos. The church was gutted by fire in 1976 and has not been rebuilt.

St Mary of the Mongols

At the top of the stepped lane that borders the Patriarchate of Jerusalem, turn left and you will see, immediately in front of you, a deep red Byzantine church with a high drum. This is the church of the Theotokos Panaghiotissa, the All-Holy Mother of God, more usually known as the Panaghia Mouchliotissa, or St Mary of the Mongols (in Turkish Kanlı kilise; *map p. 343, B3*). This is the only Byzantine sanctuary continuously in Greek hands since before the Conquest. It was either founded or rebuilt c. 1282 by

Maria Palaeologina, an illegitimate daughter of the Michael VIII Palaeologus. In 1265 she was sent as a bride to the Great Khan of the Mongols and lived at the Mongol court in Persia for about 15 years. Through her influence the Khan and many of his courtiers became Christians. When the Khan was assassinated by his brother in 1281, Maria returned to Constantinople, at which time she founded the present church and convent, where she retired and spent her last years. After the Conquest Fatih, at the request of his Greek architect Christodoulos (who may be Atik Sinan, the architect of the original Fatih Camii), issued a firman confirming the right of the Greeks to keep this church. Copies of Fatih's firman and those of several of his successors are displayed on the rear wall.

The Megali Scholi

Dominating the Fener skyline as you approach by boat, and lying just behind St Mary of the Mongols as you approach on land, is the red-brick, neo–Gothic Greek High School for Boys (Fener Rum Lisesi; *map p. 343, B3*), completed in 1881. Also known as the Megali Scholi, the 'Great School', it is a secular institution of higher education founded c. 1840. Prior to that time the Patriarchate had operated a school of higher learning on this site that offered both religious and secular studies, one of the very few such institutions in the Ottoman Empire. Here many of the Greek voivodes and hospodars of Moldavia and Wallachia were educated, as well as most of the chief interpreters. This latter group includes men with the illustrious names of the Byzantine aristocracy: Palaeologus, Cantacuzenos and Cantemir. The school was closed by the Turkish government in 1971, but it has since reopened, though with a very small enrolment.

The Bulgarian church of St Stephen

Standing on its own on the waterfront between the Fener and Balat landing stages is the handsome, gunmetal green-grey church of St Stephen of the Bulgars. Designed by an Armenian architect, Hovsep Aznavur, it was built in 1896, at a time when the Bulgarian Church was asserting its independence from the Greek Orthodox Patriarchate. The fascinating thing about it is that it is constructed entirely of cast iron, not only the structure itself but all of its interior decorations, which are in an eclectic style with hints of neo-Gothic and Neoclassical. The church was prefabricated in Vienna and shipped down the Danube and across the Black Sea in sections, after which it was erected here. Inside, the sound of piped chant makes it a sea of sacred calm, a welcome retreat from the roaring road outside. The church is much loved by the small community of Bulgarians who worship here. It is surrounded by a little garden in which several metropolitans of the Bulgarian Orthodox Church are buried.

The Metochion of Mt Sinai

Much abomination of desolation is to be seen in Fener. Nowhere is there a better example than at the old Metochion of the monastery of St Catherine on Mount Sinai (*map p. 343, B3*). St Catherine's monastery was founded by Justinian, and since Byzantine times it has been under the aegis of the Patriarchate of Alexandria. The monastery, like many others, was traditionally represented in Constantinople by an archimandrite.

They are mentioned as having been in residence in a mansion on this site as early as 1686. Today's mansion, one of the oldest and grandest of the former Phanariot residences, is in a very dilapidated condition. Once upon a time it was a supreme example of an Ottoman-era Greek residence of the type known as meta-Byzantine. Its walls are constructed of alternate courses of stone and brick; the upper storey projects out over the street, with the cornice under the roof consisting of courses of sawtooth brick. The mansion is very stoutly built, with massive walls and iron doors and window-shutters, more like a fortress than a dwelling-place. It was badly damaged during the anti-Greek rioting in 1955, and a decade later it was closed by the Turkish government. It has been abandoned since then and is now falling into ruins.

BALAT

The Turkish name of this district is a corruption of Palation ('palace'), which derives from its proximity to the Byzantine Palace of Blachernae (*see p. 217*). The surrounding quarter is by turns picturesque and dilapidated, and filled with history.

HISTORY OF BALAT

Balat was traditionally a Jewish quarter of the city. Many of its residents were Greek-speaking Jews who had lived here since the Byzantine period and were absorbed by the Sephardim who came from Spain in 1492 at the invitation of Beyazıt II. There are still half a dozen ancient synagogues in the quarter, at least one of them dating in foundation from Byzantine times, although few of the present structures are of any antiquity. Although most of the area's Jews have moved to more modern neighbourhoods—or emigrated to Israel—a few still remain. There were also many Greeks and Armenians in Balat, as evidenced by the number of their churches here, though their populations too have greatly diminished.

AROUND BALAT KAPISI

There is no mistaking the former location of Balat Kapısı (*map p. 343, B3*), the Byzantine gate in the sea walls, for all the local streets converge on it. Close to it is the **Armenian church of Surp Reşdagabet** (the Holy Archangels), which stands on the site of a Byzantine church of the 13th–14th centuries, apparently rebuilt in the second quarter of the 19th century. The church originally belonged to the Greeks, but the Armenian community took possession in 1629. Beneath the church there is a crypt with an aghiasma, evidently a very old one, as evidenced by the ancient Greek funerary stelae set into its walls.

On the same street is the small **Ferruh Kethüda mosque**, a minor work of Sinan. A long inscription in Arabic over the entrance portal states that it was built in 1562–63 by Ferruh Ağa, Kethüda (Steward) of the Grand Vizier Semiz Ali Pasha. Close to the mosque is **Çavuş Hamamı**, Istanbul's oldest Turkish bath (*closed at the time of writing*), built either in the time of Fatih or of Beyazıt II.

The Ahrida Synagogue

The oldest and most historic synagogue in Balat, on Kürkçü Çeşmesi Sk., is the Ahrida Synagogue (*map p. 343, B3*), which dates back to the first half of the 15th century—the only synagogue in the city that can definitely be dated to the Byzantine period. It was built by Romaniot Jews from Ohrid in present-day Macedonia. It is now open as a museum, although permission to visit must be obtained from the office of the Chief Rabbinate (*Yemenici Abdüllatif Sk. 23; T: 0212 243 5166; map p. 344, B3*). The synagogue is noted for its association with Shabbatai Sevi, the so-called False Messiah, who in 1667 gave a sermon here to proclaim that he was the long-awaited Saviour.

The church of Haghios Dimitrios Kanabu

The Greek church of **Haghios Dimitrios Kanabu** (*map p. 343, B2*) has existed on this site since the early 14th century. The present structure is a rebuilding of 1730. The church may have been founded by the family of Nicholas Kanabou, who became emperor for a few days in April 1204, in the brief interval between the deposition of the co-emperors Alexius IV and Isaac II and the later usurpation by Alexius V. His reign was so short that he is not included in the traditional list of Byzantine emperors. Haghios Dimitrios served as the church of the Ecumenical Patriarchate from 1597 until 1601.

The churchyard is built up against a section of the Byzantine sea walls, from where you can look out over the Golden Horn. There is a view of the **Old Galata Bridge**, which was moved here after its demolition in 1992.

Eating in Balat: Köfteci Arnavut, which has been in business since the 1940s, is a tiny little place serving impeccable meatballs (*Mürselpaşa Cd. 139, T: 212 531 6652*).

HASKÖY

As the ferry comes in to land at Hasköy (*map p. 343, B2*), don't be surprised, as you look to your left, if you see an old DC3 threatening to take to the skies. It belongs to the Koç Museum, a favourite with children and for many adults too, the main reason to come to Hasköy. If you are travelling with small boys, don't miss it.

Rahmi M. Koç Industrial Museum

The Rahmi M. Koç Industrial Museum (*open 10–5, closed Mon*) is housed on two sites on either side of the main shore highway. The visit begins in the shoreside building, which has a superb display of machines (vehicles, computers, household appliances) with push-buttons that turn them on and let you see how they work (part of their body-work has been cut away so you can see inside). Another hall has a stunning array of old motor cars, including an East German Trabant, a pink Cadillac, a Rolls Royce Silver Cloud and many more. Steam engines, old trams, boats (the glorious Riva Aquarama is a highlight) and aeroplanes are displayed in further halls and outside. You can climb up steps to look inside Sultan Abdülaziz's private Birmingham-built train carriage with its power blue upholstery, and relive your own or your parents' or grandparents' youth inside the DC3. One of the most memorable exhibits is the WWII American B-24 Liberator bomber that crashed into the sea near Antalya when en route back to Benghazi from a bombing raid on oil refineries in Romania in 1943. The pilot and co-pilot were trapped and drowned, the other crew members escaped. Now dredged from the depths, it stands on permanent display, to be explored in all its crippled, sinister majesty.

The exhibit continues across the road in a beautifully restored Ottoman *lengerhane*, a forge for making ship's chains and anchors, a structure dating largely from the reign of Ahmet III (1703–30)—though once you are inside on the upper floor, you will see that it must be Byzantine in origin.

Eating in Hasköy: Within the precincts of the Koç Museum, on the landward side of the road, is an attractive, French-bistro-style restaurant called Café du Levant (*T: 0212 369 6607; closed Mon*).

The synagogues of Hasköy

Hasköy once had a large Jewish community, but only two synagogues are still functioning, and even those are used infrequently. The Jewish community here included members of the Karaite sect, who were moved to Hasköy from their original quarter in Eminönü early in the 17th century, when Yeni Cami was built. Orthodox Jews worship at the **Mualem Synagogue** on Harap Çeşme Sk. (*map p. 343, C2*) , which has a dedicatory inscription on its entryway dated 1734. The Karaite synagogue, **B'nai Mikra**, at no. 3 Mahlul Sk. (*map p. 343, B2*), is undated. The Jewish cemetery on the hill above Hasköy (*map p. 343, B1; bus 77Ç from Eminönü or Kasımpaşa to Çıksalın*) has sections for both the Orthodox and Karaite communities.

Aynalıkavak Kasrı

Aynalıkavak Kasrı, the 'Pavilion of the Mirroring Poplars' (*map p. 343, C2; open 9–5; closed Mon and Thur*) is a graceful imperial pleasure kiosk situated among trees and gardens. The original building was erected in the early 17th century by Ahmet I, on the site from where Mehmet the Conqueror watched his army breach the land walls of Constantinople. The sultans used it as a pavilion from which to view nautical spectacles, as shown in miniatures by Levni. Its orchards became famous for their peaches.

Sultan Ahmet III in Aynalıkavak watching acrobats walking on tightropes suspended from ships' masts, during the festival for his son's circumcision. Miniature by Levni.

The kiosk was rebuilt and embellished by Ahmet III (r. 1703–30). Improvements were made during the reign of Abdülhamit I (r. 1774–89), when the kiosk gave its name to the Treaty of Aynalıkavak, signed here in 1784 by representatives of Russia and the Ottoman Empire, acknowledging Russian annexation of the Crimea. The palace took on its present form under Selim III (r. 1789–1807).

The kiosk has two storeys facing the Golden Horn and a single storey at the back, an arrangement dictated by the slope of the site. Aynalıkavak is celebrated for its windows, particularly those on the upper level which have rims of decorative stained glass. The furniture and décor are from the time of Selim III, including many original works. The sultan's tuğra is by the calligrapher Yesarı, as are the other inscriptions, from poems by Enderunlu Fazıl (who wrote in praise of Selim III and was also famed for his erotic lyrics) and Şeyh Galip (author of a poem entitled *Beauty and Love*). The principal rooms are the imperial audience chamber; the Mother-of-Pearl Room, named after the inlaid suite there; and the Composition Room, so called became Selim III is thought to have written music there. The palace also houses the Turkish Musical Research Centre and Musical Instruments Museum, with a superb collection of Turkish classical instruments. Concerts are sometimes given.

AYVANSARAY

Cowering in the lee of the busy Golden Horn Bridge is Ayvansaray (*map p. 343, A2*), On Çember Sk., just in from the coastal highway, is a handsome former Byzantine church dated to the 9th century and tentatively identified as the church of SS Peter and Mark. It is now a mosque, **Atik Mustafa Paşa Camii**, and contains the tomb of a martyr called Cabir, a companion of Abu Ayyub (*see p. 219*) who died alongside him.

The aghiasma of Blachernae

On the inland side of Mustafapaşa Bostani Sk. is the entrance to the famous **Aghiasma of the Theotokos** (*map p. 343, A2*), a sacred spring enclosed by a little shrine surrounded by a garden. The aghiasma, dedicated to the Mother of God, has been venerated since early Byzantine times because its waters are believed to possess healing powers: even the emperor and empress came here to benefit from its curative waters. In 451 the empress Pulcheria built a church over the spring and a few years later, when two Constantinopolitan pilgrims brought back the robe and mantle of the Virgin from Jerusalem, these holy relics were housed here. The Virgin 'Blachernitissa' (of Blachernae) was revered as the protectress of the city; according to tradition, she appeared on the walls in 626 to confound an army of Avars and Persians, sending a miraculous hurricane to beat them back. The famous icon of the Panaghia Blachernitissa, of the Orans type, was probably destroyed during the Iconoclastic period.

The ancient church burnt down in 1434 and was rebuilt several times. The present, very simple, building dates from the 1960s. The shrine is still a popular place of pilgrimage for Greeks, who come to bathe their eyes in the holy water. Above the line of taps is a palindromic inscription in Greek: NIΨON ANOMHMATA MH MONAN OΨIN ('Cleanse my sins, not only my eyes'). It was after the repulse of the Avars that the famous Akathist Hymn was written, a paean to the Virgin which must be sung standing up (*a-kathistos* means 'not seated').

The Palace of Blachernae

Dervişzade Sk., the 'Street of the Dervish's Son', winds uphill to a broad terrace just inside the Byzantine walls. At one end of it, close to the ramparts, is the attractive İvaz Efendi Camii (*map p. 343, A2*), founded by Murat III's Lord Chief Justice in the 1580s. It stands on the site of the famous Palace of Blachernae, the imperial residence during the last centuries of Byzantine rule.

HISTORY OF THE PALACE OF BLACHERNAE

The first palace on this site was built by Anastasius I (r. 491–518). It was thenceforth used by the imperial family whenever they came to visit the shrine of the Blachernitissa. Over the centuries the palace was rebuilt and enlarged several times, particularly during the reign of the Comnenus dynasty in the 11th–12th centuries. From that time on it became the favourite residence of the imperial family, gradually supplanting the Great Palace beside Haghia Sophia.

After the Latin Occupation of 1204–61 the Great Palace was abandoned altogether, and for the remainder of the Byzantine period the imperial family lived exclusively at Blachernae. They were still in residence when the city fell to the Ottomans in 1453. Because of its proximity to the defence walls, the palace suffered much damage during the siege.

Today only two towers and some dungeons remain. The first tower, just behind İvaz Efendi Camii, is known as the **Tower of Isaac Angelus**, after Isaac II Angelus, who was imprisoned here in 1195–1203, the years between his two reigns. The tower was probably built by him during his first reign and was probably designed as a private palace with its upper level serving as a belvedere. Certainly the upper storey, on a level with the terrace, commands a superb view of the Golden Horn and the surrounding countryside; notice outside the windows the shafts of columns that once supported a balcony. The other tower is known as the **Anemas Tower** after Michael Anemas, a general who conspired against Alexius I in the 12th century and was imprisoned here. He gives his name to the **Anemas dungeons** beneath. They are very impressive, though there is little to be seen without a torch. Two nearly parallel walls, some 60m long, are joined by arched cross-walls into three tiers of cells, though the wooden floors have long since decayed.

Hacı Hüsrev Camii and Miniatürk

Situated in a green and pleasant park on the shores of the Golden Horn, with excellent views of the Byzantine walls, is the **mosque of Hacı Hüsrev** (*map p. 343, A2*). Here the faithful come to see the memorials of four companions of the Prophet who died while attempting to slay the infidel.

On the other side of the Golden Horn is **Miniatürk** (*map p. 350; Sütlüce ferry stop*), a landscaped park with over 100 miniature models of monuments from Istanbul, ancient Asia Minor and former Ottoman territory not incorporated in modern Turkey.

EYÜP

The suburb of Eyüp (*map p. 352*) is named after its great shrine, the holiest Muslim pilgrimage site in Istanbul. Indeed, after Mecca and Jerusalem, it is perhaps the third most sacred place of pilgrimage in the Islamic world.

In Ottoman times Eyüp had the reputation of being wild and picturesque. Bored by the safe European life of Pera, the narrator in Pierre Loti's *Aziyadé* comes to live on the heights above Eyüp, and notes that the mosque and shrine themselves are not places where any Christian should dare to show his face. That is not true today. Visitors are welcome; though it is important to dress modestly, behave with respect and not attempt to trespass on the holy places during prayer hours.

Approaches

Whether you approach Eyüp by bus or ferry, two buildings are prominent as you arrive. The first, right on the waterfront, is the long, low **Feshane**, or former fez factory. The original factory on this site was erected in 1833 to produce fezzes for the New Army of Mahmut II. The building was redesigned in 1843, and in 1894 it was expanded. After the fez was banned in Atatürk's clothing reform of 1925, the Feshane was converted to other uses. It is now used as an exhibition hall and trade fair centre.

Just beyond the Feshane, standing tall on the far side of the shore road, is **Zal Mahmut Paşa Camii** (*map p. 352*), a mature work of Sinan, probably completed in the 1570s. Zal occupies an unenviable place in Ottoman history: when in 1553 Süleyman decided to execute his son Mustafa, it was Zal who strangled him. Later he became Grand Vizier and married the Princess Şah Sultan, daughter of Selim II. This was a reward, it was said, for having smoothed Selim's path to the throne by the elimination of his half-brother. Little is known of Zal's subsequent career, except that in 1580 he and his wife died on the same night, for reasons unknown.

There is no other mosque quite like this one. With its four tiers of windows and its massive squareness, it looks more like a palace from the outside. Inside, it takes the form of a vast rectangular room. Though there is some fine faience decoration in the mihrab, it is certain that much tilework has perished, for Evliya Çelebi writes that 'architectural ornaments and decorations are nowhere lavished in so prodigal a way as here, in this the finest of all the mosques in the Empire built by viziers'.

Zal Mahmut Pasha and his wife are buried in the türbe garden. A door in its east wall leads to the pretty late 18th-century **külliye of Şah Sultan**, a sister of Selim III. It consists of an elaborate türbe and mektep. The undulating façades of the türbe and the amusing turned-back staircase of the mektep are very charming.

HISTORY OF EYÜP

The shrine is famous as the reputed burial-place of Abu Ayyub al-Ansari (in Turkish Eyüp), the friend and standard-bearer of the Prophet Mohammed. Long after the Prophet's death, the aged Ayyub is said to have been among the leaders of the first Arab siege of Constantinople in the years 674–78, when he was killed and buried outside the city walls. Since then his tomb has been a holy place for Muslims. During Ottoman times numerous great men and women of the Empire arranged to be buried here in splendid türbes, and many other people of humbler origins chose to be buried on the hill above the shrine. This is now one of the most extensive cemeteries in the Turkish world, and Eyüp is a veritable outdoor museum of Ottoman funerary architecture.

The street that leads to the main square of Eyüp, lined with stalls and booths, is called Camii Kebir Sokak, 'Great Mosque Street'. At the far end on the left is the **türbe of the Grand Vizier Sokollu Mehmet Pasha** (see p. 112; open 8.30–4; closed Mon), built by Sinan c. 1572 as part of a small külliye. Elegant and well proportioned, it is severely plain. The interior contains some interesting stained glass, partly ancient and partly a modern imitation, but very well done; alternate windows are predominantly blue and green.

A short colonnaded path attaches the türbe to the dershane. The door-frames of the two buildings are almost identical; the only difference is that the voussoirs of the türbe door are in *verd antique*, while those of the dershane are in red conglomerate marble.

Across the street from Sokollu Mehmet's tomb is the **türbe of the Grand Vizier Siyavuş Pasha**. This türbe is also by Sinan. Siyavuş Pasha died in 1601, outliving Sinan by a dozen years; he seems to have had Sinan build this türbe originally for some of his children who died young, and was finally buried here himself.

EYÜP SULTAN CAMİİ

The mosque (*map p. 352*) is approached through a wide outer courtyard paved with white marble slabs, each one the size of an individual prayer mat. Two undulating Baroque archways give access to the mosque precincts, shaded by plane trees.

The külliye as a whole, including the mosque and türbe, was built by Fatih in 1458. Here on their accession to the throne, the sultans were girded with the sword of Osman, the eponymous founder of the Ottoman (in Turkish, Osmanlı) dynasty, a ceremony equivalent to a coronation. By the end of the 18th century the mosque had fallen into ruins, perhaps a victim of the great earthquake of 1766 that had destroyed Fatih's own mosque. In 1798 Selim III ordered that the remains be torn down and a new mosque built in its place, a project that was completed in 1800. The mosque that is seen today dates from that time, except for the minarets, which were erected by Ahmet III early in the 18th century.

The mosque is very attractive inside, with pale honey-coloured stone, decorations picked out in gold, an elegant chandelier hanging from the centre of the dome, and a magnificent red and gold carpet covering the entire floor, with—as is so often the custom—individual prayer mats woven into the design.

The türbe of Ayyub

According to tradition, Ayyub's grave was discovered by the Şeyhülislam Akşemsettin during the Turkish siege in 1453, after which Fatih built the mosque and türbe on the site. This legend is certainly apocryphal, because the tomb is known to have been a sacred place even in the Byzantine period. Several Muslim historians note that it was made a condition of peace after the first Arab siege that the tomb should be preserved. An Arab traveller during the reign of Manuel I Comnenus (r. 1143–80) mentions it, while another traveller, Zakariya al-Kazwini (c. 1203–83) relates that 'this tomb is now venerated among them [the Byzantines] and they open it when they pray for rain in time of drought, and rain is granted them'. If the tomb was still visible in the 13th century, it seems unlikely that it should have disappeared so completely before the Turkish Conquest. Probably Fatih either restored it or rebuilt it on a grander scale.

The side of the building opposite the mosque is a blank wall, most of it covered with panels of tiles without an overall pattern and of many different periods, some of them of great individual beauty. A door in the wall leads to the türbe, an octagonal building, three sides of which project into the vestibule. The latter is itself sheathed in tiles, many of them of the best Iznik period. The türbe is sumptuously decorated with work largely of the Baroque period, though the structure itself is the original of 1458.

The exterior of the türbe of Abu Ayyub al-Ansari.

The mosque precincts

According to Evliya Çelebi, the medrese of the külliye formed the mosque courtyard; this was evidently swept away in 1798–1800, during Selim III's rebuilding programme. The hamam partially survives and extensive restoration was underway at the time of writing, with plans to include a hydrotherapy centre here.

THE KÜLLİYE OF MİHRİŞAH
& TÜRBE OF SULTAN MEHMET V

The enormous **külliye of Mihrişah Valide Sultan**, mother of Selim III, is one of the largest and most elaborate of all the Baroque complexes. Built in 1791, it includes the türbe of the foundress, together with a mektep, an imaret and a splendid sebil and çeşme. The türbe is round, but the undulating façade turns it into a polygon, with the various faces separated by slender columns of red or dark grey marble. The entrance is in a little courtyard filled with tombstones and trees; the columned portico of the mektep runs along one side. Farther along the street, another monumental gateway leads into the vast main courtyard, which is filled with more tombstones and surrounded on three sides by the porticoes of the huge imaret. This is the only imaret in Istanbul that still fulfils its original function as a soup kitchen for the poor of the city; some 1,500 people are served free food here daily at 11am, and are allowed to take away enough food for the evening meal. In leaving the imaret do not fail to notice the magnificent sebil at the end of the garden on the street side.

On Sultat Reşat Cd. is the tall Neoclassical **türbe of Sultan Mehmet V Reşat** (r. 1909–18), the penultimate ruler of the Ottoman Empire. He is the only one of all the sultans to be buried in the holy precincts of Eyüp and the last to be interred in his own country. The last sultan, Mehmet VI (r. 1918–22), died in exile and was buried abroad, as was Abdülmecit II (r. 1922–4), who held only the title of Caliph.

THE NORTHERN REACHES OF EYÜP

NB: To get to the Pierre Loti café at the top of the cemetery, you can either wind up on foot along the cobbled lane or take the cable car (it takes tram jetons).

The great **cemetery of Eyüp** is the last resting-place of many Ottoman notables as well as generations of ordinary Istanbullus. The path that winds uphill through it is lined with tombstones in picturesque disarray, the grave markers of the men topped with turbans of various styles or with tasselled fezzes, those of the women adorned with reliefs of flowers. Many of them are inscribed with the words Ruhuna Fatiha: 'Pray for His/Her Soul'.

At the top of the hill is the famous **Pierre Loti café**, named after the French novelist who frequented it during his stay in Istanbul. Inside it is decorated like an old-fashioned Ottoman coffee house, with small low tables, a brazier in the centre in winter, and an upholstered couch around the walls. Its terrace commands a superb view of

Three tombstones in the cemetery at Eyüp. Islamic grave markers are never elaborate. The topmost motif, however, does indicate the status of the deceased. For a man the stone is topped with a turban of differing styles, or with a fez. Women's gravestones are carved with flowers.

the Golden Horn and its upper reaches, where two streams flow into it. These are the **Sweet Waters of Europe**, the Alibey Suyu and Kağıthane Suyu, the ancient Barbyzes and Cydaris, respectively. They are separated at their mouth by the promontory known in Turkish as Sivri Tepe, the Semistra of the Greeks. According to Dionysius of Byzantium, it was on this hill that Io, daughter of Inachus, who had fled here pursued by the gadfly of jealous Hera, gave birth to the nymph Cereossa. According to one version of the myth, Byzas, the eponymous founder of Byzantium, was the son of Cereossa and Poseidon.

For centuries the meadows and banks of the Sweet Waters were the site of royal palaces, mansions, gardens and pavilions, and were a favourite holiday resort. But now the pleasure domes have disappeared and the upper reaches of the Golden Horn are surrounded by sprawling suburbs. Nevertheless, the view is still magnificent from Pierre Loti's café, particularly at sunset, in the early twilight of late afternoon, when the Golden Horn does indeed take on the colour of molten gold.

The view from the heights of Eyüp

The view is fine from up here. Against the backdrop of the Golden Horn is the sombre landscape of Eyüp; the holy mosque emerging in all its marble whiteness from a mysterious background, a forest of ancient trees; and then the sad hills, tinted with sombre shades and scattered with marbles—immense cemeteries, a veritable city of the dead. On the right is the Golden Horn, with thousands of golden caïques weaving to and fro; all of Stamboul in a nutshell, the mosques jumbled together, their domes and minarets blending into one. In the distance, far away, is a hill planted with white houses; that is Pera, the Christian city...

Pierre Loti, from *Aziyadé*, 1879 (Tr. AB)

GALATA & BEYOĞLU

The area at the northern end of the Galata Bridge is Karaköy, the heart of old Galata. On the hill above is the modern district of Beyoğlu, formerly known as Pera.

Galata today is a scruffy, unpretentious, workaday place, with relics of its Genoese and Jewish past and its great banking houses scattered almost, it seems, at random, amid the clustering shops and workshops. Most of these sell ironmongery of some kind. Galata is hardware heaven, with myriad outlets big and small selling tool boxes, carburettors, plugs and wires, electrical fittings, taps and shower heads, vacuum cleaner parts, audio equipment—anything you can think of to keep the DIY enthusiast browsing for days.

HISTORY OF GALATA

The origins of Galata, modern Karaköy, go back a long way. From very early times there had been settlements along the northern shores of the Golden Horn; Byzas himself is said to have erected a temple there to the hero Amphiaraus. The most important of these communities, Sykai, the 'Fig Trees', was located on the present site of Galata. As early as the 5th century AD, this was included within Constantinople itself, under the name of Regio Sycaena; it had churches, a forum, public baths, a theatre, a harbour, and was surrounded by a defence wall. In 528 Justinian restored its theatre and defence walls, grandiloquently renaming it Justinianae, though the name never caught on. The name Sykai seems to have continued in use until the 9th century, when Galata, whose derivation is uncertain, began to supplant it.

After the reconquest of Constantinople from the Latins in 1261, the Byzantine emperors granted the district to the Genoese as a semi-independent colony with its own *podestà*, or governor. Although the Genoese were forbidden to fortify the colony, they ignored the prohibition, built walls, and went on expanding their area and its fortifications for more than a hundred years. Sections of the Genoese walls are still in existence, though all in a very dilapidated state.

After the Ottoman Conquest of 1453, the outer walls of Galata were partially destroyed as the district became the general European quarter of the city. Here the foreign merchants had their houses and shops and the ambassadors of the European powers built their residences. When the Sephardic Jews were expelled from Spain by Ferdinand and Isabella in 1492, Beyazıt II invited them to his dominions and many settled in Galata. Early in the following century a large number of Moorish refugees settled here as well, joining the large number of Greeks and Armenians who had arrived from Anatolia in the century after the Conquest, giving Galata the polyglot flavour that it retained until comparatively recently.

Detail of Galata's famous Camondo Stairs (see p. 227).

Getting around Galata and Beyoğlu

The tram from Eminönü stops at Karaköy square. From there you can take the funicular (Tünel) to the lower end of İstiklal Cd., or stay on the tram to Kabataş, where another funicular takes you up to Taksim Square. Alternatively you can walk up the steep Galata streets on foot. Highlights are described below.

The Galata Tünel, the underground funicular railway, which ascends in 80 seconds to the heights of Beyoğlu, was built by French engineers in 1875 and was one of the first underground railways in the world. Galata is covered by the map on p. 344.

THE GALATA SHORE OF THE GOLDEN HORN

In the early morning there is considerable bustle on the dusty, busy Tersane Cd., the wide thoroughfare that leads between Galata Bridge and Atatürk Bridge. Around the old, dilapidated **Bedesten market hall** (originally built in the time of Fatih), vendors come to set out their wares: hosepipes, screwdrivers, drill fittings in all girths—anything, in fact, that belongs in a toolbox or a garden shed. Prominent signs on the road direct you to **Arap Cami** (*map p. 344, B4*), formerly one of the Latin churches of Genoese Galata, as one can see from its tall square tower, clearly an old campanile. The church seems to have been a Dominican foundation, dating from 1323–37 and incorporating a chapel of St Paul, by whose name it was popularly known. In the 16th century it was given to a colony of Moorish refugees, hence its Turkish name, the 'Arab Mosque'.

The interior retains the aspect of a medieval Latin church: a long hall ending in three

rectangular apses. The wooden roof and galleries date from a restoration in 1913–19. At that time also the original floor was uncovered and large quantities of Genoese tombstones of the late Byzantine period came to light. Some of the tombstones bore the date 1347, the year when the Black Death struck Constantinople before ravaging western Europe; these are now in the Archaeological Museum.

At the end of Tersane Cd., huddled in the machine-age embrace of the Atatürk Bridge, is a beautiful street-fountain, the **Azapkapı Sebili**. It was built in 1732 with funds from the Valide Sultan Saliha, mother of Mahmut I. The sebil itself, with three grilled windows, is flanked by two magnificent çeşmes whose surfaces are entirely covered with floral reliefs—roses, lemon trees, pear trees—with borders and a chronogram

Detail of the relief carving on the Azapkapı Sebili, a fine monument of the early 18th century.

Menorahs and the Ten Commandments painted on glass, above the Ark of the Torah in the Zulfaris Synagogue (Jewish Museum).

picked out in gold. Just to the south of the fountain, on the water's edge, is **Sokollu Mehmet Paşa Camii**, built by Sinan in 1577–78 for the same Grand Vizier for whom he had built the more famous mosque in Sultanahmet (*see p. 111*).

For a glimpse of the old **Genoese walls**, cross Tersane Cd. (very carefully) and walk uphill along any of the lanes that lead to Yanık Kapı Sk., the 'Street of the Burnt Gate'. Here much demolition has taken place, revealing a stretch of the walls in which gapes an ancient archway, the only surviving gate of the Genoese city. Above it is a besmirched stone tablet emblazoned with the Cross of St George, emblem of Genoa, between a pair of escutcheons bearing the heraldic arms of the noble houses of Doria and De Merode.

JEWISH GALATA

Perşembe Pazarı Cd., which runs north–south (*map p. 344, B4*), is lined with picturesque 18th-century houses and hans. The most handsome is the one at no. 10 (1735–36). The general structure is completely characteristic of Turkish buildings of that period, with masonry in alternate courses of brick and stone and pointed window arches. It has three storeys, the upper ones projecting in zigzags held up by corbels, with two zigzags in Perşembe Pazarı Cd. and more in the alley beside it.

The street intersects **Bankalar Cd.**, once the financial heart of Galata. The oldest and most famous of the changing houses here is the **former Ottoman Bank**, in a huge Neoclassical building. This is the oldest bank in Turkey. Founded in 1856, it moved into the present building in 1892. On the mezzanine floor there is a museum (*closed for restoration at the time of writing*) with exhibits dealing with the financial history of the city in late Ottoman and early Republican times.

Opposite the bank are the elegant, Mannerist **Camondo Stairs**, built in 1860 as a public works project by the wealthy Jewish Camondo family (*see box overleaf*).

The Jewish Museum

Up steps and to the right at the end of Perçemli Sk. is the entrance to the Jewish Museum in the former Zulfaris Synagogue (*map p. 344, C4; open Mon–Thur 10–4, Fri 10–2, Sun 10–4 April–Nov and 10–2 Dec–March; www.muze500.com*). The synagogue fell out of use in the 1980s and has been a museum since 2001. It has a pretty stucco ceiling and a women's gallery supported on wooden columns painted as faux marble and with gilded Corinthian capitals. The Ark of the Torah at the east end is housed in a carved marble frame (1882) with crocketed neo-Gothic spirelets. The exhibits traces the history and fortunes of Turkish Jewry. Display panels in the women's gallery tell the story of the Camondo family. Downstairs is an exhibition of costumes and a circumcision chair.

Three other synagogues remain in Galata, the Ashkenazi Synagogue on Yüksek Kaldırım (*map p. 344, C4*) and the Neve Shalom Sephardic Synagogue on Büyük Hendek Cd. (*map p. 344, B4*) and the Italian Synagogue on Şair Ziya Paşa Cd. (*map p. 344, B4*).

THE CAMONDO FAMILY

The family that was to rise to wealth and status in Galata and ultimately to perish in a Nazi concentration camp began life in Spain, from where they fled to Venice after 1492. When Napoleon transferred Venice to Austria in 1797, the family moved again, this time to Istanbul. Here their mercantile ventures prospered, and a few years later Isaac Camondo and his brother Abraham set up the family bank. For three decades until the Imperial Ottoman Bank was established in 1856, the Camondos were the main bankers to the Empire.

Abraham Camondo maintained contact with Venice and became a champion of Italian unification. In 1870, in recognition of his services, the new King of Italy, Vittorio Emanuele, ennobled him. He lies buried in the Jewish cemetery above Hasköy. His grandsons, meanwhile, had carved out financial careers for themselves in Paris. It is from there that the last members of the family were deported to Auschwitz in 1943.

GENOESE GALATA

Galata Kulesi Sk., 'Galata Tower Street', leads uphill from Bankalar Cd. The building to the right at the beginning of this street is the **former Palazzo Comunale**, the official residence and headquarters of the *podestà*, the Genoese governor. The building dates from 1316, and it retained its original appearance until the late 19th century, when its façade was rebuilt during the widening of Bankalar Cd. The building behind it, on the other side of Kartçınar Sk., is also a Genoese foundation of the same time.

On the first cross street, Eski Banka Sk., immediately on the right, is a huge dilapidated old building known as the **Han of St Pierre** (Senpiyer Han), built in 1771 by the Comte de Saint-Priest as the 'lodging-place and bank of the French Nation', as recorded in his bequest. André Chénier, the early Romantic poet guillotined during the Terror, was born in an earlier house on this site in 1762, the son of a cloth merchant who served as consul in Galata. The façade of the present buildings bears the arms of the Comte de Saint-Priest and the fleur de lys of the house of Bourbon.

Further up Galata Kulesi Sk. on the left is the entrance to the **church of SS Peter and Paul** (*open for visits Sat 3.30–5.30*). It was founded in the late 15th century by the Genoese, together with the adjoining Dominican convent. Later it came under the protection of France and became the French parish church in Galata; in more recent times it has been the parish church of the local Maltese community, several of whose tombstones are built into the courtyard wall. The present church dates from a rebuilding in 1841 by the Fossati brothers. At the rear of the monastery is a stretch of the Genoese wall with two defence towers (well seen from the top of the Galata Tower).

The street rounds a corner after the church, and the Galata Tower comes into view.

THE GALATA TOWER

Map p. 344, C4. Open 9–8 every day; restaurant and nightclub open until midnight. A lift takes you to the seventh floor after which you walk two spiral flights to the top, where there is a café and observation terrace. They serve Galata-Tower shaped cookies with the tea and coffee.
The Galata Tower, the most prominent landmark on this side of the Golden Horn, was originally built as a lighthouse in the 6th century. It was rebuilt by the Genoese in 1348 as part of the fortifications of their expanding colony and was known as the Tower of Christ. During the early Ottoman period it was occupied by a detachment of Janissaries, whose commander served as the military governor of Galata. During the 16th century it was used to house prisoners of war, who were usually consigned as galley slaves in the Ottoman arsenal on the Golden Horn. Later it became a fire observation post, a purpose it continued to serve up until 1964. During restoration as a tourist attraction in 1967 large numbers of human bones was discovered in the tower dungeon, doubtless the remains of the galley slaves who were once imprisoned there.

The tower stands over 60m high, with walls over 4m thick. The entrance is up a curving double stairway of Proconnesian marble. The inscription above the doorway records a restoration by Mahmut II in 1832, prior to which time the approach to the entryway seems to have been via a wooden gangplank or drawbridge.

The observation deck at the top commands superb views of Topkapı, Haghia Sophia and Galata itself, including the stretch of Genoese wall and two bastions within the precincts of the church of SS Peter and Paul. From the top of the tower the mid-17th-century proto-aviator Hezarfen Ahmet Çelebi, equipped with a homemade pair of wings and with a strong wind behind him, flew all the way to Üsküdar, a distance of 6km—at least according to the story told by Evliya Çelebi. Sultan Murat IV was so terrified by the bird-man's powers that he sent him into exile.

The Bereketzade fountain
On the terrace behind the tower, fixed against the remnants of the barbican, is a pretty

'Here lies Gerasimos Ioannis Kavadias'. Neoclassical grave marker on the courtyard wall of the Turkish Orthodox church of the Pahaghia Kafatiani.

street-fountain. The tap is placed between reliefs of tall cypress trees, with rose bushes and baskets of figs above. In its present form it dates from 1732, but it was originally constructed just after the Conquest by Bereketzade Hacı Ali Ağa, the first Turkish governor of Galata, and it originally stood near his mosque. When that was demolished in 1948, the fountain was moved here. The Bereketzade mosque was reconstructed in its original location in 2006.

THE GALATA MEVLEVİ TEKKE

Above the Galata Tower on Galip Dede Cd. (*map p. 344, C3*), a steep street filled with shops selling musical instruments and audio equipment as well as stalls serving fresh pomegranate juice, is the entrance of the Galata Mevlevi Tekke (Mevelvihanesi Müzesi; *closed for restoration at the time of writing*). The tekke, or dervish monastery, was founded in the last decade of the 15th century by Şeyh Muhammad Semai Sultan Divanı, a descendant of Mevlana Celaleddin Rumi, the great 13th-century divine and mystic poet who founded the religious brotherhood known as the Mevlevi, the 'Whirling

Dervishes'. The most famous sheik of the Galata tekke was Galip Dede, whose ornate türbe is on the left of the path leading into the interior courtyard.

At the back of the courtyard is the octagonal *semahane*, or dancing-room. Before restoration (and perhaps also after) it and its adjacent chambers housed the Museum of Divan Poetry. Divan poetry was a form of Ottoman court verse inspired by the mystical verses of Mevlana. The Mevlevi occupied this tekke until the mid-1920s, when all the dervish orders were abolished by Atatürk.

The **graveyard** has some interesting old tombstones. One of them marks the grave of Count Bonneval, or Kumbaracı Ahmet Pasha (a nearby street is named after him), a French officer who enrolled in the Ottoman army during the reign of Mahmut I (1730–54). He was made Commandant of the Artillery Corps, became a Muslim, changed his name to Kumbaracı ('Bombardier') Osman Ahmet, and spent the rest of his life in the Ottoman service, dying in Istanbul in 1747. A French contemporary wrote of him that he was 'a man of great talent for war, intelligent, eloquent with charm and grace, very proud, a lavish spender, extremely debauched, and a great plunderer'.

BETWEEN THE GALATA BRIDGE & KABATAŞ

The tram from Eminönü stops at Karaköy, Tophane and Fındıklı. From the last stop, Kabataş, you can take the funicular (Tünel) to Taksim Square.

Yeraltı Cami

Towards the end of the 6th century Tiberius II is said to have built a fortress at the confluence of the Golden Horn and the Bosphorus, from which a chain, kept afloat by buoys, could be stretched to the opposite shore to close the Horn to enemy shipping. Yeraltı Cami, the 'Underground Mosque' on Kemankeş Cd. (*map p. 344, C4*), is housed in the low, vaulted cellar or keep of a Byzantine tower which some scholars have identified with Tiberius' fortress.

The inside of the mosque is a forest of squat pillars supporting low vaults. Toward the rear are two large chambers bathed in a greenish light. They contain the tombs of three sainted martyrs who died in the first Arab siege of Constantinople in 674–78. The site of their graves was revealed in a dream to a Nakşibendi dervish one night in 1640.

Two historic churches

The **church of St Benoit** (*map p. 344, C4*) was founded by the Benedictines in 1427; later it became the royal chapel of the French ambassadors to the Ottoman Empire, several of whom are buried here. After being in the hands of the Jesuits for several centuries, it was given, on the temporary dissolution of that order in 1773, to the Lazarists, to whom it still belongs. In 1804 they established a school next door; this is still in operation and continues to be one of the best foreign lycées in the in the city. Of the original 15th-century church, only the tower remains, with the rest of the building dating from two later reconstructions.

The quarter between Kemeraltı Cad. and the Bosphorus is a warren of narrow, winding streets. On Ali Paşa Değirmeni Sk. stands the Merkez Meryem Ana Kilisesi, the **church of the Panaghia Kafatiani** (*map p. 344, C4*), which belongs to the Turkish Orthodox Church, whose symbol is a cross with the Turkish star and crescent in the upper right-hand quadrant. This sect was founded in 1924 by a dissident priest from Anatolia known as Papa Eftim, who took his parishioners with him in a schism with the Greek Orthodox Church. Mass is said in Turkish rather than Greek, as this is the language of the Anatolian Christians known as the Karamanlı. During the half-century from that time until his death, Papa Eftim, who styled himself Patriarch Euthymius I, engaged in a running battle with the Ecumenical Patriarchate. The Turkish Orthodox congregation has now dwindled to just a handful of followers. The most treasured possession of the church of the Panaghia is an icon of the Hodegetria known as the Black Virgin, which was brought from Kaffa in the Crimea in 1475. The walls of the church enclosure are hung with a number of grave stelae, some of them quite fine.

Kılıç Ali Paşa Camii

Kılıç Ali Paşa Camii (*map p. 344, C4; under restoration at the time of writing*) is the finest of the classical mosques on the European shore of the Bosphorus. It was built by Sinan in 1580 for the Ottoman admiral Kılıç Ali Pasha.

KILIÇ ALİ PASHA

Like so many of the great Ottoman corsairs, Kılıç Ali was not a Turk. He was an ethnic Italian who was captured as a youth by Algerian pirates and spent 14 years as a galley slave. After regaining his freedom he entered Süleyman's service, becoming a Muslim and distinguished himself in several naval engagements. In recognition he was given the post of Governor of Algiers. Süleyman's successor Selim II appointed him Admiral of the Fleet, and named him Kılıç Ali, 'Ali the Sword'.

While serving in Algiers Ali Pasha came into contact with Miguel de Cervantes, who had been enslaved there after his capture at Lepanto. The governor was apparently impressed with Cervantes, for he released him and gave him enough money to return to Spain. Cervantes paid tribute to this kindness in *Don Quixote* (Vol. II, chapter 39), 'Wherein the captive relates his life and adventures'.

Ali Pasha retired to Istanbul in 1580. When he asked permission to build his mosque from Murat III, so the story goes, the sultan sarcastically suggested that he construct it on the sea, since that was the Kaptan Pasha's domain. Ali Pasha proceeded to do just that, and commissioned Sinan to build him a mosque on infilled land along the Bosphorus.

Ali Pasha died in 1587. According to the 19th-century historian Joseph von Hammer he was, although 90 years of age, still lusty and amorous, and expired in the arms of a concubine.

Although Sinan greatly admired Haghia Sophia, he had always avoided any kind of direct imitation of it. Now in his old age—he was nearly 90 when he built this mosque—he followed its design very closely, with the dome resting on four massive piers, flying buttresses carrying the weight externally, and galleries above three sides. The mihrab is in a square apse decorated with lovely Iznik tiles.

The türbe of Ali Pasha is behind the mosque to the east. Opposite the southeast corner of the mosque is the former medrese, at the time of writing in a state or ruin. The large and fine hamam was undergoing restoration.

The hamam, which is a single bath, is next to the mosque. It is unlike other hamams in Istanbul and similar instead to bath houses at Bursa or in Buda in Hungary. The hararet is not cruciform but hexagonal, with open bathing places in four of its arched recesses. The other two recesses give access from the two separate soğukluks.

TOPHANE & FINDIKLI

Tophane, the 'Cannon House', on the left of the road as you go towards Kabataş (*map p. 344, C3–C4*), was the principal military foundry in the Ottoman Empire. The original Tophane was built on this site by Mehmet II soon after the Conquest. The present structure with its five domes was built by Selim III in 1803, doubtless in connection with his attempt to reform the Ottoman army. The building is now an art centre belonging to Mimar Sinan University. On the other side of the main road is a kiosk, **Tophane Kasrı**, built by Sultan Abdülaziz as a pavilion from which he could review troop parades.

The **Tophane Çeşmesi**, next to the pavilion (*map p. 345, D4*), is one of the most famous of the Baroque street-fountains in the city. Built in 1732 by Mahmut I, it has marble walls completely covered with floral designs and arabesques carved in low relief, which were originally painted and gilded. Its widely overhanging roof was lacking for many years (old engravings show the fountain without it) but has recently been restored.

The Modern Art Museum

Istanbul Modern is the name of the city's Museum of Modern Art, a large white building on the Tophane docks, housed in an old warehouse (*map p. 345, D4; open 10–6, until 8pm on Thur, closed Mon*). The permanent collection of works by modern and contemporary Turkish artists is displayed upstairs, rehung with a different theme each year. The ground-floor exhibition space is used for temporary shows of Turkish and international art. There is an increasing number of art galleries in Tophane. In 2010 riots accompanied one gallery opening, it was suggested because local residents feared that the influx of fashionable establishments would push up property prices. Other reports suggested that it was a symptom of Istanbul's increasingly uneasy coexistence of liberal and conservative populations.

The street-fountain (çeşme) of Tophane, built by Mahmut I in 1732, with Nusretiye Camii behind it, built almost a century later by Mahmut II.

Nusretiye and Cihangir Camiis

Nusretiye Camii (*map p. 345, D4*), the 'Mosque of Victory', was built between 1822 and 1826 by Mahmut II; it was completed just after the Sultan's extermination of the Janissaries, and its name commemorates that event. The architect was Kirkor Balyan, the founder of the large family of Armenian architects who served the sultans through most of the 19th century and who built many of the mosques and palaces along the shores of the Bosphorus. Balyan had studied in Paris and his mosque shows an interesting blend of Baroque and Empire motifs. The western façade is no longer a traditional porticoed courtyard but a palace or villa-like edifice, a feature which became a characteristic of all the Balyan mosques. Notice how slender the minarets are (so much so, in fact, that they collapsed soon after construction and had to be rebuilt).

Not far beyond the Nusretiye, on the heights above, is **Cihangir Camii**. Built for Abdülhamit II in 1890, it occupies the site of an older mosque built in 1553 by Sinan for Süleyman the Magnificent, dedicated to Prince Cihangir, Süleyman's hunchback son, who died in that year—of heartbreak, it is said, because of the Sultan's execution of his beloved half-brother, Prince Mustafa. Sinan's mosque burned down in 1720.

Between the two mosques is **Salipazarı Yokuşu**, whose nargile cafés and snack bars are very popular.

Fındıklı

In Byzantine times the area of Fındıklı (*map p. 345, D3–E3*) was known as Argyropolis, the 'Town of Silver', since it stood opposite Chrysopolis (modern Üsküdar), the 'City of

Gold'. Today it is named after the humble hazelnut. Beyond the Mimar Sinan University, named after the great Ottoman architect, is a handsome mosque on the edge of the water, built, appropriately enough, by Sinan himself. This is **Molla Çelebi Camii**, built in 1561–62; the founder was Mehmet Vusuli, also known as Molla Çelebi, Lord Chief Justice in the reign of Süleyman the Magnificent. About 100m farther along on the right the **Hekimoğlu Ali Paşa çeşmeşi**, a street-fountain built in 1732 by Hekimoğlu Ali Pasha, son of a Greek-born doctor who rose to be Grand Vizier of Mustafa I and Osman II, until Osman imprisoned him in the Maiden's Tower off the Üsküdar shore. It is a beautifully carved work in white marble, with a fountain on its two faces. On the other side of the highway, just as you reach Kabataş, there is a fine Baroque sebil doing service as a roadside café. This is the **Koca Yusuf Paşa sebili**, built in 1787 by the Grand Vizier of Abdülhamit I. It has a magnificent çeşme in the centre, flanked by the two grilled windows. The whole edifice is elaborately carved and decorated, with a long calligraphic inscription forming a frieze above the windows.

BEYOĞLU

Beyoğlu (*map pp. 344–45*) is the district above Galata. It lies strung out around its famous long shopping avenue, İstiklal Caddesi. At the height of the Ottoman Empire, when it was known as Pera, this was the foreign quarter of the city, where all the great powers had their embassy buildings and their residences. Today it is known for its shops, restaurants and hotels, and for a nightlife that is a hundred times more spirited than in the sleepy confines of the historic peninsula.

HISTORY OF BEYOĞLU

The history of Beyoğlu follows that of Galata (*see p. 224*). Its historic name, Pera, means 'beyond' in Greek. At first this was used in the general sense of 'on the other side of the Golden Horn'; later it more specifically related to the heights above. As the confines of Galata became too crowded for flourishing foreign community, they began to move out, beyond the medieval walls, to the hills and vineyards above. Here the foreign powers built enormous mansions surrounded by spacious gardens; all of them standing along the road that would later be known as the Grande Rue de Péra, today's İstiklal Caddesi. Nevertheless, the region must have remained rural until well into the 18th century; for in that period you often see references to *les vignes de Péra*. But as Pera became more and more built up, it fell a prey like the rest of the city to the endemic fires. Two especially devastating outbreaks, in 1831 and 1871, destroyed nearly all the earlier buildings, hence the dearth of anything of architectural antiquity in Beyoğlu. This is the realm of late 19th-century eclecticism, of Art Nouveau, and of 20th-century utilitarianism.

ON & AROUND İSTİKLAL CADDESİ

At the upper end of the Galata funicular (the Tünel) begins the grand promenade of İstiklal Caddesi (*map p. 344, C3*), the former Grande Rue de Péra, renamed 'Independence Boulevard' to commemorate the declaration of the Turkish Republic in 1923. Today it is a pedestrianised street (except for the old-fashioned tram that still rumbles along it) lined with shops and cafés, and with alleyways opening off it into warrens of boutiques, fleamarkets and clothing stalls. Some of the buildings are grand and architecturally interesting, but modern signage and the clamour of commerce often mask the finer details. It pays to spend time here. The street is always busy; in the afternoons in can be packed, filled with a mass of humankind, even on the coldest days in winter when the wind can whistle down it with penetrating force. The consulates on or near the street belong to those countries that have had legations here since the early centuries of the Ottoman Empire. Near the south end of the street is the **Swedish Consulate**. The Embassy of Sweden was established here on its present site in 1755; the present building was erected in 1870 by the Austrian architect Domenico Pulgher.

Directly across the street from the Swedish Consulate is the **Narmanlı Han**, which housed the Russian Embassy up until 1845, when it was replaced by another building farther along the avenue. Now filled with small shops, its most distinctive feature is the row of engaged Tuscan Doric columns along the façade. The apartment on the upper floor at the corner facing Tünel was for half a century the residence of Aliye Berger-Boronai (1904–73), one of Turkey's greatest female artists.

Diagonally opposite at no. 235 is the fire-blackened **Botter House**, 1901, an Art Nouveau building built as a shop and apartments by the Dutch-born outfitter to Sultan Abdülhamit II.

A DETOUR OFF THE AVENUE

Kumbaracı Yokuşu (named after the great bombadier; *see p. 231*) leads downhill off İstiklal Caddesi. At the lower end of the street, turn right to find the **Crimean Memorial Church**, behind a wall with a large bay tree by the gate (*map p. 344, C4*). This handsome church was built between 1858 and 1868 under the aegis of Lord Stratford de Redcliffe, known to the Turks as Büyük Elçi, or the Great Ambassador, because of the enormous influence he exerted on Turkish affairs during his three terms as British Ambassador to the Ottoman Empire during the period 1810–56. Designed by G.E. Street, the architect of the London Law Courts and the Anglican church in Rome, it is built in the neo-Gothic style with a cavernous porch, like the Law Courts themselves. The church was abandoned for a time, but recently it has been well restored and is once again in use.

Asmalı Mescit Cd. leads off the avenue to the left. It and Sofyali Sk. which leads off it are lined with meyhanes, traditional Turkish taverns. One of the finest is Asmali Cavit, halfway down Asmalı Mescit Cd. on the right. At its far end Asmalı Mescit Sk. leads into Meşrutiyet Cd. and the quarter known as Tepebaşı. On the right is the famous **Pera Palace Hotel** (*map p. 344, B3–C3*), built in the years 1893–95 by Alexander Vallaury. The hotel reopened after extensive restoration in 2010. A sedan chair of the type that would have conveyed guests to the hotel from Sirkeci Station is displayed in reception. The wonderful old elevator, the first in Istanbul, is still in working order (though not in use on a regular basis) and is a fine feature of the lobby and main staircase (its workings can be seen behind glass from the basement floor). The faithfully restored Domed Salon (it looks remarkably like period photographs of itself), with its Orientalist décor, is a beautiful place for tea or a cocktail. The room where Agatha Christie stayed and wrote part of *Murder on the Orient Express* (no. 411) is still in regular use. Atatürk's suite (no. 101), decorated in his favourite colour, sunrise pink, has been restored as a museum, with a number of his personal belongings, including a panama hat, his trademark sunglasses, his bedroom slippers and a cigarette case still full of cigarettes.

Also on Meşrutiyet Cd. (no 53) is another grand old hotel, the **Büyük Londra** (Grand Hôtel de Londres). This is truly a survival from another age, and the shabby-genteel bar with its many birdcages (many of them tenanted) is also a memorable place to stop for a drink.

Notice from the Pera Palace kitchens in 1944 advising customers that food will not be served until further notice.

OLD EMBASSIES ALONG İSTİKLAL CADDESİ

The embassies of Pera were established over the course of the 16th–18th centuries, generally by grants of land bestowed by the sultans, and each formed the centre of its 'Nation'; that is, of the community of resident merchants and officials of the various countries. These embassies came to exert a growing influence on the Ottoman Empire and collectively they dominated the life of Pera until the establishment of the Turkish Republic. Near the embassies various churches were established, more or less under their protection, and some of these foundations survive. All the embassies were relocated to Ankara when it became capital of the Turkish Republic in 1923. The old ambassadorial premises now function as consulates, all marked on the map on p. 344, C3.

Many of the buildings are quite fine, and most have interesting histories attached to them. As Philip Mansel points out in *Constantinople, City of the World's Desire*, the new embassy buildings, built in the mid-19th century after a fire had destroyed the old, were very often built in a style attaching to the Nation they represented. The **Palais de France** looks like an *hôtel de ville*, the **Russian Consulate** resembles a mansion of the Romanovs, the former **British Consulate** is a copy of the Reform Club in St James's, London. The reason for this might be deliberate national chauvinism, but it also has much to do with the ingrained taste of the architects who were given the commissions. The Russian Embassy was built in 1837–45 by Giuseppe Fossati. The Fossati brothers, of Italian-Swiss origin, had been in Moscow for several years as official architects of Tsar Nicholas I, who sent them to Istanbul to build his new embassy (they remained here for two decades as official architects to the sultan, restoring Haghia Sophia in 1847–49 and building several other structures, including the Dutch Embassy and the church of SS Peter and Paul in Galata). The architect of the Palais de France, and of its church, St-Louis des Français, was a native Frenchman. The British Embassy was designed by Sir Charles Barry, architect of the Houses of Parliament in London.

All the embassies had their own adjacent places of worship. A short way down Postacılar Sk. on the left, in the precincts of the Dutch Consulate, is the entrance to the **former Dutch Chapel**, since 1857 the Union Church of Istanbul. Below it, the street winds to the right past the dilapidated former Spanish Embassy, with only the **chapel of the Terrae Sanctae** remaining in use.

At the bottom of Postacılar Sk. is a tidily-kept square flanked by two large old buildings. The one to the left, at the top of the square, is the former **French Tribunal of Justice**, a 19th-century structure in which the legal affairs of the European 'Nations' were handled in late Ottoman times. The handsome old building on the right is the **Palazzo di Venezia**, now the Italian Consulate. The present building is believed to date from c. 1695, though it was completely rebuilt c. 1750. In Ottoman times it was the residence of the Venetian *bailio*, the ambassador of the Serene Republic and one of the most powerful of the foreign legates in the city. We learn from his *Memoirs* that Giacomo Casanova was a guest here in the summer of 1744; in his three months in the city this great lover did not make a single conquest but was himself seduced by one İsmail Efendi.

There are stories attaching to all the embassies and their Nations, some amusing, others of historic importance. The **Palais de Hollande** (Dutch Consulate) is an attractive building completed in 1855 by the Fossati brothers. It was a native of the Habsburg Netherlands, Augier Ghislain de Busbecq, who took the first tulip bulbs back to Holland. He had encountered the flowers and been much struck with them during his time in Istanbul, where he served as Ambassador of the Holy Roman Empire to the court of Süleyman the Magnificent.

France was the first European nation to establish formal diplomatic relations with the Ottoman Empire, beginning with the envoys sent by Francis I to Süleyman in 1525. Relations between the two powers were always close. This is not to say that they were always cordial. There were frequent diplomatic tensions, particularly in the 17th century when the great Köprülü grand viziers were working hard to make European ambassadors show sufficient respect. A Russian ambassador of the day was beaten up for not bowing low enough. The French ambassador Nointel almost broke off relations with the Sublime Porte over the question of where he was or wasn't allowed to place his stool during audiences with the sultan. Culturally and economically, however, France and Constantinople have derived much from each other. France was the Ottoman Empire's first great European trading partner. The Reform Movement of Selim III and Mahmut II was inspired by the ideals of the French Revolution. The European influence that entered Turkish art, architecture and literature came to it mainly from France.

British relations with the Sublime Porte have been less fraternal, partly because British imperial ambition was at times a threat to the Ottoman state. Pre-revolutionary Russia, too, made no secret of its designs on Constantinople. Seeing Russia as the custodian of the Orthodox faith, Tsar Nicholas II was explicit in his aim to annexe the great Byzantine city. Britain's Prime Minister, Asquith, was a supporter of the idea. At the end of the First World War, if Lloyd George had had his way, Constantinople would have been returned to Greece. For much of the 19th century the embassies of Pera had been obsessed with the Eastern Question, the balance of power between Russia, Britain, France and the Austrian and Ottoman empires. The Ottoman government had always done much to aid British interests in this respect. Ultimately that service was not forgotten. In 1922, Mehmet VI, the last sultan, abandoned by France, left Istanbul on a British battleship, the HMS *Malaya*, which took him into exile, first on Malta and then on the Italian riviera.

Female mascheron and moulded leaves from a European-influenced façade of the early 20th century on İstiklal Caddesi.

St Mary Draperis

The **Yemek Kulübü restaurant** at no. 172 on the left as you walk towards Taksim Square has a lovely Art Nouveau interior. Past the Russian Consulate on the other side is the Franciscan **church of St Mary Draperis**, down a flight of steps from the street level (*open 10–12 & 2–6, Sun and Tues 2–6 only*). Above the door is a distinctive, faintly Titianesque mosaic of the Assumption, and a clock has been built into the left-hand window oculus. The first church on this site was built in 1678 and the present structure dates from 1789. The parish itself, however, is a very ancient one, dating from the beginning of 1453, when the Franciscans built a church near the present site of Sirkeci Station. After the Conquest they were forced to leave Stamboul, settling first in Galata and then in Pera. The Franciscans still preserve in the church a miraculous icon of the Virgin, which they claim to have inherited from their first church in Constantinople. The walls are lined with memorials to legates, dragomans and their wives.

From the old Apollon studio to the church of Our Lady

On the corner of Balyoz Sk. is the **Mek:Med Café**, with an elaborate ceiling and an excellent breakfast buffet. Diagonally opposite, in an old building on the right, the former Apollon photographic studio, is a delightful second-hand bookshop, the **Denizler Kitapevi**. Opposite the Dutch Consulate is the **Paşabahçe glass shop** selling fine and ornamental glassware from the famous brand established at Beykoz on the Asian side of the Bosphorus (though sadly no longer made there).

A few steps further along on the right is the **Robinson Crusoe bookshop**, with a wide selection of titles in English. Further up still, on the same side, behind a tall arcade, is the Franciscan **church of St Anthony of Padua** (*map p. 344, C3*), the largest Roman Catholic sanctuary in the city. The first church of St Anthony was established on this site in 1725; the present building, a good example of Italian neo-Gothic architecture in red brick, with three rose windows and dwarf arcades above, was built in 1906 by the Istanbul-born Italian architect Giulio Mongeri.

A short way beyond the church, to the left, is **Hazzopulo**, branded a 'historical passage', a picturesque alley filled with stalls and opening out into a cobbled area with cafés. Here an alley on the left, where the café puts out cushions on the steps for overflow customers, leads through to the Greek **church of Our Lady of Pera** (*map p. 344, C3*), dedicated to the Eisodeia tis Theotokou (the Presentation of the Virgin). First consecrated in 1807, it was rebuilt in 1855. On the right side of the iconostasis there is an icon of the Virgin and Child dating from the 10th century.

Around Galatasaray Meydanı

Galatasaray Meydanı (*map p. 344, C3*) takes its name from the **Galatasaray Lisesi** (lycée), its ground surrounded by an ornate fence with gilded *fleur-de-lys* finials. Although the present building dates only to 1908, Galatasaray traces its origins back to the early Ottoman period. It was founded by Beyazıt II (r. 1481–1512) as a school for the imperial pages, ancillary to the one in Topkapı Sarayı. After a somewhat chequered career, it was reorganised in 1868 under Sultan Abdülaziz as a modern lycée on the French model, with the teaching partly in Turkish, partly in French. After the University of Istanbul, Galatasaray is the oldest Turkish institution of learning in the city, and it has produced a large number of the statesmen and intellectuals who have shaped modern Turkey.

Sahne Sk. leads left under a metal arch marked Balıklı Pazarı, 'fish market' (*map p. 344, C2–C3*). This street and its tributary alleyways are lined with shops and stalls selling tourist trinkets intermingled with the barrows of fishmongers and greengrocers, along with kerbside eating and drinking places and meyhanes. To the right is **Çiçek Pasajı**, 'Passage of Flowers', an L-shaped passage that has entrances on both Sahne Sk. and on İstiklal Cd. This was originally the 'Cité de Pera', built in 1870 by the Greek businessman Zographos Efendi as a *de luxe* apartment house with elegant shops along the arcade at street level. During the 1930s a number of meyhanes were opened in the arcade; the flower shops that gave the passage its name have long since been displaced by restaurants. The entrance on İstiklal Cd. is very fine, with 'Cité de Péra' inscribed between caryatids and a pretty design of flowers and fruit painted on glass.

Opening off the opposite side of Sahne Sk. from Çiçek Pasajı is the **Avrupa Pasajı**, which runs down to Meşrutiyet Cd. This was built by the Austrian architect Domenico Pulgher in 1870, modelled on a passage in Paris; it is also known as Aynalı Pasaj, or the 'Mirrored Arcade', because of the mirrors that reflected the light of the gas lamps that once illuminated it in the evening.

A short way down Sahne Sk. beyond these passages on the right is the **Armenian**

church of Üç Horon (the Holy Trinity). The symbol of the triangle and dove is repeated on the main door itself and in the Diocletian window above. A side chapel is usually open for prayer. The present building dates from 1907.

Nevizade Sk. (*map p. 344, C2*) is a colourful street lined with meyhanes. On Turnacıbaşı Cd., leading off İstiklal Cd. to the right, is the **Galatasaray Hamamı**.

Between Galatasaray and Taksim Square

The section of İstiklal Cd. between Galatasaray and Taksim Square is lined with shops, banks and eating places. This is the heart of downtown Istanbul. Many of the buildings along the avenue date to the last half century of the Ottoman era, such as Tokatlıyan Hanı, Cercle d'Orient and Cité de Roumélie (some of which were under restoration and swathed in tarpaulin at the time of writing). Halfway along this stretch, on the left, is **Ağa Camii** (*map p. 344, C2*), the only mosque on İstiklal Cd. The first mosque on this site was founded in 1597 by Hüseyin Ağa of the Galatasaray School; it was rebuilt in 1839 and restored in 1936.

The last street on the right before the end of the avenue, Meşelik Sk., leads to the courtyard entrance of **Haghia Triada** (*map p. 345, D2*), the Holy Trinity, the largest Greek Orthodox church in Istanbul, completed in 1880. The narthex is kept open for prayer. Hens live in the courtyard and nest in the oleander beds.

At no. 16 İstiklal Cd., Starbucks Coffee has set up shop in a tall building where you can still make out, in faded blue paint, the name, in Greek letters, of N. Papadakis. At the end of the avenue on the left is the **French Consulate and Institut Français**, originally constructed in 1719 as a plague hospital. Beyond that is a pretty little octagonal building that has given its name to Taksim Square and the surrounding quarter. This is the **Taksim Meksemi**, or water-distribution centre, built by Mahmut I in 1732. *Taksim* means water-channelling. There are two little bird houses on its façade, still tenanted by sparrows (*see box opposite*).

TAKSİM SQUARE

Taksim Square (*map p. 344, D2*) is the centre of modern Istanbul. In the middle of the square is the **Independence Monument**, a statue group representing Atatürk and other leaders of the Turkish Nationalist movement, completed in 1928 by the Italian sculptor Pietro Canonica. It was the scene of a suicide bombing in October 2010, during the Independence Day celebrations. The glass-walled building at the far end of the square is the **Atatürk Cultural Centre** (Kültür Merkezi), home of the Istanbul Opera; this was completed in 1969, only to burn down the following year, and repairs were not completed until 1978.

A number of streets radiate out from Taksim Square: Siraselviler Cd. heading off to the south, Taki Zafer Cd. (and its continuation, İnönü Cd.) to the west, and Cumhuriyet Cd. to the north, the first two avenues leading down to the Bosphorus and the third to the modern quarters of Harbiye, Nişantaşı, Teşvikiye and Şişli.

THE BIRD HOUSES OF ISTANBUL

A distinctive and attractive feature of Istanbul are its bird houses, known as *kuş evleri* or *kuş sarayları*. They are small constructions, usually of stone (those that were of wood have perished), attached to the exterior walls of public buildings: hamams, medreses, libraries and mosques. They were made throughout the Ottoman period, from the 15th to the 19th centuries. Early ones are simple apertures  into which birds can fly and build. Other, later bird houses from the Tulip Era and throughout the 18th century, are more elaborate, fashioned to look like mini palaces, pavilions or even mosques, complete with minarets. Some of the finest are in Üsküdar, on the Ayazma Camii and Yeni Valide Camii. The one illustrated here is also an 18th-century example, from the water distribution kiosk on Taksim Square. A modern bird house is fixed to the wall of the Koç Museum at Hasköy. Most are occupied in the nesting season by sparrows, finches and other songbirds.

The Military Museum

The museum (Askeri Müzesi; *open 9–5; closed Mon and Tues; entrance on Gümüs Cd.; map p. 345, D1*) has an extensive and interesting collection of exhibits from all periods of Ottoman military history. Among these are the beautiful cannons captured by the Turks in their campaigns in Europe and the Middle East, all of them arrayed outside the museum. The miniature Janissary costumes include all of those worn by their different ranks and units, a fascinating and colourful collection. Another notable exhibit is the huge and sumptuous imperial tent in which the sultan lived when he accompanied the army on campaign. The second of three parts of the great chain that was stretched across the Bosphorus in an attempt to keep out the fleet of Mehmet the Conqueror is also kept here. The other two sections of the chain are in the Naval Museum and the Archaeological Museum. There are also performances of Ottoman military music (*Wed–Sun 3–4*) by the Mehter Band, whose drums, cymbals and trumpets originate in the military parade music of the Janissary corps. The European music known as *alla turca* was inspired by these martial tunes.

The Atatürk Museum

At no. 250 Halaskargazi Cd., the continuation of Cumhuriyet Cd. (*beyond map p. 345, D1; open Wed, Fri, Sun 9–4*), is an old mansion where Atatürk lived with his mother and sister in 1919, just before he went to Anatolia to organise the Turkish Nationalist movement. On display are a number of Atatürk's personal effects as well as photographs, documents and memorabilia associated with his residence here. The exterior is painted in the great leader's favourite shade of pink.

THE EUROPEAN SHORE OF THE BOSPHORUS

Boats on the Bosphorus are either leisure cruises (run by a variety of companies; the best value are those operated by Şehir Hatları), or commuter ferries, all from Eminönü. However, because the ferries cater to working Istanbullus, they leave early in the morning (before 8am) and return in the late afternoon (after 5pm) and do not operate on Sun and holidays. By land your choice rests between buses and taxis. Details are included in the text.

Since antiquity travellers have praised the beauties of the Bosphorus, and in its heyday it must indeed have been one of the loveliest and most dramatic sights in the world, with lines of wooden yalıs at the water's edge and forested hills behind.

The Bosphorus derives its name from the myth of Io, a priestess of Hera who was seduced by Zeus. Zeus transformed Io into a heifer to conceal her from his jealous wife, but Hera was not deceived and sent a gadfly to torment Io. Pursued by the gadfly, Io plunged into the strait that separates Europe from Asia, and thenceforth it was known as the Bosphorus, the 'Cow Ford'. The Bosphorus also appears in Greek mythology in the legend of Jason and the Argonauts, who travelled up the strait to the Black Sea, the ancient Euxine, in their quest for the Golden Fleece. Many places on the Bosphorus are associated with their adventures.

The Bosphorus first appears in Greek literature in the *Histories* of Herodotus, with a description of the bridge of boats constructed by Darius in 512 BC to take his army across in his campaign against the Scythians. It played an important role in the history of the city founded at its southern extremity in 667 BC. As Petrus Gyllius expressed it: 'The Bosphorus with one key opens and closes two worlds, two seas.' As Philip Mansel less romantically remarks, the once beautiful strait, famed as a 'diamond between two emeralds', is now more of a 'sewer between two housing estates'. But all is not yet lost. There is still beauty to be discovered.

Topography and oceanography

The Bosphorus is some 30km long. At its narrowest it is 700m wide and over 3.5km at its widest. The average depth at the centre is between 50m and 75m, but at one point it sinks to over 100m. The predominant surface current flows at a rate of 3–5 knots from the Black Sea to the Marmara, but eddies producing strong reverse currents flow along most of the shoreline. A very strong wind may reverse the surface current and make it flow towards the Black Sea, in which case the counter-eddies also change direction. At a depth of about 40m there is a sub-surface current, the *kanal*, which flows from the Marmara to the Black Sea. These lower waters, denser and more saline than the waters above them, are for the most part prevented from entering the Black Sea by a threshold just beyond the Bosphorus mouth, which turns them so that they mingle with the upper waters and are driven back toward the Marmara. The lower current is sometimes so strong that if fishing nets are lowered into it, it may pull the boats toward the Black Sea.

Both shores of the Bosphorus are indented with bays and harbours, and in general an indentation on one shore corresponds to a cape or promontory on the other. Most of the bays are at the mouths of valley streams coming down from the hills on either side.

Both shores are lined with hills, none of them very high, the most imposing being Büyük Çamlıca (262m) and Yuşa Tepesi (201m), both on the Asian side. Nevertheless, especially on the upper Bosphorus, the hills often seem very high because of the way in which they come down to the water in precipitous cliffs. In spite of the never-ceasing development and building, both sides of the Bosphorus are still fairly wooded. The dark pink flowers of the judas trees are a famous sight in spring.

THE BOSPHORUS DROWNINGS

While the fate of unwanted royal princes was to be strangled with a bowstring, ladies of the harem who were considered to have transgressed were disposed of by drowning. When rumours began to circulate that someone had been interfering with his women, the mad sultan İbrahim is said to have ordered that over 200 women be tied in sacks and tossed into the Bosphorus. The German-born architect and painter Anton Ignaz Melling (1763–1831), who worked for Selim III and his demanding sister Hatice Sultan, left a memorable description of a nocturnal execution:

'Nothing is more terrible than the way these unfortunate women are subjected to the ultimate penalty. The Kızlar Ağa sends them to the Bostancıbaşi. There they are tied up in sacks in the bottom of which stones have been placed. The bostancıs charged with throwing them into the Bosphorus get into a boat with three pairs of oars and place the condemned women in another small barque attached to their own by a rope. They are thus conducted to the open sea, rounding the Saray point; and by various buffetings the fragile barque is made to capsize. A eunuch accompanies the bostancıs, and returns to the Kızlar Ağa to confirm that his orders have been carried out. Mr Melling, on returning one night from the Princes' Isles, witnessed an execution of this kind by moonlight: the cries of the two women could be heard from far off. The impression of horror remained imprinted in his memory for long afterwards.'

From *Voyage Pittoresque de Constantinople et des Rives du Bosphore* (Tr. AB)

DOLMABAHÇE

The end of the tramline from the old city, Kabataş (*map p. 345, E2*), is one of the principal ferry-stops on the lower Bosphorus, with boats to Kadıköy and the Princes' Islands, and a funicular railway to Taksim Square. From here you can walk (slightly over 1km, not particularly pleasant, but bearable) to Dolmabahçe or take a bus to Beşiktaş.

Detail of the neo-Baroque clock-tower outside Dolmabahçe Palace (1890–95).

Dolmabahçe Camii

The mosque on the seashore some 300m upstream from the Kabataş ferry port is **Dolmabahçe Camii** (*map p. 345, E2*). It was built in 1853 for the Valide Sultan Bezmialem, mother of Sultan Abdülmecit; the architect was Nikoğos Balyan, who worked with his father on the new Dolmabahçe Palace, also for Abdülmecit. The wide cartwheel arches of this mosque are very distinctive, divided into great segments like a wedge of lemon. The minarets are very slender, and each is in effect a Corinthian column, fluted up until the acanthus-leaf capital, above which rises a tapering witch's hat roof. The mosque is preceded not by a classical porticoed avlu but by an eclectic front resembling a villa façade. All these elements are trademarks of Balyan mosque architecture.

The neo-Baroque **clock-tower** to the north of the mosque was erected by Sarkis Balyan in 1890–95 for Abdülhamit II. There are clock faces on all sides with Arabic numbers; these were made by the French horologist Jean-Paul Garnier.

Directly across the avenue from Dolmabahçe Camii there is a **tiny külliye** with a five-windowed sebil. It was built in 1741 by the sipahi Hacı Mehmet Emin Ağa. It is flanked symmetrically by a door on one side and by a çeşme on the other; behind three barred apertures are the tombs of the members of the sipahi's family; his own tomb, unusually, is in the sebil itself.

DOLMABAHÇE SARAYI

Map p. 345, F2. Open 9–4; closed Mon and Thur. Bus 28 or 28T from Eminönü to Beşiktaş, or tram T1 to Kabataş, then walk.
Dolmabahçe Sarayı was the principal imperial residence in the late years of the Ottoman Empire, particularly under Abdülmecit I, from whose reign the current building dates. The public entrance is through the gardens to the south. The most impressive aspect of the palace is its white marble seaside façade, 284m long.

HISTORY OF DOLMABAHÇE SARAYI

The site of Dolmabahçe was originally a small harbour on the Bosphorus. On 22nd April 1453, during the Ottoman siege of Constantinople, Mehmet II had 70 ships anchored here in preparation for the strategem that turned the tide of battle in his favour. After sunset he had the ships placed on wheeled platforms and hauled by oxen over the heights of Pera and then down to Kasımpaşa on the Golden Horn, thus bypassing the chain with which the Byzantines closed the mouth of the inner harbour. This gave the Turks control of the Horn and set the stage for their final conquest of Constantinople.

Shortly after the Conquest, Fatih laid out a royal garden on this site, and early in his reign Selim I built a seaside kiosk here. Early in the 17th century, Ahmet I extended the royal gardens by filling in the seashore in front of them, a project that was completed by his son and successor, Osman II; thenceforth this site was known as Dolmabahçe, the 'filled-in garden'. By the beginning of the 19th century there was a large imperial summer residence here, and Mahmut II seems to have preferred it to the old palace of Topkapı.

His son and successor, Abdülmecit I, decided to move out of Topkapı altogether, and in 1844 he commissioned Karabet Balyan and his son Nikoğos to replace the existing structures at Dolmabahçe with a new palace. It was completed in 1855, after which time Dolmabahçe served as the principal imperial residence. The only sultan not to use it was Abdülhamit II, who preferred the greater seclusion of Yıldız (*see p. 251*).

After the establishment of the Turkish Republic, Dolmabahçe served as Atatürk's presidential residence whenever he was in Istanbul. Atatürk lived here during his last illness, and he died here on 10th November 1938, in a seaside bedroom that is still furnished as it was at the time of his death. The palace is now a museum and is used as a venue for official gala functions.

The palace

The core of the palace is a great imperial state hall flanked by two main wings containing the state rooms and royal apartments, with the *selamlık* on the south and the harem on the north; the apartment of the Valide Sultan is in a separate wing linked to the sultan's harem through the apartment of the crown prince; in addition there was another harem for the women of the princes, and still another residence at the northwest corner for the Chief Black Eunuch. The complex also included rooms for those of the palace staff who lived within Dolmabahçe, as well as kitchens, an imaret to feed the staff, an infirmary with a pharmacy, stables, carriage houses and barracks for the halberdiers who guarded the imperial residence. All in all, there were a total of 285 rooms, including 43 large salons and six hamams, with the sultan's private bath centred on an alabaster bath tub.

The palace interior was the work of the French set designer Charles Séchan, who designed the Paris Opéra. A number of European artists were commissioned to produce paintings, notably the Orientalists Jean-Léon Gérôme and Fausto Zonaro; examples of their work can still be seen in the rooms for which they were commissioned. The opulent furnishings include 4455 square metres of hand-woven Hereke carpets. The world's largest chandelier hangs in the Muayede Salon, or State Room, comprising 4.5 tonnes of Bohemian glass with 750 lights.

A great showpiece is the ornate stairway that leads up from the Hall of the Ambassadors, its balusters made of Baccarat crystal and its upper level framed with monoliths of variegated marble. Other impressive chambers are the Zülveçheyn Salonu, the Kırmızı Oda (Red Room), the Mavi (Blue) Salon, the Pembe (Pink) Salon, the Valide Sultan's apartment, the apartment of Sultan Abdülaziz and Atatürk's apartment.

IHLAMUR KASRI

The street that runs inland just north of Dolmabahçe (Şair Nedim Cd.; *beyond map p. 345, F1*) leads after 1km to an imperial Ottoman rest-house, Ihlamur Kasrı, the 'Linden Pavilion' (on Nüzhetiye Cd.; *open 9–5; closed Mon and Thur*). It takes its name from Ihlamur Deresi, the Valley of the Lindens, the once-lovely vale in which it is set (though the landscaped park around the *kasr* today is still lovely). Ahmet III, the 'Tulip King', laid out gardens here during the first quarter of the 18th century, and these would have been used in his annual Tulip Festivals. Abdülmecit erected a kiosk here early in his reign, and then in 1849–55 Nikoğos Balyan built for him the pair of kiosks that constitute the present Ihlamur Kasrı. These are Maiyet Köşkü, the Kiosk of the Retinue, and Merasim Köşkü, the Ceremonial Kiosk. The first of these, as its name implies, was used by the sultan's retinue, including the women of his harem, while the second was used for his guests, including visiting dignitaries. Ihlamur Kasrı has recently been superbly restored, along with its surrounding gardens, and there is a café serving tea and coffee.

OCCIDENTALISM & THE BOSPHORUS PALACES

Though Mahmut II never completely forsook Topkapı, he is known to have described it as a place 'fit only for deeds of blood and intrigue'. He had seen drawings of European palaces and he wanted something like them for himself, contrasting Topkapı, 'hidden behind high walls and among dark trees, as though it could not bear the light of day' with places such as Versailles and Schönbrunn, 'light, laughing palaces, open to the free air and the pure sunshine'. Such a place, he announced, was what was needed in Istanbul.

Western-style palaces were certainly erected here, but how light and laughing they ever were is open to debate. One feature that is common to all the great palaces on the Bosphorus built by the Ottoman sultans of the 19th century is the attempt to maintain an Oriental way of life in a Western-style building, and the tensions and challenges that this produces, as well as the solutions that are reached, make the buildings extremely interesting. European visitors do not always warm to Dolmabahçe and Beylerbeyi, perhaps because grandeur without human faces is alien to them. The Frenchman Émile Julliard, writing in 1892, complained of the lack of painting and statuary at Cırağan. For him the repetition of patterns and rich materials in room after room was dull. 'If, at the very least, the walls had been enlivened with a few paintings,' he moaned, 'if I had seen a few statues in the corners of these absurdly solemn salons, then I could have said that in this desert of silk and gold and silver there were a few bronzes that lived, that regarded one, that appealed to one. But there was nothing for the heart or the spirit; only a vast moronic luxury everywhere...'. The style of exterior decoration defies comparison with anything else. It is reminiscent of the Spanish plateresque, of the Lecce Baroque, of Hindu temple carving—but ultimately it is unique to itself.

BEŞİKTAŞ

Beşiktas is a busy port, with boats to Üsküdar and Kadıköy. It is on bus routes from Eminönü (nos 28 and 28T), as well as to/from Sarıyer further up the Bosphorus.

In the square behind the ferry station and taxi rank there is a **statue of Hayrettin Pasha**, the famous Ottoman admiral known in the West as Barbarossa. The statue, a vivid and lively work by the sculptor Zühtü Müridoğlu, was erected in 1946 on the third centenary of Barbarossa's death. **Barbarossa's türbe** stands in a little railed-off compound planted with oleanders. This is one of the earliest works of Sinan, dated by an inscription over the door to 1541–42.

BARBAROSSA, THE BARBARY PIRATE

Kheir-ed Din Barbarossa, or Hayrettin Barbaros, as he is styled in Turkish, was born c. 1465. He began life as a pirate, conducting raids against Mediterranean towns and harrying shipping. When he captured part of North Africa for the Ottomans, Sultan Selim I made him Bey of Algiers. His tireless aggression against coastal targets in Italy and on the islands of the Aegean kept the Istanbul slave markets well supplied—not to mention its harem. Nurbanu, consort of Selim II and later Valide Sultan to her son Murat III, was captured in one such raid. Under Süleyman the Magnificent Barbarossa served as Admiral of the Fleet and his actions safeguarded the eastern Mediterranean coasts for Turkey. He died in 1546 in Istanbul.

Portrait by Nigari of Barbarossa in a surcoat with *çintamani* design.

Across the road from Barbarossa's türbe (Beşiktaş Cd., just on the curve of the intersection with Barbaros Blv.) is **Sinanpaşa Camii**, a brick and stone edifice. This is another work of the architect Sinan, built for Sinan Pasha, Ottoman admiral and brother of the Grand Vizier Rüstem Pasha. Inscriptions on the şadırvan and over the entrance portal give the date of completion as 1555–56, two years after the death of its founder.

The Maritime Museum

To the left of Beşiktaş square as you stand with your back to the water is the Maritime Museum (Deniz Müzesi; *open 9.30–5; closed Mon and Tues; a new wing was under construction at the time of writing*). The exhibits include naval uniforms, models of ships, engravings, paintings, portraits of great corsairs, maps by the Turkish cartographer Piri Reis, carved figureheads, fire pumps and other artefacts ranging from Ottoman to Republican times. A section of the iron chain that was stretched across the mouth of the Golden Horn and which failed to keep out the fleet of Fatih Sultan Mehmet in 1453 (*for the reason why, see p. 247*) is on display here too. One of the finest exhibits is the ensign of Barbarossa, which once served as the pall on the cenotaph in his türbe. It is embroidered with talismanic symbols such as the six-pointed star and the cleft Sword of Ali, as well as the following verse from the Koran: 'The conquest is nigh; tell the glad tidings to the people of Islam.'

Çırağan Sarayı

About half a kilometre from the Beşiktaş ferry station are two luxury hotels on the waterfront. The first is the Four Seasons Bosphorus. The second is the Çırağan Palace Kempinski. Çırağan was built during the reign of Sultan Abdülaziz; the sultan died here on 4th June 1876, five days after he had been deposed. His death was officially declared to be a suicide (he had called for a pair of scissors to trim his beard and was soon after found weltering in a pool of his own blood), but the suspicious circumstances suggested to many of his contemporaries that he had been murdered. His nephew and successor, Murat V, was deemed unfit to rule, whereupon he was deposed in favour of his brother, Abdülhamit II. For the next three decades Murat and his family were kept in Çırağan, and though the cage was a gilded one, it was definitely a cage. The sultan and his womenfolk diverted themselves with music and amateur theatricals (there were talented pianists among the women), but they were denied many basic commodities and their lives at heart were empty and hopeless. A botched attempt was made to reinstate Murat as sultan, and many died in bloody fighting in the palace. After this, Murat's confinement became even closer. He died here in 1905. After the Constitution of 1908, Çırağan was restored and used to house the new Turkish Parliament. The last act in the tragedy of this ill-starred palace occurred one night in January 1910, when it was gutted in a disastrous fire, leaving only a blackened shell. The palace has now been reopened as a luxury hotel. The old building, completely recreated inside, with a grand entrance hall with glass balusters, is used as an events and conference centre. The terrace of the new building, overlooking Kuzguncuk and the green hills of Asia, is a delightful place to have coffee.

YILDIZ PALACE

A few hundred metres beyond Çırağan, the shore highway passes the entrance to Yıldız Park (*park open daily 9–5; Şale Köşk and the Marangozhane open 10–4, closed Mon and Thur; either walk or take a bus from Beşiktaş, about 1km, or take bus no. 40 from Taksim Square*). With its gardens and former imperial kiosks, it is a delightful place to come in spring.

HISTORY OF YILDIZ PALACE

Yıldız Sarayı, the 'Palace of the Star', first began to take form during the time of Mahmut II. Before that there had been imperial gardens here and a kiosk belonging to Mihrişah Sultan, mother of Selim III. The buildings that stand here today date from the reign of Mahmut II to that of Abdülhamit II. Abdülhamit made Yıldız his main residence, and he also set up workshops here, where furniture and porcelain were made, for Yıldız Sarayı and the other imperial palaces and pavilions along the Bosphorus. The pavilions of Yıldız were abandoned after the fall of the Ottoman Empire, but in recent years they have been splendidly restored by the Turkish Touring and Automobile Club, directed by the late Çelik Gülersoy.

The lower end of the park

The mosque to the right of the park entrance is **Küçük Mecidiye Camii**, built in 1848 by Nikoğos Balyan for Sultan Abdülmecit.

A few yards beyond the lower entrance to Yıldız Park a steep but short street leads to the very picturesque **shrine of Yahya Efendi**, a foster-brother of Süleyman the Magnificent, to whom his mother acted as wet nurse. Yahya Efendi died in 1570, and so the little külliye, which is a work of Sinan, must date to about that time. The külliye originally included Yahya Efendi's türbe and an associated medrese, but these have been enveloped by various wooden structures of the 19th century. The türbe communicates by a large grilled opening to a small wooden mosque with a Baroque wooden dome. The various buildings are picturesque, but the surroundings are even more so: topsy-turvy old tombstones lie scattered among a lovely copse of trees, through which you catch occasional glimpses of the Bosphorus. This is one of the most popular religious shrines in the city, and it is always thronged with people at their devotions.

After entering the grounds, you can take any one of a number of very pleasant paths through the park, which is virtually the last extensive tract of woodland left on the European shore of the Bosphorus. A number of kiosks and greenhouses have been converted into cafés by the TTOK, including the Malta Köşkü, the Çadır Köşkü, the Lale Sera (Tulip Conservatory) and the Yeşil Sera. The setting of the café outside the **Malta Köşkü** is superb, with a romantic view of the Bosphorus through a screen of greenery, giving you some idea of how beautiful the shores of the strait were in days gone by.

Şale Köşk and the Municipality Museum

The most palatial of the surviving residences at Yıldız Sarayı is **Şale Köşk** so called because of its resemblance to a Swiss chalet. It consists of two buildings, the first erected in 1889 and the second in 1898; the latter is apparently the work of the Italian architect Raimondo d'Aronco, who brought to Istanbul the Art Nouveau style of architecture under the name of the Stile Floreale (the striking **türbe of Zafir Efendi**, also in the park, is a good example). Şale Köşk has some 50 rooms, the largest and grandest being the magnificent Reception Hall, other splendid chambers being the Mother-of-Pearl Hall and the Yellow Parlour. Şale Kösk was used principally as a residence for visiting royalty, most notably Kaiser Wilhelm II, who during his visit to Abdülhamit in 1895 formed an alliance between Germany and the Ottoman Empire.

D'Aronco also built the Çin Fabrıkası, or **Porcelain Manufactory**. Other buildings of interest include the **Büyük Mabeyn**, where the state apartments were located, and the Marangozhane, or **Carpentry Shop** (Abdülhamit was a skilled carpenter and made some of the palace fittings himself).

The **Municipality Museum** (*open 9.30–4.30; closed Thur*), just outside the upper entrance to Yıldız Park, contains mostly works of art from the late Ottoman period, including paintings of the Bosphorus and its shores in the latter years of the Empire.

Outside and to the south of the upper entrance (Dağ Kapısı) on Barbaros Blv., is the **Hamidiye Camii**, built in 1886 by Abdülhamit II.

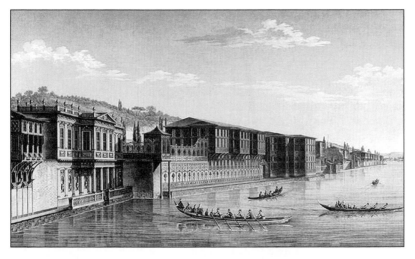

Anton Ignaz Melling: view of the waterfront palace of Hatice Sultan, sister of Selim III, at Ortaköy.

THE MIDDLE BOSPHORUS

The stretch of the Bosphorus between the two bridges includes the former villages of Ortaköy, Anravutköy and Bebek (*see maps on pp. 351 and 340–41*). Most of the Bosphorus settlements began life as Greek fishing villages. Today they have all become more or less continuous conurbation and the ethnically mixed populations of Greeks, Armenians and Jews have nearly all left. But in the very centres some of the villages still retain personality and charm. Rumeli Hisarı, the fortress built to guard the narrowing of the strait, is an impressive sight in any season.

Bus 40B from Beşiktaş to Sarıyer, with stops at Levent, İstinyePark shopping mall, İstinye, Yeniköy, Kalender, Tarabya, Kirçeburnu and Büyükdere. Line 40 also stops at Sarıyer, İstinye, Yeniköy, Kalender, Tarabya, Kirçeburnu, Büyükdere and then Emirgan, Boyacıköy, Baltalimanı, Rumeli Hisarı, Boğaziçi University, Bebek, Robert College, Arnavutköy, Ortaköy, Çırağan before going up to Taksim Square.

ORTAKÖY

Although Ortaköy, the 'Middle Village', is now part of the urban sprawl of Istanbul, it still has a village atmosphere about it. In recent years it has become known for its art galleries and this has attracted a fashionable young crowd. Ortaköy is busy and lively, with a 'happening' feel to it. A number of its old wooden houses have been restored,

particularly in the area around the ferry-landing, where there are numerous outdoor cafés, bars and restaurants.

As you approach Ortaköy, it is instantly recognisable from its large mosque on the waterfront and the graceful sweep of the Bosphorus Bridge soaring above it. The settlement was known in Byzantine times as Haghios Phocas, after a famous church of that saint which stood here. There is still a Greek church of Haghios Phocas just in from the ferry landing; this was built in 1856 but its parish undoubtedly dates back to the Byzantine period. Ortaköy was known historically for the ethnic mix of its inhabitants. Most have left now, but a block away from Haghios Phocas, at the southern entrance to the village, is the Etz Ahayim ('Tree of Life') Synagogue, in origin dating back to the Byzantine era, though the present building dates only from 1913.

Major sights of Ortaköy

The most prominent monument in Ortaköy is the waterfront mosque, **Büyük Mecidiye Camii**, an elaborate Baroque building dramatically situated on the water's edge. The mosque was built for Sultan Abdülmecit in 1854 by Nikoğos Balyan, architect of Dolmabahçe Camii and Dolmabahçe Palace. But Mecidiye Camii is a much better building than either of those two edifices; the style is exuberantly eclectic and there is a real verve and movement in the undulating walls of the tympana of the great dome arches.

The conspicuous brick building on the far side of the cobbled waterfront square is the **Esma Sultan Yalısı**, presented to Esma, daughter of Sultan Abdülaziz, on her wedding in 1889. It was gutted by fire but has now been refitted inside in a completely contemporary design. It is used as a venue for private functions and is very popular for weddings. On the shore road there is an ancient **hamam**, built by Sinan for Hüsrev Kethüda, who served as steward for the Grand Vizier Sokollu Mehmet Pasha. It was undergoing restoration at the time of writing.

The **Bosphorus Bridge** at Ortaköy, officially Atatürk Köprüsü, opened in 1973 on the 50th anniversary of the founding of the Turkish Republic. At the time it was the fourth longest suspension bridge in the world, 1074m in length between the two great piers on either shore and with its roadway 64m above the water.

KURUÇEŞME & ARNAVUTKÖY

Much of the shore between Ortaköy and Arnavutköy is parkland, making this one of the prettiest stretches of the middle Bosphorus. The wooden **Kuruçeşme Camii** on the shore road was built in the 18th century by one Tezkireci Osman Efendi.

At **Arnavutköy**, 'the Albanian Village', the shore road has been built out to run outside the picturesque old wooden houses along the waterfront. The interior of the village is charming and picturesque, with wooden houses lining lanes festooned with vines. On the highest hill above the shore, in a superb position, are the buildings of **Robert College**, founded in 1871 as the American College for Girls. This was the first

The graceful Bosphorus suspension bridge at Ortaköy.

modern lycée of its kind in Turkey and produced many women who played a leading part in the life of their country, the most famous being the writer Halide Edib Adıvar, prominent in the Turkish Nationalist movement. In 1971, the college was amalgamated with the boys' lycée of the old Robert College, a little farther up the Bosphorus, with the new institution taking the latter name and occupying the site above Arnavutköy. From the grounds of the school there is a superb view of this part of the Bosphorus and its shores.

BEBEK

The point that separates Arnavutköy harbour from the bay of Bebek is called **Akıntıburnu**, the 'Cape of the Current'. This is the deepest part of the Bosphorus, which here reaches a depth of some 100m at the centre of the strait. The current is extremely powerful, making it very difficult for small boats to round the point. Bebek was once one of the prettiest villages on the Bosphorus, but now, with its notorious Mc-Donald's and multi-storey apartments, it has entered the modern era. In the hinterland loom the great highrises of new Istanbul's **Skyscraper City**, tallest among them the 54-storey Sapphire Tower. The Diamond Tower in nearby Maslak, at the planning stage at the time of writing, will be even taller. Despite all this, Bebek Bay is still beautiful. As the road enters the village it passes the huge Art Nouveau palace known as **Hidiv Sarayı**. This was formerly the residence of the Khedive of Egypt, the Ottoman viceroy, and now it serves as the summer home of the Egyptian consulate. The palace was built in 1902 by Raimondo d'Aronco in the Stile Floreale (Art Nouveau). On the water's edge just past the ferry landing there is a little **mosque** built in 1913 by Kemalettin Bey, a leader of the Neoclassical school of Turkish architecture.

There are still a few old wooden houses of the late Ottoman era in the back streets. The oldest is the **Kavafyan Konağı** on Manolya Sk., 'Magnolia Street'. The house was built in 1751 by the Kavafyan, an Armenian family who still own it.

Boğaziçi Universitesi

On the hill between Bebek and Rumeli Hisarı stand the buildings of Boğaziçi Universitesi, the University of the Bosphorus (*map p. 341*). This new Turkish university was established in 1971, occupying the buildings and grounds of the old Robert College.

Robert College, which in its time was the finest institution of higher education in Turkey, was founded in 1863 by Cyrus Hamlin, an American missionary who had baked bread and washed clothes for Florence Nightingale's hospital in Üsküdar. The College was named after Christopher Robert, an American philanthropist who provided the initial funds to build and run the institution. During the 108 years of its existence the College had among its staff and graduates a number of prominent men (and women after 1958). Its graduates number two Prime Ministers of Turkey: Bülent Ecevit and Tansu Çiller, the latter being the first woman to hold this post.

The site of the University is superb, and its lovely terrace commands a stunning view of this exceptionally beautiful stretch of the Bosphorus. Just below the terrace is the attractive old house called **Aşıyan** ('Nest'), which once belonged to Tevfik Fikret (1867–1915), for many years professor of Turkish Literature at Robert College and one of the leading poets of his time. The house has been converted into a museum to exhibit memorabilia of the poet (*open 9–5; closed Thur and Sun*).

The point below Aşıyan is known as Kayalar, 'the Rocks'. This gives its name to **Kayalar Mescidi**, the little wooden mosque beside the road, built in 1877 by Şeyh Ahmet Niyazi Efendi, head of a tekke of the Kadiri dervishes.

RUMELİ HİSARI

Above the narrowest part of the Bosphorus, only about 700m wide, rise the walls of Rumeli Hisarı, the magnificent fortress that dominates the European shore of the strait (*map p. 341; open 9.30–5 every day except Mon, and also when performances are being held*).

HISTORY OF RUMELİ HİSARI

When Darius chose to cross the Bosphorus in his campaign against the Scythians in 512 BC, the crossing was accomplished on a bridge of boats. As his army crossed the strait, the king watched from a stone throne cut into a cliff on the European shore. This throne, located about where the north tower of the fortress now stands, was later flanked by two columns raised to commemorate the historic crossing; these were still standing in early Byzantine times.

Soon after he came to the throne in 1451, Mehmet II began preparations for his siege of Constantinople. His first step was to cut off the city from its grain supply on the Black Sea; to do this he decided to build a fortress on the European shore. The young sultan himself selected the site, directly across from Anadolu Hisarı, the fortress constructed on the Asian shore by Beyazıt I in 1395. Mehmet drew up the general plan of the fortress, and hired 1,000 artisans and 2,000 labourers for the task, which began in April 1452. He entrusted the construction of each of the three main towers of the fortress to one of his chief viziers: the north tower to Saruca Pasha, the sea tower to Halil Pasha, his Grand Vizier, and the south one to Zaganos Pasha. The project was completed early in August 1452, less than four months after it had been started. The castle was then garrisoned with a force of Janissaries, whose bombardiers trained their huge cannon on the strait, warning foreign captains not to try and get to Constantinople from the Black Sea. One Venetian captain made the attempt, but his boat was sunk by the Turkish artillery, and he and his surviving crewmen were impaled.

After the Conquest the fortress lost its military importance and it became a garrison post and prison, particularly for foreign ambassadors and prisoners of war. It was restored in 1953, in time for the 500th anniversary of the Conquest. Today it is used for performances during the Istanbul Festival.

The fortress

The fortress spans a steep valley with two tall towers on hills at either end and a third at the water's edge. The towers are linked by a curtain wall defended by three smaller towers, forming an irregular enceinte some 250m long by 125m wide at its maximum. The north tower, built by Zaganos Pasha, was used as a prison in Ottoman times; it now houses a small museum showing objects used by the Janissaries. The area inside the fortress has been made into a park, and the circular cistern on which once stood a small mosque (part of the minaret has been left to mark its position) has been converted into the acting area of a Greek-type theatre.

The cemetery and village

The **cemetery** under the walls of Rumeli Hisarı is the earliest Turkish burial-ground on the European side of the city, its oldest tombstone dating back to 1452. The little mosque on the shore beneath the castle is **Hacı Kemaleddin Camii**. This was originally founded by Hacı Kemaleddin, perhaps during the reign of Mehmet II (r. 1451–81), and then in 1746 it was rebuilt by Mahmut I.

Beyond the fortress is the **village of Rumeli Hisarı**, one of the most picturesque on the Bosphorus. The mosque on the corner opposite the landing stage was founded by Ali Pertek, an admiral in the reign of Murat IV (r. 1623–40), and it was rebuilt in the 1960s. In the village there is an Armenian church dedicated to Surp Santuht, still used by the small Armenian community that has lived in Rumeli Hisarı since at least the time of the Conquest. The original church on this site may have been founded in Fatih's time, though the oldest inscription (on one of the tombstones used to build the present church in 1856) bears the date 1756.

Just upstream from Rumeli Hisarı is **Fatih Sultan Mehmet Köprüsü**, the second Bosphorus Bridge. This was opened in the summer of 1988, exactly 2,500 years after Darius constructed his bridge of boats across the same stretch of the narrows.

THE UPPER BOSPHORUS

The village of **Baltalimanı** (*map p. 341*) is named after the Ottoman admiral Balta Oğlu, who built Fatih's fleet here at the outset of the 1453 siege. On the approach to the village is a large seaside palace, now a hospital, built in the mid-19th century by Sarkis Balyan for Mustafa Reşit Pasha, who served six terms as Grand Vizier during the reign of Sultan Abdülmecit I (r. 1839–61). **Boyacıköy** is a pretty village with many old Ottoman houses along its back streets.

Emirgan

Emirgan is named after the Persian prince Emirgüne, who in 1638 surrendered the city of Yerevan to Murat IV without a fight. Emirgüne later became the sultan's favourite companion in drinking and debauchery, and was rewarded with the gift of palace in this village. On the left side of the shore road, not far from the ferry landing, there are the remains of a handsome old yalı, believed to stand on the site of that palace. Parts of the structure may go back to that time, but most of it dates to the 19th century, when a new or at least rebuilt mansion was erected by a *şerif* of Mecca named Abdullah Pasha. The mansion is now known as the Şerifler Yalısı.

The village square is very picturesque, with outdoor cafés and teahouses shaded by giant plane trees. Beside the square stands a Baroque mosque, partly of wood, built in 1781–82 by Abdülhamit I. It consists of a large rectangular room, almost square, but curiously asymmetrical, with elegant décor.

Just above the village are the famous tulip gardens of Emirgan, which are at their most glorious during the annual Tulip Festival in April. The Turkish Touring and Automobile Club has restored a number of Ottoman structures around the Emirgan gardens, converting them into cafés: Pembe Köşk, Sarı Köşk, Beyaz Köşk and the Kır Kahveleri.

Maslak Kasrı

After leaving Emirgan the shoreline curves to the left as it approaches the deeply indented bay of İstinye. A road left (Sarıyer Cd.) leads inland into the suburbs that occupy the heights above the European shore. Signs direct you to Maslak Kasrı (*open 9–5; closed Mon and Thur*), an imperial Ottoman lodge originally set in spacious parklands with a view of the upper Bosphorus and its entrance from the Black Sea. It is built on a site first used as a country retreat during the reign of Mahmut II, though the present buildings appear to date mainly from the time of Sultan Abdülaziz.

İstinye

Petrus Gyllius writes of İstinye that 'after the Golden Horn it must be acknowledged the largest bay and the safest port of the entire Bosphorus, rich as this is in bays and ports'. The Turkish name İstinye is a corruption of the Greek Sosthenion; according to one version of the legend Jason and the Argonauts erected a statue here, in thanksgiving (*sosthenion*) for aid given by a winged genius of the place against their enemy on the opposite shore, King Amycus, ruler of the savage Bebryces (*see p. 276*).

Today İstinye is famous for its huge luxury shopping mall, İstinyePark, behind the shore on İstinye Bayırı Cd.

Yeniköy

Yeniköy is one of the prettiest villages on the Bosphorus. Known in Byzantium as Neapolis, its Greek name has the same meaning as its Turkish: 'New Town'. There are a number of handsome yalıs along the seafront around the ferry landing, the oldest being the Dadyan Yalısı, built by an Armenian family in the late 18th century.

There are four churches in the village, three Greek and one Armenian. There is also a synagogue on the shore road by the ferry landing; this was founded in 1870 by Count Abraham de Camondo (*see p. 228*), who had a summer home here. At the northern extremity of the village is the former summer residence of the embassy of Austria-Hungary. This was presented by Abdülhamit II in 1883 to the Emperor Franz Joseph I. The Greek poet Cavafy wrote a poem to Yeniköy, his mother's native village.

Tarabya and Kireçburnu

With its deeply indented azure bay, Tarabya once vied with Bebek in its claim to be the most beautiful village on the Bosphorus. Its loveliness has made it prey to the pressures of tourism, and though attractive enough, it is no longer the loveliest place on the European shore. Tarabya is a corruption of the old Greek name Therapeia (cure, healing): this name was apparently given to it by the Patriarch Atticus (r. 406–25), because of its salubrious atmosphere. The ancient name of the village was Pharmakeus, the 'Poisoner', based on the legend that Medea, in her pursuit of Jason, there threw away the poison with which she had intended to kill him.

By the intersection at the beginning of Tarabya is the Greek church of Haghia Paraskevi, built in the mid-19th century. In the courtyard there is an aghiasma, also dedicated to Haghia Paraskevi, whose shrines are often associated with sacred springs.

Beyond Tarabya the shore road is lined with the **summer embassies** of several European powers, some of which have lovely gardens. The first is the summer residence of the Italian Embassy, built in 1906 by Raimondo d'Aronco. Beyond it is the French Embassy, formerly the yalı of the Ypsilanti family, presented by Selim III to Napoleon in 1807. Then comes the Russian Embassy, built in 1840 for General Nikolai Ignatiev, the Tsar's ambassador to the Porte.

The next village beyond Tarabya is **Kireçburnu**, a small cluster of houses and fish restaurants at a bend in the Bosphorus. This was known in Byzantium as Kledai tou Pontou, the 'Keys of the Pontus'; here for the first time you can see directly into the Black Sea.

BÜYÜKDERE & BELGRAD FOREST

Büyükdere (*map p. 341*) is a big village along the northern side of a large bay. Its Turkish name means 'Large Valley', while in Byzantium it was known as Kalos Agros, the 'Beautiful Meadow'. It is indeed a very lovely and fertile valley with fine old trees through which a road leads into the Belgrad Forest.

HISTORY OF BELGRAD FOREST

The forest takes its name from the village of Belgrad that once stood in its midst. This was founded by Süleyman the Magnificent after his conquest of Belgrade in 1521, when he transported a number of the inhabitants of that city and settled them here to look after the reservoirs and aqueducts with which the forest abounds. The village of Belgrad became a popular summer retreat for European residents of Istanbul in the Ottoman period, particularly in times of plague. Lady Mary Wortley Montagu lived there during her stay in Istanbul, 1716–18, and her encomiums made the village famous. The site was abandoned in late Ottoman times and the village has now vanished.

The **aqueducts and reservoirs** scattered throughout Belgrad Forest are very impressive. Many of them were built for Süleyman the Magnificent by Sinan during the period 1554–65, some of them replacing or restoring Byzantine works. The nearest aqueduct to Büyükdere is at the top of the hill along the road leading inland from the Bosphorus. This grand structure was founded by Mahmut I and completed in 1732, and conveys the waters from his reservoir and several others to the distribution centre in Taksim Square.

Büyükdere still has a small Greek community and the church of Haghia Paraskevi is one of the oldest churches on the upper Bosphorus, first mentioned in 1604. There is also an Armenian church dedicated to Surp Boğos (St Paul). This was originally a small chapel erected by Boğos Bilezikçiyan in 1847; then in 1893 the architect Kirkor Hürmüzyan expanded it into a stone church in the Gothic style.

Near the far end of the village is the oldest of the European summer embassies, that of Spain. The Spanish ambassador, Juan de Bouligny, bought this mansion from the Franciscans in 1783, so that his legation could escape the cholera epidemic then raging in Istanbul.

The Sadberk Hanım Museum

The old Azaryan Yalısı, at the northern end of Büyükdere, was built in the late 19th century by an Armenian named Manuk Azaryan Efendi, who served in both the Parliament and the foreign service during the last years of the Ottoman Empire. Today the yalı houses the Sadberk Hanım Museum (*open 10.30–5 every day except Wed; closed Feb*), a unique and rich collection of antiquities and Turkish works of art. The museum was founded by Sadberk Koç, late wife of Vehbi Koç, one of Turkey's leading businessmen, who died in 1995. The museum opened in 1980 under the direction of their daughter Sevgi Gönül. Its collection includes examples of the pattens that were worn at hamams and a tambur, a long-necked lute (*tambur*) that is believed to have belonged to the composer-sultan Selim III.

The archaeological section has some 7,000 antiquities arranged in chronological order beginning with the Late Neolithic and Early Chalcolithic periods and going on through the Bronze Age, the Assyrian Trade Colonies, the Hittites, the Urartians, the Phrygians, the Mycenaeans, and the successive periods of Greek and Roman history, ending in the Byzantine era. Among the exhibits are terracotta figurines, pottery and ceramics, jewellery, inscribed tablets, glass and crystal objects, ivories, and objects made from bronze, silver, gold and electrum.

The Turkish and Islamic Art section has exhibits ranging in date from the Early Islamic era through the Ottoman period. The objects include metalwork, imperial monograms in silver, jewel-encrusted timepieces, jewellery, Chinese porcelain, and Turkish tiles and pottery from İznik, Kütahya and Çanakkale. On the upper floor there are dioramas of traditional Turkish scenes, including a bridal shower and a circumcision bed. There are also beautiful examples of Ottoman costumes and Turkish embroideries.

Sarıyer and Rumeli Kavağı

Sarıyer is the largest village on the European shore of the upper Bosphorus and has given its name to the entire administrative area between Rumeli Hisarı and Rumeli Feneri. The most picturesque part is on the shore behind the mosque, where there is a small fishing port. The fish-market is particularly colourful, and on the pier are a number of good restaurants with splendid views of the Asian shore.

Sarıyer and **Yeni Mahalle** (where there are more fish restaurants) are the last heavily settled area on the European shore. About midway between Sarıyer and Rumeli Kavağı, on the coast road on the right, is the **türbe of Telli Baba**, a Muslim saint. This is one of the most popular Muslim shrines in the city, and it is much frequented by women who pray to the saint for a husband. Those who are successful return to give thanks, usually fastening strands of gold wire on his tomb.

Rumeli Kavağı consists of a small cluster of houses and fish restaurants around the ferry-landing. On the hill above the village are the few scattered remains of a defensive castle, known locally as Kara Taş, 'Black Stone'. On the Asian shore directly opposite are the ruins of another fortress, which, together with the castle here made up the Byzantine control points on the upper Bosphorus. The batteries below the castles on either side are relatively modern Turkish works; they were built in 1783 by Toussaint and strengthened in 1794 by Monnier, two French military engineers in the Ottoman service.

HISTORY OF RUMELİ & ANADOLU KAVAĞI

The villages of Rumeli and Anadolu Kavağı are probably to be identified with the ancient Serapion and Hieron, respectively. These were the Byzantine customs control points, and a chain was strung between them to prevent ships from passing to and from the Black Sea without paying their tolls. Both of these posts were guarded by fortresses on the hills above; that on the European side was built by Manuel I Comnenus (r. 1143–80) while the one on the Asian side was founded at some time early in the dynasty of the Palaeologues.

In the 14th century the Genoese seized both fortresses, after which they collected the tolls and customs fees from shipping in the Bosphorus, further contributing to the decline of the Byzantine Empire. Mehmet II captured the fortresses in 1452; they then fell into ruins in the peaceful centuries after the Conquest.

Rumeli Kavağı to Rumeli Feneri

The sightseeing ferries go no further than Rumeli Kavağı, so that those wishing to explore further must hire a motor boat there or in Sarıyer. An excursion by boat along the shores of the upper Bosphorus reveals a coast that is wild, rugged and desolate, and extremely beautiful. Now for the first time you find sandy beaches hidden away in secluded coves; grey herons haunt the cliffs and black cormorants dive for fish. Petrus Gyllius, who explored this coast in the mid-16th century, identified a number of sites with the mythical voyage of Jason and the Argonauts. These identifications, though based on myth, add romantic interest to an excursion.

Some 5–6km up the Bosphorus by sea from Rumeli Kavağı is a strangely shaped craggy point, known in Turkish as Garipçe, which means strange or curious. There is an Ottoman fortress here, built in 1773 for Mustafa III by the Baron de Tott, a Hungarian-French military engineer in the Ottoman service. The third Bosphorus Bridge will cross the strait here, from Garipçe to Poyraz.

The village of **Rumeli Feneri** that takes its name from the lighthouse (*fener*) on this last promontory on the European (*Rumeli*) shore. On the headland beyond, looking out over the Black Sea, are the remains of a fort built in 1769 by a Greek engineer.

JASON, THE ARGONAUTS & THE SYMPLEGADES

The ancient name of this place was Gyropolis, the 'Place of Vultures', by association with the myth of King Phineus, the blind prophet and son-in-law of Boreas, god of the North Wind. He was tormented by the Harpies, winged monsters who, every time a meal was set before the king, would swoop down upon it, snatch away most of the food. As a result, Phineus had almost faded away by the time the Argonauts arrived on their journey up the Bosphorus in quest of the Golden Fleece.

Among them were Zetes and Calais, the winged sons of Boreas, who took pity on their brother-in-law, flying up into the air to chase away the Harpies for ever. In return Phineus advised the Argonauts about the rest of their journey, particularly on how to avoid the baleful Symplegades. These were two huge rocks at the mouth of the Bosphorus, which were supposed to clash together, thus imperilling all shipping. Phineus told the Argonauts to let loose a dove which would fly between them; if it was caught they were to give up their journey, but if it got through safely they were to wait till the rocks opened again and then row their hardest. They did so, the clashing rocks just shaved off the tail feathers of the dove and the Argo got safely through, with only some slight damage to its stern.

The rocks that Gyllius identified as the **Symplegades**, the 'Clashing Rocks', are now connected to the mainland by a concrete mole, which extends southwards to protect the harbour. The rock formation is divided by deep fissures into several parts. On the peak of the highest rock are the remains of the so-called Pillar of Pompey. This is in fact an ancient altar, decorated with a garlanded ram's head and other reliefs now much worn; it once had a Latin inscription, no longer legible, the transcription and interpretation of which are debated. Certainly it never had anything to do with Pompey, and it is not known how it came by its misleading name. Gyllius thought that the altar was probably a remnant of the shrine to Apollo which Dionysius of Byzantium says the Romans erected on one of the Symplegades.

Now that the rocks have ceased clashing, Rumeli Feneri is a peaceful place. In season its fish restaurants set tables up outside, where you can have lunch with splendid views of the water.

THE ASIAN SIDE

ÜSKÜDAR

Ferries to Üsküdar, operated by Şehir Hatları and Turyol, leave regularly from Eminönü (west side of the Galata Bridge, behind the fish sandwich boats) and from Kabataş and Beşiktaş. Journey time approx. 15mins. There is a taxi rank and bus stop at the ferry landing.

HISTORY OF ÜSKÜDAR

Üsküdar is ancient Chrysopolis, the 'City of Gold', founded by the Athenians under Alcibiades in 409 BC. In later Byzantine times it was known as Scutari, a name that lingered on until fairly recently. The city was eventually absorbed by Byzantium and became a suburb of Constantinople. It was taken by the Ottomans about a century before the fall of Constantinople, and under Turkish rule it came to be known as Üsküdar.

The focal point of Üsküdar is the great square behind the ferry landing. Beyond it stands **Mihrimah Sultan Camii** (*map p. 339, B1*), a stately imperial mosque on a high terrace, built in 1547–48 for Mihrimah, daughter of Süleyman the Magnificent. The exterior is imposing because of its dominating position high above the square and its great double porch, a curious projection of which covers a charming fountain. The architect was Sinan, who would later build another mosque for the princess in the old city near the land walls (*see p. 202*). A charming story is attached to the two mosques. It is said that Sinan fell in love with Mihrimah. Her name means 'Sun and Moon' in Persian, and those who pay attention to such things have noticed that every year on the princess's birthday (21st March), as the sun sets behind the Mihrimah mosque on the European side, the moon can be seen rising behind her mosque on the Asian side. Mihrimah was Süleyman's only daughter, and she enjoyed a relationship with her father of great affection and trust. Her husband, Rüstem Pasha, became Grand Vizier, and Rüstem's brother Sinan was appointed Admiral of the Fleet. Mihrimah is buried beside her father in his türbe at the Süleymaniye.

Along Hakimiyet-i Milliye Caddesi

On the main avenue of Üsküdar, on the left as you walk away from the water, is a supermarket housed in the remains of an ancient hamam. It is known as **Sinan Hamamı** or Mimar Sinan Çarşısı (*map p. 339, B1*), names which ascribe the bath to Sinan. He was probably not the architect, though it certainly dates from his time. It was a double bath, but the main entrance chambers were destroyed when the street was widened.

A little farther on there is an ancient and curious mosque, **Karadavut Paşa Camii**, built by Nişancı Kara Davut Pasha toward the end of the 15th century. It is a broad shallow room divided into three sections by arches, each section having a dome, an arrangement unique in Istanbul.

Across the street and opening into the square is the large complex of the **Yeni Valide Camii** (map p. 339, B1). This was built in 1708–10 by Ahmet III, who dedicated it to his mother, the Valide Sultan Rabia Gülnuş Emetullah. At the corner is the Valide's charming open türbe, looking like a large aviary, and next to it a grand sebil.

Along the seafront

On the promontory beyond the ferry port is **Şemsipaşa Camii** (map p. 339, A1), one of the most delightful of the smaller mosque complexes in the city, built of glittering white stone and standing in a very picturesque location right at the water's edge. Built by Sinan for the vizier Şemsi Pasha in 1580, the mosque is of the simplest type: a square room covered by a dome with conches as squinches. Şemsi Pasha's türbe opens into the mosque itself, from which it is divided by a green grille, a most unusual and pretty feature. The well-proportioned medrese forms two sides of the courtyard, while the third side consists of a wall with barred windows opening directly onto the quay and the Bosphorus.

Şemsipaşa Caddesi leads away from the water up a low hill to an ancient mosque. This is **Rum Mehmetpaşa Camii**, built in 1471. Mehmet Pasha, the founder, was a Greek (*Rum*) who converted to Islam and became one of Fatih's viziers This is the most Byzantine in appearance of all the early mosques in the city: note the high cylindrical drum of the dome, the exterior cornice following the pie-crust curve of the round-arched windows, and the square dome base broken by the projection of the great dome arches. Behind the mosque is Mehmet Pasha's türbe.

Ayazma Camii and the Maiden's Tower

The imposing Baroque mosque known as **Ayazma Camii** (map p. 339, A1) was built in 1760–61 by Mustafa III and dedicated to his mother, the Valide Sultan Mihrişah. It is one of the more successful of the Baroque mosques in the city, especially on the exterior. A handsome entrance portal opens onto a courtyard from which a pretty flight of semicircular steps leads up to the mosque porch; on the left is a large cistern and beyond that an elaborate two-storeyed colonnade gives access to the imperial loggia. The upper structure is also diversified with little domes and turrets, and many windows give light to the interior. The interior is less successful, though the grey marble gallery along the entrance wall, supported by slender columns, is effective. At the back of the mosque there is a picturesque graveyard with some interesting old tombstones.

On the waterfront at this point is the location of the Asian terminus of the Marmaray Tunnel (*still under construction at the time of writing*). It passes just to the north of Kız Kulesi, the **Maiden's Tower**, which stands on a tiny offshore islet. The Turkish name of the islet is derived from a legend concerning a princess who was confined there by her father to protect her from the fate foretold by a dire prophecy: that she would die from the bite of a serpent. However, the princess was eventually bitten by a serpent, which had been smuggled out to the islet, and she died instantly. In English the place is sometimes called Leander's Tower, in the mistaken notion that Leander drowned here in his attempt to swim the strait to see his lover Hero: this mythical tragedy actually happened on the Hellespont—which Byron then swam and didn't die. According to Nicetas Choniates, Manuel I Comnenus (r. 1143–80) built a small fortress on the islet, using it to attach one end of the great chain which he stretched across the mouth of the Bosphorus, fastening the other end at a tower just below the acropolis. Since then the islet has served as the site of a lighthouse, semaphore station, quarantine post, customs control point, and a home for retired naval officers. The present structure dates from the 18th century; it now houses as a restaurant and café (*boats from Üsküdar or Kabataş; reservations necessary for dinner; T: 0216 342 4747, www.kizkulesi.com.tr*).

Just south of where Doğancılar Cd. meets Salacak İskelesi Cd. (*map p. 339, A2–B2*) is the severely plain **türbe of Hacı Ahmet Pasha**, who died in 1559. A work of Sinan, it stands on an octagonal terrace covered with tombstones and overshadowed by a dying terebinth tree.

The Ahmediye külliye

The attractive külliye of the Ahmediye mosque and medrese (*map p. 339, B2*) was built in 1722 by Eminzade Hacı Ahmet Pasha, comptroller of the Arsenal under Ahmet III. The building complex is essentially still in the classical style, though elements of it lean towards the Baroque. It is roughly square in layout, with the porticoes and cells of the medrese running along two sides. On the third side is the library, one entrance portal, and the mosque. The main gate, with the dershane above it and a graveyard alongside, occupy the remaining side. The whole plan is, however, very irregular because of the alignment of the surrounding streets and the slope of the ground.

The dome of the little mosque is supported by scallop-shell squinches and has a finely carved mimber and Kuran kursu. Scallop-shell decoration is in fact a feature of the whole complex, as seen in the pretty niches of the sebil and çeşme. The whole külliye ranks with those of Amcazade Hüseyin Pasha and Bayram Pasha as being among the most charming and inventive in the city.

ATİK VALİDE CAMİİ

Eski Toptaşı Cd., the 'Old Avenue of the Cannon Ball', winds uphill through a picturesque neighbourhood. Towards the top of the hill and somewhat towards the left is Atik Valide Camii, the great mosque complex that dominates the skyline of Üsküdar. The precinct is entered by an alley beside the mosque graveyard. This is one of the most beautiful of all the mosque courtyards in the city, a grandly proportioned cloister with domed porticoes supported on marble columns; in the centre are the şadırvan and a copse of ancient plane trees and cypresses. The mosque is entered through an elaborate double porch, the outer one with a pentise roof, the inner domed and with handsome tiled inscriptions over the windows.

NB: At the time of writing the entire complex was being restored, and it was not be possible to visit all of the buildings.

HISTORY OF ATİK VALİDE CAMİİ

The imperial külliye of Atik Valide Camii was built by Sinan in 1583 for the Valide Sultan Nurbanu, favourite consort of Selim II and mother of Murat III. This is the most splendid and extensive of all Sinan's constructions in Istanbul, with the exception of the Süleymaniye. In addition to the mosque itself, the külliye consists of a medrese, a hospital, an imaret, a school for reading the Koran, a caravansaray and a hamam. Altogether this is certainly one of the half-dozen most impressive monuments of Ottoman architecture in the whole of Turkey. Its name, 'Old Valide Mosque', distinguishes it from the Yeni Valide Camii, built for the mother of a later sultan (*see p. 265*). Nurbanu ('Lady of Light') is thought to have begun her life as Cecilia Baffo, daughter of the Venetian governor of one of the Aegean islands, captured when the island was taken by Barbarossa (*see p. 250*) in 1537. She is not buried in her complex here, but in the türbe of Selim II at Haghia Sophia.

The prayer hall is a wide rectangular room with a central dome supported by a hexagonal arrangement of pillars and columns; to the north and south there are side aisles, each with two domed bays. The aisles were added at a later date. There are galleries around three sides of the room, and the wooden ceilings under some of them preserve the rich painting typical of the period: floral and arabesque designs in black, red and gold. The mihrab is in a square projecting apse entirely revetted in magnificent Iznik tiles; notice also the window frames of deep red conglomerate marble with shutters richly inlaid with mother-of-pearl. The mihrab and mimber are fine works in carved marble.

The **medrese** stands at a lower level than the mosque and is entered by a staircase in the west wall of the courtyard. Its courtyard is almost as pretty as that of the mosque itself. Leaving the medrese by the gate in the south side, you can walk around the building and pass under this picturesque arch. At the next corner beyond it stands the large *hankah*, or **dervish hospice**, also an attractive building.

The **hamam**, which has been restored and is once again in use, is two blocks west of the medrese and on the same street.

Çinili Cami

East of Atik Valide Camii lies Çinili Cami, the 'Tiled Mosque', built in 1640 by another powerful Harem lady with an Aegean Greek background, the Valide Sultan Kösem, mother of Murat IV and Crazy İbrahim (*see p. 107*). The mosque, in a pretty garden filled with flowers and trees, is small and simple: a square room covered by a dome. The mosque is decorated both on the façade and in the interior by a revetment of tiles, chiefly pale blue and turquoise on a white ground. The mimber of white marble has its own carving very prettily picked out in gold, red and green, and its conical roof is tiled. The porch of the mosque is a Baroque addition, as is the minaret, of which the şerefe has a corbel of very pretty folded-back acanthus leaves, unique in the city.

ENVIRONS OF ÜSKÜDAR

Büyük Çamlıca

Büyük Çamlıca, the 'Great Hill of Pines', is the highest peak in the immediate vicinity of Istanbul; its summit, surmounted by television antennae, is the most prominent landmark along the lower Bosphorus. The peak is about 4km east of the ferry landing (*beyond map p. 339, C1*). There is a pleasant café and teahouse on the summit, which commands an extraordinary view of Istanbul, the Golden Horn and the lower Bosphorus.

Karaca Ahmet Cemetery

'*The cypresses of Scutari In stern magnificence look down On the bright lake and stream of sea, And glitt'ring theatre of town: Above the throng of rich kiosks, Above the towers in triple tire, Above the domes of loftiest mosques, These pinnacles of death aspire.*' So wrote Lord Houghton, biographer of Keats and amateur poet, and in an Istanbul context most famous as the rejected suitor of Florence Nightingale. For those who love cemeteries, this historic Turkish burial-ground in the hills above Üsküdar, some 1.5km from the ferry landing (*map p. 339, C3*), is even more romantic and atmospheric than Eyüp. According to tradition, it was founded at the time of the Turkish conquest of the surrounding area in the mid-14th century and is named after Karaca Ahmet, a sainted warrior who was killed when the Turks took Chrysopolis and Chalcedon. As so often happens, Karaca Ahmet's grave was rediscovered later, revealed in a dream to a dervish. A türbe was then erected to house his remains (the present structure dates from the 19th century), and alongside it a monument was built to his favourite horse, whose skeleton was also found here. As time went on other prominent people chose to be buried here, their türbes and tombstones now shaded by spectral cypresses.

Enthusiasts of the eclectic architecture of the Balyan family will want to follow the road (Nuh Kuyusu Cd.) to its end, where it joins Gazi Cd. There on the right is the **Armenian Cemetery**, where the great architects are buried (except for Sarkis, who died in Paris and was laid to rest in Père Lachaise).

HAYDARPAŞA

The most prominent monument along the Marmara shore south of Üsküdar is the enormous, four-towered **Selimiye Barracks** (*map p. 339, B3*), famous as the site of Florence Nightingale's hospital during the Crimean War. At night its outline is illuminated in electric light, and is well seen from the European shore.

Boats to Harem run by İDO leave from Sirkeci, weekdays only, journey time 30mins (www.ido.

com.tr). More frequent ferries operated by Şehir Hatları run from Eminönü to Kadıköy, from Kabataş to Kadıköy and from Karaköy to Haydarpaşa and Kadıköy (www.sehirhatlari.net).

*Permission to visit the **Florence Nightingale Museum** must be sought in advance by calling the Protocol Office (T: 0216 553 1009). Allow 48hrs notice. You will need to fax a copy of the photo page of your passport (F: 0216 310 7929).*

HISTORY OF THE SELİMİYE BARRACKS

The first barracks here were built by Selim III in 1799 to house the men of his New Army, with which he hoped to replace the Janissaries. After Selim had been deposed and killed in a Janissary insurrection, new barracks were erected by Mahmut II in 1828, within two years after he finally destroyed the Janissaries. Three further wings were added by Sultan Abdülmecit in 1842–53.

During the Crimean War the barracks served as a British military hospital; during the first months of its operation conditions there were so bad that the death toll was more than 20 percent of the patients admitted. In October 1854 Florence Nightingale organised a party of 38 nurses, mostly from various religious orders, for service in the Crimean War. When her party arrived in Istanbul the following month she took charge of the medical services at the barracks in Scutari, as it was then called, and also at the other military hospital at Kuleli on the Bosphorus. Before she left Istanbul, in the summer of 1856, shortly after the end of hostilities, the death rate at the two hospitals had dropped to two percent.

After the war the Selimiye Barracks was once again used to house Turkish soldiers, a function it still performs today.

The building consists of four enormous wings, each of three storeys, surrounding a vast quadrangular parade ground; at the corners there are five-storeyed towers with tall turrets above, the one to the northeast rising above the **chambers where Florence Nightingale lived** when she was directing the hospital here. One of the downstairs rooms has been converted into a museum in her honour by the Turkish Nurses Association.

Opposite the main entrance to the barracks is the **Büyük Selimiye Camii**, the mosque that Selim III built for the men of his New Army. Constructed in 1803–04, it is the last and one of the most handsome of the Baroque mosques. Not only are its proportions and details most attractive, but it is placed in an exceptionally lovely garden shaded by three of the finest old plane trees in the city. The interior of the mosque is a little stark, though of impressive proportions. The western gallery, the mihrab and the mimber are all of highly polished grey marble and give the place a certain charm.

Prominent to the south of the Selimiye Barracks is the **Marmara University**, a huge building with twin towers flanking its entrance. This was built by Alexander Vallaury in 1894 to house the Military Medical Academy, which remained here until 1933, after which it became a secondary school for boys.

Farther to the south is **Haydarpaşa Railway Station**, a grand building with a façade flanked by twin towers, built in 1906–08 by the German architects Otto Ritter and Helmut Cuno. The roof was damaged by fire in 2010. The restaurant can be recommended: not for a gastronomic feast but for a slice of Istanbul life in one of the most scenic spots in the city. The tiled ferry station in front of the station was built in 1915–17 by the architect Vedat Tek. The **Crimean War Cemetery** is almost hidden away to the east of the railway station, in the angle formed by the two highways that intersect there. The cemetery was founded as a burial place for the British soldiers who died in the Selimiye Barracks when it was being used as a hospital during the Crimean War, and among the tombstones there are a number marking the graves of some of Florence Nightingale's nurses. Also buried here are British soldiers who fell at Gallipoli and others who died in the Middle East during World War II, along with British and other civilians who have died in Istanbul during the past century. The principal funerary monument is an obelisk of grey Aberdeen granite, with, in several languages, an inscription paying tribute to the dead by Queen Victoria. There is also a plaque dedicated by Queen Elizabeth II, honouring the pioneering nursing work done by Florence Nightingale and her staff during the Crimean War.

The famous Haydarpaşa station, terminus of the *Taurus Express* between Constantinople and Baghdad.

KADIKÖY

Ferries operated by Şehir Hatları run to Kadıköy from Eminönü, Karaköy and Kabataş (www. sehirhatlari.net).

HISTORY OF KADIKÖY

Kadıköy (*map p. 351 and beyond map p. 339, C4*) is ancient Chalcedon, founded by the Megarians from mainland Greece c. 675 BC, some two decades before Byzantium. The city was eventually absorbed by Byzantium and became a suburb of Constantinople. In 451 a famous ecumenical council was held here, which pronounced a ruling on the dual nature of Christ. This led to the so-called monophysite schism, with those who disagreed with the council's ruling clinging to the conviction that Christ's human and divine nature was single and indivisible. Chalcedon was conquered by the Ottomans at the same time as Üsküdar (mid-14th century), and under Turkish rule it came to be known as Kadıköy.

Major sights of Kadıköy

Across the shore road from the ferry-station, the site of the **Kadıköy street market** is now an attractive pedestrian mall. The famous Tuesday market (Salı Pazarı; *taxi or bus 8A*) has moved inland to Hasanpaşa. İskele Camii on the shore road opposite the ferry station, originally built in 1761 by Mustafa III, was rebuilt after a fire in 1858.

Further into the market quarter is a little square flanked by two churches. The one on the right as Armenian. That on the left is the **Greek church of St Euphemia of Chalcedon**, believed to stand on the site of the original church that was founded early in the Byzantine period. Euphemia was martyred c. 300 and became the patron saint of Chalcedon. The church dedicated to her here was the site of the historic Council of Chalcedon in 451. Euphemia's remains were removed to Constantinople when the Persians occupied Chalcedon early in the 7th century, and her casket is now in the church of St George in Fener (*see p. 210*). The present church was founded in 1694 and was rebuilt in 1830. It has recently been superbly restored, using a number of columns and other architectural members from an earlier Byzantine structure. In the narthex there is a painting by a local artist, dated 1882, showing the Council of Chalcedon in session in the original church of St Euphemia.

One block to the east of St Euphemia is **Osman Ağa Camii**, the oldest mosque in Kadıköy, founded in the reign of Ahmet I (r. 1603–17). The founder, an Egyptian named Osman Ağa, also built the nearby fountain, which is dated 1620.

Another block farther to the east brings you to the **Armenian church of Surp Levon** (St Leo). This is the only Armenian Catholic church on the Asian side of the city, all of the others being Gregorian. The present church was built in the mid-19th century by the architect Boğos Bey Maksadar, replacing an earlier wooden structure.

THE ASIAN SHORE OF THE BOSPHORUS

Bus E2 links Beykoz, Paşabahçe and Kanlıca; bus 15B links Beykoz with Anadolu Feneri; bus 15A links Anadolu Kavağı, Yuşa Tepe, Beykoz, Paşabahçe, Kanlıca and Çubuklu. Bus 15 runs all the way between Üsküdar and Beykoz with stops at Beylerbeyi, Çengelköy, Vaniköy, Kandilli, Küçüksu, Anadolu Hisarı, Kanlıca, Çubuklu and Paşabahçe. Maps pp. 351 and 341.

Kuzguncuk

Kuzguncuk (*map p. 351*) is perhaps the most delightful village on the Bosphorus. In an age when Istanbul's multi-ethnic character is largely just a memory, Kuzguncuk preserves a functioning Greek church and two synagogues. During Ottoman times Kuzguncuk had one of the largest Jewish communities in the city, at its peak numbering some 10,000, so that it was called 'little Jerusalem'. The Jewish cemetery on the hill above town is one of the oldest burial grounds in Istanbul, with tombstones dating back to the 16th century. At the southern extremity of the village is the Fethi Ahmet Paşa Yalısı, also known as the Pembe (Pink) Yalı. This was originally built in the 18th century, and then restored in the second quarter of the 19th by the vizier Fethi Ahmet Pasha. The İsmet Baba restaurant is a pleasant place to come for lunch, overlooking the Bosphorus, Ortaköy and the skyscrapers beyond.

BEYLERBEYİ

Lying almost directly under the Bosphorus bridge is Beylerbeyi Sarayı (*map p. 351; open 9.30–4; closed Mon and Thur*), the largest Ottoman palace on the Bosphorus after Dolmabahçe. The palace and the village were named after a *beylerbeyi*, an Ottoman title that literally means 'Lord of Lords'; this was Mehmet Pasha, governor of Rumelia in the reign of Murat III. He built a mansion on this site, and though it eventually vanished, the name Beylerbeyi lived on. The first sultan to reside here was Mahmut II, who built a summer palace that was destroyed by fire in the mid-19th century. The present palace was built for Abdülaziz in 1861–65 by Sarkis Balyan. It was used mainly as a summer lodge and as a residence for visiting royalty, one of the first being Empress Eugénie of France, who stayed here in 1869; later visitors included Emperor Franz Joseph of Austria, Shah Nasireddin of Persia and King Edward VIII of England with Mrs Simpson. Abdülhamit II lived out the last years of his life in Beylerbeyi after his return in 1913 from exile in Salonica, dying here in 1918.

Visiting the palace

The palace is divided into the usual selamlık and harem. The building has three storeys, although only the upper two are visible along the Bosphorus façade. The ground floor houses the kitchens and other service apartments of the palace; the state rooms and imperial apartments are on the two upper floors, a total of 26 elegantly appointed chambers, including six grand salons, with a magnificent spiral staircase leading up from the central reception hall.

Beylerbeyi is as sumptuously furnished and decorated as Dolmabahçe; its adornments include Hereke carpets, Bohemian crystal chandeliers, French clocks, vases from China, Japan, France and the imperial Ottoman workshops at Yıldız, which also manufactured all of the furniture. It is decorated with a number of murals by the Armenian Romantic artist Aivazovsky, court painter to Abdülaziz.

Beylerbeyi village

The village of Beylerbeyi lies just above the Bosphorus bridge. Adjoining the landing stage is Beylerbeyi Camii, built in 1778 by Mehmet Tahir Ağa for Abdülhamit I. It has two minarets, the lower part of each consisting of a square base above which there is a bulbous foot, rather like a flattened bell-jar, from which rises the fluted shaft, with a single şerefe and a bulbous stone crown with a tall horned *alem*, or crescent-like symbol. This is the first appearance of this type of minaret which, particularly its bulbous foot, became a characteristic feature in mosques of the late 18th and the 19th centuries.

ÇENGELKÖY TO ANADOLU HİSARI

Çengelköy

Çengelköy 'Hook Village' (*map p. 351*), took its name, according to Evliya Çelebi, from the fact that shortly after the Conquest Fatih found a store of Byzantine anchors here. The village is exceptionally pretty and has a very picturesque square on the sea, shaded by plane trees and graced by a Baroque fountain. Just north of the main part of the village, on the main shore road (Kuleli Cd. 51) is a luxury hotel called Sumahan on the Water, a beautiful place to stop for coffee.

Kuleli, Vaniköy and Kandilli

The imposing building on the shore south of Vaniköy is the **Kuleli Officer Training College**. The original military training school and barracks here were built c. 1800 by Selim III, as part of his attempted reform of the armed forces. The present structure dates from a rebuilding and enlargement by Sultan Abdülmecit, completed in 1860. The older building served as a military hospital during the Crimean War. It was one of two hospitals which were under the supervision of Florence Nightingale, the other and larger one being in Üsküdar (*see p. 269*). It was more or less on this site that the empress Theodora, wife of Justinian the Great, established her famous home for reformed prostitutes. Procopius, the court chronicler, writes in his *Secret History* that some of the women 'threw themselves from the parapets at night and thus freed themselves from an undesired salvation'. Above **Vaniköy** itself is the tower of the Istanbul Rasathane, an astronomical observatory and meteorological station. It has a small exhibition of the antique astronomical instruments used by the 16th-century astronomer Takiuddin.

At **Kandilli** (*map p. 341*) the waters of the Bosphorus rush past the point with such speed that they are known as the Devil's Current. On the hill above is the palace of Adile Sultan, sister of Sultan Abdülaziz, built in 1856 and now home to the Kandilli branch of the Borsa restaurant chain.

Küçüksu

Küçüksu, 'Little Water' (*map p. 341*), is named after one of the two streams that make up the Sweet Waters of Asia. In Ottoman times it was a favourite resort; just south of the ferry landing is **Küçüksu Kasrı** (*open 9–4; closed Mon and Thur*), a small Rococo palace built by Nikoğos Balyan in 1856–57 for Sultan Abdülmecit. The same architect had earlier built Ihlamur Kasrı (there are stylistic similarities). On the seashore near the palace is the fountain of the Valide Sultan Mihrişah, mother of Selim III, built in 1796. It is square with upturned eaves and colonnettes set in its corners, with the spigots and their basins framed in round arches. The situation of the fountain is extremely picturesque, and has been a favourite subject for painters and engravers.

Just beyond the Küçüksu stream is the **Kıbrıslı Yalısı**, the longest seaside mansion on the Bosphorus. It was originally built in the mid-19th century by the Grand Vizier İzzet Mehmet Pasha, who sold it to the Grand Vizier Kıbrıslı ('from Cyprus') Mehmet Emin Pasha. A short way farther along is the beautiful **Kırmızı Yalı** (Red Yalı), also built in the mid-19th century, for the Ostrorogs, a noble French-Polish family who moved to Turkey in the late Ottoman period. The last of the line, Count Jean Ostrorog, died here in 1975.

Anadolu Hisarı

The port of Anadolu Hisarı (*map p. 341*) is just north of the mouth of Göksü ('Blue Water'), the second of the Sweet Waters of Asia. Just north of the ferry landing is the small fortress of Anadolu Hisarı, a medieval castle which well deserves its Turkish name of Güzelce, 'Beautiful One'. It was built in 1395 by Sultan Beyazıt I and was rebuilt and perhaps extended by Mehmet II in 1452, when he was constructing the great fortress of Rumeli Hisarı across the Bosphorus.

ABOVE THE FATİH BRIDGE

Kanlıca

Kanlıca (*map p. 341*) is a pretty place, still retaining something of its old village feel. It is famous for the number of fine old yalıs that line the coast here, which include the oldest yalı on the Bosphorus, the Amcazade Hüseyin Pasha Yalısı. Hüseyin Pasha, the fourth member of the illustrious Köprülü family to serve as Grand Vizier, is thought to have built it in 1698, the year in which he represented Mustafa II in the negotiations between the European powers and the Ottoman Empire at Carlowitz. The final articles of the Peace of Carlowitz, where the Ottoman Empire recognised the loss of much territory in Eastern Europe, were signed here on 26th January 1699. All that remains of the original house is the wreck of a once very beautiful room built out on piles over the sea.

Kanlıca is traditionally also famous for its delicious thick, creamy yogurt. Made of a mixture of sheep's and cow's milk, it was praised by Evliya Çelebi as the best in Istanbul. It is still served here: traditionally you eat it with sugar sprinkled on top. On the far side of the pretty square around the ferry landing there is a mosque which is a minor work of Sinan; an inscription over the entrance portal records that it was founded in 1559–60 by the vizier İskender Pasha. The founder's türbe is nearby.

The Rococo stairway of the mid-19th-century Küçüksu Kasrı, built by Nikoğos Balyan.

Çubuklu and Paşabahçe

Çubuklu (*map p. 341*), known in Byzantine times as Eirenaion, 'Peaceful', had a famous monastery founded in 420 by St Alexander for his order of Akoimatoi, the 'Unsleeping', who prayed in relays throughout the day and night. Half a century later a branch of this order was installed in the newly-founded monastery of St John of Studius in Constantinople (*see p. 190*), where they became renowned for their piety and scholarship. On the hill above the village is the **Hidiv Kasrı**, a palace built in 1907 by the Italian architect Delfo Seminati for Abbas Hilmi Pasha, the last Khedive of Egypt, the hereditary viceroy under Ottoman rule. Its distinctive tower is one of the most conspicuous landmarks on this part of the Bosphorus. The palace is now a hotel, restaurant and café.

Paşabahçe, the 'Pasha's Garden', named after the palace and gardens established here by Hezarpare Ahmet Pasha, Grand Vizier under Murat IV. The village was once home to a glass factory, set up by Selim III, who wanted a domestic source of fine glassware to reduce reliance on Venetian and Bohemian imports. The Paşabahçe manufactory became famous for its fine crystal and glassware, 'Beykoz ware', and for its delicate *çeşme-i bülbül* ware, literally 'eye of the nightingale', distinctive for its swirling patterns. Glass is still made under the Paşabahçe name (though the Bosphorus factory is now closed), and can be bought at outlets all over the city (there is one on İstiklal Caddesi).

Beykoz and Hünkar İskelesi

The large village of Beykoz, 'Governor's Walnut' (*map p. 341*), boasts a handsome 19th-century seaside mansion, the Halil Ethem Yalısı, south of the landing stage. On the main square there is a fountain, built in 1746 by one İshak Ağa, Inspector of Customs; it forms a domed and columned loggia and is quite unlike any other fountain in the city.

According to legend, Beykoz was the home of King Amycus, ruler of a barbarous people known as the Bebryces. When strangers landed on this coast Amycus forced them to box with him wearing nail-studded gloves, but since Amycus, the son of Poseidon, was the best boxer in the world, he always killed his man. However, when the Argonauts landed, Amycus challenged Polydeuces, who turned out to be an even greater boxer than he, and the king finally met his death.

At **Selvi Burnu**, 'Poplar Point', the coast turns east to the valley of the Tokat Deresi. Here Fatih built a royal kiosk, as did Süleyman the Magnificent after him. It is from the royal landing stairs that the place gets its modern name, Hünkar İskelesi, the 'Emperor's Landing-Place', which in turn gave its name to the peace treaty signed here in October 1833 between Russia and the Ottoman Empire. The palace that now stands on the site was built in the mid-19th century for Sultan Abdülmecit by Sarkis Balyan.

Anadolu Kavağı

The village of **Anadolu Kavağı** (*map p. 341*) is the last ferry stop on the Asian side. The fortifications here, like those at Rumeli Kavağı, were built in 1783 by Toussaint and improved in 1794 by Monnier (*for the history, see p. 262*). To the south of the village is **Yuşa Tepesi**, a hill named after the Muslim saint called Yuşa Baba, with a shrine at the top.

On the long stretch of concave coast called **Keçili Limanı**, the 'Harbour of the Goats', is the place that Gyllius called the Fane of Jove, the temple of Zeus Ourios, Zeus of the Favouring Winds. In the temple there was a hieron, or sacred precinct, dedicated to the Twelve Gods. According to one myth, it was founded by Jason on his return from Colchis with the Golden Fleece. In Byzantine times the name Hieron applied to the toll and customs station at this point, which was guarded by the huge **fortress**. This fortress is often called 'the Genoese Castle', though it is actually Byzantine in foundation. It is the largest fortress on the Bosphorus, enclosing almost twice the area of Rumeli Hisarı. Until recently it was garrisoned by the Turkish army, but now it is open to the public; it is an easy walk from Anadolu Kavağı and is a wonderful spot for a picnic, commanding a superb view of the upper Bosphorus and its mouth on the Black Sea.

The shore beyond this point is wild and rugged, a line of jagged promontories and inlets so precipitous that they can hardly be called harbours. The promontory called **Poyraz** is named after the fierce northeast wind that howls down the Bosphorus from the Black Sea in winter; it is the equivalent of the Greek Boreas. On Poyraz Burnu is a fortress built in 1773 by Baron de Tott for Mustafa III, a twin of the fortress across the strait; there is also a small village on the cape.

Anadolu Feneri Burnu takes its name from the lighthouse on the promontory above. Below it the village of **Anadolu Feneri** clings perilously to the cliff, and just to the south is Çakal Limanı, 'Jackal Harbour', fringed by savage and rocky precipices. At the mouth of the Bosphorus is **Yum Burnu**, the 'Cape of Good Omen', anciently known as the Ancyrean Cape, 'of the Anchor', from the legend that it was here that Jason took on a stone anchor for the Argo.

THE PRINCES' ISLANDS

Old steamers (vapur) for the islands (Adalar) operated by Şehir Hatları leave from Kabataş. Boats stop at the four largest and most populous of the islands, the closest of which is Kınalı, followed by Burgaz, then Heybeli, and finally Büyükada, the largest in the archipelago. Journey times (approx.) are: to Kınalıada 45mins; Burgazada 1hr; Heybeliada 1hr 20mins; Büyükada 90mins. You will need to buy a token from the ticket office (a different type from tram and funicular tokens) and use that to get through the barriers. Fast ferries operated by İDO, also from Kabataş, are much less frequent but the journey time is considerably less (under an hour to Büyükada).

The Princes' Islands (*map p. 338*) are a little suburban archipelago just off the Asian coast of the Marmara. There are nine islands in total, all but four of them tiny. The nearest is some 15km from the Galata Bridge, the farthest about 30km, though in spirit they seem at a far greater remove than that, being so different in atmosphere and appearance from the rest of the city.

HISTORY OF THE PRINCES' ISLANDS

In the medieval Byzantine period the archipelago was known as Papadonisia, the 'Islands of the Monks', from the many monasteries there, monasteries which became famous because of the many emperors and empresses who were shut up in them after losing their thrones. According to the Byzantine chronicler Cedrenus, Justin II built himself a palace and a monastery on the largest of the isles in 569. This island became known as Prinkipo, the Island 'of the Prince'.

The first regularly scheduled ferry service to the islands began in 1846. This brought a large influx of visitors who built summer houses, and many settled in as year-round residents. These were largely well-off Greeks, but included substantial numbers of Armenians, Jews, resident foreigners and a few wealthy Turkish families. The ferries also brought crowds of people on summer weekends, particularly to Büyükada, resulting in the construction of hotels, restaurants, cafés and bathing establishments.

Motor vehicles are not permitted on the islands, and the only public transport is provided by phaetons, picturesque horse-drawn buggies which can be hired at the ferry-landings.

KINALIADA

Kınalıada has a few sandy coves where you can picnic, and it has fine views from the summits of its three bare hills: Çınar Tepesi, Teşvekiye Tepesi and Monastir Tepesi. Otherwise there is little to do on the island, which has no hotels and restaurants.

HISTORY OF KINALIADA

The Greeks have always called the island Proti, 'First' since it is the nearest in the archipelago to the city. In Byzantine times there were two monasteries on the island, one of them dedicated to the Panaghia and the other to the Transfiguration, and there was also a convent of unknown name. All three of these establishments housed royal exiles at one time or another. From the 9th to the 11th centuries these included Michael I, the family of Leo V, Romanus I Lecapenus and his sons Stephen and Constantine, the empress Theophano, widow of Romanus II and Nicephorus II, and Romanus IV Diogenes. The island takes its Turkish name ('Henna-Red') from the colour of the sandstone cliffs that plunge into the sea at its eastern end. The population has traditionally been largely Armenian.

The modern Greek **church of the Panaghia**, which can be seen to the left of the ferry-landing, a few streets in, is believed to stand on, or near, the site of the Byzantine monastery of the same name. Around the church, and also in a nearby park, there are architectural fragments that almost certainly belonged to it.

The second street to the south of the church, Kınalı Fırın Sk., leads inland past a **Byzantine cistern** thought to have supplied water to the monastery of the Panaghia. It was undoubtedly from here that the British Admiral Duckworth obtained water for his fleet when he anchored off Kınalı during his show of force against Istanbul in 1827. While watering his fleet Duckworth learned that a party of Turkish troops had taken refuge at the Monastery of the Transfiguration, which was just a short distance outside the town to the southwest. He thereupon ordered a bombardment which utterly destroyed the monastery, which had probably been in existence for a thousand years.

One block beyond the cistern the street leads to a path which heads out into the countryside. A short way along, on the left, is the modern Monastery of the Transfiguration; this was founded in the mid-19th century by Simon Sinosoğlu to replace the Byzantine structure destroyed by Duckworth. A bust of Sinosoğlu stands beside the church, which has a superb iconostasis of dark wood and some fine icons. All that remains of the Byzantine monastery are a few fragments.

The path passes between Monastir Tepesi (south) and Teşvekiye Tepesi (north), after which it turns right to pass between Teşvekiye Tepesi and Çınar Tepesi. From either of these two hills there is an excellent view of Sivri (to the right) and Yassı (to the left).

SİVRİ & YASSI

In Byzantium Sivri was known as Oxya and Yassı as Platy: both the Turkish and Greek names mean the same thing: 'Pointed' and 'Flat'. Sivri is nothing more than a tall craggy reef rising to a height of 90m, taller than any of the Seven Hills of Constantinople. Because of its remoteness and barrenness this and its flat neighbour Yassı have been used for centuries solely as places of exile and imprisonment.

During the last century of Ottoman rule Sivri was used on several occasions to dispose of the street dogs of Istanbul, who were rounded up in their thousands and left to starve and tear each other to pieces. Yassı formerly boasted what Murray's Handbook of 1892 describes as 'a dilapidated Anglo-Saxon castle' built by Sir Henry Bulwer, English ambassador to the Sublime Porte and brother of the novelist Bulwer-Lytton; here he is popularly supposed to have engaged in frantic orgies.

Some remains of the castle were still visible until 1960, when they were largely engulfed in the buildings erected for the trial of the deposed Prime Minister, Adnan Menderes, and 14 of his associates. After a lengthy trial they were all convicted and sentenced to death, but twelve of the sentences were commuted to life imprisonment and only Menderes and two of his former ministers suffered the death penalty. They were hanged in September 1961 on the island of İmralı, farther west in the Marmara.

BURGAZADA

Burgazada, some 4km from Kınalı by sea and traditionally inhabited by Greeks, is one of the most pleasant in the archipelago. It is just as beautiful as the two larger and better-known islands to its east, Heybeli and Büyükada, but it has escaped virtually all of the ravages of uncontrolled development.

HISTORY OF BURGAZADA

In antiquity the island was known as Panormas, but in Byzantine times it was called Antigone, a name which is still used by Greeks. Burgaz, its Turkish name, is a corruption of *pyrgos*, the Greek word for tower, because there was a watch-tower on the highest point, a landmark which was noted by travellers until the early 19th century. During Byzantine times the island had a large monastery dedicated to the Transfiguration.

The only famous personage exiled on Antigone during the Byzantine period was St Methodius, Patriarch of Constantinople, who was imprisoned here by Michael II during the years 822–29. After his death in 846 he was recognised as a saint in the Greek Orthodox Church, and a shrine was built here by Theodora, widow of the emperor Theophilus. Later, a church dedicated to St John the Baptist was built around the shrine.

The town of Burgaz is the prettiest in the islands, with white and pastel-coloured houses ringing a crescent bay. There are two prominent landmarks as you approach from the water: to the left is the high dome of the Greek church of St John the Baptist, and to the right the Burgazada Camii, with pretty waterfront cafés at its foot. There are views over to Kaşık with Helybeli beyond and, further away, the coast of Asia, with its teeming blocks of new housing.

The **church of St John the Baptist** is a modern structure, but it stands on the site of the Byzantine church of the same name that was built over the shrine dedicated to St Methodius. According to tradition, the shrine occupies the dungeon where the saint was imprisoned; it is located behind the door at the left end of the narthex, marked 'I Phylaki Patriarchou Methodiou'. One block beyond the church, on Çayır Sk., is the former **home of the writer Sait Faik** (1907–54), now a museum (*open Tues–Fri 9–1 & 2–5, Sat 9–1*).

At the south end of the village the second road in from the seashore leads to a path that runs up the slopes of the heavily wooded Christos Tepesi, the highest peak on the island (170m). The modern Greek church of **Haghios Christos** at the top is surrounded by some impressive architectural fragments from a large medieval sanctuary, probably the Monastery of the Transfiguration. According to tradition, this was founded by Basil I (r. 867–86), and it appears to have stood until 1720, when it was probably demolished by the Turkish authorities.

The road that leaves the north side of the village passes on the right a modern Greek church dedicated to St George, beside which there is a café pleasantly situated by the sea.

KAŞIK

A narrow strait, less than 1km wide, separates Burgaz from Heybeli. In it lies the tiny islet of Kaşık, or 'Spoon', a name vaguely suggested by its topography. Its Greek name is Pitta and it is the smallest island in the archipelago, too minute to support a monastery. In recent years a number of villas have been built here, and in summer it is linked to Burgaz by motor launch.

HEYBELİADA

This is perhaps the most beautiful of all the Princes' Isles, although many would argue in favour of its neighbour, Büyükada. The village is a pretty cluster of white-washed stone houses and pastel-hued villas on the eastern side of the island.

HISTORY OF HEYBELİADA

The island has always been known to the Greeks as Halki, a name bestowed upon it in antiquity because of its copper-mines, long ago exhausted. Its general outline as seen from the sea, two symmetric hills separated by a rounded valley, is responsible for its Turkish name, which derives from *heybes*, or saddle-bag.

In Byzantine times there were two monasteries on the island. One of these was the Monastery of the Holy Trinity, believed to have stood on Ümit Tepesi, the northernmost of the hills, which is now surmounted by the impressive buildings of the Greek Orthodox Seminary, founded in 1841. According to tradition, the monastery was founded in 857 by the patriarch Photius, who was deposed by Michael III in 886 and exiled to his monastery here, where he died four years later. This monastery continued in existence until the construction of the present seminary, which operated until 1971, when it was closed by the Turkish Parliament. Today there is much debate about its potential reopening.

The second of the two Byzantine monasteries stood on the western slope of Değirmen Tepesi, the more westerly of the two peaks that flank the village. Dedicated to the Panaghia, it was founded by John VIII Palaeologus (r. 1425–48) and was the last monastic establishment to be founded in the Byzantine Empire. The original monastery was destroyed by fire in 1672, was rebuilt, only to be destroyed again in the anti-Greek riots in 1821. In 1833 it was restored and converted into a Greek commercial school; this continued in operation until 1916, when it was converted into an orphanage. In 1942 the building and grounds were taken over by the Turkish government. The only part of the original Byzantine structure that seems to have survived is the chapel of the Panaghia Kamariotissa, founded some time between 1427 and 1439 by Maria Comnena, third wife of John VIII Palaeologus and the last Empress of Byzantium.

The buildings and grounds of the **Turkish Naval Base** are to the left of the ferry landing. Until recently this was the site of the Turkish Naval Academy, which has now been moved across to the mainland.

A paved road leads around the coast of Heybeli, with a branch road cutting across the waist of the island. **Phaetons** can be hired near the ferry station; to go all the way around the island tell the driver 'Büyük (Grand) Tour', or to circle only the northern half say 'Küçük (Small) Tour'.

The Panaghia Kamariotissa

At the intersection of the coast road and the road leading across the waist of the island are the buildings and grounds of the inland branch of the Turkish Naval Base. Normally civilians are not permitted to enter, but sometimes the officer in charge will allow you to see the chapel of the Panaghia Kamariotissa. It is of the quatrefoil or tetraconch type; that is, with a central dome surrounded by four semidomes over exedrae, three of which project from the outside of the building, with the fourth being contained within the narthex. This is the only Byzantine church of this type to have survived in the city.

Buried in the courtyard are seven patriarchs of Constantinople. Four of them died violently in the 17th–18th centuries. The most famous of these is Cyril Lucaris, six times Patriarch of Constantinople and once of Alexandria, who was executed by Murat IV in

1638. His body was flung into the Bosphorus and was washed ashore several days later, when it was taken secretly to Halki for burial. Thus ended the remarkable career of the man whom Pope Urban VIII had called 'the son of darkness and the athlete of Hell'.

On the hillside above there is a very interesting old graveyard. The most striking sepulchral monument there is a large statue of an angel holding the imperial Russian coat of arms, which, like that of Byzantium, is inscribed with the figure of a double-headed eagle. This is a memorial to the three hundred or so Russian soldiers who died in the nearby monastery, imprisoned there after having been captured in the Russo-Turkish war in 1828. Only the names of the officers are inscribed on the monument.

BÜYÜKADA

Büyükada, the largest of the Princes' Isles, is the summer resort *par excellence*.

HISTORY OF BÜYÜKADA

During Byzantine times there were at least four monasteries and a convent on Prinkipo. The convent sheltered several imperial exiles during the medieval period. It had originally been founded by Justinian in the mid-6th century, but it was completely rebuilt and considerably enlarged in the last years of the 8th century by the empress Eirene (r. 797–802), one of the very few women to rule Byzantium in her own right. In 797 Eirene usurped the throne from her son and banished his daughter, Euphrosyne, to Prinkipo so that she could not contest the throne. In 802 Eirene was herself deposed and after her death was buried here. Euphrosyne remained in the convent on Prinkipo for 26 years, while five emperors in turn succeeded one another on the throne of Byzantium. The last of these, Michael II, the Stammerer, suddenly grew tired of his wife, the empress Thecla, and when rumour reached him of the pretty princess-nun on Prinkipo, he sent for her, banishing Thecla to Prinkipo in her stead. Later that same year Michael died and was succeeded by his son Theophilus. The new emperor restored his mother Thecla to the palace and sent Euphrosyne back to her convent.

Two centuries later, in 1041, this same convent sheltered the empress Zoë after she had been exiled by her adopted son, Michael V. She was freed a few weeks later however, when the people of Constantinople deposed Michael and raised Zoë and her sister Theodora to the throne, where they ruled in their own right before being succeeded by Constantine IX, whom Zoë married.

Anna Dalassena, mother of the future Alexius I Comnenus, was imprisoned here in 1060, before being allowed to return to the capital. In 1115 the empress Eirene, wife of Alexius I, entered the convent voluntarily so that she could be near her husband, who was suffering a slow and painful death in one of the monasteries on Prinkipo. He died here in 1118.

The island consists of two large hills separated in the middle by a broad valley, so that the road around it makes a figure of eight. There are **phaetons** for hire from the top of the main square, and here again ask for 'Büyük Tour' for a ride all the way around the island or 'Küçük Tour' to go around the northern half only—or to get to the monastery, just ask for 'Aya Yorgi'. You should really take the Grand Tour, for the southern end of the island is almost totally unspoiled and in places it is extraordinarily beautiful. But the best way to tour the island is on foot, for you can then wander off on pathways up into the hills or down to the sea, where there are secluded coves, ideal for picnicking.

The town

There are some beautiful old houses in the little town, and the phaeton ride takes many of them in. The most prominent is the **Hotel Splendid** at 23 Nisan Cd., built in 1911 by the Greek architect Laskaris Kaloudis for Sakizli Kazım Pasha. The İzzet Pasha Köşkü at 55 Çankaya Cd., built in the latter half of the 19th century by the Greek banker Konstantinos Ilyaso, passed to İzzet Pasha, head of the secret police during the reign of Abdülhamit II. Leon Trotsky lived here during the first years of his exile on Büyükada (1929–33), and it was here that he began to write his monumental *History of the Russian Revolution*. Also on Çankaya Cd. is the Con Pasha Köşkü, the grandest of all the old mansions on Büyükada. This was built in the late 19th century by the Greek architect Achilleos Politis for Con Pasha (Tarasivolos Yannaros), an Ottoman statesman of Italian-Greek ancestry who started the first commercial steamboat service between Kadıköy and Büyükada.

The monastery of the Transfiguration

Both of the island's hills are surmounted by monasteries. The one on İsa Tepesi, the Hill of Christ, is dedicated to the Transfiguration. Virtually nothing is known of the history or date of foundation of this monastery, other than that it was restored in 1597; the present buildings date from the 19th century. It is well worth climbing the hill to see it, for it is in a very picturesque location in the midst of a pine forest.

The monastery of St George

Yüce Tepe, the southern hill, also thickly forested, rises to 202m, the highest in the archipelago. The picturesque Monastery of St George (Aya Yorgi) stands in a beautiful clearing at the top. The phaeton will take you to a carpark almost at the top, from where you have to walk (bikes can be hired too, but it is very steep). The route takes you up a cobbled path (about 20mins), covered for much of its length with lengths of cotton, because on St George's Day thousands of supplicants come here, by no means all of them Christian, unravelling a reel of thread and making a wish as they go. There is a very pleasant café at the top, where you can enjoy a simple meal in an incomparably lovely setting (www.yucetepe.com).

There is evidence that there was a monastery on this site as early as the 12th century, though most of the present structure is modern. The monastery is known to the Greeks as Haghios Georgios Koudonas, 'St George of the Bells'. One version of the foundation

Bas-relief of St George on the chapel on Büyükada, the site of a mass pilgrimage by Christians and Muslims alike on 23rd April, St George's Day.

legend has it that a shepherd was grazing his flock on the hill when he heard the sound of bells coming from under the ground. When he dug down he found an icon of St George, which he and the other islanders enshrined on the spot.

The present building consists of six separate chapels on three levels, the older sanctuaries being on the lower levels. On the ground floor is the chapel of St George, built early in the present century. A flight of stairs leads down to the first level below. Just beside the steps is a chapel of the Blachernitissa, Our Lady of Blachernae. Beyond that is a shrine of St Charalambos, and past that is another chapel of St George. Small iron rings set into the floor of these chapels were for controlling the madmen who were brought here in the hope of being cured, for in Byzantine times the monastic complex included an insane asylum. The room at the bottom of the stairs is a tiny shrine with an aghiasma, a sacred spring. Beyond it you come to the final chapel, dedicated to the Twelve Apostles.

The building abutting the church to the west is a hostel for those who come to visit the monastery on the feast days of the saints who have sanctuaries here. The most important festival is that of St George, 23rd April, when hundreds of Greeks as well as other pilgrims flock to visit the church.

SEDEF & TAVŞAN

From the summit of Yüce Tepe you can see the two tiny islets beyond Büyükada, Sedef Adası, or 'Mother-of-Pearl Island' (to the east), and Tavşan Adası, 'Rabbit Island' (to the south). In Byzantine times Sedef was known as Terebinthos and Tavşan was called Nyandros. Tiny as they are, both were the sites of religious establishments in Byzantium, with a monastery on Terebinthos and a convent on Nyandros. Both were founded in the mid-9th century by the patriarch Ignatius, eldest son of Michael I. Ignatius served as patriarch until his death in 877, after which his remains were brought back for burial in his monastery on Terebinthos. He is now venerated as a saint in the Greek Orthodox Church.

Both Sedef and Tavşan can be reached by boats hired at the port in Büyükada. Sedef has a colony of summer villas, but Tavşan is uninhabited. On Tavşan there are still some scattered ruins of Ignatius' convent.

PRACTICAL INFORMATION

When to go

Spring is the most beautiful season, when judas trees blossom along the Bosphorus and the tulips are out. The heat of summer is usually tempered by the *meltem*, the breeze that blows down the Bosphorus from the Black Sea, though when the dreaded *lodos* blows in from the south across the Marmara, the heat and humidity can be unpleasant for two or three days at a time. Early autumn is also a wonderful time, marked by the annual migration of storks, which rise from their nesting places in great thermal spirals before flying south along the meridians to Egypt. Winters are cold and often rainy.

Visa requirements

United States and most European citizens need a visa to enter Turkey. These can be purchased at the port of arrival, for dollars, pounds sterling or euro (credit cards accepted). Check the status of reciprocal arrangements between your country and Turkey before you travel.

Customs regulations

Apart from the occasional spot-check, visitors to Turkey are seldom asked to open their baggage for inspection. Antiquities may not be taken out of Turkey under any circumstances, so if you buy anything old (and the definition of antique is quite vague) be sure to have it validated by the merchant from whom you purchase it. It is also necessary to do this for Turkish rugs and carpets.

GETTING AROUND

Getting in from the airport

There is a shuttle bus service from both Atatürk Airport on the European side and Sabiha Gökçen Airport on the Asian side (www.istanbulairportshuttle.com). Taxis are also plentiful and the drivers are reliable. Allow plenty of time to catch your plane when travelling back; traffic can be very heavy at peak times of day.

By bus

The city has an extensive network of buses, which are the quickest way to get up and down the Bosphorus shores or the south bank of the Golden Horn. All buses have signs with their route and destination. You can buy a single ticket (*bilet*) at kiosks along the route or from central bus stops, or on the bus itself.

By tram and funicular

An old-fashioned tramway runs along the whole length of İstiklal Cd. A modern tramline goes from Kabataş to Eminönü and Sultanahmet and then along Divan Yolu through the centre of the old city to the bus terminal outside the Theodosian walls beyond Top Kapı. To use the tram you need jetons, which you can either buy from booths at major tram termini or from Jetonmatik machines. In Istanbul there is no such thing as running for a tram. You have to put your jeton into the slot at the turnstile before you can get onto the platform. Many a tram has been missed by people fumbling for jetons.

The funicular from Kabataş to Taksim takes the same kind of jetons as the tram. The Tünel funicular between Karaköy and the top of İstiklal Cd. has its own type of ticket.

By metro
One metro line begins at Aksaray, after which it runs under Adnan Menderes Cd. out beyond the walls to the Otogar; from there it curves back to the domestic terminal at Atatürk Airport. Another line runs from Şişhane to Ayazağa, stopping at Taksim, Osmanbey, Şişli, Levent and Maslak.

By taxi
Taxis all have meters and are required to use them, so it should not be necessary to bargain about fares. If the meter is not on just say *saat* (which means 'clock') to the driver. Most drivers are honest and courteous. Taxis are good value and easy to hail in the street, and there are plenty of taxi ranks.

By train
The Orient Express has its terminus at Sirkeci Station. A commuter train runs out along the Marmara coast from Sirkeci to the beach resort at Florya; service is frequent and inexpensive. Trains on the Asian side have their terminus at Haydarpaşa Station in Kadıköy.

By ferry
Fairly frequent ferry services link the old town with all parts of the city and its suburbs. The main ferry terminuses are around the Galata Bridge, at Kabataş and at Beşiktaş. The landing stages are marked with the places served by ferries, e.g. Haliç (Golden Horn), Boğaz (Bosphorus) and Adalar (Princes' Islands).

Ferries on the upstream side of the Galata Bridge, behind the Eminönü bus station, go up the Golden Horn. Ferries for Üsküdar, Kadıköy and the Bosphorus leave from landings on either side of the bridge, depending on which company you use. Boats for the Princes' Islands leave from Kabataş. The main municipal ferry company, Şehir Hatları, has a good website where you can look up timetables: www.sehirhatlari.net or www.sehirhatlari.com.tr. Fares are very low and the ferries are quite comfortable and usually not too crowded. Other competing companies also offer alternative services. Another reliable one is Turyol (www.turyol.com).

Reading a ferry schedule and buying a ticket
There are two sets of timetables, one for Sundays and holidays (*Pazar Günü ve Tatil Günü*) and one for weekdays (*Pazardan Başka*). Before you board a ferry you need either

a ticket or a jeton, depending on what system the operating company uses. The following vocabulary might be useful:

Kalkış (K.)	Departure time
Varış	Arrival time
Hat, Hattı	Itinerary, line, route
Günleri yapılı	Days operating
Günleri yapılmaz	Days not operating
Hergün	Daily
Expres	Express
İyi yolculuklar	Have a pleasant journey

WHERE TO STAY

Hotels in Istanbul range from luxurious establishments with international standards to very simple inns. The list that follows is a personal selection of places that are either particularly handy or particularly charming or particularly historic. Omission from this list does not imply any adverse judgement, nor does inclusion imply any guarantee of satisfaction. Hotels are grouped according to location and price. Star ratings follow those allocated by the Turkish Ministry of Tourism. For Blue Guides Recommended (■), see p. 291.

The Old City

*****

Eresin Crown. Luxurious hotel behind the Blue Mosque on the site of the Palace of Byzantium. Jazuzzis in every room, two restaurants and a bar. Seaview terrace. *Küçük Ayasofya Cd., Sultanahmet; T: 0212 638 4428, www.eresincrown.com.tr. Map p. 349, D4.*

Four Seasons. Luxury hotel in a late Ottoman former prison, overlooking the archaeological site of the Great Palace of Byzantium. The restoration has been well done. Outstanding restaurant serving western dishes as well as traditional Ottoman cuisine. *Tevfikhane Sk. 1, Sultanahmet; T: 0212 638 8299, www.fshr.com. Map p. 349, E3.*

****

Arcadia. A large modern hotel centrally located behind the palace of İbrahim Pasha; restaurant with roof terrace looking out over the monuments of the First Hill. *Dr Imren Öktem Sk. 1, Sultanahmet; T: 0212 516 9696, www.hotelarcadiaistanbul.com.Map p. 349, D3.*

Armada. A modern hotel in the old quarter on the Marmara slope below the Hippodrome and the Blue Mosque; restaurant serving traditional Turkish dishes. *Ahırkapı Sk. 24, Sultanahmet; T: 0212 455 4455, web www.armadahotel.com.tr. Map p. 349, E4.*

Ayasofya Konakları. A street of charming old Ottoman mansions along the walls of Topkapı Palace, elegantly restored and furnished in period decor by the Turkish Touring Club. Several restaurants, including one in a converted Roman cistern (Sarnıç; *see p. 296*), an outdoor café, bars, a Turkish bath, and a library with a unique collection of books about Istanbul as well as old prints and maps. *Soğukçeşme Sk., Sultanahmet; T: 0212 458 0760/1, www.hoteldersaadet.com. Map p. 349, E3.*

İbrahim Pasha. Small but well-appointed hotel on the Hippodrome, with a roof terrace commanding a panoramic view. *Terzihane Sk. 5, Sultanahmet; T: 0212 518 0394, www.ibrahimpasha.com. Map p. 349, D4.*

Kariye. Old Ottoman building restored by the Turkish Touring Club on the street next to Kariye Camii; restaurant (Asitane) serving traditional Turkish cuisine, dining al fresco in garden during summer. *Kariye Camii Sk. 18, Edirnekapı; T: 0212 534 8414, www.kariyeotel.com. Map p. 343, A3.*

Konuk Evi. Old Ottoman mansion beautifully restored by the Turkish Touring Club, set in a spacious courtyard with its restaurant in a former greenhouse. *Soğukçeşme Sk., Sultanahmet; T: 0212 513 3660, info@ayasofyapensions.com. Map p. 349, E3.*

Kybele. Two town houses converted into a hotel near the Basilica Cistern and Haghia Sophia; colourful lobby lit by 1,002 oriental lamps and adorned with innumerable Turkish antiques. *Yerebatan Cd. 35, Sultanahmet; T: 0212 511 7766, www.kybelehotel.com. Map p. 349, E3.*

Sirkeci Konak. ■ Exceptionally well-run hotel close to Haghia Sophia with some rooms overlooking Gülhane Park. Free afternoon tea, superb breakfast buffet, friendly, helpful and professional staff. An excellent place to stay in the old town. With restaurant, spa and roof terrace. *Taya Hatun Sk. 5, T: 0212 528 4344, www.sirkecikonak.com. Map p. 349, E2.*

Yeşil Ev. An old Ottoman *konak*, made of wood, between the Blue Mosque and Haghia Sophia, beautifully reconstructed by the Turkish Touring Club; restaurant with tree-shaded garden. *Kabasakal Sk. 5, Sultanahmet; T: 0212 517 6785, www.istanbulyesilev.com. Map p. 349, E3.*

* * *

Celal Sultan. Housed in a converted and elegantly appointed town house; roof terrace with panoramic view of Haghia Sophia. *Salkımsöğüt Sk. 16, Sultanahmet; T: 0212 520 9323, www.celalsultan.com. Map p. 349, E3.*

Empress Zoë. An imaginatively restored Ottoman house in the old quarter below the Blue Mosque; roof terrace looking out over the Marmara and garden café adjoining picturesque old Turkish bath. *Akbıyık Cd., Adliye Sk. 10, Sultanahmet; T: 0212 518 2504, www.emzoe.com. Map p. 349, E3.*

Fehmi Bey. Housed in a restored town house off the southwest corner of the Hippodrome, with a sauna, and roof terrace commanding a view of the Blue Mosque and Haghia Sophia. *Üçler Sk. 15, Sultanahmet; T: 0212 639 9083, www.fehmibey.com. Map p. 349, D4.*

Nomade. One of the oldest of the converted town house hotels, a favourite among journalists and academics, with a roof-terrace looking out at Haghia Sophia and the Blue Mosque. *Divanyolu Cd., Ticarethane Sk. 15, Sultanahmet; T: 0212 513 8172, www.hotelnomade.com. Map p. 349, D3.*

Pierre Loti. Small, centrally located

hotel just off Divan Yolu. *Piyer Loti Cd. 5, Çemberlitaş; T: 0212 518 5700, www. pierrelotihotel.com. Map p. 349, D3.*

**

Artefes Hotel. A large wooden house with flower-filled window boxes and a roof terrace. *Çayıroğlu Sk. 12; T: 0212 516 5863, www.artefes.com. Map p. 349, E4.*

Berk Guesthouse. Small family-run hotel on the Marmara slope of the First Hill; all rooms with bath. *Kutlugün Sk. 27, Sultanahmet; T: 0212 517 6561, www. berkguesthouse.com. Map p. 349, E3.*

Park. Comfortable, well-run hotel with Marmara views from the terrace. *Utangaç Sk. 26, Sultanahmet; T: 021 517 6596, www. parkhotelistanbul.com. Map p. 349, E3.*

*

Alp. Simple but clean hotel with en-suite bathrooms; on the Marmara slope of the First Hill; terrace in garden. *Akbıyık Cd., Adliye Sk. 4, Sultanahmet; T: 0212 517 7067, www.alpguesthouse.com. Map p. 349, E3.*

Alzer. Decent hotel with small but comfortable rooms; centrally located on the Hippodrome, with roof terrace. *Atmeydanı 72, Sultanahmet; T: 0212 516 6262, www. alzerhotel.com. Map p. 349, D4.*

Hanedan. Cheap but clean hotel on the Marmara slope of the First Hill. *Akbıyık Cd., Adliye Sk. 3, Sultanahmet; T: 0212 516 4869, www.hanedanhotel.com. Map p. 349, E3.*

Merih 2. Cheap, clean and well-run hotel centrally located on the First Hill; cafeteria on garden terrace. *Alemdar Cd. 20/24, Sultanahmet; T: 0212 526 9708, www. hotelmerih.com. Map p. 349, E3.*

Poem. Cheap, clean and well-appointed hotel on Marmara slope of the First Hill. The owner has inscribed in each room a different Turkish poem, hence the name. *Terbıyık Sk. 12, Sultanahmet; T: 0212 638 9744, www.hotelpoem.com. Map p. 349, E4.*

Beyoğlu, the Bosphorus and the Marmara

*****

Bosphorus Pasha. Housed in a late Ottoman yalı on the Asian side of the Bosphorus near Beylerbeyi Palace, with an outstanding Italian restaurant that is a branch of the renowned Cecconi's in London. All the front rooms have views of the Bosphorus and the skyline of the old city. *Yalıboyu Cd. 64, Beylerbeyi; T: 0216 422 0003, www.bosphoruspalace.com.*

Çırağan Palace Kempinski. Outstanding luxury hotel housed partly in a recreated mid-19th-century Ottoman palace (*see p. 251*). Turkish and Italian restaurants; outdoor swimming pool. *Çırağan Cd. 32, Beşiktaş; T: 0212 326 4646, www.kempinski.istanbul.com.*

Conrad International. *De luxe* hotel overlooking the Bosphorus and the gardens of Yıldız Palace. Turkish and Italian restaurants; indoor and outdoor swimming pools. *Yıldız Cd., Beşiktaş; T: 0212 227 3000, www.conradistanbul.com.*

Four Seasons Istanbul Bosphorus. Luxury hotel on the European shore of the Bosphorus, part of it in a reconverted Ottoman palace. Excellent restaurant. *Çırağan Cd. 28, Beşiktaş; T: 0212 381 4000, www.fourseasons.com/bosphorus.*

Marmara. De luxe hotel on Taksim Square; restaurant with Turkish, Italian and French specialities as well as brasserie for lunch and supper; rooftop lounge with panoramic view. *Taksim, T: 0212 251 4696, www.themarmarahotels. com. Map p. ???, ??.*

Sumahan on the Water. ▪ Luxury hotel in an imaginatively restored rakı distillery on the Asian shore of the Bosphorus; excellent restaurant. Free shuttle boat across the water. *Kuleli Cd. 51, Çengelköy; T: 0216 422 8000, www.sumahan.com.*

Tomtom Suites. ▪ Stylish, comfortable home from home in an old Franciscan convent. *Tomtom Kaptan Sk. 18; T: 0212 292 4949, www.tomtomsuites.com. Map p. 344, C3.*

****

Galata Residence. Housed in the converted late 19th-century mansion of the Camondos, the famous Jewish banking family of Galata; it comprises one- or two-bedroom apartments, each with a study, a bathroom and a fully-equipped kitchen. The rooms on the upper floors have views of the harbour and the skyline of the old city. *Bankalar Cd., Felek Sk., Galata, T: 0212 292 4841, www.galataresidence.com. Map p. 344, C4.*

Kervansaray. Modern hotel on Taksim Square; Turkish and European restaurants; roof terrace. *Taksim; T: 0212 235 5000, www.kervansarayhotel.com. Map p. 345, D2.*

Merit Halki Palace. Wonderful hotel on Heybeliada island. *T: 0216 351 0025, www.halkipalacehotel.com.*

Pera Palace. ▪ The first of Istanbul's grand hotels, opened in 1895 for travellers arriving on the *Orient Express*. It has been the setting for a number of murder mysteries, most notably those of Agatha Christie and Eric Ambler. The decor of the public rooms is evocative of the cos-

mopolitan Pera of late Ottoman and early Republican times; these include a restaurant with Turkish and Western dishes, a charming patisserie, and the famous bar that was the setting for so many real and fictional Levantine intrigues, with a terrace café outside where in summer you can watch the sun setting over the Golden Horn. *Meşrutiyet Cd. 52, Beyoğlu; T: 0212 377 4000, www.perapalace.com/en. Map p. 344, B3–C3.*

Richmond. Great location in the heart of Beyoğlu, next to the old Russian Embassy. *İstiklal Cd. 445, Beyoğlu; T: 0212 252 5460, www.richmondhotels.com.tr. Map p. 344, C3.*

Splendid. Elegant, old-world hotel on the island of Büyükada. *T: 0216 382 6950, www.splendidhotel.net.*

***

Bebek. Small hotel on the European shore of the middle Bosphorus; seaside rooms have superb view across to the Asian shore; café-bar with waterfront deck. *Cevdetpaşa Cd. 113–115, Bebek; T: 0212 358 2000, www.bebekhotel.com.*

House Hotel Galatasaray. ▪ Beautifully converted late 19th-century mansion, the former Zenovitch Apartments, with stylish rooms and top-floor lounge, all in a cool grey-biege palette. *Bostanbaşı Cd. 19; T: 0212 252 0422, www.thehousehotel.com. Map p. 344, C3.*

Villa Zurich. A 45-room hotel near the centre of the modern town in Cihangir; all rooms with private bath, central heating and air-conditioning; two restaurants, patisserie and terrace bar. *Akarsu Ykş. 44–46, Cihangir; T: 0212 293 0604, www.hotelvillazurich.com. Map p. 345, D3.*

**

Büyük Londra. The oldest hotel in the

city, built in the late 1870s on what was then a fashionable avenue overlooking the Golden Horn. Charming old-fashioned lobby with caged parrots in the bar. *Meşrutiyet Cd. 53, Tepebaşı; T: 0212 245 0670, www.londrahotel.net. Map p. 344, C3.*

Monopol. Inexpensive but clean, comfortable and well-run; centrally located. *Meşrutiyet Cd. 223, Beyoğlu; T: 0212 251 7326, www.hotelmonopol.net. Map p. 344, B3.*

*

Santa Ottoman Hotel. Very close to Taksim Square, overlooking an Armenian Catholic church. *Zambak Sk. 1, Taksim, T: 0212 252 2878, www.santaottomanhotel.com. Map p. 345, D2.*

Art Suites. Good-value, well-located place with simple rooms with kitchenette. *Balyoz Sk 14, Beyoğlu; T: 0212 245 8205, www.artsuiteshotel.com. Map p. 344, C3.*

Villa Rifat. Charming old house on Büyükada with garden and view of the sea. *Yilmaz Türk Cd. 80, T: 0216 351 6068.*

Prenset Pansiyon. Cheap but spotless and well-run hotel on Heybeliada; sauna and small swimming pool on roof terrace. *Ayyıldız Cd., T: 0216 351 0039, www.prensetpansiyon.com.*

BLUE GUIDES RECOMMENDED

Hotels, restaurants and meyhanes that are particularly good choices in their category—in terms of excellence, location, charm, value for money or the quality of the experience they provide—carry the Blue Guides Recommended sign:■. All these establishments have been visited and selected by our authors, editors or contributors as places they have particularly enjoyed and would be happy to recommend to others. To keep our entries up-to-date, reader feedback is essential: please do not hesitate to contact us (www.blueguides.com) with any views, corrections or suggestions, or join our online discussion forum.

FOOD & DRINK

Turkish cuisine is one of the best and most varied in the world, and in Istanbul you can dine like a sultan—at least in terms of the menu. You will probably dine more convivially than his highness did, as the sultan always ate alone. The trick is knowing what to order. This is no problem in a *lokanta*, the simple places where working people eat, for you simply walk up to the counter and choose what you want from the pots on the steam table. In higher-class restaurants the procedure is as follows: you begin with cold hors d'oeuvres (*soğuk meze*), which you are invited to choose from a huge tray brought to your table. To supplement them you can order some hot hors d'oeuvres (*ara sıcak*) from the menu. You also order the main course that will follow, and later a sweet and/or coffee.

Cold hors d'oeuvres (soğuk meze)

beyaz peynir white goat cheese
beğin brain
biber dolması stuffed green peppers
cacık grated cucumbers with yogurt and garlic (tzatziki)
domates dolması stuffed tomatoes
imam bayıldı (literally, The Imam Fainted) stuffed aubergines

kaşar peynir hard cheese
lahana dolması stuffed cabbage
lakerda salted bonito tuna
midye pilakısı mussels cooked with olive oil and served cold
tarama carp roe
yaprak dolması stuffed green peppers
zeytin olives

Salads (salata)

çoban salata chopped peppers, tomatoes, lettuce, cucumbers, and celery
domates salatası tomato salad
fasulye ezmesi dried bean salad
ispanakoku salatası spinach salad
marul Romaine (Cos) lettuce
pancar salatası beet salad

patates ezmesi mashed potato salad
patlıcan salatası aubergine salad
piyaz dried white bean salad
salatalık salatası cucumber salad
yeşil salata green salad
yoğurtlu kabak salatası zucchini with yogurt

Warm hors d'oeuvres (Ara sıcak)

Among the most popular hot meze dishes are the various types of *börek*, thin puff pastry with various fillings, such as the following:

etli börek with minced meat filling
ispanaklı börek with spinach
mantarlı börek with mushroom
pastırmılı börek with a filling of dried spiced beef
peynerli börek with cheese filling
tavuklu börek with chicken filling

Other popular hot *meze* dishes are:

arnavut ciğer chopped liver and onions
beğin tavası fried brain
et sauté thin slices of meat sautéed in

tomato and pepper sauce
izgara köfte grilled meat balls
kabak kızartması fried zucchini
koç yumurtası fried sheep's testicles
menemen eggs scrambled with green and red peppers and white cheese
midye tavası fried mussels
midye dolması fried mussels served in the shell and stuffed with rice
patates köfte potato croquettes
patates kızartması fried potatoes
patlıcan kızartması fried aubergines

Meat (etler), Poultry (tavuk) and Fish (balık)

Meat and fish may be prepared in several ways: grilled (*izgara*), fried (*tava*), roasted (*kızartma*), in casserole (*güveç*), grilled on a skewer (*şiş*). Among the most popular meat dishes are the various types of kebabs.

alabalık trout

bahçevan kebabı meat cooked with vegetables one would find in a typical kitchen garden

barbun red mullet

bıldırçın quail

Bursa kebab döner kebab served with yogurt and tomato sauce, sometimes called *Iskender kebab*

çerkez tavuk Circassian chicken, with walnut sauce

cığer liver

çinakop a species of small bluefish

çulluk woodcock

dana veal

dil sole

döner kebab pressed lamb cooked on a rotating spit over a charcoal fire and carved off in thin slices

güveç meat, poultry or seafood baked together with vegetables in a casserole

hindi dolması stuffed turkey

hünkar beğendi ('The Sultan's Favourite') puréed aubergine served with chicken or meat

islim kebabı meat and aubergines cooked in a covered casserole

kadın budu ('The Lady's Thigh') ground meat and rice formed into patties and then dipped into beaten eggs and fried

kağıt kebab meat, vegetables, and herbs in a wine sauce, and cooked in a wax-paper envelope

kalkan turbot

karnıyarık ('Belly Split-Open') ground

meat cooked together with aubergines

kaz goose

keklik partridge

kılıç swordfish

kış türlüsü a meat and vegetable stew

mantı meat-filled mini ravioli

kiyma minced meat

kuzu budu rostosu roast leg of lamb

kuzu lamb

levrek bass

lüfer bluefish

mercan bream

ördek duck

palamut bonito

pılıç young chicken

pılıç dolması stuffed roast chicken

pılıç kağıta chicken cooked in a wax paper envelope

pirzola lamb chops

sığır beef

şiş kebab lamb skewered on a spit with tomatoes and onions and grilled over a charcoal fire

somon balığı salmon

sülün pheasant

tas kebab lamb stew with rice and vegetables

tavuk chicken (also poultry in general)

tavukklu beğendi chicken in egg purée

tavuklu güveç chicken casserole

tekir small red mullet

üskümrü mackerel

yaban domuz wild boar

Soup (*Çorba*)

domateslı çorbası tomato soup

domateslı pirinç çorbası tomato and rice soup

düğün çorbası ('Wedding Soup') soup with meat, vegetables, eggs, and paprika

işkembe çorbası tripe soup

kırmızı mercimek çorbası red lentil soup

mercimek çorbası lentil soup

tavuk çorbası chicken soup

yayla çorbası beef soup with yogurt

Vegetables (*sebze*) and Fruit (*meyva*)

bezelye peas
bamya okra
biber green pepper
çalı fasulye green string beans
çilek strawberry
domates tomatoes
elma apple
enginar artichoke
erik plum
fasulye green beans
fasulye pılakısı white beans
greyfurt grapefruit
havuç carrots
hıyar cucumber
incir fig
ispanak spinach
kabak zucchini
karnıbahar cauliflower

karpuz watermelon
kavun melon
kereviz root celery
kiraz cherry
kuşkonmaz asparagus
lahana cabbage
maydonoz parsley
muz banana
pancar beets
patates potatoes
patlıcan aubergine
pirasa leeks
pirinç rice (*pilav* when cooked)
portakal orange
salatalık cucumbers
şeftali peach *soğan* onion
üzüm grapes
vişne sour cherry

Desserts (*tatlı*)

aşure ('Noah's Pudding') sweet pudding
with walnuts, raisins, and peas
ayva kompostu stewed quince
ayva marmaladı quince marmalade
baklava many-layered pastry filled with
walnuts, baked and soaked in syrup
bal kabağı tatlısı pumpkin dessert
bülbül yuvası ('Nightingale's Nest') shred-
ded wheat with pistachios and syrup
dondurma ice cream
ekmek kadayıfı crumpet in syrup
gül receli rose jam
helva dessert made with ground sesame
seeds
kadın gobeği ('Lady's Navel') doughnut

soaked in syrup
lokma pastry ball fried in oil and soaked
in syrup
muhallebe pudding made from milk, rice,
and rosewater
portakal peltesi orange pudding
revani dessert made with sesame, flour,
and eggs soaked in syrup
sarığı burma rich, flaky dessert with nut
filling
sütlaç rice pudding
tulumba tatlısı rich flour dessert with
almond flavouring
yogurt tatlısı custard made with yogurt
and eggs

DRINKS

When dining, Turks traditionally like to drink rakı, a strong (87 percent proof) anise-
flavoured drink, similar to Greek ouzo. They rarely drink it straight, mixing it half-

and-half with water, which turns it milky white. It goes very well with Turkish food. However, recent very high taxes on alcohol means that it is expensive. There is very good Turkish wine (*şarap*) available, but waiters are often inexpert on the subject, largely because they rarely drink it themselves. Nevertheless, most restaurants have a wide selection of red (*kırmızı şarap*), white (*beyaz şarap*), and rosé (*pembe şarap*) wines. A reliable large-scale producer is Kavaklıdere, whose white wine is labelled Çankaya and the red Yakut.

Turks wash down their food with copious quantities of bottled water (*su*) and mineral water (*maden suyu*), which is excellent and cheap (still water is particularly good value, often offered free). They also drink *ayran*, a kind of liquid yoghurt, which goes very well with Turkish foods. Here and there in the old city you can find a *bozahane* or *bozacısı*, a café that sells *boza*, a delicious drink made from millet. An excellent breakfast drink, particularly in winter, is *salep*, a thick beverage made from powdered orchid root and served piping hot. Salep goes very well with a *simit*, a kind of ring-shaped pretzel, often covered with sesame seeds, which are carried in huge stacks by itinerant vendors. They are quite delicious and make an excellent snack when strolling around town.

All Turkish meals end with coffee (*kahve*), served in a small cup with varying amounts of sugar (*şeker*). If you want no sugar in your coffee say *sade*. A little sugar is *az şekerli*; medium-sweet is *orta şekerli*; sweet is *şekerli*. You can also order tea (*çay*), which is served in a small bell-waisted glass with sugar on the side. The tea is often well stewed and quite bitter, an acquired taste for some but a basic element in the Turkish way of life. A popular variant is apple tea.

RESTAURANTS

Istanbul is particularly well-endowed with excellent restaurants, which cater to every taste and social class. The gastronomic spectrum includes de luxe Western-style restaurants in the modern sections of Istanbul, excellent kebab lokantas in the old city, famous fish-restaurants along the Bosphorus, and simple little working-men's cookshops dotted all over town. It would be impractical to list all the good restaurants in the city, for there are hundreds in every category; what follows is just a selection.

Travellers wishing to experience something of the flavour of Turkey are advised to eat in those restaurants which the Turks themselves frequent. The most popular are the old-fashioned meyhanes, taverns that serve traditional Turkish meze.

The least expensive restaurants are designated as $ and the most expensive as $$$$.

Restaurants are listed separately for three general areas: the Old City, Beyoğlu, and the Bosphorus. For Blue Guides Recommended (■), see p. 291.

The Old City

$$$$
Asitane. Well-regarded restaurant just beside Kariye Müzesi, serving revived

recipes from the courts of the sultans. Fatih Mehmet was particularly fond of *mantı* (ravioli). *Kariye Camii Sk. 6,*

Edinrnekapı; T: 0212 635 7997, www. asitanerestaurant.com. Map p. 343, A3.
Darüzziyafe. Outstanding restaurant in the former imaret (public kitchen) of the Süleymaniye; specialises in Ottoman cuisine. *Şifahane Cd. 6; T: 0212 511 8414, www.daruzaffiye.com. Map p. 348, B2.*
Zeyrekhane. An elegant restaurant built on the terrace behind Zeyrek Camii, the church of the Pantocrator, with a stunning view of the Süleymaniye and the Golden Horn. Excellent food and service, with both western dishes and traditional Turkish cuisine. *İbadethane Arkası Sk. 10, Zeyrek; T: 0212 532 278, www.zeyrekhane.com. Map p. 348, A1.*

$$$
Develi. Meat restaurant, founded in 1912, on the Marmara shore in Samatya, with specialities from southeastern Anatolia; terrace in summer. *Balıkpazarı, Gümüş Yüzük Sk. 7, Samatya; T: 0212 529 0811, www.develikebap.com/samatya/iletisim.asp. Map p. 346, B3.*
Hamdi. Famous *lokanta* near Yeni Cami. The top floor has views of the Golden Horn. Specialises in kebabs and baklava. No vegetarian. *Tahmis Cd., Kalçın Sk. 17; T: 0212 528 0390, www.hamdi.com.tr. Map p. 349, D1.*
Konyalı. Historic restaurant in the Fourth Courtyard of Topkapı, founded 'to promote Turkish Cuisine to foreigners'. Don't expect an 'authentic' Istanbul experience, but the views are superb. Lunch only. Closed Tues. *Topkapı Sarayı, Sultanahmet; T: 0212 513 9696, www. konyalilokantasi.com. Map p. 349, F2.*
Pandeli. Old Greek restaurant above the entrance to the Spice Bazaar; Turkish cuisine as well as international dishes; beautifully tiled interior. *Mısır Çarşısı,*

Eminönü; T: 0212 527 3909, www.pandeli. com.tr. Map p. 349, D2.
Sarnıç. In a cavernous, brick-built ancient cistern, with tables placed among the pillars. Very atmospheric in the candlelight. Good food and service. Memorable atmosphere. Evenings only. *Soğukçeşme Sk; T: 0212 512 4291, www. sarnicrestaurant.com. Map p. 349, E3.*

$$
Karışma Sen. Traditional place near the Marmara shore; its name means 'Mind Your Own Business'. *Kennedy Cd. at Ahır Kapı; T: 0212 458 0081, www.karismasen. com. Map p. 349, E4.*
Safa. Wonderful old-fashioned restaurant in Samatya. *İmrahor İlyasbey Cd. 169, Samatya; T: 0212 585 5595. Map p. 346, B3.*

$
Havuzlu. An old restaurant by the fountain in the Grand Bazaar, a favourite place to eat before or after shopping. *Gani Çelebi Sk. 3, Kapalıçarşı; T: 0212 527 3346. Map p. 348, C3.*
Caferağa Medrese. Simple but excellent eating-place in the picturesque court-yard of a 16th-century medrese opposite Haghia Sophia. Lunchtime only. *Caferiye Sk; T: 0212 513 3601. Map p. 349, E3.*
Subaşı. Located just opposite the entrance to the Grand Bazaar from the Nuruosmaniye Mosque. *Nuruosmaniye Cd. 8, Çarşıkapı; T: 0212 522 4762. Map p. 348, C3–D3.*
Tarihi Sultanahmet Köftecisi. Famous *köfte* restaurant, said to serve more customers a day than anywhere else in Turkey. There are many imitations; the Tarihi is the original. *Divanyolu Cd. 12A; T: 0212 520 0566, www.sultanhametkoftesi.com. Map p. 349, E3.*

Beyoğlu

$$$

Hacı Baba. Touristy but time-honoured restaurant, just off Taksim Square; terrace overlooking courtyard of the church of Haghia Triada. *İstiklal Cd. 49; T: 0212 244 1886, web www.hacibabarest.com. Map p. 345, D2.*

Meze by Lemon Tree. ■ Excellent small restaurant opposite the Pera Palace hotel serving beautifully prepared mezes in well-decorated surroundings. Here tradition takes on a new lease of life. Turkish favourites are prepared with real flair; clever taste combinations and well chosen ingredients make this place stand out. *Meşrutiyet Cd. 83B; T: 0212 252 8302, www.meze.com.tr. Map p. 344, C3.*

Sensus. Wine bar and café near the Galata Tower stocking good Turkish wines. *Büyük Hendek Cd. 5; T: 0212 245 5657. Map p. 344, C4*

Asmalı Cavit. Excellent old meyhane with good mezes and a wonderful atmosphere, in a cosy, wood-panelled setting. *Asmalı Mescit Cd. T: 0212 292 4950. Map p. 344, C3.*

$$

Café Ara. Wonderful café-restaurant off Galatasaray Square, owned by the photographer Ara Güler, whose images of Istanbul adorn the walls. *Tosbağa Sk. 8A, Galatasaray, T: (0212) 245 4105. Map p. 344, C3.*

Gurme Boncuk. Friendly, reliable

meyhane catering to a mix of locals and visitors. Simple, short lunch menu. Good fish dishes. Cheerful atmosphere. *Asmalı Mescit Cd. 29, T: 0212 245 3169. Map p. 344, C3.*

Hacı Abdullah. Old-established place serving traditional Turkish food since 1888. No alcohol. *Sakız Ağaçı Cd. 17; T: 0212 293 8561, www.haciabdullah.com.tr. Map p. 344, C2.*

Hacı Salih. One of the oldest restaurants in Beyoğlu; simple but excellent food. *İstiklal Cd. 201; T: 0212 243 4528 (closed Sun). Map p. 344, C3.*

Imroz. Owned by a Greek from the island of Imroz (Gökçeada); specialises in Greek and Turkish meze. *Nevizade Sk.; T: 0212 249 9073, www.krependekiimroz.com. Map p. 344, C2.*

Kahvedan. Relaxed café-restaurant in Cihangir, for coffee and a snack or full dinner with wine and rakı. *Akarsu Yks. 1; T: 0212 292 4030, www.kahvedancafe.com. Map p. 345, D3.*

Refik. Old meyhane under the same management for 40 years; good food and old Beyoğlu atmosphere. *Sofyalı Sk. 10–12; T: 0212 243 2834, www.refikrestaurant.com. Map p. 344, C3.*

$

Karaköy Lokantası. Good neighbourhood restaurant near the seafront in Galata. *Kemankeş Cd. 37A; T: 0212 292 4455. Map p. 344, C4.*

The Bosphorus

$$$$

Körfez. A de luxe fish restaurant in a cove on the Asian shore of the middle

Bosphorus; customers are ferried across by a boat from Rumeli Hisarı. *Körfez Cd. 78, Kanlıca; T: 0216 413 4314, www.*

korfez.com.

Rumeli İskele. Outstanding fish-restaurant housed in the old Rumeli Hisarı ferry landing just below the upper Bosphorus bridge; superb view of the most beautiful stretch of the Bosphorus. *Yahya Kemal Cd. 1, Rumeli Hisarı; T: 0212 263 2997, www.rumelihisariiskele.com.*

Façyo. The oldest fish restaurant in Tarabya, the beautiful cove on the European shore of the Bosphorus. *Kireçburnu Cd. 13, Tarabya; T: 0212 262 0898.*

$$$

Ali Baba. Historic fish restaurant founded in 1923 by Ali Baba, who originally operated a barber shop here; traditional Turkish sea-food, with view of the middle to upper Bosphorus. *Kireçburnu Cd. 20–22, Kireçburnu; T: 0212 262 0889, www.tarihialibaba.com.*

Boğaziçi. The oldest fish-restaurant in Beykoz on the Asian shore of the upper Bosphorus; excellent food and service. *Fevzipaşa Cd. 3/1, Beykoz; T: 0216 323 9768, www.bogazicibalik.com.*

Borsa. Chain of restaurants that are excellent for getting acquainted with Turkish cooking. Excellent food in a slightly formal three-course setting which means you can go there for a leisurely dinner. There are two main ones: the Adile Sultan Borsa in an old imperial villa at Kandilli on the Asian shore of the Bosphorus (*T: 0216 460 0304*) and the Boğaziçi Borsa in the Lütfi Kırdar Convention Centre (*Gümüş Cd,; T: 0212 232 4201; map p. 345, D1*).

Ciya Sofrası. A sort of gastronomic museum from around Turkey, in Kadıköy. *Güneşlibahçe Sk. 43, Kadıköy, T: 0216 330 3190, www.ciya.com.tr.*

Deniz Park (Aleko'nun Yeri). The only Greek fish restaurants remaining on the Bosphorus; superb view of the strait, particularly under a full moon. *Daire Sk. 9, Yeniköy; T: 0212 262 0415.*

House Café. ■ Beautifully renovated old house close to the waterfront at Ortaköy. International cuisine with Turkish undertones, in a cheerful, fashionable atmosphere. Outdoor eating in fine weather. Delicious fresh fruit juices and imaginative salads. Doubles as a hotel, part of the House Hotel group (*see p. 290*). *Salhane Sk. 1, Ortaköy; T: 0212 227 2699, www.thehousecafe.com.*

İsmet Baba. Long-standing restaurant on the waterfront at Kuzguncuk. Good for dinner or for a long, leisurely lunch. Fine mezes and fish. *Çarşı Cd. 96, Kuzguncuk; T: 0216 553 1232, www.ismetbaba.com.tr.*

Kanaat. Venerable institution in Üsküdar serving Turkish home cooking. Best to choose yourself from the large array of simmering dishes. *Selman-i Pak Cd. 9, Üsküdar; T: 0216 341 5444. Map p. 339, B1.*

Kordon. Elegant fish restaurant in the Sumahan on the Water hotel (though the restaurant was here first), just north of Çengelköy. Expansive waterfront terrace. Seasonal fish from the Bosphorus, Black Sea, Marmara and the Aegean. *Kuleli Cd. 51, Çengelköy; T: 0216 321 0473, www.kordonbalik.com.*

Marina. Excellent fish restaurant housed in the old Kuruçeşme ferry-station; panoramic view of the middle Bosphorus. *Vapur İskelesi, Kuruçeşme; T: 0212 287 2653.*

ADDITIONAL INFORMATION

Money and banks

The currency is the Turkish lira, whose unit of small change is the kuruş. There are plenty of ATM machines which work with most international debit cards. Any bank with a 'Kambiyo' sign will change money, though private exchange bureaux (*Döviz Bürosu*) usually offer better rates. Banks are open 9–1 & 2–5 (9–2 in summer); Sat 9–12. For information on exchange rates, check online before you travel. Travellers' cheques can be quite difficult to cash, and a substantial fee is usually charged.

Museums and monuments

Hours of admission to the various museums and monuments in Istanbul are given in the text of this guide. The opening hours quoted may vary by half an hour or an hour depending on the season. Ticket prices can be surprisingly high. There is often a different, cheaper price for Turkish nationals.

Mosques are open during the five occasions of daily prayer, and often at other times as well. Do not to disturb the faithful at their prayers. The larger mosques are open throughout the day. Smaller ones may be closed between the hours of prayer, but if you stand patiently by the front door someone will usually fetch the caretaker, who will open up the mosque for you (tips are expected). Shoes must be taken off at the door and either left outside or placed on a shelf inside. Shorts should not be worn when visiting mosques, and women should wear a headscarf and cover their arms.

National holidays

The Turkish National Holidays, when all offices, shops, schools, banks, museums and monuments are closed, are as follows:

23rd April (National Sovereignty Day and Children's Day)
1st May (Spring Day)
19th May (Sport Day)
27th May (Constitution Day)
30th August (Victory Day)
29th October (Republic Day).

There are also two religious holidays when all of the above places are closed; these are Şeker Bayram (3 days) and Kurban Bayram (4 days). The dates of these holidays are regulated according to the Muslim lunar calendar and thus occur 11 days earlier each year.

Newspapers, books and local information

Most British newspapers and the *International Herald Tribune* are on sale in the highest-class hotels, in foreign-language bookshops, and at a few centrally-located kiosks. There is a good English-language newspaper, the *Daily News*. The best shops for English-language books are Homer (Yeni Çarşı Cd. 12; *map p. 344, C3*); Robinson Crusoe (İstiklal Cd. 389; *map p. 344, C3*) and Galeri Kayseri English Bookshop (Dıvanyolu Cd.

58; *map p. 349, D3*). Other good sources of English-language books are the museum shops, for example in Topkapı Palace and the Museum of Turkish and Islamic Arts.

Time Out Istanbul, published in magazine form and online (*www.timeout.com/istanbul*), has restaurant, entertainment and events listings. The magazine on Turkish culture par excellence is *Cornucopia*, published three times a year (*www.cornucopia.net*).

Opening hours

Banks 9–1 & 2–5 (9–2 in summer); Sat 9–12.
Grand Bazaar 8–8 every day except Sun and major holidays (8.30–7 in winter).
Offices: weekdays 9–12 & 1.30–5; Sat 9–1; closed Sun and holidays.
Shops (varies): weekdays 9–1 & 2–7; Sat 9–12 & 1–7; closed Sun, holidays.

Personal security and behaviour

Crime in Istanbul is low by US or European standards, and most areas of the city are perfectly safe at night. Having said this, women are advised not to walk unaccompanied at night. You should be alert for bag-snatchers and pickpockets, even in the daytime. Codes of dress are in theory much the same as in cities in Europe or the US, although again, women would be advised to dress demurely, particularly in some of the more conservative parts of the old town. When visiting mosques and other holy places (for example türbes) women must wear a scarf and long sleeves. Everyone is required to remove their footwear before entering mosques and türbes.

Post offices

Post offices (PTT). Central Post Office, Büyük Postane Cd., near Sirkeci Station (*open 8am–9pm daily, including Sun; map p. 349, D2*); branch post offices on İstiklal Cd. just off Galatasaray Square (*open 9–5 Mon–Fri, 9–1 Sat; map p. 344, C3*), and just off Taksim Square (*open 9–7 Mon–Fri, 9–1 Sat; map p. 345, D2*).

Stamps (*Posta pulu*) are sold only at post offices (*for locations, see above*). Special delivery is called *expres* (*patınıtuker*) and registered mail is *taahhütlü*.

Religious services (non-Islamic)

Protestant: Christ Church (Anglican), Serdarı Ekrem Sk. 82, Tünel; T: (0212) 251 5616.
Union Church: (non-denominational), Postacılar Sk. 4, Beyoğlu; T: (0212) 244 5212.
Roman Catholic: St Espirit, Cumhuriyet Cd. 250B (across from the Hilton), T: (0212) 248 0910; St Anthony of Padua, İstiklal Cd. 325, Beyoğlu, T: (0212) 244 0935; St-Louis des Français, Postacılar Sk. 11, T: (0212) 244 1075.
Jewish: Neve Shalom Synagogue, Büyük Hendek Sk. 67, Galata; T: (0212) 244 7566.
Greek Orthodox: Haghia Triada, Meselik Sk. 11/1, Taksim; T: (0212) 244 1358.

Telephones

The country code for Turkey is 90. The prefix for the European side of the city is 212 and for the Asian side and the Princes' Islands 216. Add a zero at the beginning if calling from within Turkey (0212 and 0216).

Your mobile phone will work for a time on Turkcell but not indefinitely. Mobile handsets brought into the country for longer than a month or so have to be registered and you will need to buy a Turkish SIM card.

Toilets

Signs read WC or Tuvalet. Men is *Bay*; Women is *Bayan*. There are public toilets in most mosque courtyards.

Tourist police

Headquarters in Bahçekapı (near Sirkeci Station), T: (0212) 527 4503; also offices at Alemdar Karakol, near the Blue Mosque; the Maritime Passenger Terminal in Karaköy (Galata); Sirkeci Station; and at Atatürk International Airport.

Turkish pronunciation

All letters in the Turkish alphabet have one and only one sound; no letters are silent, although the ğ is almost silent. Vowels have their short continental value; i.e. a as in 'father', e as in 'get', i as in 'sit', o as in 'doll', u as in 'bull'; ı (undotted) is between i and u, somewhat as the final 'a' in 'Anna', ö is as in German or the 'u' in 'further'; ü is as in German or the French 'u' in 'tu'. Consonants are sounded as in English except for the following:

c as j in 'jam'
ç as ch in 'church'
g always hard as in 'give', never soft as in 'gem'
ğ is almost silent, tending to lengthen the preceding vowel
s is always unvoiced as in 'sit', never like z
ş is as s in 'sugar'.

'Th' as in 'thin', 'sh' as in 'ship' and 'ph' as in 'philosophy' do not exist in Turkish. The consonants must be pronounced separately, so 'ders-hane', 'kütüp-hane' etc.

Turkish is very lightly accented, most often on the last syllable, but all syllables should be clearly and almost evenly articulated.

GLOSSARY

NB: Turkish words appearing in brackets are the form that they take when modified by a preceding word or when rendered in the genitive: e.g. Sultanahmet Camii (the 'Mosque of Sultan Ahmet'), whereas Yeni Cami ('New Mosque').

Ağa, within the Ottoman administration, the head of an organisation or corps, appointed to enforce discipline; a civil or military leader, e.g. *Kızlar ağası*, 'Ağa of the Girls', the eunuch in charge of the imperial harem

Abacus, flat-topped slab at the top of a column capital on which the architrave (*qv*) rests

Aghiasma, a holy well (in Turkish, *ayazma*)

Ambo (pl. *ambones*), pulpit in a Christian basilica; one of two pulpits on opposite sides of a church nave from which the Gospel and Epistle were read

Ambulatory, a passageway around and behind the high altar of a church, between the back of the altar and the apse

Annunciation, the appearance of the Angel Gabriel to Mary to tell her that she will bear the Son of God

Antae, projecting pilasters ending the lateral walls of a Greek temple; columns between the *antae* are said to be *in antis*

Apostles, those who spread the Christian word, traditionally twelve in number, being the eleven disciples (without Judas) plus St Paul

Apse, the circular or polygonal termination of a church sanctuary, at the liturgical east end

Arabesque, type of decoration involving interweaving tendrils, foliage and scroll motifs

Arasta, a series of shops built beneath or near a mosque. Rent from the shops provided money for the maintenance and repair of the mosque and its dependent institutions

Arcade, a series of piers or columns linked by arches (*cf colonnade*)

Archaic, period in Greek civilisation preceding the Classical era: from about 750 BC–480 BC

Architrave, the horizontal beam or lintel stone running above the columns in ancient architecture; the lowest part of the entablature (*qv*)

Arcosolium (pl. *arcosolia*), a tomb where the sarcophagus or funerary bed is in a recessed niche surmounted by an arch

Atrium, a forecourt, either of an ancient Roman house or of a Byzantine church

Avlu, the forecourt of a mosque

Ayazma, *see aghiasma*

Barbican, an outwork of a fortress, designed to protect a gateway

Barrel vault, a vault of semicircular cross-section, like a prolonged archway (*see illustration opposite*)

Basilica, originally a Roman hall used for public administration; in Christian architecture, an aisled church with a clerestory and apse and no transepts

Bema, in a Byzantine church, the chancel or sanctuary

Bedesten, a multi-domed hall, usually in the centre of a Turkish market, where valuable goods are stored and sold

Black Eunuch, a castrated African slave who served in the imperial harem

Buttress, a mass of masonry built up against a wall to resist the outward pressure of an arch or vault

Cadde (*caddesi*), avenue

Caliph, the head of the Muslim 'nation', the earthly vicar or viceroy of Allah

Camekan, the reception room or entrance foyer of a Turkish bath, sometimes also doubling as the changing room

Cami (*camii*), mosque

Capital, the crowning feature of a column or pilaster

Caravansaray (also *caravanserai*, in Turkish *kervansaray*), a *han* (*qv*), an inn arranged around a spacious courtyard with accommodation for travellers and their animals

Çarşı (*carşısı*), market

Catechumen, in the early Christian Church, a novice preparing for baptism

Cenotaph, literally, 'empty tomb', a funerary monument either placed above an actual grave or serving as commemoration in cases where there is no body

Çeşme (*çeşmesi*), fountain

Chi-Rho, Christian symbol formed by the superimposition of the first two letters of Christ's name in Greek, X and P

Ciborium, in a church, a receptacle or small structure for storing the Communion bread

Çintamani (also *çintemani*), popular motif used in Turkish ceramics and textiles in the 16th century consisting of double wavy lines and often also three circles with smaller circles within (*see illustration on pp. 34 and 250*)

Classical, in ancient Greece, the period from 480–323 BC; in Ottoman terms, the period c. 1500–1650, when some of the greatest mosques were built, in a style that blended Islamic traditions and liturgical needs with the great design of Haghia Sophia

Colonnade, a series of columns linked by a horizontal architrave (*qv*), not by arches as in an arcade

Colonnette, small column, with a decorative, not a load-bearing, function

Corbel, a block of stone or wood, often carved or moulded, projecting from a wall, and supporting the beams of a

1: Barrel vault; 2: Cross or Groin vault; 3: Dome on pendentives.

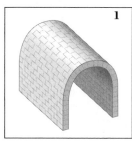
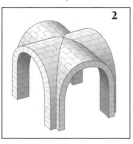
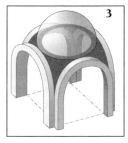

Corinthian capital.

roof, floor, vault or other architectural member **Corinthian**, order of Classical architecture easily identified by its column capitals decorated with curling acanthus leaves

Cornice, topmost part of a temple entablature (*qv*); any projecting ornamental moulding at the top of a building beneath the roof (outside) or ceiling (inside)

Crenellations, the indentations in the parapet of a fortress wall

Cross vault, also known as a groin vault; vaulting characterised by arched diagonal groins, formed by the intersection of two barrel vaults (*see illustration on previous page*)

Cruciform, cross-shaped

Cuerda seca, ceramic technique that developed c. 1500. Pattern outlines were traced in an oily manganese compound (potassium permanganate) that prevented different colours from running into each other

Curtain wall, a wall with no load bearing function, built to close the space between two vertical members, e.g. defence towers in a castle

Dar-ül Hadis, 'School of Tradition', where the deeds and sayings (*hadis*) of the Prophet are taught

Dar-ül Kuran, a school for learning the Koran

Darüşşifa, an Ottoman hospital

Deësis, a scene of intercession for the sins of mankind, with Christ shown flanked (usually) by the Virgin and St John the Baptist

Dershane, the lecture hall of a medrese (*qv*)

Dervish, a Sufi Muslim, a member of one of the ascetic, mendicant and often mystical orders, founded by saints

Devşirme, periodic levy of Christian youths inducted into the Ottoman army

Diaconicon, in Byzantine churches, the sacristy, an auxiliary chamber usually next to the apse, where the sacred vessels were stored

Doctors of the Church, see *Hierarchs*

Dormition, the 'falling asleep', in other words death, of the Virgin Mary, in Greek the *Koimisis tis Theotokou*

Domical vault, a dome rising directly from a square or polygonal base, without the intermediary of a drum, pendentives (*qv*) or squinches (*qv*)

Dragoman, an interpreter between the Sublime Porte (*qv*) and the courts of Europe

Efendi, a term of respect or courtesy, broadly the equivalent of 'Sir'. *Hanımefendi* is used for women

Engaged column, a column partly embedded in the wall

Entablature, the upper part of an Order of architecture (*qv*), comprising architrave, frieze and cornice, supported by a colonnade

Eunuch, see *Black Eunuch, White Eunuch*

Epistyle, the Greek word for the architrave

Evangelists, the authors of the four Gospels, Matthew, Mark, Luke and John, often depicted in art through their symbols, respectively the man/angel, lion, bull and eagle

Exedra (also, properly, exhedra), recessed area projecting from a room or other space, originally with benches

Exonarthex, the outer vestibule of a church

Eyvan, a vaulted or domed recess or side chamber, open on one side

Faience, glazed earthenware, often ornamented, used for pottery or as revetment on the walls of a building

Fatih, 'Conqueror', the name given to Sultan Mehmet II who took Constantinople from the Byzantines in 1453

Firman, a decree from the Sultan; in Turkish, *ferman*

Forum (pl. *fora*), open space in an ancient Roman town serving as a market or meeting-place

Four-column church, a design where the dome over the nave is supported on columns (*see p. 27*)

Fresco, a painting executed on wet plaster

Frieze, strip of decoration usually along the upper part of a wall; in a temple this refers to the horizontal feature above the columns between the architrave and the cornice

Gigantomachia, in ancient Greek sculpture, a representation of the battle between the Olympian gods and the giants

Göbektaşı, the 'belly-stone', the heated stone platform in the hot room of a Turkish bath

Grand Vizier, the Sultan's chief minister

Groin, the curved edge formed by the intersection of two vaulted surfaces, as in groin vault

H., abbreviation for *hijra*, the year (corresponding to AD 622) when Mohammed and his followers migrated from Mecca to Medina. Dates in the Islamic calendar are calculated from this time. Thus H. 1200 is AD 1787 (the Islamic year is a lunar year, thus making the calculation is not simply a matter of subtracting 622 from the Gregorian year). Also written 'AH' (*anno hijri*)

Hacı, 'pilgrim', a popular given name; also a title applied to persons who have made the *hajj*, the pilgrimage to Mecca

Hadis (also *hadith*) the deeds and sayings of the Prophet Mohammed, forming a separate tradition not contained in the Koran and studied as precepts for Islamic living

Haghia, Haghios, holy, saint (Greek)

Halvet, in a hamam, a very hot chamber opening off the main steam room

Hamam (*hamamı*), a Turkish bath

Han (*hanı*), an Ottoman inn

Hararet, the steam room of a Turkish bath

Harem, the family quarter of an Islamic home, where the women and children live secluded from men who are not members of their immediate family

Hazrat, literally 'prophet', used in Turkish as an honorific title, particularly for saints and martyrs

Haseki, a favourite woman who had borne a child or children to a sultan; a *kadın* (*qv*)

Hellenistic, Greek culture of the period from the death of Alexander the Great to the victory of Rome over Antony and Cleopatra (323–30 BC). Art from this period often displays more sentiment than Classical works

Hereke, town on the bay of İzmit east of Istanbul, known for its carpets, produced using a distinctive technique, often in silk, and with double knots

Hierarchs, the three pre-eminent

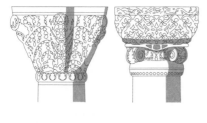

Three types of Byzantine Capital: melon (top left) and two variants of pseudo-Ionic, each preserving the scrolls or volutes.

Doctors of the Eastern Christian Church: St Basil the Great, St Gregory of Nazianzus and St John Chrysostom. Their relics are preserved in the church of the Ecumenical Patriarchate

Hisar (*hisarı*), an Ottoman fortress

Hodegetria, icon type representing the Virgin with the Child seated on her lap. It functions as a 'guide', presenting the infant Christ as 'the Way'. Traditionally based on the prototype said to have been painted by St Luke

Hünkar kasrı, royal pavilion attached to an imperial mosque

Hünkar mahfili, the sultan's loggia in an imperial Ottoman mosque

Hücre, a student's cell in a medrese

Hypocaust, a series of small chambers and under-floor flues through which the heated air was distributed to the rooms of a bath

Hypogeum, an underground chamber, often, but not necessarily, a tomb

Iconoclastic, in the Byzantine world, the period in the 8th and early 9th centuries when representations of the

human form (icons, graven images) were banned from sacred art

Iconodule, a worshipper or adorer of icons; the opposite of an iconoclast

Iconostasis, screen inset with icons, placed between the nave and chancel of an Orthodox church to separate the sanctuary from the laity

İkbal, a harem favourite, a woman with whom the sultan had sexual relations

İmam, the cleric who presides over public prayers in a mosque

İmaret, the public kitchen in an Ottoman pious foundation.

Impost, block or projecting corbel above a capital or pier on which the spring of an arch rests

Ionic, order of architecture developed in coastal Asia Minor in the late 6th century BC, and identified primarily by its style of capital, which has paired volutes (*see illustration left*)

İskele (*iskelesi*), quay, landing stage

Janissaries, properly *Yeni Ceri*, 'New Troops', the élite corps of the Ottoman army, traditionally formed of recruits taken from the non-Muslim population

Jinn (also *djinn*), a spirit, able to assume human or animal shape, and intervening in men's lives, either for good or evil

Kadın, literally 'woman'; the 'wife' of a Sultan. Though not legally wed, the *kadın* enjoyed the legal status of a wife. By Islamic law, the sultan was permitted four *kadıns*.

Kafes, the 'cage', an apartment in the harem at Topkapı Sarayı where the brothers of a reigning sultan were kept under house arrest, to prevent them from staging coups, interfering in state affairs or challenging their brother's authority. The system was introduced by Ahmet I in 1603. Prior to that all brothers of new sultans had been strangled

Kaptan Paşa, naval commander, Admiral of the Fleet

Kasr (*kasrı*), a small palace, a pavilion

Kayık, a barge or caique

Kible, the direction of Mecca; in Arabic *qibla*

Kilise (*kilisesi*), church

Kızlar ağası, literally 'Master of the Maidens', the Chief Black Eunuch (*qv*)

Koimisis tis Theotokou (pron: ***kee**-mis-is*), Dormition (*qv*) of the Virgin

Konak, an Ottoman mansion

Koran (in Turkish, *Kuran*), the Holy Book of Islam, containing God's law as revealed to his prophet Mohammed in the early 7th century. Devout Muslims look upon it not only as a spiritual guide but also as a manual for daily living, political, social and domestic

Köşk (*köşkü*), a Turkish kiosk or pavilion

Kouros (pl. *kouroi*), free-standing statue of the Archaic period, an idealised representation of a young man, placed as dedicatory offerings in temples of Apollo.

Kore (pl. *korai*), Archaic Greek sculpture of a young woman, dedicated to Artemis

Külliye (*külliyesi*), an Ottoman mosque complex or pious foundation, with attendant buildings such as baths, schools and public kitchens

Kuran kursu, the chair on which the imam, or preacher, sits when he is reading the Koran to the congregation

Kütüphane, Turkish library

Lancet, tall narrow window ending in a pointed arch

Latin, in the Byzantine world, pertaining to Western Christians, those adhering to the Church of Rome

Levha, a plaque

Lintel, the horizontal member, of wood or stone, that spans a door or window aperture

Loggia, covered gallery or balcony

Lozenge capital, Islamic style of capital decorated with carved diamond shapes, or lozenges (*see illustration below*)

Lunette, semicircular space in a vault or above a door or window, often decorated with a painting or relief

Medrese (*medresesi*), Islamic school of higher studies

Mektep, an Ottoman primary school, also called a *sibyan mektebi*

Melon capital, Byzantine style of capital carved as if in undulating segments, resembling a large melon or pumpkin (*see illustration opposite*)

Meryem, Mary; *Meryem Ana Kilisesi* is 'the church of the Mother Mary'

Mescit (*mescidi*), a small mosque

Meta-Byzantine, type of building constructed after the Ottoman conquest, but in the earlier Byzantine style

Mevlevi, the dervish (*qv*) order known

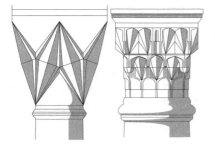

Two types of Ottoman capital: lozenge (left) and stalactite (right).

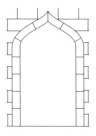

Ogive or ogival arch.

for its whirling dance

Mihrab, the niche in the wall of a mosque that indicates the *kible*, the direction of Mecca

Mimber, the pulpit in a mosque (also written *mimbar*, *minbar*)

Minaret, the spire, beside a mosque, from which the *müezzin* (*qv*) gives the call to prayer. In function, a minaret is to a mosque what a bell-tower is to a church

Monolithic, made from a single piece of stone

Mosaic, decorative surfaces formed by small cubes (*tesserae*) of stone, glass, or marble

Müezzin, cleric who chants the responses to the prayers of the imam (*qv*) in a mosque and gives the call to prayer from the minaret

Müezzin mahfili, the raised platform where the *müezzins* chant their responses to the prayers of the imam

Müneccim, in the Ottoman world, a time-keeper, astronomer and caster of horoscopes

Muvakkithane, the house of the *müneccim*, or mosque astronomer

Namazgah, an outdoor place of prayer

Nargile, a water-pipe, hubble bubble, or hookah

Narthex, the entrance vestibule of a Byzantine church, stretching across the façade before the west entrance to the nave

Nike, in Classical art, the personification of Victory, depicted as a winged woman

Ocak, a Turkish fireplace

Oculus (pl. *oculi*) a round opening, a circular window

Oda (*odası*), in Turkish, room, hall or chamber

Ogive arch, a rounded arch where the curved sides meet in a peak (*see illustration left*)

Opus alexandrinum, Byzantine style of revetment for floors and other surfaces in which small pieces of stone or glass paste are arranged in expansive geometric patterns interspersed with larger discs of marble and other coloured stone

Opus sectile, ornamental paving or wall covering made from thin pieces of marble or glass (larger than mosaic tesserae; *qv*) arranged in geometric or figurative designs

Order, an Order in ancient Greek architecture comprised a column, with base (unless Doric), shaft and capital, the whole supporting an entablature (*qv*)

Osmanlı, 1. the House of Osman, the dynasty of the Ottomans; 2. Perso-Arabic script in which Ottoman Turkish was written

Panaghia, the 'All Holy' Virgin (Greek)

Pantocrator, literally 'He who Controls All', a representation of Christ in Majesty traditionally featured in the central dome of Orthodox churches and in the apse of an Early Christian basilica

Parecclesion, subsidiary chapel in an Orthodox church, often with a funerary function

Paşa (pasha), honorific title borne by certain Ottoman dignitaries

Pendentive, one of four concave spandrels (triangular spaces) descending from the 'corners' of a dome, and converting the square lower space into the circular upper space (*see illustration on p. 303*)

Penetralia, in architecture, the innermost parts of a building, especially of a temple or palace

Pent roof (also pentise roof), a lean-to roof, such as the sloping roof of a verandah or porch

Peristyle, a colonnade (*qv*) surrounding a courtyard or garden

Pier, a mass of masonry with a load-bearing, supportive function

Pilaster, a shallow pier or rectangular column projecting only slightly from the wall

Pitched roof, roof made of two sloping sides, meeting in a ridge at the top

Platytera, representation of the Virgin and Child as a symbol of the Incarnation. The Christ Child is placed in the centre of the Virgin's lap or abdomen. She holds her hands out in prayer. The full name of the icon type is *Platytera ton Ouranon*, 'Wider than the Heavens'. It illustrates the paradox that a human womb yielded space to the godhead, Creator of the universe

Polychrome, many-coloured

Porphyry, dark blue, purple or red-coloured igneous rock, much prized in the ancient world and used almost exclusively for imperial commissions

Portico, a covered space or porch, with the roof supported on at least one side by columns

Proconnesian, fine white marble from an island in the Sea of Marmara (the etymology of the word marble), known as Marmara in Greek and Proconnesus in Latin. It is used primarily in architecture and for sarcophagi

Prothesis, the part of a Byzantine church dedicated to the preparation of the Communion bread and wine

Pseudo-Ionic, type of column capital having scrolled volutes like an Ionic column, though these are smaller and more peripheral to the overall structure (*see illustrations on p. 306*)

Qur'an (*see Koran*)

Ramadan (in Turkish, *Ramazan*), Islamic period of fasting, beginning with the first sighting of the moon of the ninth month, the time when Mohammed received God's Word as recorded in the Koran

Refectory, the dining-hall in a monastery, convent, hostel or imaret (*qv*)

Revak, in Turkish, a domed or vaulted colonnade enclosing a porch

Revetment, cladding; a facing of stone, ceramic tile or other material, for decorative or protective purposes

Rum, literally 'Rome', used in an Ottoman context to describe Europeans or, ecclesiastically, Catholics or Orthodox Christians

Şadırvan, an ablution fountain in the courtyard of a mosque

Sanctuary, the part of a church at the far east end; the chancel, the holy of holies

Saray (*sarayı*), an Ottoman palace

Sebil (*sebili*), an Ottoman fountain-house from which water was distributed free to passers-by

Şehit, martyr

Şehzade, the son of a sultan; a prince

Selamlık, the male quarters of an Ottoman home or palace; also the sultan's ceremony of Friday prayers

Selsebil, decorative cascade fountain, where the water falls successively into basins of gradated size

Semahane, the room in a Mevlevi (*qv*) dervish lodge where the *sema*, or dancing ritual, takes place

Şerefe, the balcony of a minaret, where the *müezzin* gives the call to prayer

Şeriat, the sacred law in Islam

Şeyülislam, head of the Islamic religious hierarchy; the chief cleric

Sibyan mektebi, see *mektep*

Sipahi, a cavalry knight

Soğukluk, the chamber of intermediate temperature in a Turkish bath

Sofa (*sofası*) a raised, carpeted seating area

Soffit, the underside of an arch

Sokak (*sokağı*), street

Son cemaat yeri, the raised, carpeted front porch of a mosque where latecomers pray

Spolia, elements of masonry from an older building reused or 'recycled' in a newer one

Squinch, a small arch, bracket, or similar device built across each angle of a square or polygonal structure to form an octagon or any appropriate base for a dome

Stalactite, distinctive style of carving or moulding seen in much Islamic architecture, over doorways, in squinches (*qv*) and on column capitals (*see illustration on p. 307*). Stalactites are also known as *muqarna*

Sublime Porte, originally the gate leading to the offices of the Grand Vizier, close to Topkapı Palace; by extension the whole apparatus of the Ottoman Empire

Su terazi, a Turkish water-control tower

Syenitic, of granite, an igneous rock composed largely of feldspar and/or hornblende, coarse-grained, ranging in colour from pinkish tan to grey

Synnada marble, white to brownish puce marble from Synnada, modern Şuhut, in central west Turkey

Synthronon, semicircular bench or tiered seats for the clergy in the apse of a basilica

Tabhane, a hospice for travelling dervishes

Taksim, a Turkish water-distribution system

Tekke, a dervish lodge

Tessera (pl. *tesserae*), a small cube of marble, glass etc., used in mosaic work

Theotokos, in the Greek Orthodox Church, the Mother of God

Tip medrese, an Ottoman medical school

Torah, the Books of Moses, the Pentateuch (Genesis, Exodus, Leviticus, Numbers, Deuteronomy), revealed to Moses on Mt Sinai

Trabeated, construction where the apertures (doors, windows) have vertical supports and horizontal lintels as opposed to arches

Trompe l'oeil, literally a deception of the eye. Used to describe illusionist decoration, painted architectural perspectives, etc

Tuğra, the elaborate calligraphic signature of an Ottoman sultan, appearing on all official documents (*see illustration on p. 74*). The tuğra has four main constituent parts: at the bottom is the *sere*, where the sultan's name and attributes are written; to the left is the *beyze*, two billowing egg-shaped strokes, curving back to the right to end in trailing ribbons; extending from the *sere* into the *beyze* is the *kol*, a horizontal stroke; rising above the whole is the *tuğ*, three tall vertical strokes resembling flagstaffs

Türbe (*türbesi*), an Ottoman mausoleum, a one-roomed structure, typically octagonal, often lavishly decorated with tiles. The interior contains the cenotaphs of the deceased, often in the shape of coffins (men's cenotaphs have a turban at the head) and covered with a pall, often of green baize. The actual body or bodies are in the ground beneath

Tympanum (pl. *tympana*), the semicircular space enclosed by an arch. In Haghia Sophia and the imperial mosques based on its design, the four vast tympana below the central dome are a memorable feature. Also the space enclosed by a pediment above a door or window. In Classical architecture the tympanum is the triangular space enclosed by the pediment on a temple façade

Vakıf, the deed of a pious foundation

Valide Sultan, the mother of a reigning sultan

Vault, an arched roof or covering in stone, brick or concrete

Verd antique, green marble from Thessaly, Greece; Thessalian green

Vizier, a minister in the Ottoman civil service

Volute, scroll-like decoration at the corners of an Ionic or pseudo-Ionic capital (*see illustration on p. 306*)

Voussoirs, wedge shaped blocks forming the curved part of an arch, fanning upwards from the side piers; the central voussoir is the keystone

White Eunuch, a castrated European, who served the Palace School or imperial civil service

Yalı (*yalısı*), an Ottoman waterside mansion, traditionally of wood

Zaviye, religious establishment to accommodate pilgrims or travelling dervishes

BYZANTINE EMPERORS

Constantine the Great	324–37	Constantine VII Porphyrogenitus	913–59
Constantius	337–61	Romanus I Lecapenus	919–44
Julian the Apostate	361–63	Romanus II	959–63
Jovian	363–64	Nicephorus II Phocas	963–69
Valens	364–78	John I Tzimiskes	969–76
Theodosius I	379–95	Basil II	976–1025
Arcadius	395–408	Contantine VIII	1025–28
Theodosius II	408–50	Romanus III Argyrus	1028–34
Marcian	450–57	Michael IV	1034–41
Leo I	457–74	Michael V	1041–42
Leo II	474	Theodora and Zoë	1042
Zeno	474–91	Constantine IX	1042–55
Anastasius I	491–518	Theodora (second reign)	1055–56
Justin I	518–27	Michael VI	1056–57
Justinian the Great	527–65	Isaac I Comnenus	1057–59
Justin II	565–78	Constantine X Ducas	1059–67
Tiberius II	578–82	Romanus IV Diogenes	1067–71
Maurice	582–602	Michael VII Ducas	1071–78
Phocas	602–10	Nicephorus III	1078–81
Heraclius	610–41	Alexius I Comnenus	1081–1118
Constantine II	641	John II Comnenus	1118–43
Heracleonas	641	Manuel I Comnenus	1143–80
Constantine III	641–68	Alexius II Comnenus	1180–83
Constantine IV	668–85	Andronicus I Comnenus	1183–85
Justinian II	685–95	Isaac II Angelus	1185–95
Leontius	695–98	Alexius IV Angelus	1195–1203
Tiberius II	698–705	Isaac II Angelus (restored)	1203–04
Justinian II (restored)	705–11	Alexius V Ducas	1204
Philipicius Bardanes	711–13	Theodore I Lascaris (in Nicaea)	1205–21
Anastasius II	713–15	John III Ducas (in Nicaea)	1221–54
Theodosius III	715–17	Theodore II Lascaris (in Nicaea)	1254–58
Leo III, the Isaurian	717–41	John IV Lascaris (in Nicaea)	1258–61
Constantine V	741–75	Michael VIII Palaeologus	1261–82
Leo IV	775–80	Andronicus II Palaeologus	1282–1328
Constantine VI	780–97	Andronicus III Palaeologus	1328–41
Eirene	797–802	John V Palaeolologus	1341–47
Nicephorus I	802–11	John VI Cantacuzenus	1347–54
Michael I	811–13	John V Palaeologus (restored)	1354–76
Leo V	813–20	Andronicus IV Palaeologus	1376–79
Michael II	820–29	John V Palaeologus (restored)	1379–90
Theophilus	829–42	John VII Palaeologus	1390
Michael III	842–867	John V Palaeologus (restored)	1390–91
Basil I	867–886	Manuel II Palaeologus	1391–1425
Leo VI	886–912	John VIII Palaeologus	1425–48
Alexander	912–13	Constantine XI Palaeologus	1448–53

OTTOMAN SULTANS
(& CALIPHS OF ISLAM AFTER 1517)

Rulers in Bursa and Edirne

Osman Gazi, chieftain, founder
of the dynasty — 1288–1326
Orhan Gazi — 1326–62
Murat I — 1362–89
Beyazıt I — 1389–1403
Interregnum 1403–13
Mehmet I — 1413–21
Murat II — 1421–51

Rulers in Istanbul

Mehmet II, the Conqueror
son of Murat II by Hatice Hüma,
an (?)ethnic Greek — 1451–81
Beyazıt II, son of Mehmet II
by Mükrime, an Anatolian — 1481–1512
Selim I, son of Beyazıt I by
Gülbahar, a (?)Greek — 1512–20
Süleyman I, the Magnificent,
son of Selim I by Ayşe Hafsa,
a Crimean — 1520–66
Selim II, son of Süleyman by
Hürrem, a Ruthenian — 1566–74
Murat III, son of Selim II by
Nurbanu, a Venetian — 1574–95
Mehmet III, son of Murat III
by Safiye, a Venetian — 1595–1603
Ahmet I, son of Mehmet III
by Handan, a Greek — 1603–17
Mustafa I, son of Mehmet III
by Fuldane, an Abkhazian — 1617–18
Osman II, son of Ahmet I by
Mahfiruze, a Greek — 1618–22
Mustafa I (restored) — 1622–23
Murat IV, son of Ahmet I by
Kösem, a Greek — 1623–40
İbrahim, also son of Ahmet I
by Kösem — 1640–48

Mehmet IV, son of İbrahim by
Turhan Hatice, a Ruthenian — 1648–87
Süleyman II, son of İbrahim
by Saliha, a Serbian — 1687–91
Ahmet II, son of İbrahim by
Hatice, a (?)Polish Jew — 1691–95
Mustafa II, son of Mehmet IV
by Rabia Gülnuş, a Greek — 1695–1703
Ahmet III, also son of Mehmet
IV by Rabia Gülnuş — 1703–30
Mahmut I, son of Mustafa II
by Saliha, a ?Greek — 1730–54
Osman III, son of Mustafa II
by Şehsuvar, a Serbian — 1754–57
Mustafa III, son of Ahmet III
by Mihrişah, a Frenchwoman — 1757–74
Abdülhamit I, son of Ahmet III
by Rabia, a (?)Frenchwoman — 1774–89
Selim III, son of Mustafa III
by Mihrişah, a Genoese — 1789–1807
Mustafa IV, son of Abdülhamit
by Ayşe, a Bulgarian — 1807–08
Mahmut II, son of Abdülhamit
by Nakşidil, a (?)Frenchwoman — 1808–39
Abdülmecit I, son of Mahmut II
by Bezmialem, a Circassian — 1839–61
Abdülaziz, son of Mahmut II
by Pertevniyal, a Wallachian — 1861–76
Murat V, son of Abdülmecit
by Şevkefza, a Georgian — 1876
Abdülhamit II, son of Abdülmecit
by Tirimücgün, an Armenian — 1876–1909
Mehmet V, son of Abdülmecit
by Gülcemal, a Circassian — 1910–18
Mehmet VI, son of Abdülmecit
by Gülüstü, a Circassian — 1918–22
Abdülmecit II (Caliph only),
son of Abdülaziz by Hayranıdil,
a Georgian — 1922–24

ECUMENICAL PATRIARCHS

Andrew the Apostle	38	Sisinius	426–27
Stachys the Apostle	38–54	Nestorius	428–31
Onesimus	54–68	Maximian	431–34
Polycarp I	71–89	Proclus	434–46
Plutarch	89–105	Flavian	446–49
Sedekion	105–14	Anatolius	449–58
Diogenes	114–29	Gennadius I	458–71
Eleutherios	129–36	Acacius	472–89
Felix	136–41	Fravitas	489
Polycarp II	141–44	Euphemius	489–95
Athenodorus	144–48	Macedonius II	495–511
Euzois	148–54	Timothy I	511–18
Lawrence	154–66	John II	518–20
Alypios	166–69	Epiphanius	520–35
Pertinax	169–87	Anthimus I	535–36
Olympian	187–98	Menas	536–52
Mark I	198–211	Eutychius	552–65
Philadelphus	211–17	John III the Scholastic	565–77
Cyriacus I	214–30	Eutychius (2nd reign)	577–82
Castinus	230–37	John IV	585–95
Eugenius I	240–65	Cyriacus	595–606
Titus	242–72	Thomas I	607–10
Dometius	272–84	Sergius I	610–38
Rufinus I	284–93	Pyrrhus	638–41
Probus	303–06	Paul II	641–53
Metrophanes I	306–14	Pyrrhus (2nd reign)	654
Alexander	314–37	Peter	654–66
Paul I	337–39	Thomas II	667–69
Eusebius of Nicomedia	339–42	John V	669–75
Macedonius I	342–46	Constantine I	675–77
Paul I (restored)	346–51	Theodore I	677–79
Macedonius I (2nd reign)	351–60	George I	679–86
Eudoxius of Antioch	360–70	Theodore I (2nd reign)	686, 687
Evagrius	370	Paul III	687–93
Demophilus	370–80	Callinicus I	693–705
Gregory of Nazianzus	379–81	Cyrus	706–11
Maximus the Cynic	380	John VI	712–14
Nectarius	381–97	Germanus I	715–30
John I Chrysostom	398–404	Anastasius	730–54
Arsacius	404–05	Constantine II	754–66
Atticus	406–25	Nicetas I	766–80

Paul IV	780–84	Chariton	1177–78
Tarasius	784–806	Theodosius II	1178–83
Nicephorus I	806– 15	Basil II	1183–86
Theodotus I	815–21	Nicetus II	1187–89
Antonius I	821–36	Leontius Theotokites	1189–90
John VII Grammaticus	836–42	Theodosius III, Dositheus	1190–91
Methodius I	842–46	George II	1191–98
Ignatius I	846–58	John X	1198–1206
Photius I	858–67	Michael IV	1207–13
Ignatius I (2nd reign)	867–77	Theodore II	1213–15
Photius I (2nd reign)	877–86	Maximus II	1215
Stephanus I	886–93	Manuel I	1215–22
Antonius II	893–901	Germanus II	1222–40
Nicholas I Mysticus	901–07	Methodius II	1240
Euthymius I	907–12	Manuel II	1240–55
Nicholas I (2nd reign)	912–25	Arsenius	1255–60
Stephanus II	925–28	Nicephorus II	1260–61
Tryphon	928–31	Arsenius (2nd reign)	1261–67
Theophylact	931–56	Germanus III	1267
Polyeuctus	956–70	Joseph I	1267–75
Basil I Scamandrinos	970–74	John XI	1275–82
Antonius III the Studite	974–80	Joseph I (2nd reign)	1282–83
Nicholas II Chrysoberges	984–95	Gregory II	1283–89
Sisinius II	996–99	Athanasius I	1289–93
Sergius II	999–1019	John XII	1294–1304
Eustathius	1020–25	Athanasius I (2nd reign)	1304–10
Alexius the Studite	1025–43	Nephon I	1311–15
Michael I	1043–59	John XIII	1316–20
Constantine III	1059–63	Gerasimus I	1320–21
John VIII	1063–75	Isaias	1323–34
Cosmas I	1075–81	John XIV	1334–47
Eustratius Garidas	1081–84	Isidore I	1347–49
Nicholas III	1084–1111	Callixtus I	1350–54
John IX	1111–34	Philotheus	1354–55
Leo	1134–43	Calixtus I (2nd reign)	1355–63
Michael II	1143–46	Philotheus (2nd reign)	1364–76
Cosmas II	1146–47	Macarius	1376–79
Nicholas IV	1147–51	Nilus	1380–88
Theodotus I	1151–53	Antonius IV	1389–90
Neophytus I	1153	Macarius (2nd reign)	1390–91
Constantine IV	1154–56	Antonius IV (2nd reign)	1391–97
Luke Chrysoberges	1156–69	Callixtus II	1397
Michael III	1170–77	Matthew I	1397–1410

Euthymius II	1410–16	Matthew II (3rd reign)	1603
Joseph II	1416–39	Raphael II	1603–07
Metrophanes II	1440–43	Neophytus II (2nd reign)	1607–12
Gregory III Mammas	1443–50	Cyril I Lucaris	1612
Athanasius II	1450–53	Timothy II	1613–20
Gennadius II	1454–56	Cyril I Lucaris (2nd reign)	1620–23
Isidore II	1456–62	Gregory IV	1623
Sophronius I	1463–64	Anthemus II	1623
Joasaph I	1465–66	Cyril I Lucaris (3rd reign)	1623–33
Mark II	1466	Cyril II	1633
Symeon I	1466	Cyril I Lucaris (4th reign)	1633–34
Dionysius I	1467–71	Athanasius III	1634
Symeon I (2nd reign)	1471–74	Cyril I Lucaris (5th reign)	1634–35
Raphael I	1475–76	Cyril II (2nd reign)	1635–36
Maximus III	1476–81	Neophytus III	1636–37
Symeon I (3rd reign)	1481–86	Cyril I Lucaris (6th reign)	1637–38
Nephon II	1486–88	Cyril II (3rd reign)	1638–39
Dionysius I (2nd reign)	1488–90	Parthenius I	1639–44
Maximus IV	1491–97	Parthenius II	1644–46
Nephon II (2nd reign)	1497–98,	Joannicius II	1646–48
Joachim I	1498–1502	Parthenius II (2nd reign)	1648–51
Nephon II (3rd reign)	1502	Joannicius II (2nd reign)	1651–52
Pachomius I	1503–04	Cyril III	1652
Joachim I (2nd reign)	1504	Athanasius III (2nd reign)	1652
Pachomius I (2nd reign)	1504–13	Paesius I	1652–53
Theoleptus I	1513–22	Cyril III (2nd reign)	1654
Jeremias I	1522–45	Paesius I (2nd reign)	1654–55
Joannicius I	1526	Joannicius II (3rd reign)	1655–56
Dionysius II	1546–56	Parthenius III	1656–57
Joasaph II	1556–65	Gabriel II	1657
Metrophanes III	1565–72	Parthenius IV	1657–62
Jeremias II	1572–79	Dionysius III	1662–65
Metrophanes III (2nd reign)	1579–80	Parthenius IV (2nd reign)	1665–67
Jeremias II (2nd reign)	1580–84	Clement	1667
Pachomius II	1584–85	Methodius III	1668–71
Theoleptus II	1585–86	Parthenius IV (3rd reign)	1671–73
Jeremias II (3rd reign)	1587–95	Dionysius IV	1671–73
Matthew II	1596	Gerasimus II	1673–74
Gabriel I	1596	Parthenius IV (4th reign)	1675–76
Theopanes I	1597	Dionysius IV (2nd reign)	1676–79
Meletius I Pigas	1597–98	Athanasius IV	1679
Matthew II (2nd reign)	1598–1602	James	1679–82
Neophytus II	1602–03	Dionysius IV (3rd reign)	1682–84

Parthenius IV (5th reign)	1684–85	Callinicus IV (2nd reign)	1808–09
James (2nd reign)	1685–86	Jeremias IV	1809–13
Dionysius IV (4th reign)	1686–87	Cyril VI	1813–18
James (3rd reign)	1687–88	Gregory V (3rd reign)	1818–21
Callinicus II	1688	Eugenius II	1821–22
Neophytus IV	1688–89	Anthimus III	1822–24
Callinicus II (2nd reign)	1689–93	Chrysanthus	1824–26
Dionysius IV (5th reign)	1693–94	Agathangelus	1826–30
Callinicus II (3rd reign)	1694–1702	Constantius I	1830–34
Gabriel III	1702–07	Constantius II	1834–35
Neophytus V	1707	Gregory VI	1835–40
Cyprian I	1707–09	Anthimus IV	1840–41
Athanasius V	1709–11	Anthimus V	1841–42
Cyril IV	1711–13	Germanus IV	1842–45
Cyprian I (2nd reign)	1713–14	Meletius III	1845
Cosmas III	1714–16	Anthimus VI	1845–48
Jeremias III	1716–26	Anthimus IV (2nd reign)	1848–52
Paesius II	1726–32	Germanus IV (2nd reign)	1852–53
Jeremias III (2nd reign)	1732–33	Anthimus VI (2nd reign)	1853–55
Seraphim I	1733–34	Cyril VII	1855–60
Neophytus VI	1734–40	Joachim II	1860–63
Paesius II (2nd reign)	1740–43	Sophronius III	1863–66
Neophytus VI (2nd reign)	1743–44	Gregory VI (2nd reign)	1867–71
Paesius II (3rd reign)	1744–48	Anthimus VI (3rd reign)	1871–73
Cyril V	1748–51	Joachim II (2nd reign)	1873–78
Paesius II (4th reign)	1751–52	Joachim III	1878–84
Cyril V (2nd reign)	1752–57	Joachim IV	1884–86
Callinicus III	1757	Dionysius V	1887–91
Seraphim II	1757–61	Neophytus VIII	1891–94
Joannicius III	1761–63	Anthimus VII	1895–97
Samuel I	1763–68	Constantine V	1897–1901
Meletius II	1768–69	Joachim III (2nd reign)	1901–12
Theodosius II	1769–73	Germanus V	1913–18
Samuel I (2nd reign)	1773–74	Meletius IV	1921–23
Sophronius II	1774–80	Gregory VII	1923–24
Gabriel IV	1780–85	Constantine VI	1924–25
Procopius	1785–89	Basil III	1925–29
Neophytus VII	1789–94	Photius II	1929–35
Gerasimus III	1794–97	Benjamin	1936–46
Gregory V	1797–98	Maximus V	1946–48
Neophytus VII (2nd reign)	1798–1801	Athenagoras	1948–72
Callinicus IV	1801–06	Dimitrios	1972–91
Gregory V (2nd reign)	1806–08	Bartholomew	1991–

INDEX

Major references, in cases where many are listed, are given in bold. Numbers in italics are picture references.

contd. from p. 6

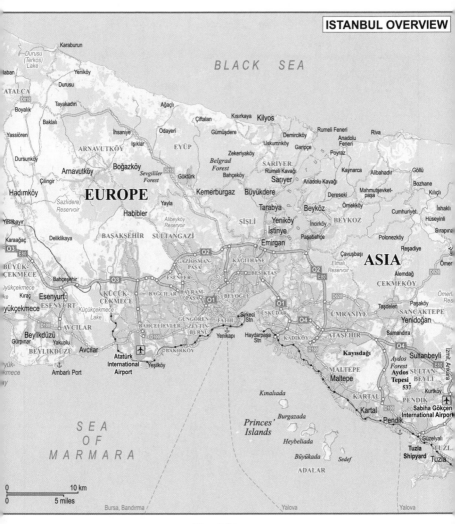

ISTANBUL OVERVIEW

City Maps

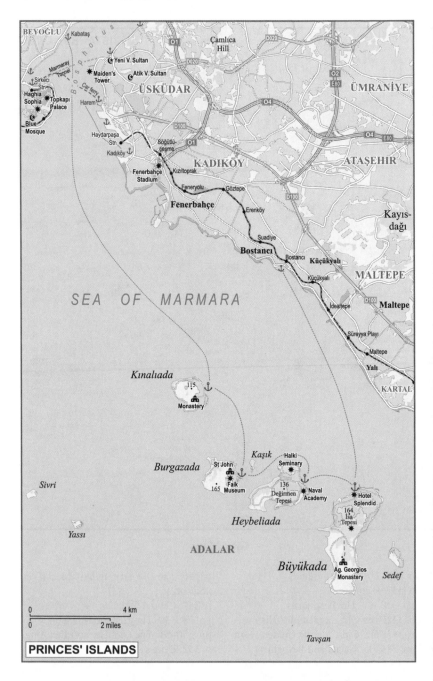

PRINCES' ISLANDS

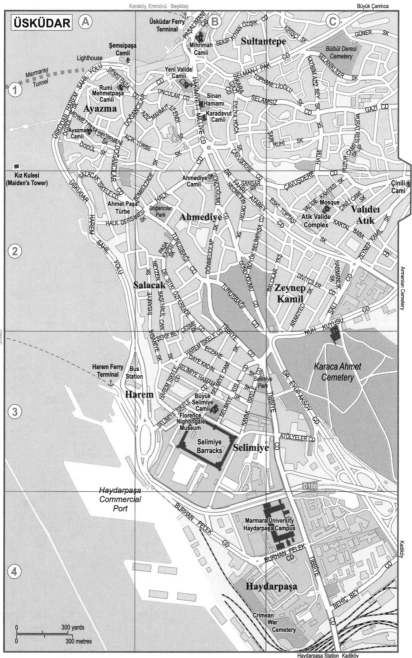

ÜSKÜDAR (A)

Karaköy, Eminönü Beşiktaş

Büyük Çamlıca

Üsküdar Ferry Terminal (B)

(C)

Şemsipaşa Camii

Mihrimah Camii

Sultantepe

KIRISCI SK

GÜNER SK

Lighthouse

SEKIP AYHAN ÖZIŞIK CD

SELANIKLILER SK

Bülbül Deresi Cemetery

Marmaray Tunnel

Yeni Valide Camii

SELMANI PAK

TOPHANE LIOGLU

KATIBIM AZIZ BEY

GAZI CD

Rumi Mehmetpaşa Camii

UNCULAR CD

Sinan Hamamı

EVLIYA HOCA

SELAMSIZ

(1)

Ayazma

Ayazma Camii

Karadavut Camii

ŞAIR RUHI SK

MURAT REİS SK

Kız Kulesi (Maiden's Tower)

Ahmediye Camii

DR. FAHRI ATABEY CD

ÇAVUŞDERE CD

Çinili Cami

(2)

Ahmet Paşa Türbe

Doğancılar Park

Ahmediye

Mosque

Atik Valide Complex

Valıde Atik

Salacak

SALACAK İSKELE CD

HALK DERSANESI SK

TUNUSBAĞI CD

Zeynep Kamil

ZEYNEP KAMIL SK

DIVITCILER SK

Karaca Ahmet Cemetery

Harem Ferry Terminal

Bus Station

Selimiye Park

Harem

Büyük Selimiye Camii

Florence Nightingale Museum

(3)

Selimiye Barracks

Selimiye

ATOLYELER CD

Haydarpaşa Commercial Port

D100

BURHAN FELEK CD

Marmara University Haydarpaşa Campus

BURHAN FELEK CD

(4)

Haydarpaşa

BEHİÇ BEY

Crimean War Cemetery

0   300 yards
0   300 metres

Haydarpaşa Station Kadiköy

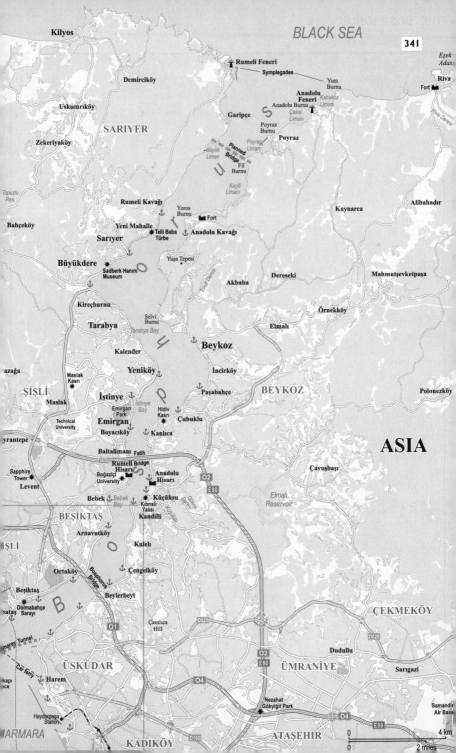

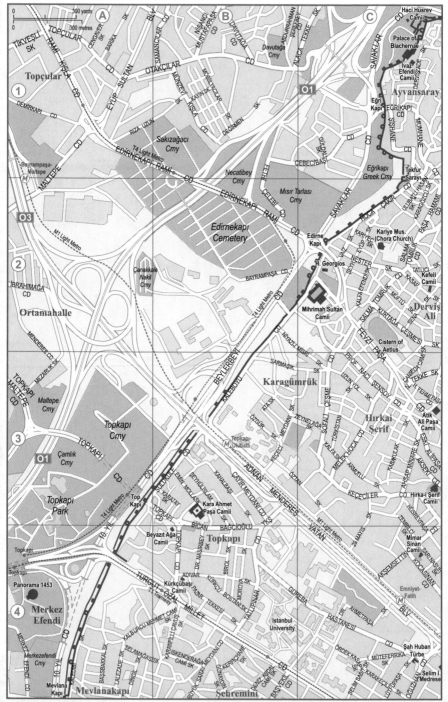

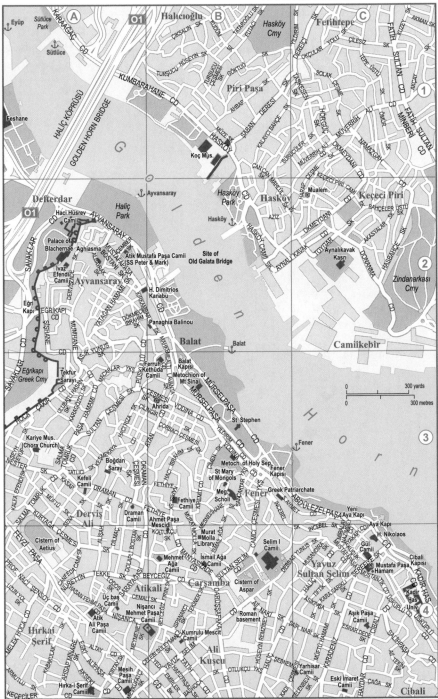

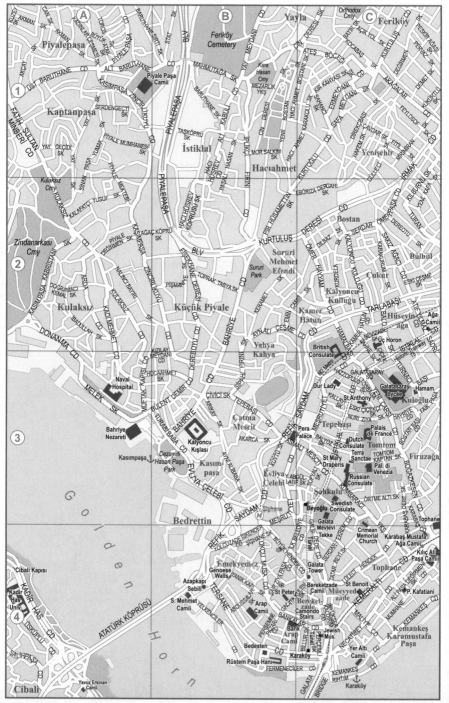

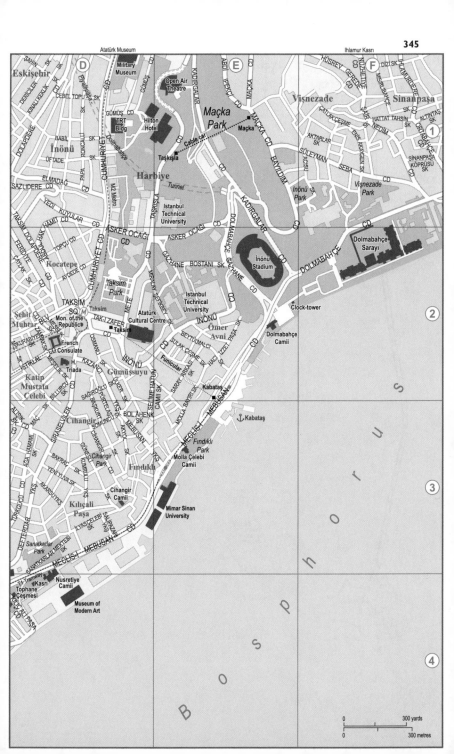

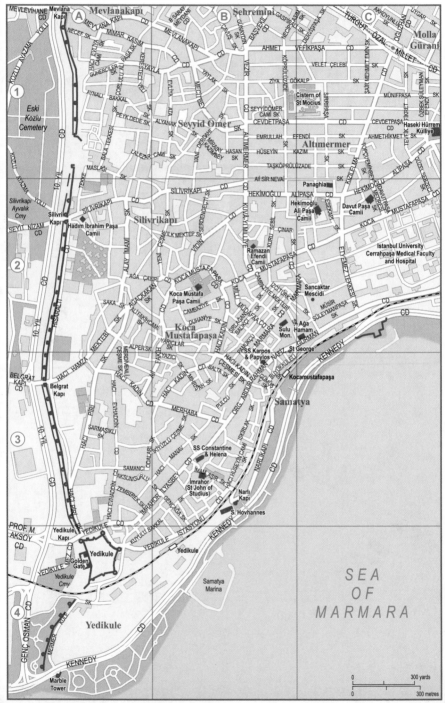

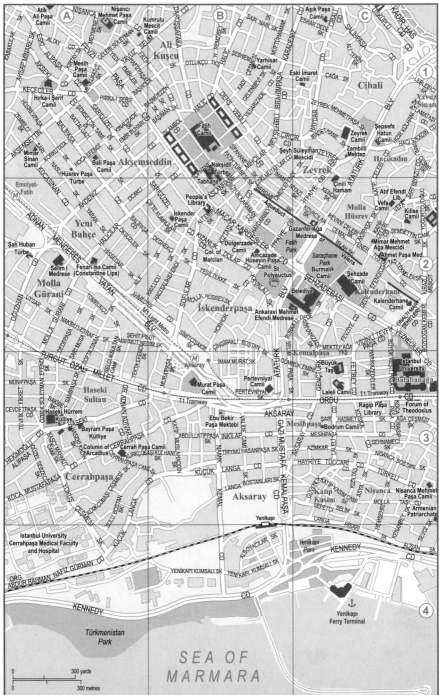

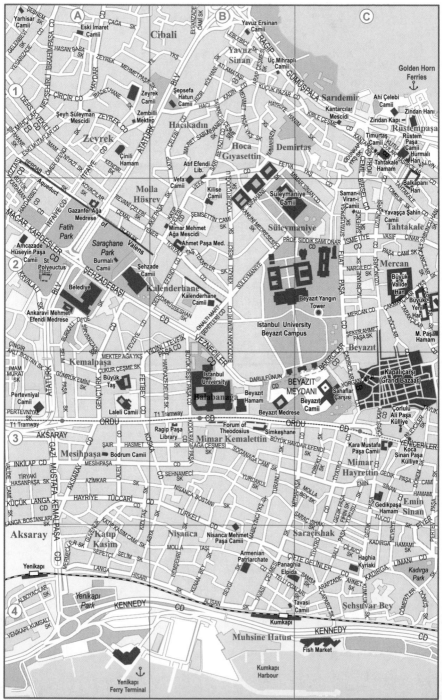

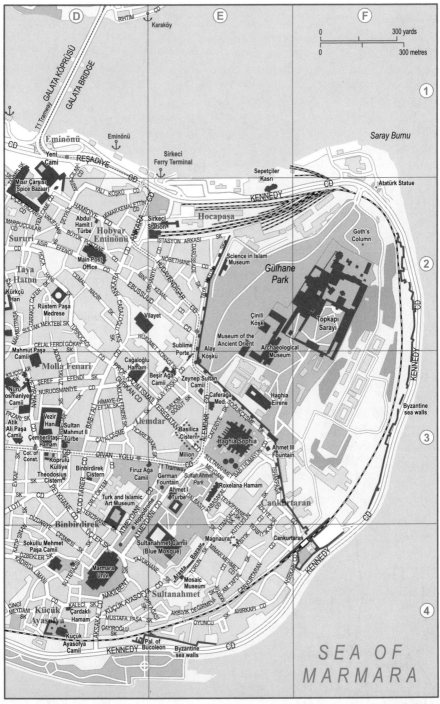

RIHTIM
Karaköy

D · E · F

0   300 yards
0   300 metres

GALATA KÖPRÜSÜ
T1 Tramway
GALATA BRIDGE

1

Saray Burnu

CD

Eminönü
Eminönü
RESADIYE   CD

Yeni
Cami

Sirkeci
Ferry Terminal

Sepetçiler
Kasrı

KENNEDY

Atatürk Statue

Misir Çarşısı
(Spice Bazaar)

HAMIDIYE
MIMARKEMALETTIN
Sirkeci
Station

Hobyar
Eminönü

Hocapaşa

Goth's
Column

2

Abdul
Hamit I
Türbe

Sururi

ISTASYON ARKASI

Science in Islam
Museum

*Gülhane
Park*

Main Post
Office

NOBETHANE
DARÜSSADE

Taya
Hatun

EBUSSUUD

Çinili
Köşk

Topkapı
Sarayı

KENNEDY

Kürkçü
Han

Rüstem Paşa
Medrese

Vilayet

Museum of the
Ancient Orient

Alay
Köşk

Archaeological
Museum

Mahmut Paşa
Camii

Molla Fenari

Sublime
Porte

Cağaloğlu
Hamam

Beşir Ağa
Camii

Zeynep Sultan
Camii

Byzantine
sea walls

Nuru-
osmaniye
Camii

Vezir
Han

Sultan
Mahmut II
Türbe

Alemdar

Caferağa
Med.

Haghia
Eirene

3

Atik
Ali Paşa
Camii

Çemberlitaş
Hamam

Basilica
Cistern

Milion

Haghia Sophia

Ahmet III
Fountain

Col. of
Const.

Köprülü
Külliye

DIVAN YOLU

Binbirdirek
Cistern

Firuz Ağa
Camii

T1 Tramway

*Sultan Ahmet
Park*

Roxelana Hamam

Cankurtaran

Theodosius
Cistern

German
Fountain

Ahmet I
Türbe

Turk and Islamic
Art Museum

Binbirdirek

Hippodrome

Sultanahmet Camii
(Blue Mosque)

Magnaura

Cankurtaran

KENNEDY

4

Sokullu Mehmet
Paşa Camii

Marmara
Univ.

Mosaic
Museum

Sultanahmet

Küçük
Ayasofya

Çardaklı
Hamam

Küçük
Ayasofya
Camii

KENNEDY

Pal. of
Bucoleon

Byzantine
sea walls

CD

*SEA OF
MARMARA*

THE OLD CITY & ITS ENVIRONS

0   0,5 mile

0   1 km

Miniatürk

Eyüp
Cmy

p.352

Eyüp

O1

Sütlüce

Eyüp Sultan
Camii

Hasköy

p.343   p.344

Nişancı

G. Horn

Bridge

Golden

p.342

O3

Defterdar

Ayvansaray
Eğri
Kapı

Balat

BEYOĞLU

Edirnekapı
Cmy

Kasımpaşa

Cihang

Edirne
Kapı

Kariye
Mus.

Horn

Galata
Tower

Topha

Fener

Selim I
Camii

Atatürk

Karaköy

O1

Top
Kapı

FEVZİPAŞA CD.

ADNAN MENDERES VATAN BLV.

D100

Mevlana
Kapı

TURGUT ÖZAL MİLLET CD.

Galata

Bridge

Bridge

p.348

Fatih
Camii

BLV.

Süleymaniye

Eminönü

Sirkeci
Station

FATİH

GAZİMUSTAFA

YKUTLU

Grand Bazaar

Haghia
Sophia

Haseki

Aksaray

KEMALPAŞA CD.

Beyazıt

Silivri
Kapı

Kumkapı

Sultanahmet

Blue
Mosque

Yenikapı

Kumkapı

KENNEDY

ZEYTİN-
BURNU

Belgrat
Kapı

Samatya

Kocamustafapaşa

p.347

Yenikapı
Ferry Terminal

Yedikule
Kapı

CD.

Yedikule

Kazlıçeşme

Yedikule

KENNEDY

SEA OF

p.346